There have been moments during the last week or so when I had grave doubts as to whether I should see tomorrow.

Compiled from the almost daily letters home and a diary written in the immediate aftermath of the First World War, *We Are All Flourishing* is a remarkable first-hand account of one man's service during 1914-19. Walter Coats was an officer with the 9th Highland Light Infantry (Glasgow Highlanders) – one of the first territorial battalions dispatched to the Western Front. Anticipation builds from mobilisation in August 1914, through intensive training in and around Dunfermline, up to eventual embarkation for France the following November. Sent into action, Walter describes winter days and nights in open trenches equipped with kilts and ordinary-issue footwear. As battalion machine gun officer, he participated in the Battles of Neuve-Chapelle, Loos and Arras; Third Battle of Ypres and the Somme – notably at High Wood in July 1916, where the Highlanders were almost wiped out, losing over 800 men killed, wounded and missing. In between the big battles and line-holding in less active sectors, we hear tales of ordinary trench routine, training, sudden movements, billeting expeditions, billets and interactions with the local populace. Walter's story is also one of amusing anecdotes, descriptions of wartime entertainments and humorous verse that reflects how morale was maintained in times of unrelenting terror and occasional boredom. In 1917, torn between battalion loyalty and a promise to his family to take on 'safer' employment, Walter is transferred to 100th Infantry Brigade Staff – his subsequent experience providing rare insights into a staff captain's life and responsibilities. This part of his account also sheds new light on the mid-level command administration of the British Expeditionary Force and the consequent daily challenges that, more often than not, affected the life-or-death situations encountered on the battlefield. While Walter's life was still fraught with personal danger and narrow escapes, his kindness and consideration to officers and men, love of family and dry sense of humour continue to shine through. Walter's story is illustrated with an impressive array of images and maps. Compiled and edited by his great-nephew, Jan Chojecki – and co-edited by military historian Michael LoCicero – *We Are All Flourishing* is a comprehensive and moving work offering new and unique insights into life at the sharp end of conflict and on the home front.

Dr Jan Chojecki (Editor)

Jan Chojecki is the great nephew of Walter Coats, his maternal grandmother being Walter's sister, Helen "Ellie" Rowett. He transcribed the collection of letters posted home from the Western Front by Walter, collated these with the diary account written in 1919 and has researched much of the related information on people and events described in *We Are All Flourishing*. Jan has a degree in Natural Sciences and PhD in genetics, both from the University of Cambridge (Christ's College).

Dr Michael Stephen LoCicero (Co-editor)

Michael LoCicero is an independent scholar and Helion & Company commissioning editor. Having earned a PhD from the University of Birmingham in 2011, he has been previously employed as a contracted researcher at the National Archives in London and Soldiers of Oxfordshire Trust. He is currently engaged in a wide range of academic and editorial activities including advisement for the University of Birmingham's MA programme. His publications include a chapter on Brigadier-General Edward Bulfin in the highly regarded Spencer Jones (ed) *Stemming the Tide: Officers and Leadership of the British Expeditionary Force 1914* (2013), *A Moonlight Massacre: the Night Operation on the Passchendaele Ridge, 2 December 1917* (2014) and a chapter chronicling the forgotten battle of International Trench in Spencer Jones (ed), *Courage Without Glory: The British Army on the Western Front 1915* (2015).

We Are All Flourishing

The Letters and Diary of Captain Walter J.J. Coats
1914-1919

Edited by Jan Chojecki & Michael LoCicero

Helion & Company Limited

Helion & Company Limited
26 Willow Road
Solihull
West Midlands
B91 1UE
England
Tel. 0121 705 3393
Fax 0121 711 4075
Email: info@helion.co.uk
Website: www.helion.co.uk
Twitter: @helionbooks
Visit our blog http://blog.helion.co.uk/

Published by Helion & Company 2016
Designed and typeset by Mach 3 Solutions Ltd (www.mach3solutions.co.uk)
Cover designed by Paul Hewitt, Battlefield Design (www.battlefield-design.co.uk)
Printed by Short Run Press, Exeter, Devon

ISBN: 978-1-911096-39-9

British Library Cataloguing-in-Publication Data.
A catalogue record for this book is available from the British Library.

For details of other military history titles published by Helion & Company Limited contact
the above address, or visit our website: http://www.helion.co.uk.

We always welcome receiving book proposals from prospective authors.

Contents

List of Illustrations

List of Maps

Acknowledgements

The research and preparation of *We Are All Flourishing* has been made possible with the help of several people for whose contributions I am extremely grateful. In particular, I would like to thank: my colleague Rebecca McIntosh for typing up Walter's diary; Jon Cooksey for his initial advice and for introducing me to Helion and Company; Fraser Skirrow; Colonel Tom Bonas; Alec Weir, author of *Come on Highlanders!*; Sandy, Joyce and Kevin at the Royal Highland Fusiliers Museum in Glasgow; Marcus Pilleau; Anthony Morton, Curator of the Sandhurst Collection; Paul Hewitt of Battlefield Design for his design of the cover; George Anderson of Combat Cartography for preparing the maps; Kim McSweeney of Mach 3 Solutions Ltd for typesetting/ design; Liz McGowan of Glasgow Academy; Vicky Harris at Woodside Place; Jamie Stormonth-Darling; and Edward Hasell McCosh and Mungo McCosh for kindly providing information and photos from the McCosh family archives.

Several family members have been of great help, especially my sister, Maryla Green, and my cousin, Diana Hastings (granddaughter of Walter's brother, Jack Coats); also Jack's grandson, Doug, and his wife Angela in New Zealand.

Very special thanks to Kurt Jackson for allowing the use of his painting of French Flanders, *Across the Field*, as the backdrop for the book cover; to Alexander McCall Smith for kindly writing the foreword and, via *Espresso Tales*, for helping me find the living relatives of Walter's school friend and comrade, Edward McCosh; to Trevor Royle for his very kind words; and to David McDowell, James Weatherby and especially Craig Marshall of Fettes College for helping with many of the pieces of the Fettes College jigsaw that is a theme throughout the story.

Most of all, I am very grateful to Helion & Company proprietor Duncan Rogers for publishing this volume and to his colleague and my co-editor, Michael LoCicero, for his endless enthusiasm, meticulous attention to detail and his deep historical knowledge that has provided such intriguing insight into so many aspects of Walter's wartime experiences.

Jan Chojecki
Reading
June 2016

Foreword

In 2014 the one hundredth anniversary of the Outbreak of the First World War brought forth a plethora of studies of that immense and tragic conflict. The questions posed by these publications were wide ranging: how was it that Europe drifted into such a wasteful carnage? How was it that military tactics allowed for such relentless slaughter? Who was to blame for the great disasters and ignominies – the Somme, Passchendaele, Gallipoli? Such questions and the books that pose them are, of course, of undoubted interest, but they do not always deal with the ordinary reality of soldiering and the experience of those caught up in the day to day business of backwards and forwards fighting for the possession of contested trench-ridden territory. For that we need to look to the accounts of soldiers themselves. This remarkable book, dealing with the experience of Walter Coats, an officer in the Highland Light Infantry, provides us with just such a picture.

A striking feature of this collection of letters and diary entries is that it provides a complete and personal story, from the very beginning of the War to its ending and the early days of peace. That in itself is remarkable, as it defies the odds that prevailed against survival at the front. Walter Coats made it, even though he spent a great deal of the war right up at what he describes as the firing line. This lends a certain completeness to his account: we see him joining up, spending early days training at Dunfermline, travelling to France, going up to the front and then back again, and eventually awaiting demobilization at the end of hostilities. So many other letters and memoirs were cut short; so many others who wrote widely-read poetry or prose were cut-off mid-sentence. Wilfred Owen was perhaps the best-known of those, dying just a few days before the Armistice came into effect.

Walter Coats was not a literary figure in the way in which Wilfred Owen, Siegfried Sassoon, or Robert Graves were. He was a straightforward young trainee lawyer from Glasgow who volunteered at the outset with all the enthusiasm of those who had no idea of what lay ahead. His letters and diary entries make fascinating reading, but they do not reveal any of the anguish of Owen or Sassoon, or indeed any of the other writers who were hurt into recording war's horrors. Coats is matter-of-fact. He is concerned in his letters to reassure his family that he is flourishing, and in his diaries he sets out to record what actually happens. There is little dwelling on the human cost of war and its futility; what we see here is an account of what had to be done and how one young man did it.

Yet there is a change in tone as one goes through these letters. At the beginning, especially when he and his fellow volunteers are in training in Scotland, there is a rather school-boyish dwelling on a life that actually seems to have been fairly healthy, active, and unstressful. There was time for plenty of exercise and for classes in bayonet fighting conducted, for the most part, by those who had never wielded a bayonet in anger. The machine gun, a ruthlessly efficient instrument of killing, is simply portrayed as an interesting bit of kit with complicated screws and levers, all to be mastered before being turned on the enemy. There is time for swimming and for billiards, and France and its trenches are still far away.

Then comes the journey to the battlefields, and slowly the tone changes. There is still very little complaint and no railing against the sheer awfulness of war. There is, however, a lot about mud – acres of it, often knee deep, through which those in the trenches must wade. This mud pervades many of the letters, even if rather little is said about killing. And then comes the extraordinary confession that the writer's feelings about going into the trenches were the same as those he had before going to a dance. Here and there, the deaths of close friends are alluded to, even if in a matter-of-fact way. There is no doubt but that Coats felt these losses deeply, but there is no lamenting, no self-pity.

And that, I think, is one of the most remarkable things about these fascinating letters and diary entries. This is the account of a man who saw a horrifying task through with integrity, a measure of cheerfulness, and, most importantly, without self-pity. We live today in an age of ready and strident complaint. We put up with very little before we begin to wallow in victimhood. This was simply not the case with Walter Coats, whose bravery and lack of self-pity shines through his writing.

A broader point is served by this collection. It is another example of how the vanishing art of letter-writing could tell a story in such a way that one hundred years later we can read it with undiminished interest. And it is an astonishing and ultimately very moving story. He could have told his correspondents – and his diary – so much more about the discomfort, the tragedy, the terror. He does not. He simply gets on with the business of living through a nightmare that had to be lived through, and recording the contours of that experience. He was not to become a great war hero; he was not to become a celebrated chronicler of suffering; he was, simply, one who was there, who did his duty, who did not want to alarm those to whom he wrote or to bring them to despair. He was obviously a fine man, a strong man, who lived by all accounts a good life and who did not allow a momentous historical disaster to ruin that life. As such, he can still be an inspiration to us after all these years. Our own times may not be quite the vale of tears that his were, but we have our challenges, and to read about how difficulties were met with dignity and generosity of spirit by a previous generation certainly helps remind us of what we owe to such people, and how much, perhaps, we have lost.

Alexander McCall Smith
Edinburgh
May 2016

Preface

I have no news except that I have been writing a sort of outline of a diary of the war since 1914. So far, I have got the general outline as far as December 1916, and I think with the help of my letters home, I should manage a fairly connected diary.

Walter Coats, letter from France, 2 May 1919

My great Uncle, Walter Coats, served in the British Army throughout the First World War. He left a large box of letters that he had sent home to his family, plus documents, photographs, maps and other artefacts relating to his experiences at the front. From mobilisation in 1914 with his Territorial battalion, the Glasgow Highlanders, he wrote letters or postcards home almost daily, even from the thick of the action. Their

Documents and artifacts comprising the Walter Coats collection. (JC)

frequency suggests that, as well as letting his family know he was safe and a means of preserving his sanity, there was, perhaps, an element of superstition that writing daily would keep him lucky. Straight after the war, Walter wrote a further account that fills out the parts that he could not, because of censorship, include in his letters. He also assembled albums of over 140 photographs purchased from the Imperial War Museum in late 1919. One hundred years on, it is time that Walter's story is told.

Walter's words are presented in their entirety other than, for sake of size, some editing out of some superfluous or inconsequential parts such as the conveying of thanks for letters and parcels, sending miscellaneous wants and giving personal banking instructions. I have left the addressee in the letters, and sometimes the address, but have removed, more often than not, his signature, "Walter J.J. Coats", which he affixed to each and every letter. In some instances, I have indicated the identity of the censoring officer. Only a few of the Field Service Post Cards (FSPCs) that Walter sent on many of the days that he did not compose a letter (and on several that he did) are included. The letters are reproduced in regular font; his War Diary entries are prefixed "**WD**" and are in a sans serif font.

A brief mention of the GPO and Army Postal Service is also deserved. Walter's letters, like those of hundreds of thousands of others generally took just two days to reach home even from remote corners of the Front, and even during intense action. With similarly huge volumes of letters (estimated at 12 million per week) and parcels travelling out to the forces, it was a remarkable logistical exercise and must have been very important in preserving morale amongst the troops – huge credit is due.[1]

Jan Chojecki
Reading
June 2016

---

1   Army Postal Service and GPO 1914-18: "With the onset of trench warfare, all mails bound for troops on the Western Front were sorted at the London Home Depot by the end of 1914. Covering five acres of Regents Park, this was said to be the largest wooden structure in the world employing over 2,500 mostly female staff by 1918. During the war the Home Depot handled a staggering 2 billion letters and 114 million parcels." See 'The Post Office and the First World War', *The British Postal Museum and Archive* <http://www.postalheritage.org.uk/explore/history/firstworldwar/> 'How did 12 million Letters Reach WW1 Soldiers Every Week', *BBC Guides* <http://www.bbc.co.uk/guides/zqtmyrd> (Accessed 3 September 2015).

Introduction

Walter John Jackson Coats was born in 1891, the sixth of seven children of John Jackson Coats (1850-1932) and his wife Helen (*née* Graham). Walter's father was a lawyer and a partner at the law firm, A J and A Graham, of 198 West George Street, Glasgow. John Jackson Coats, also known as "Jack" (or "Jacky Jackson Jackets"), was a much respected arbiter, often specifically referred to in contracts for purposes of dispute resolution, and a "Writer" – a member of the Society of Writers to Her Majesty's Signet, an independent society of Scottish solicitors.

Walter's mother, Helen (also "Ellie") (1850-1926), was the daughter of John Graham (1815-1876) who was also a lawyer and partner at A J and A Graham. On the announcement of Helen's engagement to John Jackson Coats, the newspaper misspelt John's profession as "Waiter" instead of "Writer", much to Helen and her family's mortification. Helen's brother, James Graham was also a partner in the family law firm and close colleague of Walter's father.

Two of Walter's uncles, both brothers of John Jackson Coats, are mentioned in Walter's letters, Uncle Jim (1848-1919) and Uncle Walter (1856-1941). Uncle Jim had been a Lieutenant Colonel in the Royal Army Medical Corps and also was Lord Joseph Lister's House Surgeon at the Glasgow Royal Infirmary in the late 1860's, during the infancy of antiseptic practices. Uncle Walter was a Doctor of Divinity and Minister of Brechin Cathedral (1901-1941). During the War he was acting Chaplain to the 4th Scottish General Hospital, Glasgow and the 1st Scottish General Hospital, Aberdeen.

The Coats family lived at 27 Woodside Place, Glasgow. Walter, who was nick-named "Wat" by the family, had three sisters and three brothers. His sisters were Jean (b. 1881), Helen or, like her mother, "Ellie" (b. 1882), and Janet, also known as "Jenny" or "Jint", who was born in 1884. Jean and Jint were living at home at the outbreak of war in 1914, while Ellie had married John Quiller Rowett in 1913, and was by then living in Forest Hill, London at "Perry Mount" on Mayow Road. Ellie and John Rowett are the grandparents of the editor, Jan Chojecki. John Rowett (1876-1924) was a businessman and philanthropist whose wine and spirit company, Rowett, Leakey & Co., supplied rum to the forces during the war, as referred to in several of Walter's letters. The Rowetts moved to 9 Hyde Park Terrace, London during 1918. As a schoolboy, at Dulwich College, John Quiller Rowett had encountered Ernest Shackleton, and in 1921, Shackleton persuaded him to finance the "Quest" expedition to the Antarctic during which Shackleton died, upon reaching South Georgia. In 1922, he founded the Rowett Research Institute in Aberdeen, still a leading research institute for nutrition and health.

Walter had two elder brothers, John – or "Jack" – who was born in 1886, and James ("Jim"), born 1889, and one younger brother, Douglas (b. 1892).

All four boys were educated at Glasgow Academy and then at Fettes College in Edinburgh (Carrington House). Many other Fettes College boys feature in Walter's account, such as Mathew Anderson, Edward ("Ted") McCosh,[1] Hew Hedderwick,[2] John Hay Beith (who returned to Fettes as a schoolmaster)[3] and John ("Jack") Lamberton.

Walter, aged about six, poses for the camera along the drive of a country house rented by the Coats family during a summer holiday. (WJJC collection)

---

1   Edward McCosh. Born 14 December 1890 to Andrew Kirkwood McCosh and Mary Smith McCosh of Cairnhill, Airdrie; educated at Fettes College (Moredun House, 1905-10) and Clare College, Cambridge University (Rugby Blue, 1910); 1/9th HLI.
2   Hew C. Hedderwick. Educated at Fettes College (Carrington House, 1906-09); sub-lieutenant, Royal Naval Volunteer Reserve 1914; Antwerp 1914; Gallipoli 1915; Grand Fleet 1916-18; Lieutenant Commander 1919.
3   John Hay Beith. Fettes College (Carrington House 1890-95) and St John's College, Cambridge University. Returned to Fettes College as a master (1906-1912).

The Coats brothers, 1898: L to R:
Walter, Jack, Jim, Douglas.
(WJJC collection)

The Coats Family, 1897: L to R:
Jim, Jint, Jean, Jack, Douglas (on
Jean's knee), Walter, Ellie.
(WJJC collection)

The Coats Family, 1902: L to R: Back: Jim, Walter, Jack, Douglas; Front: Ellie, Jean, Jint. (WJJC collection)

Fettes College Officer Training Corps on parade in 1909, Walter's final year at school. John Hay Beith, back at Fettes as a schoolmaster, bearing sword to the left of the parade (Fettes College collection). Beith (who wrote under the pseudonym Ian Hay) later wrote of this parade "I wonder how many of them dreamed, as they posed stiffly for that photograph, that in ten years' time their names would be inscribed on a Fettes War Memorial erected almost on the very spot on which they were standing". (Anon, *Fifty Years of Fettes: Memories of Old Fettesians, 1870-1920.* (Edinburgh: Constable,1931))

The Coats siblings at Braidwood House in May 1912 when Ellie became engaged to John Quiller Rowett: Back L to R: Jack, Ellie, Jint, Walter; Front L to R: Jean, Jim, Douglas. Sandy the Scottish terrier. (WJJC collection)

The Coats siblings, except Jack, and parents c. 1913: L to R: Walter, Douglas, Jint, Ellie, Jim, Jean. Seated: Helen Coats and John Jackson Coats. Sandy, the Scottie. (WJJC collection)

By 1914, after graduating with a Law degree from the University of Glasgow, Walter was employed as an apprentice lawyer by the Glasgow law firm McGrigor Donald & Co, who are referred to in many of Walter's letters (usually as "McG D & Co"). Meanwhile, he had joined the 9th Battalion, The Highland Light Infantry (HLI) of the Territorial Force (TF) – known as the Glasgow Highlanders, being commissioned as a 2nd Lieutenant in 1910.[4]

Jack, like Walter, also joined the Glasgow Highlanders and, having been commissioned in 1909, he was a Captain at the outbreak of the War. In 1913, he married Emilie Sarah Dunlop Anderson – known as "Esda" – the daughter of James Reddie Anderson, who was a sponsor of the artist John Ruskin. Esda's parents lived at Lairbeck, Keswick, England, the destination of Walter's letter of 15 January 1915, and which is now the Lairbeck Hotel.

Jim, too, had joined the Territorial Force, and during the War fought in Egypt and Palestine with the Royal Field Artillery. Meanwhile, Douglas was still studying Medicine at Glasgow University at the start of the War and initially enlisted in the Army as a Private but was sent back to complete his degree. In 1916, after graduating, he was sent to India where he joined the Royal Army Medical Corps.

Several other family members appear in Walter's letters. Cousins Marjory (b. 1894) and Elsie (b. 1897) are Marjory and Elspeth Graham, the daughters of James Graham, Walter's mother's brother. Elsie became a nurse and served in Army Hospitals in St Omer and Treport. Patrick ("Pat") Graham (b. 1892) is also a first cousin, the son of another of Walter's mother's brothers. Cousin Victor is John Humphrey James Victor Coats (b. 1898), son of Uncle Jim. Victor was educated at Fettes College like his cousins and served in the Royal Army Medical Corps in Ypres, Salonica and Egypt. Cousin Jock is John Dundas Orr Coats (b.1893), the son of Uncle Walter. Educated at Edinburgh Academy and Balliol College, Oxford, Jock served throughout the War in France and Mesopotamia, with the 5th Royal Highlanders (Black Watch) and also with the Machine Gun Corps, eventually as Acting Captain.

A close friend of the Coats family was Mathew Anderson, known as "Math". Math was born in 1886, the son of William Boyd Anderson[5] of solicitors Anderson and Pattison, of 137 St Vincent Street, Glasgow. He was educated at Glasgow Academy and Fettes College, where he was a contemporary of the two elder Coats brothers, Jack

---

4   With a regimental lineage dating back to 1860 and the popular Volunteer Force movement, the 1/9th HLI (Glasgow Highlanders) was, in summer 1914, headquartered at Greendyke Street, Glasgow as part of the HLI Brigade of the Lowland Division (TF). See TNA WO 95/2431: 1/9th HLI War Diary, Ian F.W. Beckett, *Riflemen Form! A Study of the Rifle Volunteer Movement 1859-1908* (Barnsley: Pen & Sword, 2007) and Alec Weir, *Come on Highlanders!: Glasgow Territorials in the Great War* (Thrupp – Stroud: Sutton, 2005) for a recent history of the Battalion during the First World War.
5   Mathew's father, William Boyd Anderson (b. 1849), had twenty years' military service, during which he held the position of Brigade Major, 2nd (Volunteer) Battalion Highland Light Infantry.

Walter (at right), Jack (second from left), Ted McCosh (next to Walter) and three
unidentified Glasgow Highlander officers, Gailes Camp, July 1914. (WJJC collection)

and Jim, in Carrington House. Math had five sisters and, being of similar ages to the
Coats children, it seems the families were very close. Math took a degree in Law at
Glasgow University. By 1914, he was a junior partner at Anderson and Pattison and,
like Walter, was already commissioned in the Glasgow Highlanders.

The Coats family traditionally took a summer break of several weeks each year,
often at Braidwood House, Braidwood, near Carluke in Lanarkshire (1914 and 1916),
but also at The Manse, Edinburgh Road, Abington (1915), Longcroft, Thornton Hall,
Lanarkshire (1917) and Kirkland Park, Strathaven (1918).

In July 1914, the Glasgow Highlanders convened at their annual training camp at
Gailes, north of Troon on the Ayrshire coast.

At the end of the month, when the camp finished, Walter went to join the rest of
the family at Braidwood House.

1

Mobilisation

Be in Glasgow over weekend.

Saturday 1st August 1914

TELEGRAM
To: COATS, Braidwood House, Braidwood, Nr Carluke
Be in Glasgow over weekend.
Officer Commanding, 9th H.L.I., Glasgow

WD: On Saturday 1st August 1914, I received a wire "Be in Glasgow over weekend." I was then at Braidwood having just finished the annual training at camp the day before. I got the evening train into Glasgow and found that Mathew Anderson had booked a room for me at St. Enoch Station Hotel where a lot of other officers were also staying.

The next day was spent at Battalion H.Q. in Greendyke Street getting things in order for mobilisation which was expected to commence at any time. As nothing happened on Monday however, we all returned to our work though we were again obliged to stay in town that night.

4th August 1914[1]

TELEGRAM
To: Lieutenant Coats, 198 West George Street, Glasgow
Attend headquarters at 4pm today
Adjutant

WD: On Tuesday 4th I received another wire ordering me to attend at Battalion H.Q. at 4 pm. This was the only order I got to mobilise. Orders were sent out that day to

---

1 Great Britain was at war with Imperial Germany from 11:00 p.m. on this day.

mobilise and the men began to arrive on Wednesday morning. The next few days we were fully occupied filling up forms of all sorts with the names and addresses of each man, the name of his next of kin, whether married, number of children, names and ages of children etc. What eventually became of all this information has always been a mystery to me as it was all left lying about in the drill hall when we left suddenly two days later. The Medical Officer, especially, was a very busy man as in addition to the recruits that were pouring in, every man in the Battalion was again medically examined. If anything was found to be wrong with a man, however slight, he was at once thrown out. We lost a good many otherwise excellent men through bad teeth but so many recruits were arriving we could afford to let them go.

Wingate, my Company Commander,[2] and McCosh, the other subaltern in the Company, went off with the Company on Thursday afternoon to guard the railway bridge at Castlecary and I was left behind with about half a dozen men to get things straightened up and to take over the new men that were being allotted to the Company. Shortly after they had gone, I was handed a bag with about £500 in cash with which to pay the men their gratuity of £5 each which they received for their boots, razors etc. which they brought with them when they joined up and which were taken over by the Government. As I was only able to pay out about £30 of it at the time, I found the balance rather a nuisance as I did not dare to leave it lying about.

On Thursday night, I slept in the Officer's room at H.Q. but on Friday moved over with about half the Battalion to the People's Palace on the Green. I was just getting comfortably to sleep here when the whole Battalion was turned out. Each man was immediately issued with his ammunition, kits were packed and everything got ready to move. After waiting for about half an hour or so wondering what the matter was we were told we could turn in again but were to parade early next morning.

Next morning [Saturday 8 August] we paraded as ordered and were marched off to Queen Street Station where we entrained at 6 a.m. for our war station at Dunfermline. We were the first Glasgow Territorial Battalion to get away. When we got to Dunfermline, we found we were billeted in the Carnegie Institute and Public Baths. Much to my relief, Wingate turned up with the rest of the Company and I was able to get rid of the cash that I had been carrying round.

9th August 1914

My dear Mother,

As you may know, we are now on our war station. We got the order about midnight the day I saw Dad, to be ready to move in an hour and as you can imagine we had a pretty cheery hour. However, we did not move off until next morning. We have got a

---

2   Captain George Wingate MC of Mossyde, Kilmacolm, Scotland (b.1874); joined Glasgow Highlanders 1894.

most glorious billet here [Carnegie Institute and Public Baths, Dunfermline] with a swimming bath and about 30 hot and cold water baths on the premises but we may be turned out if the place is wanted for a hospital. It is just possible you know where we have gone but we have strict orders not to let anyone know. My address is simply "9th Highland Light Infantry".

It is very hard to realise we are on active service just now, we are in such palatial quarters, but discipline is very strict and we shall probably realise it in a few days. Do you think you could find in my tin box the following books: "Field Devices Pocket Book" (the newest of the two), "Infantry Training" and "Field Service Regulations-Part I". There is no hurry for them and if you cannot find them it does not matter. Has Jim moved off yet and has Doug joined anything?

Your loving son, Walter J. J. Coats

PS I shall write as often as I can but do not be surprised if it is not very often.

12th August 1914

My dear Dad,
We have offered to go abroad as a Battalion at least 800 strong. It is improbable of course that we will be sent into the firing line at once and it is possible we may simply be sent to Malta or some place like that but I believe we <u>will</u> be sent abroad somewhere sometime, though the adjutant says probably not for a month at least. (I hope you can follow this). He said we would at any rate get two or three days leave before going.

We had quite a little excitement here the other night. One of our sentries at the Post Office thought he saw someone moving on the roof, so the guard surrounded the building and someone was sent up to look for anyone. No one was discovered but the sentry again thought he saw something move on the roof so he fired. When they went to see what he had fired at it was discovered he had hit one of those chimneys with a moving hood.

I have just heard that Jim is going to be stationed here too. In fact, someone said he is probably arriving just now but I don't know whether that is true or not.

We are feeling rather bucked with ourselves here as we are the first Territorial battalion in Glasgow, if not the Kingdom, to be mobilised as a complete battalion. I was speaking to a Regular officer the other day who kept rubbing into me that his lot had mobilised in 3 days although they should have been given five. As a matter of fact, we mobilised in 3 days also. I hope you and the rest of them at home are all flourishing. We are here. I have already found my belt getting tight although I have plenty of exercise. I wish I could have had some more gooseberries when I was at home. I don't think there is any more news so I may as well bottle up.

Your loving son, Walter J.J. Coats

Sunday 16th August 1914

My dear Jean,

Many thanks for your letter which I got the other day. I don't think there is much news to tell but I am simply writing to let you know that we are all flourishing here. The weather is simply ripping. I hope you are getting as good at Braidwood. It is funny to think I shall probably not be back at Braidwood again this summer.

A great many officers here have got colds just now. I think it is an overdose of swimming pond.

The people here are extraordinarily decent, as Doug would say. I believe the local barber is only charging half price and I know for a fact that the local dentist has offered to look after the teeth of the Glasgow Highlanders for nothing. One of the leading citizens has put his motor at our disposal, another has given us two packing cases per company, one for food and another for rubbish. We are told we need not worry about the paintwork of the building and altogether everyone is doing his best for us.

We had a Church parade in the Abbey here today. The old bit is very fine but the new bit is an absolute scandal by way of restoration.

Have you heard if Victor or Jock [Walter's cousins] have joined anything, if so what?

I have the pleasure of sleeping on a mattress every second night now. I and another officer take turns sleeping in the telephone room here and there is a mattress that goes with the duty. I am getting to be quite a good sleeper so I warn the military policeman outside to wake me if the telephone bell rings. The place here is simply swarming with sentries over various places and I hear today that notices have been put up through the town warning the inhabitants to stop and answer when they are challenged as otherwise they are liable to be shot.

There is really nothing more to talk about so I shall stop, with love to all.

Wednesday 19th August 1914

My dear Dad,

I am just writing a line to let you know that we are still flourishing. The officers have just been warned that we may have to move off at a moment's notice tonight and if we do I do not know when I shall be able to write you again. I shall however write as soon as possible. None of us knows where when why or how we are to move but we are ready to go anywhere. The inspecting officer today told us our regimental transport was the most efficient he has yet seen which is satisfactory from the point of view of our comfort.

I know now that Jim is here, as Math met him in the street yesterday but I have not run across him myself yet.

We are having an officers' polo match in the swimming baths this evening which ought to be rather amusing as none of us know how to play.

No more news. Love to all

20th August 1914

My dear Mother,

We did not have to move last night after all though I got rather a shock when I was roused at about 12 o'clock at night by the telephone bell ringing in my ear.

Jim was here last night and I told him to come and have a bathe today but I have not seen him here. We are going on a trek tomorrow and are sleeping out tomorrow night. We expect to be home on Saturday afternoon though we may not get back till Sunday. We were out today from 9am till about 4.40pm. So far as we can make out, we are the only Battalion here that is making any effort to get into training. Two of our men more or less collapsed today when we were climbing up the side of a very steep hill. They both recovered after a while but I expect we will try and get them discharged as unfit. There is such a crowd just now we can choose from, we can get rid of any doubtful ones.

Sunday 23rd August

My dear Jean,

I wrote Mother last so far as I can remember so I will write you now though I don't suppose it matters who I write to.

We got back from our bivouacs last night about six. I think I told you we were going to spend a night out. We left on Friday morning and got to a place about 15 miles from here in the afternoon. Each man had a blanket and a waterproof sheet with him and when we halted for the night the men were divided into groups of four. Each four made a hut for itself by stretching a string between the muzzles of two rifles and hanging two blankets over the string and a waterproof sheet at the end. Each bivouac held four men who had two blankets and three waterproof sheets left between them. The thing only takes about five minutes to put up and is quite comfortable. The officers slept in the open in what are called "flea bags" (i.e. sleeping bags) and Wolseley Valises. One Company was on outpost duty all night and it was rather funny at the first halt coming home yesterday. The whole Company laid their heads on their equipment and we were sound asleep in about two minutes.

On the way out on Friday, we were passed by Jim and some of his guns. He told us he would not be back at Dunfermline again. He says the Artillery are being scattered all over the place. At present we have two Companies in detached work. Yesterday, when we were coming home, the Brigade Major drove up in a motor and the next thing we knew was that two Companies were turned back with their blankets and the rest of us came home. I don't know what their job is.

Last night again there was quite a little excitement. There was a report that a German spy had been having a pot shot at a sentry at the Post Office so all our sentries round the billet were made to load with five rounds and everyone that came along the street was challenged and made to pass on the other side of the road.

I don't know if I ever told you that when my Company was out guarding a railway bridge and tunnel shortly after we were mobilised, one of our sentries stopped a man who was going along the line. The man said he was a Railway guard going to his job and tried to get past so the sentry asked him for his pass. The man said he had not got a pass and still tried to get past so the sentry told him he had 95 rounds of ammunition in his pouches and 5 rounds in his rifle and that if he did not go away he would shoot the legs off him. I believe the Guard did a record sprint out of sight. Several of our officers were stopped by one of our sentries a few days ago until they sent back for the password.

I can't think of anything else to write about except please give my love to all at home and excuse scribble.

PS We are all flourishing.

27th August 1914

My dear Doug,

Many happy returns of your birthday. I am sorry there is nothing here I can send you as a present except my best wishes. If you remind me next birthday, I shall give you a double present, price at least 1/-.

We are working fairly hard here just now. Physical drill and running before breakfast, marching and fighting etc. from 9am till any time in the afternoon and a lecture for officers at night. I have got the job of understudy for the machine gun officer. I have to spend my time before breakfast with the gun learning its innards etc. and I spend the rest of the day either with the gun or my Company, day about. It is very interesting. I may have to ride a horse but I rather hope not as I enjoy the walking.

I am becoming a great pro in the swimming line now. I only swallow about a quarter of the bath when I get in now instead of three quarters as I did at the beginning. As a matter of fact most of the quarter was swallowed when I tried to swim on my back.

I must stop now as I have got to inspect the Machine Gun. After that I intend to have a game of cricket then tea, then possibly do some shopping and maybe referee a football match then a swim then a lecture then Dinner then either some reading or billiards then bed then Reveille.

Love to you all

WD: While we were at Dunfermline, the transport consisted of some ordinary Glasgow lorries, a spring van and two barrel type street watering carts, the horses being some old crocks that had been palmed off on the officer detailed to collect the transport when we mobilised. The whole were under command of the fattest officer in the Battalion who required a miniature Clydesdale to carry him. This officer was quite incapable or riding and used to wait till the Battalion had started before being shoved onto his horse by his groom assisted by other members of the transport. On one occasion when we were on the march, the Adjutant rode back to see the transport. When he found it straggling all over the road he ordered the transport officer, who was riding along in front of it, to trot back and get it together and, as he told us afterwards, he nearly fell off his horse with laughing when the transport officer solemnly dismounted and trotted back on his feet.

There are also two good stories about the gentlemen who were in the ranks. On one occasion, some of these men were on guard at Brigade H.Q. which was quartered in a hotel in the town. Knowing the General was out, they were exploring the hotel when they came across his bathroom. This was too much for them and they proceeded to have a bath, incidentally using the General's own towels to dry themselves afterwards. The other story is about some of them who were out in the town after hours. They were wondering how to get in again past the sentry when one of them had a brilliant idea. He remembered that there were always pickets round the town after dark so he formed the others up in line and marched them in past the sentry as a picket and coolly dismissed them in front of the Orderly Room.

28th August 1914

My dear Jean,
Many thanks for your letter which I got today. I don't suppose there can be much news at Braidwood just now.

While I remember, Math says he would be delighted if you could send some lettuce or radish or peas or flowers here. Don't take any trouble about them. Only send them if they are to spare.

I have been working with the machine gun all day today. It is frightfully interesting. The "guts" are simply beautiful. I have learnt the nuances of about 100 nuts and screws and parts etc. already but I am not anything like through yet.

The officers are playing against Dunfermline at cricket today. I expect we will be absolutely sat on as Dunfermline are supposed to be very good. Unfortunately, I shall not be able to play as I have to sit on a board of enquiry this afternoon. It is rather a nuisance as I sat yesterday from about 2pm till about 7.30 pm at the Company pay and from about 9 till 11 pm at the machine gun and I rather wanted a day off. However, someone has got to do the work and the more work one does the more efficient one gets. I wish all the same I had not this job as I am a subaltern of the day tomorrow and shall not get outside the building unless I have to march the Roman Catholics or some such people to Church.

30th August 1914

My dear Jenny,
It is a long time since I wrote you last so I shall write you now though I suppose the letters are common property.

There is not much news just now though today has been fairly busy for me. I was subaltern of the day so I had to get up at Reveille, 6 am, and see that the men were getting a move on. I had to attend cookhouse at 7.30 and then go round asking for complaints. I then had breakfast and at 9.30 paraded the Roman Catholics and marched them to Church. I went in to see what the service was like and found it quite interesting.

When I got back I was called for by the Commanding Officer who said he was going to inspect the billets. As a rule the whole building is cleaned up by the sick while we are out, but this time there were no sick to be had as the Doctor could not see the men till after Church, so all men had to go to Church. I was responsible that the place was clean so I sent for all the defaulters and turned them onto clean-up. The inspection of the billets is a most imposing procession. First there is the Commanding Officer, then the senior Major, then the Adjutant, then the Doctor, then the Quartermaster, then the Captain of the day, then the Subaltern of the day, then the Battalion Orderly Sergeant and finally the Battalion Orderly Corporal. There is not much left unseen by the time we get round.

After the inspection, I stood easy till Dinner at 1pm when I again went to cookhouse and asked for complaints. At the Officers lunch, my Captain suddenly told us he was going out and that I must take the afternoon parade for teaching the NCOs the various kinds of knots and hitches, so I had to go and refresh my memory at that and had no time to myself till 3.30 when I helped Math to make up the Mess accounts and generally slacked around till tea at five when I had to go and see the tea issued. I then had tea myself and studied machine gun till 6.30 when I had to go and inspect the guard and picket and see them mounted and here I am.

I have still to go round with the Brigade Field Officers and inspect the guards at the Post Office, Gas Works, Brigade Headquarters, Supply Depot and the Quarter guard here and I have also to see lights out at 10.30, collect absentee reports and write my own report; and am responsible along with the Captain of the day if anything happens until 5.30am tomorrow morning when the next man takes the job.

Please excuse the recurrence so often of the word "I" but I thought you might be interested in a day's programme of the work.

Love to you all, no more news

31st August 1914

My dear Dad,
I got your letter and Mother's this morning, for which many thanks.

It is now about 2.30 pm and I have been fairly hard at it since I wrote last. I did not get to bed till about quarter past one this morning as we took a long time inspecting the various guards etc. and I was up by six this morning and have been working till now.

A funny thing happened to the subaltern of the day today. He was going round the billets seeing that the men were up in the morning, when he came across a man who was not up so he kicked him up and discovered that it was his own young brother. It was the first he had heard of his joining. Doug may know the man. His name was MacKay and he was at Fettes.[3]

With much love to Mother and the rest.

PS I got a cheque on Saturday for £17. 3/-. This is a more paying job than a law apprentice.

1st Sept 1914

John J. Coats, Braidwood

My dear Dad,

There is no news here but I like to write each day if possible to let you know we are still here and are both flourishing.

Today has been rather wet for a change but we did the usual work in spite of the rain. We did physical drill in the morning and in the afternoon we went for a march. We did about 15½ miles and are just back about an hour ago. Our average rate of marching was one mile in 17 minutes which is quite good going.

Three old officers have just joined us, Carmichael Frame, Gibson Fleming and Weir Grieve. Car. Frame tells me that Ian Graham has grown a moustache, apparently they all do in Egypt. Jack has grown one here, like most of the others, but I have set my face against one (metaphorically).

Please thank Mother for her letter which I got when we came in today and thank her for sending on the eatables. They have not arrived yet as far as I know but I have no doubt they will arrive all right. Our feeding here only costs us about 2/- a day including the hire of crockery so any extras are pretty welcome.

I had a long letter from Ellie today. I wonder how John's business is getting on.[4] I hope it is all right.

I believe there is a story going about in Glasgow that we are going to Malta. So far as we know here it is absolute drivel. No one here knows where, when or how we will be moved. It may be any minute. In a way I wish we could get moved as we know all the roads round here almost with our eyes shut. I am glad to say that if the Battalion is

---

3   The late-sleeper was Pte 2284 Ian Norman Mackay of Fettes College (1908-13) and Glasgow University; died on active service 19 January 1915. The nonplussed subaltern was 2nd Lieutenant, later Captain, Alastair Moray Mackay.

4   Ellie is Helen Rowett, Walter's sister, who was married to John Quiller Rowett, whose business supplied rum to the British armed forces.

sent abroad I shall probably <u>not</u> be left behind with those who are not going as I have understudied the Machine Gun Officer. Some officer will have to stay behind and it will be bad luck on the one who has to do so.

I hear we got either 62 or 66 recruits at Headquarters yesterday. We are taking no recruits who are not willing to serve abroad. We have permission to recruit our full strength with men willing to serve abroad.

Thursday 3rd September 1914

Mrs Coats, Braidwood

My dear Mother,

I meant to write to you yesterday but I was so sleepy I simply could not do it. I started a letter to Ellie and stuck half way.

We have at last got a move from here. C Company goes off tomorrow by itself for training somewhere between 6 and 10 miles from here. I expect we will be very hard worked but it will be interesting. We will be billeted in farm houses. I expect our food will be sent to us daily. We expect to be away for several weeks.

I suppose Jack would tell you all the news when he was with you. I shall not apply for leave again until we get back when you will probably be back in Glasgow and I shall stay the night.

I shall try and write you as often as I can but don't know what postal arrangements there are.

I don't think there is any news except that the Battalion is now full up with men qualified and volunteered for service abroad,

I must stop now as I must pack up for tomorrow.

Friday 3rd September 1914

Douglas H Coats

My dear Doug,

I have just got a letter from Jimmy saying that they are giving no more Commissions except on special conditions. If you think of joining the ranks at all I believe the Glasgow Highlanders are forming a second Battalion. Col Fleming phoned us the other day that, if he got permission, he thought he could raise a Battalion in a week. Apparently he has been promised a company of writers, a company of accountants etc. though I don't know if this is a fact. I see also that the Glasgow Academicals are going to raise a Company to be attached some battalion. If you think of either of these schemes, you could apply to either Col Fleming or to Major Couper at the

Glasgow Academy. I saw the advertisement of the Academy Company in the front of today's Herald. Please do not tell anyone about the 2nd Battalion of the Glasgow Highlanders as we want to keep it quiet and if possible go ahead of the other battalions and get the best men.

Seeing you have brothers in this Battalion we might manage to have you put into a Company of this Battalion. You may have a totally different scheme you want to try but I am writing to you in case you have absolutely no ideas and you want to join.

Saturday 5th September 1914

My dear Jean,

I had a bed to sleep in last night for the first time for a month. It was quite funny. I had a glorious sleep and was very unwilling to get up this morning. I return to the floor tonight as there is only one bed between two.

The place where we are just now is about 12 miles from Dunfermline [Glassmount, farm near Kinghorn]. There is a simply glorious view from the place and I expect I shall have a good time.

Today we spent the morning paying the men. In the forenoon some men were lent to the farmer to help with his harvest and the rest did a squad drill. This afternoon we are simply slacking and I am at present perched on top of a hill overlooking the farm and watching a torpedo boat out at sea though my glasses. It is a glorious day.

The billets we have here are very comfortable except that we lack water. We were spoilt for that in Dunfermline. The officers have two bedrooms and a sitting room in the farm house so we are very well off. I hope we stay here for some time.

I did not see Jack last night as I was off before he got back but I expect he is as flourishing as I am.

I have a slight cold just now. I think I got it the day we got soaked on the march and had to let our clothes dry on us.

There is only one post here per diem so I don't know when you will get this. One of our cyclists comes out here daily with letters and the transport brings the parcels with the food. I think he has been and gone now.

There is no more news so I shall bottle up.

PS Excuse the writing as I am writing on my knee. I believe Jim is somewhere near here so I may see him some day. I may not be able to write so often now I am here but I shall try.

I forgot to tell you that I slept last night with several tons of dynamite and a lot of gun cotton, gelignite etc under my windows. As the person who told me last night said "If you hear a noise during the night you will know what it is". It was taken away elsewhere today.

Sunday 6th September 1914

My dear Jenny,

I am sleepy and it is now about half past nine, but unless I write tonight I don't know when I shall be able to do so as I believe we are going for a long march tomorrow.

We are living on the fat of the land just now. Today we had fried eggs, fried ham and sausages for breakfast with toast and bread and butter and jam. We then went to Church leaving here about quarter to ten and getting back at 1. At 2 we had lunch consisting of fried sausages, potatoes, cold tongue, stewed damsons and stewed fruit of various kinds, biscuits and cheese and jam, ending with coffee. We then did a certain amount of work taking the ranges until tea when we had boiled eggs, toast, bread and butter and jam and biscuits. Wingate and McCosh are dining out tonight with one of the surrounding gentry while I stayed at home and dined off cold grouse, cold tongue, stewed damson and fruits, biscuits and cheese, followed by chocolate and a smoke.

We got a whole heap of rabbit yesterday which we handed over to the men.

Unfortunately I have got to dine out tomorrow night. It is rather a fag. I would about as soon do without dinner altogether.

Jim walked over here this afternoon. He appears to be going strong and flourishing.

It is my turn in the bed tonight. Cheer Oh! As a matter of fact I can now sleep anywhere quite comfortably.

It is very funny the way one settles down into someone else's house just as a matter of course. I might have been here for weeks I feel so much at home. I don't know how the farmer likes being turned out of half his house.

I forgot to tell you that one of the sergeants is a butcher and he selects the steak, kidneys etc. for our use. He says they would be lost in the general stew which is given to the men so we might as well have them. We had mushrooms for dinner last night. I don't like them but it shows what war is like. It is fifty times better than the best picnic I was ever at.

Tomorrow morning we have bayonet fighting. The men are taught to start with a lunge, then to draw the bayonet back smartly as if pulling it out of a man to the shorten arms position in which they run on and meet the next man whom they stick with the mere force of the charge. They then draw the bayonet out of that man by swinging the butt of the rifle either up into the face of or down on the head of the next man. They then go on to trip up the next man and kick the man after. They only go through the motions here at present but that is the sort of way they would do in a charge. It is a cheery thing to teach and I think they all like it.

7th September 1914, Monday

My dear Doug,

I did not get my letter to Jenny posted last night or today so I shall enclose this with it.

We had a very good march today. We left about half past nine and got back about half past four. We took lunch with us and did about 18 or 19 miles.

We had a rather amusing sick parade before we started. We have no doctor here so Wingate acted as doctor. One man complained of pains inside so Wingate prescribed a pill and sent me off to the medicine chest that is left with us to give him one. I found in the chest a box marked 'Pills' which I opened and discovered about 30 bottles with various pills in them, all numbered and, in the lid of the box, the names. Unfortunately all the names were in Latin so I was rather up the tree. However I sent for a private of the RAMC that is attached to us and he selected two pills, one a small brown one and the other a large white one. He said the brown ones were mild and the white ones were very strong so I chose the white one. When I did so, he at once asked if the man was going on parade. As he was not, I whistled up the man and had the pill administered with all formality. I have not seen the man since to speak to but I expect he will be out tomorrow.

The Company has erected a very fine field oven which we shall try tomorrow. The architects are frightfully proud of it and I hope it works. It looks alright and is quite warm inside.

The Company have each subscribed 1d and bought a mincing machine, so as I said we are living off the fat of the land. Guess what I had for breakfast this morning. Grilled steak. It was very good. The kidney we had with it was not so good as it was rather hard.

Mathew Anderson dined here with McCosh tonight. He, Chalmers[5] and Gibson Fleming are billeted in a farm about two miles from here. Wingate and I were up dining with some people called Dobie. It was quite funny using napkins and silver again. The family consisted of Dobie and his wife, and three daughters. They could all talk for which I was thankful. They told us we had created quite a sensation at Church parade yesterday and are being held up as models to the other troops in the place.

Good night and good luck

9th September 1914

My dear Dad,

Yesterday I had more of less of a slack. I simply had to stand in the trenches and watch an attack on the position. It was quite interesting. I was told to write a report on the trenches after the attack and made it rather cutting but Wingate said he would send it in and take the responsibility for it.

---

5   Major John Stuart Chalmers DSO, 1/9th HLI, a High School of Glasgow pupil, Glasgow University (LLB 1903) graduate, qualified lawyer and close friend of the Coats family. One of six brothers who served in the war, three of whom fell. See *University of Glasgow* <http://www.universitystory.gla.ac.uk/ww1-biography/?id=2279> (Accessed 27 November 2015).

Today we had to attack in German formation just to show what the attack would look like. It is a beastly feeling coming on in a solid body, you feel so conspicuous. When the attack was over I went to look for someone and ran into what we call "brass hats" at our cookhouse. The brass hats turned out to be General Ewart the G.O.C-in-C. Scottish Command, General Egerton the G.O.C. Lowland Division and their staffs.[6] I got rather a shock, however I went forward, saluted and wished them good morning. They had been admiring the field oven which our men had made out of some mud and some scraps of iron. The General was good enough to say the men were showing some intelligence in looking after themselves. I tasted some steak that was done in the oven and found it excellent.

To return to the Generals, they were most affable. They asked several questions about the place, asked how long I had been in it, where I was staying, whether I was comfortable etc. etc. and we parted the best of friends.

I was glad to see them off the premises as I was afraid they would ask for Wingate and I was not sure where he was at the time.

Nothing much else happened except that two of the officers turned up in a motor with their wives and we gave them afternoon tea. Guess who was driving the car! Private Kenneth McClelland, at least so I was told. I don't know him by sight. I have a sort of idea he is going to take a commission.

10th September 1914

My dear Mother,
There is not much doing here today. I spent the forenoon teaching the men bayonet fighting and giving them various muscle exercises. It takes a long time as I have to take each man individually as there is no one else in the Company except the officers who can do it and the other two were not on parade. The men however are very interested in it, which makes it more pleasant. We had a visit from the Brigadier at lunchtime and I was quite bucked when he agreed with me that there was a lot to be done to the trenches. Unfortunately, he rather spoilt our lunch by making us half an hour late for it.

We intend to do another march of about 20 miles tomorrow when the officers are going to wear mens' kits and carry rifles to show that their kit is just as easy to carry as ours. I should like to rig some of the men up in our kit to see how they like it. I think they would be glad to get back their own.

---

6   Lieutenant-General John Spencer Ewart (1861-1930) and Major-General Granville George Algernon Egerton (1859-1951), GOC Lowland Division (re-designated 52nd (Lowland) Division May 1915). The latter's experience of command during the Gallipoli campaign proved unhappy and short-lived. See Compton Mackenzie, *Gallipoli Memories* (London: Cassell, 1929), pp. 165-67 and Elaine McFarland, *A Slashing Man of Action: The Life of Lieutenant General Sir Aylmer Hunter-Weston MP* (Oxford: Peter Lang, 2014), pp. 205-08.

By the way, the man I gave the pill to reported in the morning that he was feeling much better. Unfortunately, the doctor has removed his case of medicine so my doctoring days are over in the meantime. It was rather fun. Wingate has been let in for a bathe this afternoon with the misses Dobie. I hope he is enjoying it. He is already ¾ of an hour late for dinner so it is probably spoilt, like lunch. However, nil desperandum, it will at least be swallowable and will keep us from starving.

I have absolutely no more drivel so I shall shut up, with love to all.

11th September 1914

My dear Mother,
Please thank Dad for his letters which I got this evening. I did not go for the march today as I had to go into Dunfermline for the day but I walked into Dunfermline and a good deal of the way back with about £40 of silver, about 15 miles altogether.

We expected to have a slack tomorrow but this evening we have been ordered into Dunfermline tomorrow for an inspection so we shall do about another 20 miles tomorrow. I hope I see Doug.

By the way, we have been ordered to hold a very particular inspection of the mens' kits "in view of the prospect of an early move abroad". However I don't know if there is anything in this, as we sent for the instruments for our band a few days ago.

The General inspecting us tomorrow is General Capper.[7] If we go on at this rate I shall have seen and been seen by about all the Generals in the British Army by Christmas. I must say if we interest them as little as they interest us they must be pretty bored men.

13/9/14

My dear Jean,
We have been fairly busy lately. On Friday, the Company did a march of about 22 miles with full kit on and were told we going to have a day of complete rest on Saturday as we have not had a free day since we mobilised. However about 7 on Friday night we were told that we must go in on Saturday to Dunfermline for an inspection by General Capper, so on Saturday morning we started to walk to Dunfermline which is about 11 miles away. When we got to Dunfermline, we had another 1½ miles to go to the

---

7   Probably Major-General Thompson Capper (1863-1915). Inspector General of Infantry; appointed GOC 7th (Regular) Division 27 August 1914; killed in action at Loos 27 September 1915. See Richard Olsen, 'An Inspirational Warrior: Major General Thompson Capper' in Spencer Jones (ed), *Stemming the Tide: Officers and Leadership in the British Expeditionary Force 1914* (Solihull: Helion & Company, 2013), pp. 189-208.

inspection ground and on the way back to the billet at Dunfermline got soaked by a thunder plump. We got some tea in Dunfermline and then started back for here at about half past five. We did the last few miles in pitch darkness and got here about half past eight. We were out altogether about 11 hours. We fairly sprinted home. The times we took for six consecutive miles were 15 mins, 15½ mins, 15 mins, 14½ mins, 14 mins and 14 mins which is quite good going.

We had a Church Parade and a full blown kit inspection today, and tomorrow is a day of rest though strictly speaking we should be beginning our serious training.

Some of the officers have been inoculated for typhoid already and I expect I shall be done shortly. I believe it makes one feel rather seedy for two or three days and some people are completely laid up with it for some time, so if there is a break in my letters sometime you will now what is the cause. I think all the men are going to be done.

We have been spending all tonight doing a review of kit deficiencies. It is a rotten job. I wish we could get rid of all paper.

We had roast for dinner tonight done in the field oven. It was a great success.

By the way, would you ask Dad if he would mind ordering a Service Revolver for me? I could not get one when I was in Glasgow last and I forgot to order one. I think the best kind are Webley's. I can pay for it when it arrives.

14th September, 1914

Englemere, Ascot, Berks.

To: J.Q. Rowett, Esq.,
Perry Mount, Mayow Road, Forest Hill.

Dear Mr Rowett,
I write a line to thank you warmly for your kind response to my appeal for field glasses. Your glasses will be of the greatest possible service to our Non-Commissioned Officers in the field.

I am asked by the Commanding Officers of Units which are shortly expected to go to the front to convey their gratitude to the owners of the glasses distributed amongst their men,
Yours very truly,
Roberts, FM.[8]

---

8   Victorian military hero Field Marshal Frederick Sleigh Roberts (1832-1914). See also letters of 19, 25 September and 6 December 1914.

15/9/14

My dear Jean,
I think it is your turn for a letter but I am not sure and I don't suppose it matters.

I believe I am going to be inoculated this afternoon so I may be too seedy tomorrow to bother writing. I think you feel as if you had influenza for two or three days. I shall be quite glad of the rest at any rate.

I did not have a rest yesterday after all as I had to march the non-foreign service men into Dunfermline. They are being formed into two separate Companies and their places taken by others. Chalmers is being given charge of one of the Home Service Companies and someone else is getting his present Company. I don't think he is overly strong and he certainly can't stand much sun.

The march into Dunfermline yesterday was not particularly cheery. The weather was beastly, pouring wet and very windy and the men did not know what was going to happen to them. It took three and a half hours to get them in. I was brought back in the carrier of McCosh's motorbike in next to no time and got back about 7pm.

Today we spent the morning parade getting the men to sign Army Form E673 or something equally exciting and the forenoon parade was simply Company drill. I saw Jack in Dunfermline yesterday. He said he had seen Doug that morning. He had been marched up with a towel round his neck for a bath at the Carnegie Institute where we are billeted. Jack said he was quite cheery.

I nearly had to administer another pill yesterday, which was sent across by the Doctor but McCosh did it instead. However, I today prescribed no dinner for a man who acknowledged he had been eating too much yesterday. The man is an ex-school-master so he should have known better. He is a regular board schoolteacher, at least, I should imagine. He has absolutely no idea of discipline and has been on the defaulters roll 29 days since we mobilised. I am sorry for the people he had to teach.

I have absolutely nothing more to gas about so I shall switch off.

17th September 1914

My dear Jenny,
The Doctor did not turn up yesterday to inoculate us but he turned up all right this afternoon. There were 37 of the Company inoculated including myself. I gave them the lead. I was done about half past five and my arm is already pretty sore at half past nine. Otherwise I am so far quite flourishing. Unfortunately, Wingate is on leave just now and as McCosh and three of my best sergeants were also inoculated I cannot afford the time to lie up as I have to run the Company while Wingate is away. The way the Doctor inoculates is to take a small squirt armed with a steel needle about an inch long which he runs into the arm about the place where one is vaccinated and scoots dead typhoid germs into the arm. The idea is that the anti-typhoid germs in the body eat up the dead typhoid germs and as it were acquire the taste for them so that when

live typhoid germs appear they are simply gulped down by the anti-typhoid germs before they can say Jack Robinson. When I was told of the idea, it rather reminded me of acquiring a taste for oysters. I wonder if dead typhoids are as beastly. The stuff was all sealed up in a bottle and looked rather like some grouse soup we had for dinner the other night. I believe we go through the same performance in about 10 days.

Unfortunately, I think I shall go into Dunfermline tomorrow for the weekly pay. I think I shall take the train from Kinghorn. I have generally walked in for the pay but I expect I shall find tomorrow that the anti-typhoids are little tough worms and I shall have to take it easy. The men seemed much interested when I told them what was happening in their insides. Some of them are pretty sorry for themselves already. Personally I feel unusually cheery.

Math and Gibson-Fleming dined here tonight. Math was inoculated a few days ago and Fleming today. They are billeted in a farm about a mile from here.

The farmer is an awful old miser. He gets about £18 a fortnight for billeting us in an old barn and two rooms in the house. We have lent him two men a day for a fortnight to help with the harvest and he was today complaining that the men had broken two windows and burnt about 3/- worth of stobs. I told him that we would square up when we left, which may mean anything, and he was quite pleased.

Please thank Dad for his letter. It is rather interesting about the Germans shooting their sailors.

PS Please thank Dad for troubling about a revolver. I have sent in my name for one through the Orderly Room but I don't know if I shall get one. Meantime, I shall just carry on without one.

18/9/14

My dear Mother,

I have had quite a long day today in spite of the inoculation. I took a bayonet fighting class in the morning of those who had not been inoculated. I then gave a lecture in the forenoon to the men who had been inoculated as they were not supposed to do much. About half past 12, I walked to Kinghorn and took the train to Dunfermline to draw the Company pay. I got back about a quarter to seven and had dinner, and then got the men paid. I am not quite so chirpy tonight as I was last night but I can still enjoy my food so there is not much wrong. The Doctor was round today and was very surprised to find us all so cheery. I think some of them are beginning to feel the effects a bit tonight. They have all got sore arms and it is very funny to see them all going about with their arms bent. It hurts when you try to straighten the arm.

I believe we leave here for Dunfermline next Monday. I shall be very sorry to leave. Our place is being taken by another Company as we have had our share of the fun for a bit.

The weather has been pretty beastly here recently, strong wind and heavy rain but it doesn't worry us much.

There is absolutely no more news, so I shall stop as I am rather sleepy. It will take about six months for me to get my sleeps out when the war is over. All our sick men sleep for about 3 days straight on end when they are sent to bed. It is my turn for the bed tonight.

Your loving and practically sleeping son,
Walter J.J. Coats

PS The Doctor has now given us a cough mixture out here so we are having some more fun. He told us what men to give it to so tonight we had the table laid out with each man's pay and several tumblers of the mixture and when any man came in who was due the mixture, he had to swallow it before he left the room. The first man said he liked it so he told the next it was quite good but judging from his face he did not think so. It took away from the usual monotony of paying.

19/9/14

My dear Dad,

I am sorry to say we are leaving here for Dunfermline on Monday. However we have had our fair share of the fun.

I have had a fine slack day today. Wingate got back last night and told me I need not worry about getting up for early parade as he would take it. It was nearly half past seven when I actually got up. The forenoon parade was also easy as the men were all rather seedy. We simply got some rope and taught them various knots etc.

I see from tonight's orders that they are starting classes for the men in French 3 nights a week, and in German 2 nights. The classes are optional and I don't know how many will go but I expect a fair number will.

By the way if you have not given away your field glasses do you think you could let me have them? Wingate wants every sergeant in the Company to have a pair and they should be returned at the end of the war. If you have already given them away, of course don't go out and get others.

I hope I shall be able to get from Dunfermline to see you soon, but I don't know if I shall be able to get the night as to do so it is necessary to go to the Division. I should like to see a dentist before I go abroad and I may make that an excuse. As a matter of fact we have quite a good dentist in the Company as a private so I shall be all right as to the teeth. He told me he was making an income of over £1,000 a year before he rejoined us. We have a wonderful lot of miscellaneous talent in the Company. We have one man in the Company who is generally known as_____ M.A., C.B. He is the schoolmaster who has been confined to Barracks practically ever since we first mobilised. I heard him tell someone the other day that he wouldn't mind if "C.B." meant confined to bed.

I can't say any more. My think tank's too empty.

22/9/14

My dear Mother,

Here we are again at Dunfermline, worse luck. I would much sooner be away.

Please thank Dad for his offer to get anything I want. I have been sleeping in a sleeping bag ever since we mobilised except the odd occasions when I got a bed. We all got one as soon as we mobilised and also valises which are large canvas waterproof bags which we sleep in when outside and which carry all our kit. The officers don't get blankets issued so we would have all been frozen if we had not had them. We cannot afford to lose sleep through cold so you can be sure I shall get plenty of warm clothes.

Tomorrow I attend a Court Martial for instruction. The Sergeant Major told me the other day not to be surprised if I suddenly found myself appointed President of a Court Martial as they were chasing up all the legal men so I told him I had never been in a Court in my life, with the result I have to attend one tomorrow. I would not mind being a member but at present I have no desire to be President of one. However, it is all in a day's work.

I don't know if it is public knowledge yet but the whole of the Lowland Division has now volunteered and been accepted for foreign service. The General says however that we shall not get away until at least the 19th of December. Please don't tell anyone this news unless you find it is already public property.

I believe the officers are going to be kicked out of this billet during the winter to give the men more room. A few are staying here, about 8 are going to the Women's Institute up the street [6-8 Pilmuir Street] where there are 7 very comfortable cubicles with beds and chests of drawers in them, one being double bedded. The rest are being billeted with the inhabitants, at least I think that is the present intention. I don't know where I shall get but I hope it is the Women's Institute as the rest of the Mess premises, viz the Mess Room and a sitting room are in the same building.

Jack was inoculated last night and is pretty seedy today though he is not so bad as some of the others who were done last night. Chalmers especially was absolutely laid out today and has been ever since about quarter of an hour after he was done. It is funny how it takes some people worse than others. So far as I can make out, it affected me less than anyone else I have come across. I am absolutely all right now. I think my second dose is due on Saturday.

With any luck I think I shall apply for leave home next week but I shall see how things are going to turn out so you need not be disappointed if I don't turn up. Probably the first intimation of my coming will be when I walk in the front door.

Today, we did about 15 miles marching, about 3 or 4 miles being across a moor but after the training we got when we detached it was more or less of a picnic.

There is absolutely no more news so I may as well bottle up, with love to all

Your ever cheery son,

Walter J.J. Coats

PS We have just got another alarm, time 10.30 pm. Every man is to sleep fully dressed tonight and all ammunition is being issued.

24/9/14

My dear Jean,
The Court Martial was quite amusing for a bit but after a while, it began to bore and several of those who were there for instruction fell sound asleep. They were mostly majors and people like that so they did not get jumped on. What struck me about the whole performance was that the President was as much in need of instruction as anyone else. The show was pretty well run by one of the Members.

The night alarm the other night resulted in nothing but a very uncomfortable night through having to sleep in our uniforms. I found the boots the worst bit.

I was not on parade today as I am what they call subaltern of the day and have to look after the place when the others are out and see that it is cleaned up. It is a rotten job as the people who do the scrubbing are those who are too sick to go on parade. It is poor fun chasing about a dozen sick around with buckets and scrubbing brushes.

I moved into my new billet today at the Women's Institute. I have bagged a very fine cubicle opposite where the bath is and a fine, clear outlook from the window. As far as I can make out it is the only cubicle with a hot pipe through it so I should be pretty comfortable during the winter.

25/9/14

My dear Dad,
Many thanks for the field glasses, which arrived all right this afternoon. They are every bit as good as some prism glasses which I have tried. They will be returned at the end of the war if it can be managed. If they are not they will have died a very useful death.

I am due my second inoculation tomorrow but I don't expect to have a bad time. At any rate, I shall have Sunday to lay up on.

27/9/14

My dear Jean,
I was not inoculated yesterday after all but I expect to be done tomorrow. Some people say that if one does not take badly the first time, one is bound to take badly the second time, but I can't believe it and have no intention of feeling bad if I can help it which I think counts for a good deal.

I suppose you saw in the papers the other day that Uncle Walter has been appointed to the first or second something general hospital in Glasgow, at least I think that is it.

Would it trouble someone very much to send over a pair of khaki bags and puttees which I think are in the bottom left hand drawer of the wardrobe. Also a pair of brown boots which are in my room and a pair of football boots which are in my uniform tin. I also left a balaclava helmet on the seat in the billiard room which I should like sent, if it can be found. I hope it will not be too much worry.

I went to a local music hall last night but it was pretty feeble and I found the paper I had with me very useful at some turns.

The night operations I had the other night were quite successful. We went out to some ground about two miles out. We heard our bugler sounding "First Post" quite distinctly at half-past nine, everything was so quiet. We were very bucked with ourselves that morning when the Brigadier came to look at us with the machine gun. He just arrived in time to see us finish taking the gun off the limber and mounting it onto its tripod, so he asked us to do it again. We got the gun off the limber, mounted, aimed and loaded in 42 seconds which is the time allowed to mount the gun when it is all laid out ready for mounting.

We played hockey against Dunfermline and were beaten but gave them quite a good game. There is some talk of our taking a footer team through to play Fettes but I don't know if it will come to anything. I think I shall try and call there tomorrow afternoon for something to do.

Monday 28/9/14

My dear Jenny,
I am finding my present billet more comfortable every day. Upstairs in this building there are six cubicles done up in white enamel with beds, chests of drawers, radiators and mirrors in them, one of which I have managed to get. There is a bathroom just across a passage from my cubicle door and two basins and the Carnegie Trustees are supplying us with blankets and sheets. From my cubicle window I can see right across part of Dunfermline to the Forth. Downstairs there is a reading room done up with oak and a tea room done up in white, which we use as Mess rooms, and there is a hoist to the kitchen.

I had my second inoculation today and so far am only feeling a little tender where I was pricked in the arm. One man collapsed entirely within two minutes of being done and had to be assisted home.

I don't think there is any immediate prospect of our moving from here as the authorities have taken 18 of our transport horses to give to some other people. I believe they are going to give us pit ponies in exchange for some of them.

We had great fun this morning when we were out for a run. I spotted a wall about nine feet high at the highest and seven at the lowest and suggested to the O.C. Coy. that we might amuse ourselves by seeing if we could get over it. So we all rushed at it like mad bulls and most of us got over. We did it several times, just for practice. We want to try and teach the men to get over walls like that in full kit and also to vault instead of climbing fences.

I don't think there is any more news so I shall stop.

PS I am understudy for the Machine Gun Officer.

Wednesday 30/9/14

My dear Dad,

I am sorry to say that owing to information received last night all leave has been stopped until further orders so I am afraid I shall not get home for the weekend after all. It is a pity but it can't be helped.

My arm is practically all right now, it was only a little stiff this time and I did not even feel sleepy. I am going for a ride this afternoon with Wingate. I hope I don't fall off.

Thursday 8/10/14

My dear Dad,

At the present moment I am more or less of a stray. For drill purposes, I am attached to 'A' Company one day and Machine Gun the next. I am running 'C' Company as regards interior economy etc. as Wingate is away. I was with A Coy yesterday, Machine Gun today, I am subaltern of the day tomorrow when I go with neither and I am on a Court Martial on Saturday, when I cannot go with either, and all the time I am more of less responsible for 'C' Company. As Shakespeare says, "a man in his life plays many parts".

We are playing rugger against Rosyth Dockyard on Saturday, the proceeds to go to one of the funds and we are also trying to get up a performance by this Battalion in the local music hall, the proceeds also going to some fund like the Prince of Wales'. It should be quite good as we have at least two professional performers and some other very good people.

Leave is on again and I shall try and get some if I am not detached with the Machine Gun. The Machine Gun is going off on its own for some time tomorrow but I am still in the usual delightful state of uncertainty as to whether I am to go with it or not.

The ladies of Dunfermline meet in our Mess every Wednesday afternoon and knit socks etc. while we 'do the polite' and hand out teas etc. It was very funny last Wednesday to see the Adjutant winding a ball of wool and carrying on a polite conversation with a fair female who was holding the wool. I managed to escape them all except the dregs as I had another job on. Judging from the look of the dregs I hope I have the same luck next Wednesday.

There is absolutely nothing else I can think of to drivel about so au revoir or rather au re-gaser as they would say in France.

Saturday 10/10/14

My dear Mother,
I am off for detachment with the Machine Gun in half an hour but it is only to a place about 4 miles from here [Craigluscar Reservoir] so I expect I shall be in fairly often.

We played Rosyth Base at Rugby this afternoon and won by 6-0, which was quite good.

There is not much more news to tell you expect that I was a member of a Court Martial this forenoon. We tried two men. Unfortunately, I was the junior member so had to state my opinion, first as to whether the men were guilty or not, and then as to what sentence should be given. As a matter of fact, there was very little doubt about either case and we got the job done in about 3 hours.

14/10/14

My dear Jean,
This is a fine place out here. We are guarding the Dunfermline water supply, or at least part of it, at night and doing machine gun firing by day.

We put armed Military Policemen on duty during the day so that we can get shooting and then we mount a guard of about 12 men every night.

I have not fired the gun yet but I hope to get a few shots to try what it is like. In a fight I would probably not have any firing to do so it does not matter whether I fire it or not.

We had all the Battalion and Brigade horses out today to see how they stood the noise. Some of them are pretty bad. The transport officer's horse never even blinked when the firing was going on although it was standing within 10 yards of one of the guns.

I may as well stop, I have got to visit the sentries at any rate.

18/10/14

My dear Dad,
We are having great times here. One of us has to go and visit the sentries at night and it is the most amusing work. I fell down three times the other night. It was so dark I could hardly see my hand. I started by side slipping on a bank when I was going to the first sentry. I then sat down when I was coming off the bank of the reservoir where the second sentry was, and then ended up by falling over a wall when I was going for a

third sentry. It is quite safe and only adds a little entertainment to the night's activity. I don't use a light as I want to see if the sentries are doing their job properly.

I have got a most excellent book on Machine Gun tactics, which is keeping me busy just now in my spare time. I am very glad I took up the job as it has great possibilities and is most interesting as the book says "Annihilation should always be the final aim of machine-gun fire". One gun fires anything from 400 to 600 rounds in a minute and is estimated by the Germans to be equal to the fire of about 120 men. We have 2 new guns per Battalion.

I don't know how much longer I shall be out here. We may go home tomorrow or may stay here for another week. The authorities go pretty much on the principle of wait and see, when we ask them when we will be moving.

22nd October 1914

My dear Jean,

Many thanks for your letter which I got yesterday. I was hoping to get leave on Friday and Saturday of this week but I find that the other man in charge of the Machine Guns is hoping the same thing, so as his reason for getting leave is more urgent that mine I let him go instead.[9] He didn't want to take my leave from me but as he was obviously very keen to get away, I said he had better go. I hope to get home on Monday or Tuesday next week.

If you are going to motor up and look at the barbed wire entanglements etc., I would warn the driver to look out for sentries. They are swarming round the place like flies and some of them, at any rate, insist on stopping everything that passes and asking where you are going and what is your business.

I don't know how much longer I shall be out here but I expect to be in at the end of the week. It is just possible however that we shall be sent from here to Leven without going into Dunfermline at all.

If you motor up here on Saturday and find I am not in Dunfermline, you might ask if I am at Craigluscar and if I am, motor out here in the afternoon. It is quite a short run out and is very nice when you get out.

Thanks for your offer to bring out any grub I want but I think I am better without it. I get as much plain food as I can eat and I don't want extras.

I was dining out here last night and was very much struck by the whiteness of a clean table cloth (ours has been on for a week and is grey) and the brightness of the spoons etc. (ours are generally wiped on the table cloth before use).

Your loving brother,

Walter JJ Coats

---

9   Second Lieutenant, later Captain and Acting Major, William MacIntyre Todd MC.

25th October 1914

My dear Jenny,

We are going back to Dunfermline in about half an hour now and are all just waiting for the transport to take our stuff. We are marching to Leven tomorrow for field firing so all hope of leave is again gone until we get back which should be in about a week. It is just bad luck and can't be helped. If I had not taken up the Machine Gun I could have been home long ago but I would rather be the way I am. Math has been put in charge of the cyclists much to his disgust and Weir Grieve, who has re-joined, has been given the transport much to his disgust so I am very lucky where I am.

It is a regular October day here and pouring wet so I am not looking forward to the march to Dunfermline. Fortunately, it is only about four miles easy road. If it is like this tomorrow, it will be poor fun.

We have just got word that the 7th Highland Light Infantry transport officer who was to arrange for all the people here coming in, has just made a fearful hash of his arrangements and there is no hope of us moving for another hour and a half, so we shall not get to Dunfermline till 6 at the least and we <u>should</u> have been in by 3. Our last transport officer has had his job taken from him for incompetence (much to his open delight) and I expect the 7th HLI man will lose his job over this. In my present mood, I hope he does. As you will see, I have now got something to grouse about which I must say I rather enjoy occasionally when there is nothing else to do.

We had a most successful Church parade this morning. The Brigade Chaplain sent word he would hold a service here at 12, so we had to have one which none of us wanted as we were cleaning up to move. As luck would have it, there is a very cold wind and when he turned up we took him into a field where he got the full benefit of it. He suggested we might hold a service inside the billet, however we informed him we didn't think there was a room big enough to hold all the men at once so he had to hold the service outside. The whole service only lasted about 10 minutes as a result, and we got back to work.

I must stop now as I have absolutely no news except that I am always merry and bright.

Your grousy but strong on the wing brother,

Walter J.J. Coats.

27th October 1914

My dear Mother,

I am now at Leven and I have struck the best billet possible. I have a bedroom to myself with a bed about twice the size of the one at home and the three of us have a sitting room about half the size of the parlour at home. The Landlady of the place simply can't do enough for us. She is a decent old sort who thinks we will starve if we don't get afternoon tea. Leven is rather a nice place as far as I have seen, but I haven't seen much of it yet. We arrived last night in pitch darkness and were busy all morning today. The march yesterday was all right except for a long straight bit of road between Kirkaldy and Leven [Standing Stane Road], which got rather boring before we had finished. Kircaldy is about the most unique jumble of houses I have ever walked through. We halted just outside the place and a wee kid of about 5 with very bandy legs took up a position in the middle of the road and sang 'Onward Christian Soldiers', much to the amusement of the men who encored him and gave him pennies.

We expect to leave here at the end of this week or the beginning of next, when I shall plump for leave if it can be got.

There is no more news here except that I have ceased to be grousy. I was in a fearfully bad temper all yesterday but I am quite approachable again today.

Your loving son
Walter J.J. Coats

29/10/14

3, Berea, Leven

My dear Dad,
There is absolutely no news from here just now and I am only writing to let you know that I am still flourishing. We have most comfortable billets here with an old lady who thinks we will get cold if we sit in a room with the window open though she always opens it when you are out, and who thinks we will starve if we don't get tea at the proper time.

The country round Leven is very nice in fine weather and we have a view from our windows of the sea. There generally appears to be a torpedo boat or something like that at sea and yesterday a hydroplane flew along the coast. I don't know when we leave here but I rather think it will be Monday.

31/10/14

My dear Mother,
I don't know when I will get back to Dunfermline as we have to stay here until our shooting is done and so far we have not been able to do any, as we can only shoot out to sea and it has been too rough to put out the targets.

I am eating the most wonderful things just now, even grouse, and rice pudding. Last night, we had sardines, cocoa, hot toast, jam, rice pudding, pears and pineapple for supper. I stuck at the sardines, through if I had been starving I would have taken them too. At the end of the war, I may even be broken in to tomato soup.

The weather here in the last two days has been simply beastly, pouring wet with a very high wind.

Leven, 31/10/14

My dear Dad,

We have just got word here (9pm) that we are to entrain for Dunfermline tomorrow as the whole Battalion is leaving Dunfermline at 3pm tomorrow for the South. I believe we are going to be billeted somewhere near London, though I don't know for certain. One thing is certain, however, and that is I shall not get home for leave in the meantime at any rate. I may have a chance of seeing Ellie. I hope so.

I must switch off now, as I have to pack.

PS I shall let you know my address as soon as possible. The rest of the Brigade is rather sick that they are not coming too.

Dunfermline, 1/11/14

My dear Jean,

I believe we are not going south today after all. All our transport however is away this afternoon and the Battalion is understood to be prepared to move abroad at any moment. No one knows when or where we are going. It will be fearfully uncomfortable here, I expect, until we actually move. I wish I could have got leave before going but all leave has been stopped.

We had rather a rush getting in from Leven this forenoon. We had reveille at 4.30, breakfast at 5.30, started to load the transport at 6, and started to put the transport into the train at 7. We had a fearful job to get the horses onto the train. We had 12 horses and it took us an hour and a half to get them and 3 two-horse carts and a spring van. Some of the horses had to be pushed into the trucks by brute force. One horse, especially, took at least 10 men to load. It only took us 10 minutes to unload everything at this end.

It is just possible that if you come through some day this week, I may see you but it is equally possible that I won't.

Did you notice in the papers the other day that Graham Young's baby, who was born, I believe, on the day of the mobilisation, has died?[10]

There is absolutely no news here except that Math has resigned from being Mess President, as some of the "dug-outs" as we call them, eg Gibson Fleming, have been groaning at the way the Mess was run. They little know what a mess everything will now be in. Cowie is now Mess President and I expect he will either starve us or feed us on the fat of the land at about 15/- a day.[11] Math is thankful to be out of the job at any rate.

---

10 Captain (later Major) John Graham Young MC of the 5/9th HLI Glasgow Highlanders, educated at Glasgow Academy and Fettes College, just before the Coats brothers. Reference is to his son, Hector James Young who died in infancy.

11 Lieutenant J Archibald Cowie (later Captain), a former Glasgow Academy pupil.

WD: Mother and Father came through to see us and say good-bye on Monday [2 November] and we left in two trains on Monday night. The train I was in went straight through to Southampton which we reached on Tuesday morning. The second train went round by Edinburgh, where they picked up several hundred new men who had been drilling in Glasgow with the 2nd Bn (which had been formed there and subsequently took our place in Dunfermline). The train with the new recruits arrived at Southampton some hours after us and the rest of the day was spent getting these men told off to Companies etc.

Southampton, Tuesday 3/11/14 10.30pm

My dear Mother and Dad,

We have just got a telegram (10.30pm) to say that we are to move to France tomorrow afternoon. I was half asleep when I got the news but as I will have no time to write tomorrow and say goodbye, I am doing so now. We arrived here today about midday, after a fair journey and marched to a rest camp where we expected to be for two or three days. I expect there must be something up, they are in such a hurry. I expect I will be sending some money home tomorrow if I have time. It is Company money and I will send a note saying what it is. Could you put it on Deposit Receipt in name of Captain George Wingate, me and 2nd Lieut Edward McCosh, all of The Glasgow Highlanders and their successors in trust for 'C' Company, The Glasgow Highlanders and keep the D/R with the note of what it is pinned to it. I may not of course have time to send the money.

   I believe we are going to be in the fighting in the north of France.

   There is not much more to say except good bye and God bless you all.

   Your very loving son,

   Walter J.J. Coats

PS Please say goodbye to all relations, especially Jean, Ellie and Jenny and also to McG D & Co.

   Off at 2.30 today (Wednesday). No money being sent. Please thank Jean and Jenny for letters. Address probably Expeditionary Force. Absolute chaos, 400 recruits to equip in about 2 hours.

4th November 1914

My dear Dad,

We are now on board the steamer bound for, I believe, France. We have been on the rush ever since we left Dunfermline and the ship sailed about 7 tonight.

   While I remember, our address is Expeditionary Force, GPO, London, with of course our regimental name too.

There is no news but I can get this posted by the pilot at 12 tonight so I am writing while I can. You may find some of my kit turning up in Glasgow someday. I shoved it in an old sack and addressed to home, but I don't know if it will arrive. It doesn't much matter if it does not.

The boat we are on is called the "SS Novian".[12]

Please thank Jean and Jenny for their letters, which I got.

I have absolutely nothing to say so I may as well stop as all lights go out at 9.30.

Your loving son

Walter J.J. Coats

---

12 F. Leyland & Co. steamer SS *Novian*. Built by D & W Henderson LTD (Glasgow) 1913; scrapped at Pola 1934.

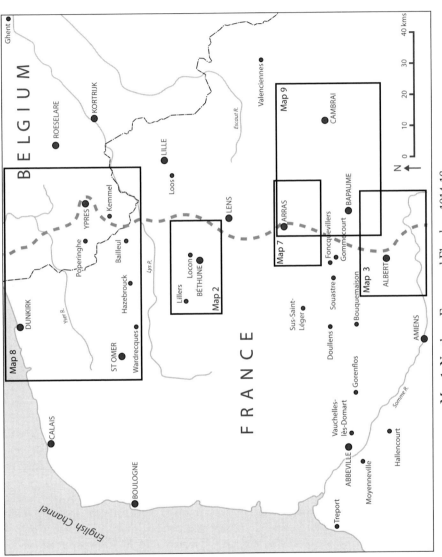

Map 1 Northern France and Flanders, 1914-18.

2

France

Somewhere where the sun is shining …

WD: 5th November 1914, hill top rest camp outside Le Havre. After getting the men settled in as well as possible, we hung around waiting for the transport to arrive but as there was no sign of it by dinner time the officers all went off to a neighbouring estaminet for something to eat. This place was the most theatrical I ever saw off the stage. There were two or three groups of villainous looking Frenchmen sitting drinking at small tables in front by the light of a very poor oil lamp and the moon and the building itself completed the picture. When we got inside, we walked, or rather fell, up a very narrow and pitch dark stairway and found ourselves in a large empty sort of loft with two tables running down it from end to end. It certainly did not look very promising but they gave us quite a good meal of soup, omelette and I think chipped potatoes with beer and red wine to drink. We finished up with the usual round slabs of bread with butter and cheese. As this was the first decent meal we had had since breakfast on the steamer, I ate not wisely but too well. I would probably have eaten more unwisely if I could have got something to drink, but I did not care for the beer or wines and was afraid of the water.

After dinner we returned to camp expecting to find the transport but it did not turn up till about 11 p.m. We found that the guide who was left to bring it up had tried to take a short cut which the transport could not get up and had then been unable to find his way onto the proper road. As we had been told we would not be moving next day, we unloaded it in order to get our kits out and then turned in expecting to get a decent rest.[1]

6th November: We had not been lying down more than an hour or so however before we were roused up and warned that we must be ready to move by 6 a.m. and were eventually turned out about 4am in order to get breakfast and have the camp cleaned before we left. We moved off in due course about 6 and marched to the Railway Station where we found several other battalions waiting to entrain.

---

1   The strength of the Battalion upon arrival in France was "30 officers, 1008 men, 63 horses, and 22 vehicles." See TNA WO 95/2431: 1/9th HLI War Diary.

As my company had done the unloading the day before we now had a stand easy while the other companies took turns at loading the train. I seized the opportunity to have a wash and a shave with a mugful of water from my bottle and then went and had a second breakfast at a hotel opposite the station.

We eventually left Havre about noon and after a very uncomfortable journey as there were eight in the carriage and someone had put his head through the window shortly after starting, we arrived at St Omer between 11 and 12 next day.[2]

7th November: Here we were put into a siding as no one seemed to know where we were supposed to go and while the men were having breakfast the officers were allowed to wander round a bit. Math and I went off to try and find something to eat but not knowing the town of course found our way into the poorer part of it. We thought at the time however that the whole town was probably the same so after some hesitation went into a very dirty looking estaminet where they gave us the inevitable omelette and coffee.

When we got back to the train we found that orders had been received to detrain and that the men were all out. Even now however no one seemed to know where we were to go and it was dark before we eventually moved off. After marching 7 or 8 miles, during the latter half of which smoking was prohibited, we arrived at Wardrecques where we were to billet. There was considerable delay here while billets were being found but eventually half the Battalion was put into a paper mill and the other half into a tile factory with the officers in a very second rate house attached to the factory.

Sunday, 8/11/14

Somewhere where the sun is shining

My dear Mother,

I am sorry I have been so long in letting you hear from me but we have been very busy ever since we left Dunfermline. Today is the first day since we left that we have not spent some time either in a boat or on a train. We have already done a 24-hour train journey in this country. I can't tell you where we are as we have orders not to say, and I believe both incoming and outgoing letters are censored. The weather has been very fine ever since we left and I have seldom felt so hot marching as I did the other day when we marched from the Coast to a rest camp and we were hurried out of it the morning after we arrived.

The matches here are the absolute limit. Would it be possible to send some out, perhaps safety ones or, if not, the other kind?

---

2   St Omer was the headquarters of BEF C-in-C Field Marshal Sir John French from 13 October 1914.

It is funny how one settles down to everything here just as a matter of course. All the officers are in an old, semi-deserted xxxx-house and the men in buildings round about.[3] The worst of the country is the lack of decent drinking water. The wine is as beastly as it was when I was over here last, but if it comes to a pinch it can be swallowed.

Thank goodness I know enough French to push on with. I expect to be quite a French scholar by the time I get home. The chief words here are 'du pain', 'de l'eau a boir' and 'bougie' [wax candle]. Do you think you could send me out a ball of the strongest string you can find, not rope?

Math has already had a smash with his motor bike. He was gaily riding along the <u>left</u> side of the road in the dark without a light when he bumped into another of our officers on another motor bike. The other officer got the worst of it and smashed his wrist.[4]

Jack sent a printed post card and sends all the usual good wishes and so do I. We are all most flourishing. No more news.

10/11/14

9th H. L. I.
Expeditionary Force, France

My dear Dad,

We are still flourishing here. My Company is outpost Company tonight so I am writing this at 3am. One officer has to be awake all night and my turn is from 2 to 4.30am. I am glad to say that things are settling down a bit after our rush across here. We are still in the place I wrote Mother from last and as far as I can see at present there is no immediate prospect of our moving but one never knows we may be off today. We are within sound of the battle but so far I have not seen a shot fired in anger. We are being put up to all the lessons so far learnt in the war.

So far the only news I have had here is what could be gathered from two rotten old rags of French papers which gave absolutely no news.

I am enjoying the life here very much although we are rather pigging it. We are fed very well though at irregular intervals and it is funny how one is absolutely satisfied lunching of a couple of Army biscuits and possibly a drink of water. The biscuits are excellent, though very hard. They are sent out in large wooden boxes lined with tin.

We are living in a funny old château with one room lit with gas and the rest of the place as dark as pitch and absolutely devoid of furniture.

---

3   An old paper mill and tile factory at Wardrecques, near St Omer.
4   The 'other officer' was Lieutenant Andrew Currie Murray (a Glasgow Academical). He was killed in action at the Hindenburg Line near Fontaine-lez-Croisilles, 20 May 1917.

I have just been helping to censor some of the mens' letters. It is quite amusing at first but one gets fearfully bored looking at about 50 letters per diem.

10th November 1914

My dear Ellie,

Nous sommes voici enfin, as they would say here, at least I think they would. My French is weird enough to make a French cow laugh but, so far, I have been able to get along all right. We are billeted in a funny old château within sound of the battle but as far as I can see, at present there is no immediate prospect of getting into the trenches. The trenches are very narrow, so once we get into them I think that we shall be a good deal less comfortable than we are here. The feeding here is rough but there is plenty of it and the weather has been splendid, although it gets very cold at night.

I have been helping to censor some of the men's letters. It is a very stale form of amusement. The idea is they that they are first censored by the O.C. Company, then by a bigger bug, in our case a Major, who stamps them as censored, and they are then liable to be opened by still bigger bugs. All the Officers' letters are censored by the Major.

PS: 15 bags of letters arrived, so you can imagine the confusion getting them sorted out. My remarks about the weather were rather premature. We got simply soaked last night and today there is a very cold wind. We had a day's most strenuous physical workout today, but no brainwork, thank Goodness. When I get home, I shall take a holiday before going back to the office. It will be very funny settling down to a desk after this sort of thing. I shall have to learn my Law all over again.

Must stop for dinner.

14/11/14

My dear Jean,

We are still flourishing here and I am now allowed to tell you some of our movements. We sailed from Southampton to Le Havre on Wednesday night, leaving at about 7pm and arriving at about midday on Thursday. We marched to a rest camp, several miles out where we were dumped down for what we thought would be several days. The officers messed in a café close by in a room that reminded one of "The Only Way". We retired to bed early as we had very few candles with us.

About 3am on Thursday morning, we were roused by people shouting for the transport officer and at about 4 we were all roused up and told to be ready to move off in 2 hours. It was frightfully cold getting up before sunrise. We got some sort of scratch breakfast, and moved off to the station where we spent the morning getting the transport horses etc. onto the train. I got a shave and a wash on the platform with water from my bottle. We got away about midday, the men being put 30 in some cattle trucks and the rest 8 in a compartment. I was in a compartment with 8 other officers and it was a fearful squash with all our swords, haversacks and rucksacks. The train went very slowly. About 6 o'clock at night, one of the men in my compartment unfortunately put his head through one of the windows. The result was we sat in a howling gale for the rest of the journey. To add to the general excitement the gas would not work as the mantle was broken. We dined off bully beef and biscuits and water with some wine we got at a stop, by the light of two candles stuck on the arm of the seat. There was only about 1 plate, 2 knives and 2 spoons in the compartment so the meal was rather scrappy. We travelled all that night and arrived [St Omer] about 8 miles from here [Wardrecques] about midday the next day. The towns we passed through which we are allowed to mention are Boulogne and Calais. We started to unload shortly after we arrived and then marched out here arriving after dark. Of all the beastly things I ever marched on, greasy cobble stones are the worst. I can't mention any more of our doings in the meantime.

Please tell Mother not to worry about my sending home 2 pairs of pyjamas. I am sleeping in my clothes when they are dry enough, as they generally are, and 35 lbs of baggage gives us very little room for luxuries.

We got soaked yesterday and today the weather has gone to bits. After getting soaked yesterday, the men all got rum, which those who took had to drink in the presence of an officer. It was more amusing to them than the field administration. Math sends kind regards.

Love to all.

PS I am enjoying myself top hole and am very fit.

WD: We spent about three weeks here digging trenches 18 inches wide which we were told was the correct width, and training generally. The chief incidents of interest were a collision between Math and Murray on their motor bikes as a result of which Murray retired to hospital; the lack of chocolate and tobacco; the beginning of the censorship of letters and the perpetual guard that was kept on duty all round the billets.

The Officers' messing arrangements, as with most battalions when they first came out, completely broke down and we lived for days on bully beef and biscuits, with occasionally bread and tinned butter. The messing turned out to be fairly expensive as the officer who had been appointed Mess President [Cowie] the day we left Dunfermline had put the mess money in one pocket and his own in another and had left all the accounts behind. He then proceeded to forget which pocket was which and we found ourselves paying several times over. As he was wounded shortly after [27 November 1914], we never got his accounts properly squared up.

19/11/14

My dear Jenny,

I am on duty again tonight from 1.30 till 4 am so I am taking this opportunity to write to you. Many thanks for your last letter. Please also thank all the others for theirs, they are most welcome. I have been spending my spare time censoring letters just now. I have sent off several and as you will see from the dates, they were written very soon after we left, though you had not received any a few days ago. Please thank Dad for the "Times". It is about all the definite news we get though it is a week old. I expect by the time you get this we will be actually in the firing line as we expect to move tomorrow or the next day. The weather has now changed from rain to frost which is a fine change though it is very cold. There was ice on the water yesterday. The thing I should like best just now is a soft warm bed with clean sheets in a clean room with no time limit. While I remember, please thank Mother for the intention of sending chocolate and tobacco. It is impossible to get chocolate here but I get more tobacco than I can smoke. Matches are scarce. It is funny what a craving one gets for something sweet. I suppose it is habit. Could you send me some cheap coloured handkerchiefs. White ones are no use for this sort of work. One or two cheap ones fortnightly would be better than expensive ones.

The big guns have been going very strong these last few days so I expect there is something doing. We hear nothing here.

I shall stop as it is nearly 4 o'clock.

Love to all.

PS We are both flourishing and fit to stand anything in the way of bad weather. It has been snowing heavily today and the ground was covered about an inch in a few hours.

21/11/14

My dear Dad,

We are moving to the front on Monday. This is definite. It is very cold here as we have had hard frost ever since the snow fell. It is much better than rain. We had three local French officers spending the evening here tonight and treated them to bagpipes etc. The senior one who was rather a jolly old boy got fearfully excited and the others all seemed to enjoy it. I expect we shall have a slack tomorrow as we are moving on so soon. We have been spending a great deal of our time here digging trenches. It has been fearfully hard work as the ground is practically solid clay. The trenches are only 18 inches wide and one has to dig oneself in up to the chin. It seems funny to think that we may spend a great part of the winter in an 18 inch hole in the ground. There are of course places behind, where one can get rest and I believe they try and work it so that gets one day in and one day out of the trench.

By the way, one of the French officers reminded me very much of John Rowett. How are he and Ellie getting on? I wonder if it is his rum we are getting here. There is not much in the way of news here except that we are both very flourishing. It is still hard to think we are at war. As a matter of fact I don't suppose we shall realise it till it is all over. It must be a great deal harder for you than for us. We are all as cheery as crickets. Please don't trouble to send tobacco as we get a free issue every week and it is more than I can smoke. I shall keep this open in case there is any more tomorrow. Meantime, Good night.

[Cont.] 22/11/14

This is a glorious frosty day with bright sunshine and we are busy getting ready to move today. All the officers are sending their swords back as they are more danger than use. I am glad to see the last of mine. I expect we will only carry revolvers and possibly a bayonet. I believe we are going to be put into the XX [5th] Brigade 2nd Division, but I am not sure as this is only a rumour, and not official.

The men were paid today for the first time since we left Dunfermline. They got Fr 12.50 each, which should keep them going for some time. I expect I shall be able to tell you where we are just now in about a fortnight's time.

PS I may not be able to write so often from now but I shall try and get some official postcards which will let you know that I am still flourishing.

WD: We eventually left Wardrecques on 22nd November to join the 5th Brigade, 2nd Division[5] in place of the 2nd Connaught Rangers who had been practically wiped out.[6] We reached Hazebrouck on the 22nd, where we spent a very uncomfortable night, and on 23rd, after being inspected by General C C Monro,[7] who was then commanding the Division, we moved off and joined the 5th Brigade under General Haking[8] at Bailleul. The

---

5   The 2nd (Regular) Division, consisting of 4th (Guards), 5th and 6th infantry brigades, was mobilized and dispatched to the continent in August 1914 as part of the original British Expeditionary Force (BEF). See Major A.F. Becke, *Order of Battle of Divisions Part I – The Regular British Divisions* (London: HMSO, 1935), pp. 41-47 for full orders of battle.

6   The 2nd Connaught Rangers had suffered crippling losses (Rear guard affair of Le Grand Fayt, 26 August 1914) during the Retreat from Mons. As a first-line Territorial unit, 1/9th HLI was dispatched to France in order to reinforce Regular formations worn down by heavy losses during the first months of the conflict.

7   Lieutenant-General Sir Charles Monro (1860-1929) GOC I Corps from December 1914; GOC Third Army July-October 1915; GOC First Army February-August 1916; C-in-C India 1916-20.

8   Brigadier-General Sir Richard Cyril Byrne Haking (1862-1945) GOC 5th Brigade 20 November-20 December 1914; Major-General and GOC First Division 1915; Lieutenant-General and GOC XI Corps 1915-18. See Michael Senior, *Haking: A Dutiful Soldier: Lt. General Sir Richard Haking, XI Corps Commander 1915–18: A Study in Corps Command* (Barnsley: Pen & Sword, 2012).

5th Brigade then consisted of the 2nd Ox and Bucks L.I., 2nd Worcestershire Regt and 2nd H.L.I. The 2nd Division consisted of the 4th Guards Brigade, the 5th Brigade and the 6th Brigade. We spent the 24th in billets in Bailleul.

24/11/14

My dear Mother,

There is practically no news to tell you except that we have been marching for two days and are going into the trenches tomorrow night. I have not received any letters from you since we started to move but I have no doubt they will arrive sometime. Please tell Dad not to worry about sending any more newspapers to me as we see them here only a day later and his generally take about a week to arrive.

Everything is flourishing with us so far and Jack and I are both in the best of health and spirits. Wingate and I are at present billeted on an old French woman who insists on coming and talking to us at the rate of about fifteen words per second. Neither Wingate nor I know much French so the result is rather amusing. I do the interpreting of the French as far as possible and he does the talking. I think I could make a better job of the talking than he does but he seems to like trying himself.

The roads in this country are easily the worst I ever struck both for machinery and motoring.

The frost has gone today entirely though there is still snow on the ground. I hope it doesn't start raining again.

Censor: E McCosh

24/11/14

My dear Ellie,

Many happy returns of your birthday, if it is not too late. I am sorry I forgot to write in time. I expect to be in the trenches tomorrow night. Mercifully I am more concerned about procuring a good dinner than anything else. I hope I can find the café we have booked. These French towns appear to me to be dumped down anywhere and anyhow. I wonder if it is some of John's rum that is being issued to us here. It is done up in Gallon jars and a ration is two jars per Company i.e. about 120 men. How is his business flourishing? I must stop now as it is time to go for that dinner.

PS The dinner was all it was held out to be. My feelings before going into the trenches are the same as before going to a dance.

WD: We left Bailleul on the evening of the 25th for the trenches near Kemmel. Before we moved off, General Haking came to see us and told us we would probably be shelled on the way up at a certain time as the Germans always sent over a few shells at that time at a certain point on the road. He said he had so arranged it, however, that we should be clear of that place by the time the shells were due, unless there were any delays on the road. We moved up though Locre and shortly after, when I was thinking of something else, I nearly sat down with surprise when there was a shriek and a bang and a shell dropped close to the road a little behind us. I then remembered what the General had said and when the first shell was followed by two others in quick succession I hoped he knew what he was talking about. As it turned out, he did, because no more came over while we were near there. This was the first time most of us had been anywhere near shells bursting and though they didn't say so, I don't think the others liked it any more than I did.

Shortly after this the Company Commanders were called away and I was sitting wondering what would happen next when suddenly the Company in front started moving and before I could get the men on their feet it had vanished in the dark. I followed as soon as we were ready but had quite an anxious time before I got in touch with them again as I had no idea where I was or where we were supposed to be going and had more than half the Battalion behind who knew even less than I did. When we did make up on the other Companies we found them assembled in a field just off the road. Wingate again turned up here and told us that A and B Companies were to go into the line with our Company (C) and D in support, the other half of the Battalion (we were then organised in 6 companies) being in reserve.

We waited here till a guide turned up from the Battalion we were to relieve and we then moved off after the two leading Companies. After walking along the road for about half an hour (there were no communication trenches), we found ourselves at our destination which was simply a series of holes dug at the side of the road. The Company we were relieving then handed over to us and we were left to our own devices.

After the men were all in, I joined Wingate and McCosh in Company H.Q. This consisted of a narrow hole long enough for two to lie down in while one sat at the foot. It was half roofed over with straw but the roof was not high enough to allow one to do more than sit up in. During the night we each took turns on duty but nothing exciting happened except for a lot of musketry fire in front.

The next day [26 November] passed fairly quietly the Germans being content to chuck over a few shells at odd intervals. None of these however landed near enough to do more than scatter the mud over us.

As soon as it got dark, I was sent off to report to Battalion H.Q. and let them know how we were getting on. The road back was inches deep in liquid mud but I was rewarded on arriving at Battalion H.Q. by a very excellent supper. I found them very comfortably settled in a farm house with plenty of straw for beds and a nice warm fire at one end of the room. After giving them the news and finding out what arrangements were being made to send up water and rations, I sat down and had supper while the ration party was getting ready and then took them up with me to the Company. This night passed as peacefully as the one before and next day, as things were getting rather monotonous, I spent the time trying to cut my hair with the assistance of a pair of nail scissors and a shaving mirror. I managed pretty well as regards the front but found the back more difficult as I could not see it and had to do it by touch.

We had been told the night before that we would be relieved that night by the Liverpool Scottish, so as soon as it was dark enough McCosh went off to guide them up while we got ready to hand over. The relief did not take long and we then moved back and rejoined the Battalion close to Battalion H.Q. We waited here for some time for the Companies who had been in the front line but as things were rather uncomfortable owing to the number of stray bullets that were coming over we were taken back to a safer distance after one of the officers [Cowie] had been hit. Shortly afterwards the other Companies arrived and we moved off for Bailleul. The march back seemed very much longer than the march up and we were all very glad when we arrived at Locre to find that the Quartermaster had brought up the cookers and had tea waiting for us. We rested here about an hour and then moved on again to Bailleul which we reached in the early hours of the morning.

Much to our surprise, Wingate and I found on our arrival that the owner of our billet, Vve. Mackereel, had supper waiting for us and had also during our absence fixed up an extra bed for me to sleep in. Unfortunately there was nothing to drink for supper but beer. As I was very thirsty I drank a fair amount of this and as a result woke up next morning feeling far from well. After half a day in bed however I was as fit as a fiddle again.

Sunday 28th November 1914

My dear Jenny,

I think it is your turn for a letter, though I don't suppose it matters. If it is not too much trouble, would you please send me the boots and puttees which I sent home. The mud is so bad here shoes simply go to bits in no time. I am sorry to trouble you but I did not know they would be wanted when I sent them home.

You will be interested to hear I have at last been in action. I was in the trenches 48 hours. I was in reserve, so inhabited a dug-out behind the fire trenches. A dug-out is simply a hole in the ground. It was very muddy and one could not stand up, but one could lie out perfectly straight so it was not so bad. Since we got back I have been suffering from a severe stomach ache brought on, I think, by two glasses of beer which I drank when we go back at 3am. I was so dry I had to drink something and could get nothing else. I am quite cheery and bright now. The first 24 hours in the dug-out were very quiet and we were only sniped getting out and in, which we did at night. The second day was more cheery as we were shelled practically all day with Black Marias and shrapnel. Damage done: 1 tin of jam laid out outside a dug-out and a little extra mud inside. It is a funny feeling at first listening to the shells coming towards one. One can hear them a long way off and has quite time enough to wonder where they will burst before they go bang, what ho! she bumps.

There is not much in the way of news to tell you except that I have a splendid billet here [Bailleul] and Madame [Veuve Mackereel] is very kind to us.

PS New address: Glasgow Highlanders, 5th Brigade, 2nd Division, 1st Army Corps, Expeditionary Force, France.

1st Dec 1914

My dear Dad,

I have just been talking to my landlady and she tells me there were 40,000 Germans in this town for 10 days during which time the inhabitants had to live as best they could. She says they kept their horses in people's drawing rooms.

Thanks for the Fettesian.[9]

PS If Mother sends shirts please ask her to send khaki ones and also an occasional khaki collar from the lot I sent home.

2nd Dec 1914

My dear Mother,

Very many thanks for the splendid parcel of stuff which arrived safely today. Please don't send any more clothes however, as I have been able to get all my clothes washed here just now so have not scrapped anything yet, and we are only allowed 35lbs of baggage.

Jenny suggested in her letter that you were worrying about the lack of warm clothes I have. You need have no worry at all on that point. I was issued about two days ago with a lined surcoat and we are all going to get sheepskin waistcoats so you can be sure we won't go wrong.

While I remember, I would like to warn you against believing all you hear about our doings in the papers, especially extracts from men's letters etc. Some of the men are given to writing the most extraordinary drivel in their letters and fairly pile up purely imaginary hardships.

I don't think I told you, we celebrated St Andrew's night with an extra special dinner. I ate not wisely, but was none the worse as the food was more or less plain.

PS It is a funny thing that since I came here I have practically given up smoking. I have only smoked about 25 cigarettes since I came over and I very seldom smoke a pipe. I think it is that when I was at home I only smoked when I wanted something to do and here I never want something to do. When I have nothing to do I have the greatest pleasure doing nothing, eg when I have finished this I intend to laze until dinner. I think I was born lazy, which is a great asset for life in the trenches.

Later: I am now allowed to say where we went after leaving Calais, We arrived at St Omer and marched from there to a place called Wardrecques, where we were billeted so long. You will be interested to learn that Jack was lucky enough to win

9   Fettes College journal.

the draw for what Captain should go to Lord Roberts' funeral and Math won the draw for the Lieutenant.[10] They said the funeral was impressive. We sent a detachment to take part in the procession and our Pipe Major was in charge of all the pipers in the show.

I saw the King today and we are to be inspected by him tomorrow.

[Cont.] Dec 4th

Still flourishing and so far no sign of moving. Have just heard we have "Hurled back the Prussian Guard". This is the first we have heard of it. Shows how much you should believe of what the papers say. Three quarters of us have not seen a German yet, myself included, though we have been potted.

Very comfortable here and hoping for a bath tomorrow. Glory.

6th Dec 1914

My dear Jean,

We are having a Church Parade today and it is wonderful how all the men look forward to it. It is the second since we came over, the first being last Sunday. While I remember, please don't send me much at Christmas. I have enough clean clothes just now to carry me till the New Year, also enough tobacco etc. In fact as usual there is nothing I want and I have as much as I can carry.

[Cont.] Monday 7th

Last night I went to the local Church. It is a great big place and the music is supposed to be very fine but I must say it seemed too squeaky for me. Today is inclined to be wet and beastly again, in fact a regular winter day. Most of us have been or are suffering from influenza. I think I got my spell over the day after I was in the trenches. I slept the whole day, which is generally what I do with influenza.

I am glad to say the men have now been cut down to one letter and as many post cards as they like every four days. The censoring job was getting too much of a good thing before, as you can imagine when Wingate and I had 250 letters to censor in one night.

By the way, yesterday I censored a letter written to the Glasgow Herald for publication. It is fearful drivel but I suppose it will be published. I don't know how the man had the nerve to write it.

Madame Mackereel has asked me to get her son an English pipe – one that comes apart in two bits. Do you think you could send me one, price about 2/- or 2/6d as I

---

10 Field Marshal Roberts died of pneumonia at St Omer on 14 November 1914; Jack Coats later observed: Lord Roberts' funeral service "was most interesting – very simple and very impressive. I was standing almost beside the Prince of Wales at the service."

should like to give him one as Madame has been fearfully kind to me ever since I came here. I will pay for it when I get back. She offered to pay for it but I said I would give it as a souvenir – about the fiftieth she has got of us. She takes anything, even old envelopes with a British stamp on them.

I shall not close this until the post comes in. It is wonderful how regular the post is. It arrives every day for us to get our letters and parcels at lunchtime. Strange to say the post has broken down today and so far I have not got a letter. While I remember, would it trouble you to send me a pair of wire cutters, strong and, if possible, light and insulated if possible so that I shall not get a shock.

This is about the beastliest day we have has so far. It must be fearful in the trenches. By the way, could you send me one of those very small packs of cards about 2 inches by one inch. It will be useful to while away the time if I ever find myself in a reserve trench again. Talking of whiling away the time, I don't suppose there are any dances in Glasgow this season. Is there a pantomime and, if so, what is it called?

9/12/14

My dear Jenny,

We are still in the same old place. I got six letters yesterday, one from Jean, one from Ellie and two each from Dad and Mother. It was splendid. You have no idea how absolutely everyone in the Battalion looks forward to the mail. It is raining again here today. It seems to rain every second day. We went for a march yesterday of 8 or 9 miles and felt much the better of it. I think we are all getting soft again from lack of work. It is funny how safe we feel here compared to the periodical fits of alarm we used to have in Dunfermline. Here we take off our clothes to sleep every night and all the motor cars go about with great blazing headlights, whereas in Dunfermline we used to sleep sometimes in our clothes and headlights were forbidden.

You might tell Dad that I have not yet managed to find the man McCallum, but that Balfour[11] is in my Company and is a very decent sort. Very quiet but very willing. There is also another man in the Company he may know. Linsday, of Lindsay Meldrum and Oats, or a son of that Lindsay, I am not sure which.[12]

I spent last night filling a pair of government boots with castor oil. I bought a Franc bottle and simply poured the stuff inside the boots, scrubbed in what I could with my fingers and left the rest to soak in. It makes the boots fine and soft and, I believe, water-proof. It also keeps the feet warm, though at first it makes them rather dirty. If you have means, I believe it is a good thing to leave them standing in the oil.

---

11 Pte 2461 Andrew Campbell Balfour.
12 Possibly Pte 2631 William Archibald Lindsay, died of wounds 1 February 1915. See Weir, *Come on Highlanders!* p. 74.

I have just received a parcel of Currant Bun from Skinner. I hate the stuff myself but I gave half to Madame and half to the Mess. I also received the parcel with the shirt etc, for which many thanks. Please, however, do not send me anything more in the clothes line except one pair of the thickest socks you can find per week until you hear from me. I simply can't carry any more stuff about with me as I have all I came away with quite clean and all I have received since.

I am sorry to have to stop you sending out stuff as I know you like doing it, but I have everything I want and you have no idea what an awful amount of stuff is sent out. One officer's people wrote to him to say they had found out that they might forward something like 75 lbs of clothing to him and that they were making up his kit bag he had left at Southampton to that amount and were forwarding it on. The officer was not only distinctly ungrateful but simply furious and wrote home a letter that I should certainly not have done at a time like this. His people were rather fools however, e.g. they sent his blue patrol which we use for messing in at camp.

Please don't believe all you hear about us in the papers. Cowie was not wounded by a sniper and was not such a silly fool as to get wounded the way the papers said. He was about a mile from the trenches when he was hit by a stray bullet, which passed over my and two other officers' head and then picked off Cowie from a group of three officers. It was dark at the time and just a case of bad luck. There were about 700 of us standing around who might just as well have been hit.

Friday 11/12/14

My dear Dad,
I am as happy as a King. In the first place, I have just had a warm bath, two buckets of hot and one of cold water in a decent bathroom. In the second place, I have managed to raise a Christmas present for Mother and the girls. I don't know exactly how they will manage to divide it up but I have no doubt they will manage somehow. It is two bits of true 'Valenciennes Lace', guaranteed hand-made by the daughter of the house, who makes excellent lace herself, and a larger bit of 'Calais Lace' (silk – not hand-made). The daughter of the house is also giving me a bit for "mes trois soeurs" which she made herself. She will not take anything for it though. It is the finest bit of lace I have seen and is about 4 yards long. I will mark which bit it is and if Jean is not too busy, do you think she could write and thank her for it? I know Jean is fearfully busy in that line, but Madame and her daughter have been so fearfully decent to me I would like if she could write and thank her, as a Christmas present to me. Her name is Noelle Mackereel, 116 Rue de la Gare, _____ though I can't in the meantime say what town [Bailleul]. If you enclose the letter to me I will see she gets it.

I have a picture postcard of my billet here, which I will send home when I am allowed by the censor.

Many thanks for your offer of money. I have plenty here as I can draw on the Field Cashier. The Currant Bun and shortbread were much appreciated by the Mess.

Please thank Mrs Robertson for her kind enquiries and wish her a Merry Christmas etc. from me. If you see Mr McLean, you can tell him that the man who is acting as Chaplain to our Battalion here just now is a Mr Connor, I don't know what Church he has or whether he is purely an Army Chaplain.[13]

I don't know when we are moving from here but so far there is no word of it.

There is really no news except that there was a man turning upside down etc. in an aeroplane today over my billet but unfortunately I missed seeing him. The weather here is fair to medium, chiefly medium.

No more news from
Your loving son
Walter

PS I am going to send all the lace to Glasgow. Please send Ellie her share. If I can raise up my courage I shall drink your health at Christmas in John's rum. Jack is flourishing though he has not such a good billet as I have. Did you notice that Hew Hedderwick has been mentioned in despatches for good work at Antwerp. I have written to congratulate him.

[Cont.] Monday 14th Dec, 9am

Moving any minute. 5pm: Not gone yet but something up. <u>Many</u> thanks for the biscuits and gloves and letters which arrived safely, also sweets just arrived. 10pm: We have not moved yet but are sleeping in our clothes tonight. I have given the plain biscuits to the Mess, the chocolate ones are nearly finished and the sweets will be very welcome in the trenches. In case I have not time to write again, a Merry Christmas and a Happy New Year to you all,

Your ever cheery son
Walter

Censor: E McCosh

16/12/14

My dear Mother,
A Merry Christmas and A Happy New Year to you all, including Ellie and John who I expect will be with you when you get this, at least I hope so as I am going to make this letter do for the whole show.

---

13 Rev. J.M. Connor, wounded at Givenchy 7 July 1915. See Weir, *Come on Highlanders!*, p. 105.

I may as well say at once that it is unlikely that I will be home on leave for a long time as our Brigade has just finished its rest cure and there other people far more deserving a rest than we are. It may quite well be March or April before we get any more leave. However, no one knows.

There is not much news here except that we are still ready to move at a moment's notice. I received a very unexpected Christmas Present yesterday from McG D & Co. Four parcels of sweets and dried fruit. It was fearfully decent of them and I wrote to them yesterday to thank them.

We had a letter from Cowie's mother the other day in which she says Cowie is getting on very well. The bullet is being left in him in the meantime.

One feels fearfully ungrateful having to give all the stuff away as soon as it arrives but it is absolutely impossible to consume it all. I can hardly look a bit of chocolate in the face and when someone asked in the Mess today if anyone would "take some chocolate off his hands" one officer out of about 15 present said he would take a little. It is the same with cakes and shortbread and every imaginable sort of eatable and woollen article, except socks. The men are all the same way and it fairly makes me sick when I see the fearful waste that is going on. I am sure the money could be far better spent on other things e.g. hospitals, sick, poor, nursing or even Foreign Missions. Personally I hope you will send me nothing except one thick pair of socks per week unless I write for it. Please excuse me writing like this in a letter of thanks, it is very ungrateful but I know you will understand. I was brought up to hate waste and the waste here makes me sick. The mail today (1 day) consisted of 57 bags so you can imagine what it is like. I wonder if they are remembering the poor chaps left at home. I heard today that someone is sending out 30 plum puddings for the officers alone – !!!! – Alas, my poor stomach. I was told today I looked as if I had put on two stones since I came out and I think it is quite possible.

Having finished my grouse I may now reassure you that we are all very grateful to be remembered and sorry we can't appreciate the presents as much as we would like to or as much as they deserve. I hope you will understand. Personally, I feel rather an imposter out here as we have so far done nothing worth making a fuss about and from all accounts people at home seem to think we are undergoing all sorts of hardships. Except for two days in the trenches I have slept between sheets every night for the last three weeks.

[Cont.] Dec 17th

While I remember, I was talking to some old hands today and they say don't stop the people at home from making things because it is better to have too much than too little. Personally, I don't see why the stuff shouldn't be stored at home and some arrangement made where our Quartermaster could write home and get as much sent when it is wanted. This would save waste and you could simply keep up a store of things at home and when the store was replenished go on to something else. We can't store things here.

Very many thanks for the wire cutters which Dad sent. The insulated ones are the very thing I wanted. I gave the other pair to Wingate who had none. They are pretty useful too and a lot of our officers have ones like them.

I am sorry for Doug having to go back to the University just now. Will he get a badge of some sort to distinguish him from the other lot? Tell him to cheer up and I will write him a letter someday extoling the beauties of a warm bed and hot baths. I wish one could have a bath by proxy.

I must wind up now as I have a lot of letters to censor. Wishing you all a Merry Christmas and Happy New Year,

Your loving son,

Walter J.J. Coats

Censor: G Wingate

22/12/14

My dear Dad,

A Happy New Year to you all. I am sorry I have not been able to write for some time but I have been pretty busy lately and there has been no news. It was rather funny the other day at Church Parade. In the middle of the service, which was in the open air, we could see a German aeroplane being shelled by our men. I don't think it was hit.

There was another funny thing happened the other day. Our signallers were ordered to go to some headquarters for instructions in telephones etc. Our signallers are all post office people and while the instructor was lecturing on the elements of the stuff one of them took a telephone to bits, tuned it up and had it all going before the instructor was half way through. The officer in charge of our signallers asked the instructor whether, when there was much noise, it was quicker to telegraph or telephone (the same machine does both). The instructor said that <u>they</u> found it quicker to telegraph, but that <u>we</u> would be quicker to telephone, so the officer asked him how many words per minute he thought good telegraphing. The instructor said about 12, so our officer turned to one of our men and asked him what rate he could send at, and the man casually said "Oh, about 34". The officer describing the scene said that the instructor's jaw nearly hit the floor. We found their best man could only do 15.

You should see the parcels that arrive every day. I found that my Company sent a whole lot of stuff to some Belgian soldiers who are here today.

There is no news except that I got soaked yesterday and spent a considerable part of the afternoon standing over the bootlaces in liquid mud. I thought I would pull the sole from the boot with each step. However, one gets used to all things and we are very cheery in spite of various chills etc.

WD: After several false alarms we actually embussed about 2 a.m. on the 23rd and after travelling all that night arrived at Locon near Béthune about 10 a.m. next morning where we found it snowing. The buses were the ordinary London buses with the windows boarded up and were very cold to travel in especially on top. Billets at Locon were somewhat scarce but we eventually got the men in. Wingate and I found we had been allotted quite a good billet in a cottage, the only drawback being a mad Belgian refugee woman who used to go about muttering to herself all day and woke us with an occasional scream at night.

[Cont.] 24/12/14

I am sorry I could not get this letter posted before as I have been on the hop since I wrote it and we are now in a different place. The people here are very decent but the billet is not so comfortable, though it might be worse. Wingate and I sat up till eleven last night playing cards with them. It was most amusing though we couldn't follow in the least what they were doing. The pipe arrived in time for Madame's son, and I gave some chocolate to Noelle, but I doubt now if I will be able to give Madame the brooch. Unless the service matchboxes which you say you sent were tied up in one of the boxes of sweets which I gave to Noelle, they have not turned up yet. Please don't send any more matches as I now get plenty here. We arrived here by London motor bus, leaving the last place about 2am and arriving here at 10am. It was a mighty cold journey. I never thought, the last time I was in a London bus, where I would be the next journey.

We are being filled up with most cheery tales of the trenches here. One is that they are waist deep in mud and water and that some of the men have to be pulled out with ropes. Others say that the trenches leading up to them are chest deep. It will be interesting to see which if any of the tales is true. I will let you know when I have been there, though I don't know when that will be.

Footnote from Mathew Anderson: Best love and Wishes for 1915. M.A.

WD: We spent Christmas Day at Locon but in the middle of the Church Parade got orders that we were to move that night. We accordingly packed up and moved off and after marching through Lacontine arrived at Richebourg St Vaast where we were put into billets.[14] We stayed at Richebourg St Vaast in Brigade reserve until about the 29th when we were moved into the trenches in front of the Rue du Bois [at Richebourg L'Avoué].

---

14 The BEF had, since the close of the First Battle of Ypres (19 October-22 November 1914), been re-organised on 26 December 1914 into two field armies on a front extending from St Eloi to Givenchy. 1/9th HLI, having left Second Army (GOC General Sir Horace Smith Dorrien) front in Belgium, was now redeployed to First Army (GOC General Sir Douglas Haig) front – extending southward from Bois Grenier to Givenchy – in French Flanders. Third, Fourth and Reserve/Fifth armies were subsequently organised in July 1915, February 1916 and May 1916 respectively.

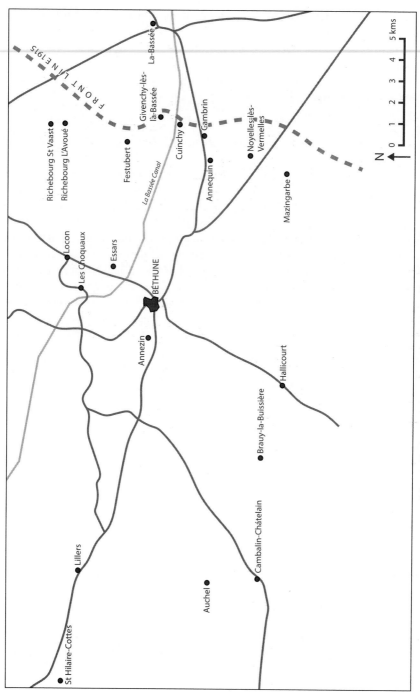

Map 2 Béthune, Givenchy/Festubert, Cuinchy sector, 1915.

30/12/14

My dear Jean,

This is really a most humorous existence. Last night about 4 o'clock we moved from our billets into the fire trenches. We arrived at a ruined village after dark and from there made our way into the trench by what is known as a communication trench. The humorous part of the performance was that the communication trench was knee deep in water through which we had to wade for about 400 yards and finally ended up by wading through a stretch of knee deep mud of about 10 yards. Two men who were wearing shoes had them pulled off and lost. When we got into the trenches our men took over the various places from the men who were in, who then filed out. After that, I found a dug-out for my abode, and then started on a tour to explore the various passages in the trench. This took some time and I finally settled down to a meal of tea, biscuits and shortbread at 1am. After that I did nothing till a man came from one of our trenches to say there were suspicious sounds in front, so I went back with him to see what it was. To get to his trench, I again had to wade through water up to my knees for about 50 yards and when I got there I found the men standing on planks an inch under water. I waited there for about three quarters of an hour half-way up to my knees in water as there was no room on the planks. I then went back to my dug-out for about half an hour, when I again started on a tour of inspection which lasted till about half past five, when I lay down and got about half an hour's sleep. We had breakfast of tea, biscuits, bacon and chocolate about half past seven, followed by some of Skinner's chocolate which I had, and a cigar, and I am now writing this from my dugout, perfectly happy in spite of the fact that my boots are full of water and are likely to remain so till we get out, which may be either tonight or tomorrow, I don't know which. There is really very little news just now except that I expect to be on the job off and on for about a month after which there is just a possibility we may get leave. I hope we do.

It is funny how one gets accustomed to this sort of life. Sleeping outside in the middle of December with a mud-caked greatcoat for cover and wet feet is treated as a matter of course and it certainly has its humorous side if you look at it in the proper way.

It is a beautiful sunny day today and with any luck will stay so till we get out.

While I remember, do you think you could get me a mess tin? A round flat one, with knife etc. inside, and also a plate and mug. I believe they have them in Wylie Hill's or Leckie Graham's. I should like one with a cover if you can manage it. Also a refill for an electrical bucket lamp.

WD: Thanks to the very wet weather and the fact that the German trenches were higher than ours and drained into them, our trenches grew steadily worse. The worst part was a listening post at the end of a sap dug-out in front of our line. The men here were standing up to their thighs in water practically all the time except for the look-out man who was perched on top of an old chair. We tried to make things more comfortable by laying a board over some more chairs for the men off duty to sit on but when this collapsed with the men on it they gave it up. There were no dug-outs in the line and we were all lucky to get a place to sleep that was anything like rainproof. I got a place where I could crawl in and lie down though my feet were in the open and when my feet got too cold to let me sleep I got up and waded about for five or ten minutes till they warmed up again.

[Cont.] 31 Dec
Still here, still wet and still flourishing. I am glad to say we get out tonight as I shall get my boots off. I was out to our lookout post about three times yesterday. The water is now over one's knees going out, and the men are standing over their boots in water. I was also into headquarters yesterday so I must have walked about 1200 yards with water up to my knees. It is a wonderful life.

We had a fine breakfast this morning, of bread, butter, jam and tea, and dates, and the man with me also had sardines. This is a regular War De Luxe. There is a large cake waiting for lunch. I don't know if all of this will interest you much as I have used the first personal pronoun rather freely but I can only speak for myself and it will at any rate give you some idea of what we are doing. If I could sketch, I would draw a picture of my very happy home but I am afraid it is beyond me. Please thank Dad and Mother for the brooch. I shall try and get it sent over.

WD: After two days here we were relieved after dark on the 31st by another Company of the Battalion and moved back to some cottage close behind the Rue du Bois where we expected to get two days rest before going in again. We had hardly got in however before we received orders to turn out and dig a new communication trench.

1915

[Cont.] 1/1/15 New Year's Day:
The humour of this life increases daily. We got out of the trenches last night about 8 o'clock and were hardly out when we were told to stand by ready to turn out in an hour. We were actually turned out at 12 midnight and given shovels and marched down to dig a new communication trench. Of all the rotten jobs I ever had I think standing up digging in bright moonlight with snipers busy all round is about the cheeriest. It was fearfully hard work too, as we kept it up for about 4 hours. It seemed a fearful long time before I managed to dig myself out of sight. I slept till about 12 o'clock today and combined breakfast and lunch. The funny thing last night was I had just got on dry socks when we were told to be ready to move, so I dipped my wet socks in warm water and put them on again. I was glad I did so, as I got fearfully muddy again. I don't think my boots will ever be dry again and my clothes are simply caked. We slacked today till about 4 when we put out 6 men to look for snipers and then about 6pm, Chalmers came in from the trenches to ask for help as two of his men had got stuck

up to the middle in mud in the communication trench and were preventing the rest of his men getting out. I was given the job of assisting him and started off with 12 men and some rope, but fortunately when we were half way there we met a man who said the stick-in-the-muds had been relieved. We are having a night in bed tonight and return to the trenches tomorrow. The communication trench is being finished off by some other men tonight. We shall be in the trenches two nights, and then I think we go back a bit for two days' rest, so we shall probably be resting when you get this. I at last feel I am earning my pay and a rest.

I had a letter from Hew Hedderwick today. He appears to be flourishing at Devonport and is very keen on getting a ship. He says he hates land fighting.

Please thank Mother and Dad for their letters which I got today. I was much amused at Doug's Christmas Dinner and only hope the story had a happy ending.

WD: We brought the New Year in digging and thanks to a fatalist beside me who had decided he was going to get through the war all right I had a very uncomfortable time, as he did not mind showing himself and I thought the chances were if the Germans tried to get him they might just as well get me instead. Shortly before dawn, we stopped digging and returned to our billets where we were allowed to remain in peace till the 3rd when we moved back to Richebourg in Brigade Reserve again. While here the Battalion was reorganised eight Companies into four. Much to my annoyance, I was posted to A Company, formed from the old A and H Coys, while my old Company, C, was joined with D Coy to make the new B Coy.

3/1/15 (cont) by the same author

I have so far been unable to get this posted so I shall continue.

We got the night in bed all right and slept well into the forenoon of the 2nd, but before the men had got their breakfasts my Company was turned out to try and clean up the communication trench the men stuck in last night. We all got spades and marched into the trench and I have never seen such mud before. I nearly stuck in it up to the knee myself and my puttee was nearly pulled off. Another man lost his shoes and we even lost the heads of some of the shovels which stuck. We had to try and dig the thing out with our hands. We were kept on this job till about five o'clock and when we got out some of us walked into a ditch at the side of the road to try and get clean while the rest didn't worry. We were no sooner back at our billets than we got orders to move, and we arrived here at about 9pm, the men having had nothing to eat all day. We have an excellent billet here and the men are all cheery and fully occupied cleaning up. I believe that we start digging again tomorrow and go on till we go back to the trenches. It is wonderful how expert we are getting with the shovel and how handy the men now are at settling down anywhere, anyhow and any time. They are a sporting lot, expert grousers but never cheerier that when they have some disagreeable job on.

While I remember, could you send two mess tins? Wingate wants one too and I said I would write. They may be sold under the name of Cavalry Mess Tins or Canteens. I should also like a folding lamp for a candle if you can find one not too heavy. I should also like a box of cigars if it is not too much to ask. There is no hurry for any of these things. As usual I have struck an excellent billet and am at present sitting smoking Princess Mary's pipe and Ellie's tobacco in my room, with a good fire going and an oil lamp burning. The house, like all the others, has been sacked by the Germans.

Could you look up "Scott's Last Voyage" or whatever it is called and see what they did for frostbite? I think it says what they did and it will be useful to know, as a lot of men are getting frostbitten feet through standing so long in cold water.

We are all in great form here including Jack and are hoping for leave after this spell of the trenches.

I am at present in the middle of a cup of most excellent soup made by one of the Tommies. Where he got the stuff and how he made it is a wonder. It tastes like chicken but I am not going to inquire too closely. He is an old Glasgow Academical.

Censor: E McCosh

3/1/15

My dear Ellie,
Here we are again! I hope you are still flourishing, likewise John.

We have just come back from a spell in the trenches. I have never seen such mud in my life. It varies from the consistency of treacle to frozen dirty water. One night I was sent with a dozen men and some ropes to pull out two men who had stuck. Fortunately I was not wanted as they had been pulled out before I arrived. It took one of our officers 20 minutes to dig out a pair of rubber boots left behind by another officer although they were only in a few inches. The deepest bit of mud I struck was up to the knee and the deepest water half way up the thigh but if you stood still you went deeper still. Apparently the Germans are as bad because the other day one of them got up and shouted to us asking us if we had not enough to do to clean our own dirty trenches without firing at them too. It is funny out here how we wade through mud and water and sleep outside in greatcoats and think nothing of it while at home if we get our feet wet at all we change at once and probably catch cold. Personally, I found that if my feet get cold the best thing to warm them was a wade. The most humorous truth about it all was when we got out and I had got my boots etc. off for the first time for about 2½ days and dry socks on, we were told to turn out and dig, so as I didn't want to get my dry socks wet I had to put on the dirty ones again. I just dipped them in warm water and then put them on. It was a cheery job but might have been worse if I hadn't had the warm water. We spent the first four hours of the New Year digging in the open with several snipers having pot shots but no damage was done. It seemed funny wishing the men a Happy New year just before taking them out to a job like that, but they were all as cheery as you make them. One man fainted while we were waiting to move off to the job and was carried away but when we went to see him before actually moving off he only said "All right Sir, I'm coming on parade". The majority are the same way, although one or two give in very easily.

I got a cup of soup today from a man in my Company. It was excellent. I rather think a chicken was responsible for it, but I don't know and didn't ask. I was telling one of the other officers about it just now, and he said he caught a mouse today and thought of making soup of it, so perhaps it was mouse soup I had. It was jolly good at any rate.

5/1/15

My dear Jenny,
Here we are again back in the trenches. The trench I have struck now is so far the driest I have seen and I am at present reclining in a comparatively comfortable dugout. Our artillery is fairly biffing the Germans and they are chucking occasional shells at us but otherwise there is nothing doing. Math is sleeping peacefully in the same dugout.

[Cont.] 10/1/15
I began this letter under the impression that we were going to have a fairly good time but I must say we had about the 3 cheeriest days I have ever spent. It began to rain the first night we were in and poured more or less until we got out, with the result that the trenches got into an awful state of mud and water and to add to the general discomfort we were not safe as the parapet kept falling in with the wet and I didn't dare to inhabit my dugout the second day as I was afraid it would fall in. You have no idea what the mud is like. My greatcoat was covered with about 1/16th of an inch of mud inside and out as far as my waist. One of my men when coming out fell in the dark about 3 feet into an old trench full of water and naturally got totally wet and another poor chap walked into a ditch that took him up to his chest. I am glad to say that so far I have never been in water deeper than half way up my thigh. We are a funny-looking set of ruffians when we get out, I wish you could see us. In spite of it all we are very cheery. For instance, after getting out of the trenches last time, we had about a 6 or 7 mile march to our billets, and the men sang all the way. Most arrived by midnight but some did not arrive till 4 am. It is a wonderful life. We came back here for a rest but have just got orders to be ready to move on half an hour's notice. The men are sticking it in a wonderful way and very few comparatively speaking have gone sick.

Please thank Mother for her letter and the socks which I got today. As far as underclothes go, I have still got plenty and have not had all my clothes off for at least the last three weeks. The furthest I have been able to undress is to take my kilt off and that only occasionally. As far as my other wants go, could you send a small bottle of brandy (enough to fill my flask)? If you wrap it up in socks etc. it will come through all right. I should also like a pair of gym shoes, size 8, and one of the rough brown towels everyone scoffs at at home. I should also like another "hunk" of milk chocolate.

I think I said I would write Doug a letter in praise of a bath. Please tell him I am sorry I can't do so now as I have forgotten what a bath is like.

You can tell the Andersons that so long as they don't hear from Jack or me to the contrary, Math is flourishing and you can be sure of the same with regard to us. If anything happens to an officer here another officer (and probably several) is sure to write to his people and let them know what it is and the same is done for the men, an officer always writes if he can find the address.

Your ever-cheery-though-his-letters-may-not-seem-like-it brother.

Censored by Mathew Anderson who added: Give my love to everyone please and let them know at Grosvenor Crescent that I am very fit, and that I am sorry they haven't heard from me but that I have written. Math.

12/1/15

My dear Doug,

Cheer Oh! I hope you are flourishing. The chief bit of news I have for you is that I am going to have a bath tomorrow. The second one since I left Dunfermline. We are out here resting just now but expect to go back to the trenches again very shortly. I hope they are a little less uncomfortable than last time.

With my usual luck I have got a bed again in my billet, though I have about a mile to walk for my meals. We are all very cheery here and there are the usual wild rumours flying about. One is that Kitchener has said the Territorials are all going to be sent home when his new army gets out and another is that Kitchener has said the war will be over in a fortnight. Personally, I don't see how the war is ever going to end. In this part of the country we are simply sitting looking at each other and as far as I can see it is the only thing to do owing to the state of the country.

I wrote to Mr McLean and thanked him for the Order of Service which he sent me. Please thank Dad for his offer to send ginger etc., but ask him not to, as large parcels have an unfortunate habit of turning up when we are on the move.

Your always merry and bright though sometimes grousing brother,

Walter J.J. Coats

Mathew Anderson – Best love from the Censor.

13/1/15

My dear Dad,

I have just had a bath!!

It was simply ripping. It was the second since I came over, the last being about 15th December. I have also got clean clothes on so am feeling most fearfully comfortable.

You have no idea what a treat it is to feel warm water on your body and as for knowing that you are more or less clean it is almost worth getting wet and dirty for. The unfortunate thing is that we go back the trenches tomorrow where we will get as dirty as ever again. Rumour has it we are going in for 12 days after which we go back for a decent rest and, I hope, leave. You have no idea how much we are all looking forward to getting leave. We have great discussions what we will do – the one thing everyone is agreed on is that we will first have a bath.

PS I forgot to tell you we have just discovered the authorities have paid us a great compliment. So far as we can discover our Battalion is the only Territorial Battalion in the country which forms the 4th Battalion in its Brigade. All the other Territorial Bns are 5th or supernumerary Bns to their Brigades and do not do exactly the same work as the Regular Battalions, as we do. It is rather a feather in our caps as even the London Scottish is a 5th Battalion in its Brigade. I have no doubt there is a certain amount of luck about it but it is something to know the authorities have sufficient confidence in us even to have put us in as 4th Battalion. Don't tell anyone.

15/1/15

My dear Mother,

The chief item of news is that Jack has been sent to hospital. I expect he will have written and told you by this time. I don't think there is much wrong with him though he certainly looked pretty washed out before he went. I think he is just run down and a rest in hospital will do him no harm. Personally, I am flourishing like a young ram and hope to stay so until the end of the war, whenever that may be.

I am sorry I gave you all so much trouble about the cure for frostbite. It was more a matter of interest than otherwise. I wanted to find out as we have a very efficient medical staff attached to the Battalion. Our Doctor is a man called Martin. Perhaps Dr Gilchrist knows him. It is useful to have the oil all the same and I shall hand it round.

We are all merry and bright here as it is now about two days since we had any decent rain. It is wonderful how a dry day improves one's spirits even if it is cold.

I don't think I told you I was removed from my Company about 10 days ago when the Battalion was reorganised but I am glad to say I have now got back to it again. I have all along been convinced that C Company was the best in the Battalion and Captain Wingate the best Captain. I think getting back has made me unusually cheerful.

Excuse writing as it is too dark to see.

Walter J.J. Coats

Mathew Anderson: Fondest love from the Censor.

17/1/15

My dear Jean,

This is Sunday afternoon and Math and I are just going to "brew" in our room, which is a sort of garret place with a bed and chair as furniture. We had a splendid brew yesterday and will improve on it today as I have just got a cake addressed to Jack which I intend to use. I have forwarded all his letters to him today but I am sorry I can't give you his address as it would give the show away.

I have two amusing stories to tell you. One is of the champion grouser of our Company. We were on Church Parade a few Sundays ago when the sun appeared for a short time (its first appearance for about 2 months). The grouser was heard to remark "I'm about fed up with this bally sun in my eyes". The other story is of a subaltern in another Battalion who had a wardrobe carried down to the trenches to use as a canoe and was fearfully annoyed when he found it would not float. The first story is true and the second is too, as far as part about the wardrobe being taken in, but I can't guarantee the rest of it.

18/1/15

I got choked off yesterday so I shall continue today. I have heard no word of Jack since he left. I suppose he has written home. I am forwarding his letters but not his parcels, I am keeping them. It is rather a joke, the cake I opened yesterday turned out to be his birthday cake. It was far too rich for me, so I pushed it on to the Mess and it vanished at a sitting.

WD: After Jack left us for hospital, we moved back from Essars to Locon. Next day (20th January) we went into the line at Le Plantin just north of Givenchy-lès-la-Bassée. The line here consisted of some loop-holed houses and a few stretches of breastwork about 1000 yards from the German trenches. As a result life was very peaceful and pleasant except for a listening post at the end of the "yellow road". This road was so called because it was marked yellow on the map to distinguish it from a road just north of it which we called the white road. The unpleasant thing about this listening post was that it was situated about six or seven hundred yards in front of our line and, except for a telephone, entirely cut off from the Battalion.[15] It was evacuated every day just before dawn and re-occupied at dusk and the latter job was rather unpleasant as it was always a toss-up whether the Germans would be there before us.

---

15 Described as a "small post on road for 11 rifles with wire in front of it. There is a gap in the line to enable a listening post to go out if required. This post is only held at night. No head cover at present." Denoted as "Post at night (C)" on the bend in "Yellow Road", see TNA WO 95/1343-2: 5th Brigade War Diary and sketch map page 82.

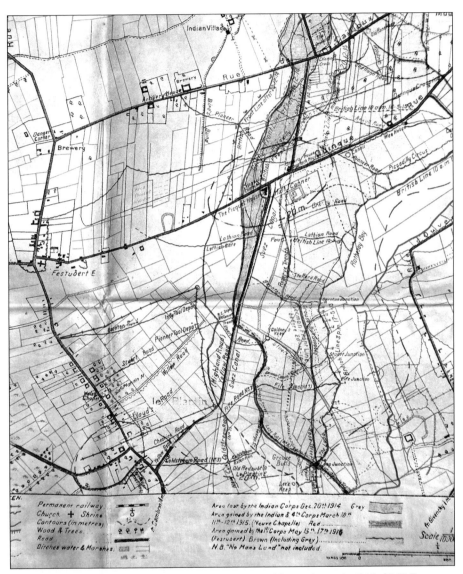

Map of Festubert-Le Plantin/Yellow Road sector N of Givenchy, early 1915. (G.F. Paterson records, Indian Corps Front Sheet 2 (Festubert), Sandhurst Collection)

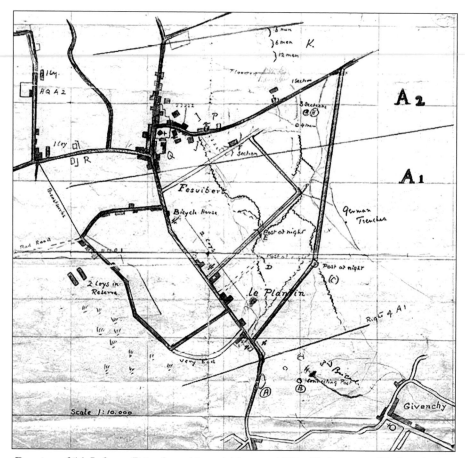

Drawing of 5th Infantry Brigade positions, 14 January 1915 – Night post at (C) described in
Walter's diary entry for 20 January 1915. (TNA WO 95/1343-2 p21)

21/1/15

My dear Jenny,

This morning, I was going round one of the trenches with an engineer officer when I
stood on what I thought was a plank, skidded off and went in over the knees in black
liquid mud. After a bit of floundering, I managed to get out and have since been going
about in a pair of borrowed boots and a kilt apron as I had my kilt, putties, boots and
coat washed. The joke of the thing is that Wingate has just gone and done exactly the
same thing in the same place, only a bit worse. His greatcoat is mud up to the chest
and his trousers mud up to the waist and he is at present being scraped in the backyard
of this billet which is behind the trenches. Everyone is fearfully amused, and fortunately he sees the funny side of it himself.

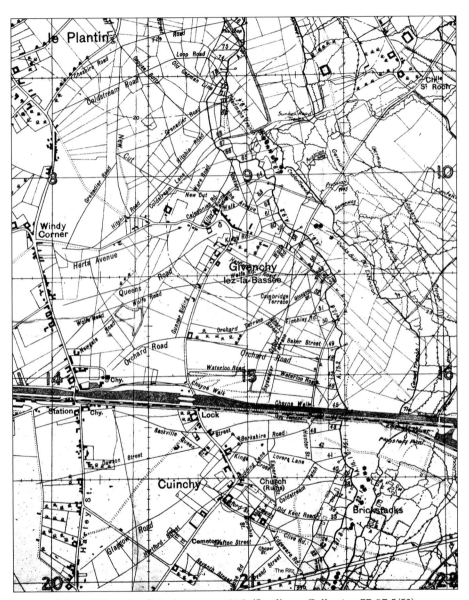

Map of Givenchy-Cuinchy sector, 1915. (Sandhurst Collection 77-97 5/52)

We expect to be here for three days, then in Battalion reserve for three days and then out for a rest. The time fairly flies when one is on a job like this. It is funny to think we have now been soldiering for six months. In a way, it seems much longer and in a way it seems no time at all.

We are all much amused at the fun that had been made about our draft. Personally, I am very sorry. I would rather they treated us like regulars.

I have just been told I am to take a few men and go and try and bag a German tonight. It will be rather muddy work but it will be worth it if I can get one. I only hope I am not bagged. I shall let you know the result before I close this letter. This is going to be a night of surprises for the Germans.

I must stop now as I have absolutely no news to tell you.

Your very merry and bright brother,

PS Headquarters would not allow me to go German chasing so here I am again, drinking cocoa in my billet. I must say, I was not sorry when I was not allowed to go out. One has got to volunteer for jobs like that but it doesn't make them any more pleasant. We all volunteered but no officer was allowed to go. The job was not considered important enough.

WD: I remember on one occasion going out to occupy the listening post when everyone was rather nervous about a reported German advance. As a matter of fact it was a false alarm and we got out quietly as usual and after things had cooled down a bit I was just thinking of leaving the post to return to Company HQ for dinner when the signaller told me to wait as there was a message coming through for me. This was rather annoying as I wanted get back for dinner but as I thought it might be important, I waited to see what it was. After waiting impatiently for about a quarter of an hour, as I knew dinner must have started, the message eventually came through to the effect that they would keep some dinner warm for me. As I might have been back by that time this was not much comfort. When I got back I found the menu and semi-cold remains of the following:

Hors d'oeuvres: Sardines and Oatcakes
Soup: Le Plantin Turtle
Fish: Salmon
Entrée: Steak a la Francais
Cold Joint: Roast Mutton, Corned Beef
Vegetables: Pommes de Terre
Sweets: Ne Peu
Tea, coffee, cocoa, cigars, cigarettes
Shortbread, Bun, Cake
Wines – Rum, Brandy, Whisky

Glasgow Highlanders No2 Coy 22nd January 1915

23 January, 1915

My dear Doug,

I expect to be in the firing line for another three days, making six in all. I shall be glad to get out though we are at the most comfortable bit of the firing line we have yet struck. I enclose last night's menu which I unfortunately missed as I had to be out at the time.

WD: We stayed here in Le Plantin for 6 days and on the 25th came in for our first heavy shelling while the Germans attacked the people on our right at Givenchy. The fighting went on all day and for a time things looked rather bad but by night everything had pretty well settled down again. We were relieved from the front line by one of our other Companies on, I think, the 26th and moved back to some houses between Le Plantin and Le Marais. While we were here, we rested during the day and worked up in the front line at night building breastworks round some orchards near Le Plantin.

27 January, 1915

My dear Dad,

This is the Kaiser's birthday, and I shall not wish him many happy returns. We got back a little from the firing line yesterday after being in for six days. The last two days were about the most cheery we have had so far. We were <u>very</u> heavily shelled on the 25th and we saw the Germans try and charge our trenches a little along the line from us. The poor brutes were simply mown down. Heavy shell fire it is, I must say, rather beastly and I am afraid I shall never get really fond of it. When it was at its worst, there was a long drawn out rumble in the air caused simply by the shells passing through it and all the time there were the explosions of the guns and shells going off. The unfortunate thing was that the silly blighters started the show just when I was trying to get to sleep about 7.30 AM. I was fearfully annoyed as I was rather sleepy.

Barring the little excitement, there is really no news to tell you. We are all in hopes of getting back a bit further tomorrow night and I believe two of our officers are going to leave then, so I am in great hopes of getting home soon for a few days.

[Cont.] 28/1/15

We are still here and don't know when we may get back. It is all the fault of the bally Kaiser having his birthday at such an unfortunate time.

We spent a long time digging last night and I must have filled about 2000 sandbags and we're going out again tonight. We are pretty expert with the shovel now.

It is very funny in our billets here, we have an old bed frame without the part one lies on and every night two officers solemnly climb over into it and go to sleep on the floor where they are more or less squashed. Chalmers and I are sleeping in a wardrobe laid on its back which has at least the benefit of keeping out the draft.

Our chaplain, who has been through the war since the beginning, tells us that the shelling the other day was the heaviest he has known. I believe by rights we should practically all have been wiped out. We have got the reputation in the Brigade of being the luckiest Battalion that ever went into action and it is certainly well earned. We have only had three killed since we came out and in all we have spent 19 days in the trenches, not to mention a lot of digging within a few hundred yards of the Germans.

Must stop now to catch post.

30 January, 1915

My dear Mother,

We have at last got back from the firing line, but not very far and we are ready to move off from here on 20 minutes' notice. I believe the reason for all the excitement is that the Kaiser is running around somewhere in this region.

I am glad to say we were not very heavily shelled after the 25th, though we have had a few chucked at us every day since, until today. It is extraordinary the number of narrow squeaks there were. I have come to the conclusion now that is it all chance whether one of us is hit or missed. The men are an extraordinary lot. The artillery officer who was with us at the last place said they were the coolest lot he has ever seen under fire. I don't think they realise yet what it is. For instance, some of our men were walking up the road the other day when the Germans began to drop some shells near them. Some of them simply turned their backs until the shell burst and the rest simply looked at things in a mildly interested sort of way and walked on until the Adjutant and told them to run for cover.

I don't think I told you too, that the other day two of our men were bringing down the mail to us in a barrow when the Germans turned a machine gun on them. Those who saw it said it was one of the funniest things they ever saw to see the men flopping down and scrambling into the nearest ditch. They were both hit but, with our usual luck, only very lightly – one in the leg and the other through the fleshy part of what in civil life would have occupied the slack of his bags or, in military terms, parados.

I am sorry to say that all leave has been stopped for officers pro tem. I expect at least until the Kaiser goes East, so it maybe some little time yet before I get home. However, everything comes to him who waits and for your sakes I do not intend to give up my turn to another when it comes.

We are all merry and bright here and C Company is going to have a concert tonight. It will be a funny affair as we are going to have songs ranging from the broadly humorous to the classical. I hope the show is a success as we are asking Madame and Co and a few gunners who are in the same billet.

By the way, I have opened all Jack's parcels and looted the whole bag of tricks. The mess tins were too large to keep for him and they are wanted here so I gave them away, and I'm going to keep the puttees for myself.

With my usual luck I have struck another fine billet, no bed this time but plenty of straw.

McLean sent me a prayer book the other day. I must write and thank him.

I must tell you of a joke we played on one of the officers the other day. The officer in question is of somewhat larger dimensions than the average and very keen on his "internal economy". One of us had had a packet of fire lighters sent out so we offered the "stout one" a cake of firelight and told him it was toffee and he actually took a bite. The joke was that we offered him some decent stuff afterwards and one of our officers whispered that it was soap and so he refused to take any.

WD: After 4 days in support we again moved up into the front line and after a second spell there the whole Battalion was moved back to Gorre behind Le Marais where we remained for some time ready to move on 20 minutes notice. While at Gorre, half the Battalion was taken up each night and was employed building breastworks 500 or 600 yards in front of our old line at Le Plantin. This was a most unpleasant job as we used to have casualties at it every night but fortunately for me I was transferred at this time to the Machine Gun Section which was not used for work of this kind.

2 February, 1915

My dear Jean,
Please thank everyone who has written to me since I last wrote. I have really no news to tell you just now as we are doing nothing here.

I am now a Machine Gunner I am sorry to say as I have been with my company for five years now and hate to leave it at a time like this, however it has its compensations.

I had Dad's letter this morning asking about Frank Carruthers.[16] So far as I know he is flourishing and certainly if there was anything serious then his officers would have written to his people about it as they always do, e.g. I have got to write to a man's people tonight. Of course, if he is only slightly seedy and sent to hospital his people might not be written to. You can tell his people however that if anything worth writing about happens, his people will be told.

3 February, 1915

My dear Jean,
We are still here where we are if that conveys anything to you and we all hope that our next move will be a bit farther back.

The Germans chucked three large shells into this place today but hurt no one except a woman and a baby. I believe the woman was hit in 30 places without much damage.

16 Pte 2523 Frank Walter Carruthers. Distinguished pupil at Glasgow Academy and Walter's contemporary; pipe major of the school cadet corps and school captain 1903; 1/9th HLI.

WD: On the 9th of February the Machine Gun Section was lent to the 6th Brigade and moved off to Givenchy-lès-la-Bassée where we were followed soon afterwards by two Companies of the Battalion, which had also been lent to this Brigade. This was possible as the 2nd Inniskilling Fusiliers had recently joined the 5th Brigade which thus had five Battalions.

When we first joined the 6th Brigade only two guns were sent into the line so I spent all my time with them but later on when all our guns came up, two being put in the front line and two in reserve, I spent my time with the guns in reserve which would have required more handling in case of attack. The guns in front were left in the charge of an N.C.O. whom I visited daily.

During the time we were with the 6th Brigade, the two Companies we lent them were relieved every few days by the other two. Todd and I also took turns of relieving each other with half the M.G. Section. When not in the line we spent our time with the reserve half of the Battalion in a Chicory Factory on the canal bank near Gorre.

11 February, 1915

My dear Doug,

We are back at work again here and I am sorry to say leave appears to have been forgotten about. I was up in the trenches from midday on the ninth till midday yesterday and return again today for another 24 hours. I don't know how long I will be going on at this job. Being a machine gunner, I spend, at present, twice as much time in the trenches as the rest, but I have a better job when I do get in as my gun is quite close to my dug-out and I don't need to get up and down the line. The dug-out I inhabit up in the trenches is or rather was a German one within quite recent times. And it is a most palatial place about 12 feet square by 4 feet high. The place I am in just now is in the support billets. I am living in a room which is almost completely below the level of the ground and so almost shell proof which is a good thing as they chuck shells about here daily.

I enclose three bits of high explosive shell which I kicked out of the walls of the upper storey of this house today. The house is in a fearful state as it has been shelled by both sides and absolutely looted as well. The bits of shell I enclose are German, judging from the way they were stuck in the wall. You can chuck them away when you are finished with them.

13 February, 1915

My dear Jenny,

As far as I can see, there is little hope of our getting a rest for some time to come yet. I got out of range of rifle bullets yesterday and expect to go back again in about four days. The other machine gun officer and I are taking turns of being four days in and four days out. The place we were in was not bad during the day but at night it simply rained stray bullets. In fact no one was allowed out alone in case he got hit and lost. Fortunately, I had no occasion to be out at night as I always went into the trench in the middle of the day. I think I made my most violent effort of the war yesterday to jump out of my skin. Just as I got to my billet and was lifting a cup of tea, the Germans landed a high explosive outside my window. I had not heard it coming. Talk of the leopard changing his skin. I bet he would do it out here all right. As far as I know, the only result of the Germans landing their shells close to us was ½ a cup of tea spilled into a bowl of sugar and the pressure of about 15,000 tonnes to the square inch on my skin not to mention the buttons of my jacket.

To return to more serious subjects, please thank various people for various letters. I had a very nice letter from Mrs. Pyatt,[17] also one from the porter in McG D & Co with five large parcels of fruit, sweets, handkerchiefs and soap from the staff. It was fearfully decent of them. I think they must have meant some of the stuff for the men as they sent 48 cakes of soap and 40 hankies among other things. I am going to write and thank them for it tonight. I understand from some of your letters you have an acknowledgement of the shawl you sent Madame Mackereel. I have not yet managed to send on the brooch, but I hope to manage to do so shortly as we are near a town where there will be a French Post office.

Mr and Mrs Pyatt, Carrington House, Fettes College, 1905. (Fettes College Archives)

17 Mrs Pyatt was the wife of the housemaster of Carrington House, Fettes College.

18 February, 1915

My dear Doug,

This is just to let you know I am still flourishing. I am going into the trenches again today for 48 hours, so will be out by the time you get this.

I am sorry to say, visions of leave are gradually receding into thin air. We are still hard at it in the same old place and there is no immediate prospect of a rest. None of our officers has got away yet. Rumour has it the end of the month will see us through but it is only a rumour. One good thing is, I believe we are making a quite good name for ourselves.

WD: While we were with the 6th Brigade, the first trench raid, I think, on record was carried out.[18] The raiding party was formed of volunteers from each Battalion in the 6th Brigade and they allowed us to supply a party also. The raid was carried out at dusk on the 20th February, the objective being to destroy some mine shafts in a part of the German line in front of Givenchy called the Duck's Bill [see map page 83].

21 February, 1915

My dear Mother,

Here we are, back from the trenches again. I was up a day longer than I expected this time, owing to a small attack which was made yesterday. I am sorry to say, however, I was not able to pop off the gun after all. Almost 10 of our men took part in the performance and did very well. I expect you will see a very flowery account of the part we took in it in the papers. As a matter of fact, the show was made up of so many volunteers from various Battalions and our men only did their share. I am told that the first 10 of our men they asked all volunteered for the job but I don't know if it is true.

My servant tells me he has got a photo from some Southampton paper showing our Battalion marching down to the docks on the way here, headed "the Lads of Bonny Scotland" or something equally exciting. He says your 'noble fils' is about the most prominent person in the picture and quite recognizable. I'm going to get him to show me it someday. It was given to him by some English Tommy out here who asked him if it was any of our crowd.

There is really very little news here as usual. The billets we are now in are about the most piggish we have yet struck but are we downhearted? No!!!! Etc. We are only somewhat! At times.

---

18 The 6th Brigade raid, carried out against the "Duck's Bill" salient near Givenchy, occurred on 20 February. See Everard Wyrall, *The History of the Second Division 1914-1918 Vol. I* (London: Thomas Nelson & Sons, 1921), pp. 185-86. The earliest recorded BEF trench raid was carried out by the Indian Corps in November 1914.

I am in charge of two machine guns. It is great sport. One of the gunners is a medical student half a year behind Doug. Sandeman is his name, he is an old Glasgow Academy boy.[19] Does Doug know him?

We are being worked nearly off our feet but we are as cheery and bright as can be. We look on a day or two's rest now in the way we used to look at a week's holiday.

Cheer Oh.

1 March, 1915

My dear Jean,

Once more out of the breach dear friend etc. I have just got back from a five day spell of the firing line about an hour ago and received the parcel with cigars etc. and also the one with the book and biscuits. Thanks very much for them all, also for various letters.

There is really very little to tell you since I wrote last. We chuck shells at the Germans and they chuck them back at us. We chuck bombs and bullets at them and they return the compliment and in our spare time we bail the trenches and patch them up. It is about the most unexciting job you can imagine. The only little excitement last time was when the Germans shelled a large distillery a few hundred yards behind the trenches. It has got a great tall chimney which they had hit several times before but never managed to bring down. Yesterday however they made a special effort and as the papers would say, 'amid scenes of great excitement', they managed to knock the beastly thing down.[20] The total result is we have now got a fresh supply of bricks to make roads with across the muddy fields. And other useful thing the shells do for us is the providing of holes to bury rubbish in. It is rather adding insult to injury to use them for this but they are very handy.

2 March, 1915

My dear Jenny,

Here we are, at last back for a three day rest with four of our officers away on leave. We are resting in the town where Jack was first taken to hospital and I have got a most excellent billet with a large bed and clean sheets. What is more, I expect to have a decent hot bath tomorrow and a change into clean clothes. To put the finishing touches, the weather today is clear and sunny, I have just had a very fine tea in a decent tea shop with fresh penny cakes, and I am now smoking one of Dad's cigars. The best thing of all, of course, is that we are out of earshot of the guns. I was beginning to

---

19 Sergeant 1466, later Lieutenant, Frank Watt Sandeman, 1/9th HLI 1914-15.
20 The chimney of the Delaune distillery (probably of sugar beet) is marked "chy" near the station on the south side of the La Bassée canal in the map on page 83.

Glasgow Highlanders marching through The Bargate, Southampton on 3 November 1914. Walter is the central figure with revolver case. On arrival, the Battalion marched to the "rest camp", probably on Southampton Common, north of the city centre. This image also appears on the dust jacket of Weir, *Come on Highlanders!* (WJJC collection)

get rather fed up with the sound of them, as when I got back yesterday I had spent 10 days out of 13 in the firing line, and where I was they were chucking shells about too freely for one's comfort.

I hope you got the postcards I sent you all right. I could have written, only I had no pad with me.

The paper in which your noble brother is figuring is 'The Hampshire Advertiser's County Newspaper', date unknown. If you are very keen they might be able to send you a decent print. As far as I could see from the copy I saw, it is quite a good photo.

Do you think it would be possible for someone to get me a pair of boots about the size of the shoes I sent home from Dunfermline? Something after the style of work-men's boots is what I want, the sole a mass of nails with bits of iron at the heel <u>and</u> toe. I would prefer them without a toecap but this doesn't really matter. If it is much trouble getting them please don't worry. One <u>can</u> get ration boots here but they are rather scarce and are all required by the men.

I hope you are now getting better and will soon be all right again. If you want to be really fit you should come out here. The open air life is the thing. I don't think I have ever felt fitter.

2 March, 1915

My dear Ellie,

> Here we are, here we are, here we are again,
> Do... Do... Do... Do ...
> Hallo, Hallo, Hallo, o – o – o
> Here we are, here we are, here we are again.

You might not think so, but this is one of the best marching songs we have got. Another good one is:

> It's a ha, he, hie,
> It's a he, he, hie,
> Germans may seem very hard to beat,
> But all they're good for is eating sausage meat,
> So they can try, try, try
> Till they die, die, die
> If the Kaiser doesn't shift
> It is certain he'll get lift
> And if anybody tells you he's as fly as George the Fifth,
> Then it's a he, he, hie
> If the Kaiser, truth to tell,
> Says he isn't feeling well,
> For the little British Army is knocking him to h___,
> Then it's no he, he, he.

Second verse, same beginning with "the truth to tell" ending.

Returning to the pleasures of prose and leaving for the time being the "Song O'Music" touch, please thank John for his very welcome letter. While I remember, would it trouble you very much to get from W H Smith and Sons, 186 Strand, London, three copies of "The Machine Gunner's Handbook", and "Vickers Light Guns" by Bostock, Limited Edition?

Leaving, for the time being, the values of prose for the needs of the inner mass, I must break off as 'tis time for Mess. I shall return anon.

Later: I am sorry to say dinner has knocked all ideas out of my head. As a matter of fact there is very little news except that we are here for three days' rest. I was out this afternoon at a teashop where I drank chocolate and ate funny cakes in the good old style. It was one of those beastly places where you have to count each cake while a waitress stands and looks on. It was quite a novel sensation, but I didn't like it. I stopped after four cakes as I didn't want to eat six and my pronunciation of the French five makes me blush. Between three of us, we ate 20 cakes.

Prospects of a bath tomorrow are very bright. Think of it, a real bath with hot water and soap. I have not had the shirt off my back for about a month now.

There is really no news to tell about, so I move that we close the meeting with a vote of thanks to the Chairman and the singing of 'He's a jolly good fellow'. The motion being seconded and carried, nem com.

Cheer Oh

PS Excuse the small talk but I am at present suffering from one of my mad fits.

WD: We were withdrawn from the 6th Brigade on 1st March and moved back to Béthune where we expected a few days' rest. This was not to be, however, for I had just finished lunch on 3rd, and was going off to watch a football match, when I received orders to be in the trenches at Cuinchy with two guns by 4 p.m. that day. Fortunately, I was able to catch the men before they went out and we started at once. Our orders were to report to Brigade H.Q. in a house beyond Annequin and receive further instructions but as I had no map, and no one I met seemed to know where Annequin was, it was dark before we got there. Here, I was told to go straight down the road to No 1 Harley Street where I was to enter the trench and proceed via Hertford Street, Edgware Road and Oxford Street to Park Lane. They gave us a map showing roughly in pencil how these trenches ran but as the map simply ignored the more complicated turnings and trench junctions we lost our way several times and it was 9 o'clock before we reached our destination.

On arriving at Park Lane, I found it was a short trench cut across the Béthune – La Bassée Road. The guns were trained to fire down this road. The accommodation for the gunners was in the cellars of a broken down house at the end of the trench which was called the Ritz Hotel.[21]

4/3/15

Park Lane,
C_____ [Cuinchy]

My dear Doug,
The three days' rest did not come off after all. Yesterday at 1.30, I got word I was to be in the trenches here by four o'clock. The trenches are only about 5 miles away, but it took us from 2.30 till 9.00 PM to get settled down as we had to lump the guns through miles of communications trenches. We entered the trenches at No1 Harley Street (dressing station), walked down Hertford Street, then along Edgware Road to Oxford Street and along Oxford Street to Park Lane (my present address). About 20 yards away is the Ritz Hotel (the cellar of a ruined house). There is an

---

21 The "Ritz" was located at the north end of the westernmost of the two trenches crossing the Béthune-La Bassée road at the south end of Edgware Road (annotated in the map on page 83).

absolute maze of trenches here so they all have to have names. It is funny asking a man you met in narrow ditch if you are still in Edgware Road. I expect to be here for anything from 4 to 6 days. It is a funny life and, strange to say, it appears to agree with me. The great thing is to see the funny side of things, and it strikes me as distinctly humorous to find myself smoking a cigar sitting on a bank of mud, with a corrugated roof overhead, a good breakfast inside and a book beside me, my outlook being a bank of mud and, in front, a glorified a ditch on either side with the Ritz Hotel in the distance.

6th March, 1915

My dear Dad,

There is really no news to tell you except that I am still flourishing, though still in the trench. Today has been simply beastly and my dug-out collapsed this morning in a regular waterfall of mud and water. However, no damage was done and we got the thing fixed up again so we are all merry and bright once more.

As there was nothing else to do, I decided to compose some poetry just to show that I am still a follower of the muses and that the goddess of war has not entirely run away with my affections. I enclose the result, which may interest you as it more or less describes a day in the trenches, though I expect the Muses will cut me dead the next time I come along. Excuse the absolute drivel but I am feeling so cheery something must be done to let off steam.

Your loving son,
Walter J.J. Coats

I
The sniper snipes the knell of parting day
The new relief come slopping down the ditch
Laden with bags of rations so that they
May pass the weary hours they sit in pitch

II
We've told the Germans be across the way
The range being seven fifty on the right
That we've been doing so and so by day
And must improve the parapet by night

III
They tell us that there are so many bags
For putting sand in, lying in that heap
That bombs are scattered down the line like fags
And S A [small arms] ammunition's going cheap.

IV

First thing to do, the old relief now gone
And disappeared like mud pies thrown in mud,
Is that needful sentries are put on,
Each with his head at least above the flood

V

At last, when all arrangements have been made
To biff the Germans, if attack they lead,
'tis quite permissible for us to wade
Down to our dug-out there to have a feed

VI

The feed being o'er 'tis time that we repair
Once more along the line to see that all
The men are working and to find out where
The beastly parapet is going to fall

VII

And so we wander up and down the night
(Poetic License for a squidgy trench)
Until the dawn comes bringing with the light
A Black Maria or some other wench

VIII

The daylight come and we being one small fed
Think of our sleep and weary start to crawl
Each had his narrow sell a dug-out said
By experts to be tottering to a fall

IX

And so it proves for sudden rattle thud
We wake and after many efforts rise
To find that Mother earth with clod of mud
Has kissed us playfully between the eyes

X

Our sleep dispelled, we start to work again
And go on working steadily till eve
And I have no doubt you will find us when
The new relief comes up and we, we leave.

22 February, 1915

To: John Bryden

Dear John,
Very many thanks for the book which you sent me. It was most interesting and I enjoyed reading it very much. It was fearfully decent of you to even think of sending it.

We are still busy here with no sign of a rest but that doesn't matter or at any rate can't be helped.

A few of our men took part in their first attack yesterday. They helped to rush part of the German trench in front, held it until it was destroyed and then fell back. There were too few of our men in it to make it one of our officer's jobs, so our men were led by a sergeant who did extremely well and may get something for it. He was hit in at least two places but is expected to recover all right. There is really no news here as life simply consists of being either in the trenches or out of them, both places being been pretty beastly.

Thanks again for the books,
Yours,
Walter J.J. Coats

[Cont.] 6/3/15
As you will see, I started writing this letter a long time ago but I was not able to send it as I couldn't remember your address and my note of it was in my valise which I could not get at.

I got back from the firing line at the last place on the 1st of March on what promised to be a four day rest but unfortunately at midday on the 3rd, I was rushed off here where I have been sitting in a trench ever since. The men with me are being relieved tomorrow but whether I shall get back with them or not, I don't know. If I get back tomorrow I shall have been 14 days in the firing line in the last 19.

The Germans appear to shell this place every day, at least they have done so every day since I came here and they are at it again just now, in fact one burst as I wrote "now". So far this morning it has all been shrapnel, for which relief, much thanks.

To add to the general comfort, it is beginning to rain. Thank goodness my dug-out is more or less waterproof.

I have really no news except that three more shells have burst.
Yours,
Walter J.J. Coats

PS Another one has just gone off.

WD: We stayed here until the 8th when we were relieved by Todd and some of the other men and moved back to Annequin where we found the rest of the Battalion. I found quite a decent billet here with an old woman who said she had once been a cook in Paris so as I did not belong to any Company I set up a mess of my own here and got her to cook for me. I believe the old woman eventually had a leg blown off by a shell.

8 March, 1915

My dear Mother,
Here we are again once more out of the trenches for, it is supposed, 4 days – though ten to one we will be pushed in again this afternoon or tomorrow. We have to be ready to move at any time.

Excuse the writing as my hands are very cold as it is snowing and very windy. I have quite a good billet here and share a bed with Math. Madame is a decent old woman and we get on alright. In fact last night I talked to her for nearly an hour. It is wonderful how far "Oui" and "Non" carry one, for barring these I don't think I spoke a dozen words all the time. The great thing is to give them a souvenir. I offered Madame a cigar but she wouldn't take it so I gave her a candle. There was a bombardment of the German lines a few days ago in the middle of the night. I don't think I ever saw such a fine sight in my life before. The sky was one mass of flame with the flashes of the guns and the noise was fearful, in fact almost loud enough to drown the rattle of the dust cart going down the lane at home. I must tell you of one fearful joke we had on the Germans for a bit. Where we are billeted, some of the houses are lit by electric light generated in a town inside the German Lines. When the Germans occupied the town, they started up the electric light with the result that our billets were lit up by electric light at their expense. The light is off now however so I expect they must have discovered what they were doing.

I don't know if you have heard at home yet but one of our sergeants has just got the DCM for the way he led some of our men in a bayonet charge.[22] To add to our general uppishness, we are today playing in the final for the B........ Cup (the town where Jack was)[Béthune]. I hope we win it as it will be a fine souvenir.

I can't say any more, my brain's too empty,
Guid nicht the noo,
Walter J.J. Coats

9 March, 1915

My dear Jean,
It is good of you writing when you are so busy. If you asked me to change jobs with you, I would refuse without hesitation as mine is a better job. I have been living in the lap of luxury for two days now. The dinner last night was quite up to what I expected

---

22 L/Sgt 1254 John Port DCM.

and Madame afterwards produced a quilt and a couple of blankets so I went to bed about 10 am did not get up this morning till nine. I breakfasted comfortably on ham and eggs at 9.30, did nothing all forenoon, lunched on soup and steak at 1.30 and am now smoking my after-lunch cigar beside the fire. Unfortunately, I have just got word that I have to go back to Park Lane tomorrow. I always thought a four days' rest was too good to be true. I am supposed to be going in for two days, but I think it is quite possible I shall be in for six. In a way I hope it is six, as this will mean the other Machine Gun officer has gone on leave, after which my turn should come. I intend to take a room at the Ritz Hotel this time.

Special Order.

To the 1st Army.

We are about to engage the enemy under very favourable conditions. Until now in the present campaign, the British Army has, by its pluck and determination, gained victories against an enemy greatly superior both in men and guns. Reinforcements have made us stronger than the enemy in our front. Our guns are now both more numerous than the enemy's are, and also larger than any hitherto used by any army in the field. Our Flying Corps has driven the Germans from the air.

On the Eastern Front, and to South of us, our Allies have made marked progress and caused enormous losses to the Germans, who are, moreover, harassed by internal troubles and shortage of supplies, so that there is little prospect at present of big reinforcements being sent against us here.

In front of us we have only one German Corps, spread out on a front as large as that occupied by the whole of our Army (the First).

We are now about to attack with about 48 battalions a locality in that front which is held by some three German battalions. It seems probable, also, that for the first day of the operations the Germans will not have more than four battalions available as reinforcements for the counter attack. Quickness of movement is therefore of first importance to enable us to forestall the enemy and thereby gain success without severe loss.

At no time in this war has there been a more favourable moment for us, and I feel confident of success. The extent of that success must depend on the rapidity and determination with which we advance.

Although fighting in France, let us remember that we are fighting to preserve the British Empire and to protect our homes against the organized savagery of the German Army. To ensure success, each one of us must play his part, and fight like men for the Honour of Old England.

(Sd.) D. HAIG, General,

9th March, 1915.   Commanding 1st Army.

1st Printing Co., R.E. G.H.Q. 673.

Special Order from General Haig on the eve of the Battle of Neuve Chapelle. On the reverse, Walter wrote down the attack briefing referred to in his letter of 10 March 1915: "No straying from billets; Ammunition at 5.30am; Officers at 7 for Brigade time; 7.30 begins; 7.40 stops; 7.50 again; 8.05 intense; 8.10 attack; Neuve Chapelle; Supporting Pt.; McKay draw ammunition in daylight". (WJJC collection)

WD: The preliminary bombardment began at 7.30 a.m. [on 10 March] and went on till 7.40 a.m. when it stopped for 10 minutes beginning again at 7.50 a.m. and becoming intense at 8.05 a.m. The assault commenced at 8.10 a.m. The attack was a complete failure.

10 March, 1915

My dear Jenny,

The war has <u>begun</u> at last. There is a big battle on today and we are all very hopeful of the result.[23] I am in support at this part of the line and am ready to move on 5 minutes' notice but I don't expect to move for a day or two yet. I will let you hear as often as I can how things are going, but don't be surprised if you don't hear as regularly as usual. I was up at five this morning and the performance began at 7.30. It is funny sitting down to a breakfast of ham and eggs with several big guns popping off within 50 yards and a regular blaze of rifle fire. I expect leave is up the pole now for some time to come. I wish I could have got a bath.

It was very interesting last night about 11pm sitting round a table getting orders about today. The great thing in this war is not to let anything put you off your feed as you never know when you will get another.

By the way, if you want to imagine what rapid fire sounds like a little way off, it is exactly like the bubbling of violently boiling water. I knew it was like something very familiar, but I couldn't think what until a few days ago when it suddenly struck me.

Your gourmandish brother.

12/3/15

The Ritz Hotel

My dear Doug,

Just a line to let you know I am still flourishing and to wish you all success on the day of your exam.

---

23 The Battle of Neuve Chapelle (10-13 March 1915). Second Division's part in the offensive was to execute a "holding attack" near Givenchy. See Sir J.E. Edmonds, *Military Operations France and Belgium 1915 Vol. I* (London: Macmillan, 1927), pp. 74-156 and Patrick Watt, 'Sir Douglas Haig and the Planning of the Battle of Neuve Chapelle' in Jones (ed), *Courage Without Glory*, pp. 183-203 for the BEF's first set-piece attack and Wyrall, *The History of the Second Division 1914-1918*, pp. 191-96 for operations carried out by 6th Brigade; 5th Brigade supported the assault with "bursts of rifle and machine-gun fire on the hostile trenches in front – Cuinchy."

There is nothing much doing here except for the battle which is going on to our left. I can't get any official information as to what is happening, but as far as I can make out things are going quite cheerily though I am afraid that casualties are fairly heavy.

I have taken a room in the Ritz Hotel this time and I am very comfortable. The place is like a glorified dungeon but it is clean, dry and warm. Last night, the Germans managed to land several bombs but they didn't break through to the cellar so no harm was done. The rotten thing about them is that you don't hear them coming as they come very slowly. You can see them if you are on the lookout but that doesn't help much if you're not.

14 March 1915

My dear Ellie,

Here we are again – once more out of the trenches. We got out last night for I think three days, but according to military calculations 1+1=3 at least 9 times out of 10, the 10th time being when we are in the trenches, when 2+2=3 or 3+3=4. C'est la Guerre, or as we would say the best laid schemes etc. I hope, however, the scheme I have made for tomorrow night's dinner holds good. I have just bought a hen. We are going to have some dinner tomorrow.

I suppose you will have heard that the War began at 7.30 am on the 10th March AD 1915. The important thing is that I expect it knocks out all prospect of leave and also of rest which could have come, I believe, on 16th. However, with any luck, I expect we will get home at the end of the War, though I have some doubts whether we won't be made to fill in the trenches before we go.

While I remember, please ask John what "S.R.D" means on the Rum bottles. I presume R stands for rum, but the S.D. beats me.[24]

I don't think I told you when I wrote last about the dugout one of our officers made in the trenches here. He was in the reserve trenches and found when he got there that he had no dugout so he went to the village a little behind during the night, and brought up a cart he found there, took off the wheels and lowered it into a hole he had cut, made a hole in the roof, stuck a chimney though, opened the door, walked in, and pulled up the window, et voila.[25] Even his dugout, however, isn't to be compared to The Ritz Hotel. The beauty of The Ritz is that it is bombproof as I discovered when I was there last. The Germans landed several bombs on top of the place when I was there but no damage done. They also landed a bomb in the back of a dugout occupied by one of my men and when the Guard by the gun rushed in to open up the place that had been

---

24 SRD: Service Rum Department. See Image on page 102.
25 Captain, later Colonel, Alexander (Sandy) Kirkwood Reid MC (1884-1948), 1/9th HLI 1914-18; married Ina Doris Law (30 April 1917) (ref letter 18 April 1915); author/editor of 'Shoulder to Shoulder', 1/9th HLI's unpublished history. See p. 103.

blown in, he found the man inside sound asleep. As the man remarked, "When ignorance is bliss!". We had a new officer out here a few days ago, who complained that he couldn't get to sleep after 5am because of the noise of the guns. It rather amused us as in the first place there was practically no noise at all, and in the second place I wonder if he thinks he is going to sleep till 9.00 every morning. Please don't trouble to send the ear plugs you talked of. A Machine Gun is nothing like the other guns. It simply fires the same ammunition as a rifle, only smaller. In proper working order it should fire about 600 shots a minute, or 10 per second, which is not bad going.

I have really no more to say so I shall wind up instead of doing as one officer I know did, viz blacked out several lines to look as if something had been censored. He told me his sister had spent a long time trying to work out what had been censored when all the time there was nothing there. It struck me as a splendid idea.

The Glasgow Highlanders' trenches at Festubert, 1915. A service rum flagon is on the parapet. (RHF Collection)

Captain Alexander Reid in the "cart dugout" referred to in Walter's letter of 14 March 1915.
(Top: McCosh family collection; Bottom: RHF Collection)

Lieutenant Edward McCosh
and Captain Alexander Reid.
(McCosh family collection)

15 March, 1915

My dear Mother,

Many thanks for the boots which I got the day before yesterday. They were a little tight to begin with but after a few days wear have become very comfortable indeed. Very many thanks for sending them so quickly. If you hadn't, I expect I would have been absolutely laid out now as the pair I had were making me lamer every day. Would you mind getting me another pair of boots ready to be sent out if I want them? If you can, please get them a bit broader and instead of the 48 nails per boot that Allan's put in, please tell them to put in at least 480 per boot if they can manage it. I don't think they have any idea of the wear and tear boots get out here. Math got a 42/- pair from Allan's which wore out in three weeks. Please have heel and toe caps put on as usual.

Please don't worry sending out souvenirs for the various Mesdames. The present one I know would value a five franc note more than any souvenir I could give her, and most of them are the same way.

I shall have my hen for dinner tonight. I have just heard it weighs 2 kilos 35, so I expect it will feed four of us alright, though I don't know what a kilo is.

Math and Madame's parrot have just been singing – Bliss, I <u>don't</u> think.

What there is of the Machine Gun Section that is out of the trenches, today beat a neighbouring battery of Royal Field Artillery. There was also a game of rugger this afternoon which I watched. In the middle, the Germans chucked a couple of shells over us. It was quite like the newspaper pictures except that the shells burst miles away.

I don't think there is any more news except that I am still hyper-flourishing,

Your ever cheery son.

PS The hen was excellent.

> Our Machine Guns, being brigaded, took their share of front line duties. Cuinchy was to the right of the British line and Lieut W.J.J.Coats as he sat in a dug-out beside one of his guns, could boast that he was literally the right hand man of the British Army.
>
> Colonel Alexander Kirkwood Reid, 'Shoulder to Shoulder'.

19/3/15

My dear Jean,

I got out of the trenches last night and expect to go in again at midday tomorrow. I am glad the Ritz Hotel is fairly comfortable or I would be getting a bit fed up. I had a cheery job of getting relieved last night. When I got out of my dugout, I found the night was as black as pitch, in fact you couldn't see your hand in front of your face. I started gaily walking down the trench but found that I bumped into every transverse I came across not to mention people etc., so I turned on my flash lamp which lit up about a couple of feet ahead of me and carried on. I thought twice that I had lost my way, but fortunately the first time the Germans sent up a flare and I recognized the bit of trench I was in, and the second time I found that there had been a new bit of trench dug since I had been there last so that instead of walking out of the trench across the road and into the trench again, I walked through the trench. When I eventually got out of trench, I was so dazzled watching where I was going by the light of the lamp that I first of all walked straight into the ditch on one side of the road I should have gone along and then into the ditch on the other side. It took me about 10 minutes before I could make out dimly the tops of the trees against the sky and by walking as nearly as possible immediately under the opening between the tops of the trees, I managed to keep on the road. To add to the general excitement it was raining and there were occasional bullets knocking around. As a rule, the darker the night, the greater the number of stray bullets.

The cutting Dad sent me from the News is the most fearful pack of lies as regards our acting as support to the Northumberland Fusiliers. As far as I know, we have never been within 20 miles of them and we have certainly never seen them since we came out. What they are trying to get at is that we are in the Fifth Brigade and have done a lot of fighting.

We lost the football Cup by one goal. We played a team of Frenchmen yesterday at rugger and beat them 9-0. I did not see the game but I believe it was marked by its absolute disregard for all rules. The referee was warned beforehand not to be too particular.

The weather here today is the absolute limit, blowing hard and snowing. You can tell Jack that the man who went to hospital with him just got back yesterday. He was on the light duty at the base for a long time.

If you see Pat [cousin, Pat Graham], please congratulate or, rather, condole with him from me. A private has the best of it. Tell him that the most necessary thing for an officer who comes out here to have is a good servant, preferably one who has the cheek to go on talking to a Frenchman in English until the Frenchman in desperation offers him everything and he takes what he has been asking for. I think that must be the principal our servants go on here because they appear to be able to get everything you tell them to get, from the shaving water in the morning to clean sheets at night.

21/3/15

The Ritz Hotel
Park Lane

My dear Ellie,

The chief bit of news here is that we are being relieved from this place tomorrow (Monday) it is <u>alleged</u> for at least eight days' rest. To add to the general cheeriness, the other Machine Gun Officer has gone on leave, so with any luck my turn will come next. You can read my poem to Mrs and Miss Rowett, as they have done their bit to become members of the family by forcing poor John to marry you.

I have really very little to drivel about just now, as nothing much has been doing here lately beyond shells by day and bombs and bullets by night. It is always the same.

I heard a steam whistle going the other day, and it reminded me at once of Glasgow. I also heard a lark and it reminded me of Biggar. It is funny but I preferred the steam whistle. It was fine.

As I said before, and I have no doubt will say many times again, I have no news therefore as the rubber doormat says, Valete!

[Cont.] 23rd

I have not had the opportunity of posting this sooner as we are now in a different position and all the time has been spent moving. The eight days' rest is up the pole.

Cheer oh!

WJ.J.C

Tuesday, 23 March, 1915

My dear Dad,

I am sorry to keep you so long without a note, but I have been rather busy lately. I got out of Park Lane on the 18th about 9.00 PM and went in again about 8.00 AM on the 20th as the other Machine Gun Officer has gone on leave. We were told we would be relieved at 11.00 AM on the 21st, but the relief didn't turn up till 4.30 PM and as we had a good long march to fresh billets, we did not get there till about 9.00 PM. The next day, I was sent for while in the middle of lunch and told to go and find out about a new position away in a different direction that we were to go into that night, so I had to borrow a bike and scoosh off at once. When I had got the information, I scooshed back and met the guns coming along the road so I hopped off and turned in with them. We eventually got out here between eight and nine. This is rather a hole, and goodness knows how long we are going to be here. I expect I shall be in the trench until the Machine Gun Officer gets back in about five days. The other people are spending one day in and three out. The funny thing is that we were told we were going for an eight day rest. However, it is my turn for leave with the next batch that goes. It is just possible, if all goes well, that I shall be home with in the week. On the other hand it is equally possible that I shall not get home within the month.

I am afraid there will be a huge lot of flies about here this summer. There are a fearful amount about already.

WD: I went into the trenches again from 11th to 14th; 16th to 18th; 20th and 21st, when we were moved back to Béthune, it was alleged for 8 days' rest. I got back to Béthune about 9 p.m. on the 21st and on the morning of the 22nd was sent off to reconnoitre some trenches near Festubert and arrange to relieve the London Scottish there that night.[26] Todd was on leave. The rest of the Battalion followed on during the day and we carried out the relief that night.

We found the line here consisted of sort of grouse butts, being built entirely above the ground of sandbags and hurdle revetting. Most of these butts were in process of being lined up but when we arrived the only connection between them was a line of brushwood hurdles. The communication trench by which we got into the line commenced at a ruined distillery at the end of the Rue de l'Epinette several hundred yards behind the line to a broken down farmhouse close behind the extreme left hand butt. It was only about 18 inches deep and here again brushwood hurdles and sacking were the only cover we had.

---

26 1/14th (County of London) Battalion (London Scottish), 1st Brigade, 1st (Regular) Division, a first-line Territorial battalion deployed in France since September 1914.

Grouse Butts near Festubert, 1915. These forward outposts were mutually supporting breastworks constructed in low-lying ground. (RHF Collection)

I took up my abode in the broken down farmhouse [possibly 'Dead Cow Farm', see map page 109] at the end of the communication trench where I found a room with a roof still on it. The R.E's. occupied the only other room in the house which they used as cover for the entrance to a mine which they were making.

24 March 1915

My dear Mother,

Just a line to let you know I am still flourishing. Last night it came down in torrents, so we had a cheery time. I got to bed at 2.00 AM and was so tired I slept solidly till nearly 10. We could hear the Germans singing and whistling in their breastworks last night. They treated us, inter alia, to "Ye banks and braes". They had a gramophone going the night before.

Map of Festubert-Rue de L'Épinette sector showing Grouse Butts, Dead Cow Farm and communication trenches described by Walter in March 1915. (G F Paterson records, Indian Corps Front Sheet 2 (Festubert), Sandhurst Collection)

We are living behind breastworks here, as trenches are impossible. They are not high enough to stand upright behind so, as one man said, we walk about like half-open pocket knives.

The ground about here is in a piggish mess and smells like _____. Inter alia, there is a cow that has been dead for goodness knows how long.

There is a lot to be done so Au Revoir,
Your loving son
Walter J.J. Coats

26 March, 1915

My dear Jean,
Here we are, still in the trenches. I have been in four days now and expect to be in for another three at least before I can get relieved. We had quite a little excitement here yesterday. I was living in an old house about 20 yards behind our breastworks and was waiting for breakfast, when suddenly there was a fearful flash in one of the rooms occupied by some engineers and before we knew what had happened the roof was blazing like a furnace. We all cleared out at once as we knew the house was also used as a bomb store but when we found it was not one of the bombs that had gone off we came back and started to get them out of the way to put the fire out. One of the boxes of bombs was on fire and had to be extinguished with some handy tea before it was got out. It was quite exciting till this was done. The house formed one side of a farmyard, so after getting the bombs etc. out we started to save the other three sides. All we had to do this with was a pump for draining trenches, two small mess tins and a Mackintosh's toffee tin. Fortunately, there was a large beam handy, so three of us lifted this up and started to use it as a battering ram to break the connection between the burning bit and the rest. How no one got a tile on the head or a lump of wood is a mystery to me. To add to the general excitement, there was a good number of spare rounds of ammunition lying about which was always going off and one man got hit on the head though not badly, I think. The Germans also started sniping but we were pretty safe from that direction. We managed to save the three sides alright though we were all like chimney sweeps before it was done. No one knows exactly how the fire started. One explanation is that an engineer laid a hot mess tin on a lot of cordite. It was a fine relief to the monotony of trench life. You would have roared if you have seen us trying to extinguish a beam 15 feet above our heads with a toffee tin.

Today has been quieter though somewhat chilly.

You will be pleased to hear my name has been sent in for leave. I hope it comes to something. At any rate, it shows that it is my turn when leave is given. I shouldn't mind a rest after a week here.

WD: As the house was quite useless after this I moved into a small shelter behind the breastwork where I stayed till I went on leave, along with Bock [Major Herman J R Bock], Whitson[27] and McNaughton.

Walter with "His Nibs" at John Rowett's home, Perry Mount, Forest Hill, London, April 1915. (WJJC collection)

---

27 Captain Ernest James Whitson (b.1886); educated at Glasgow Academy; 1/9th HLI and 100th Brigade Staff Bombing Officer; participated in Loos offensive the same day that one of his two brothers, Harold Whitson, perished nearby. Lieutenant Harold White Whitson (b. c.1896); Fettes College (Carrington House, 1911-13); 2nd HLI; wounded Battle of the Marne 1914; killed in action 25 September 1915 near Givenchy. <http://www.glasgowne-cropolis.org/profiles/harold-white-whitson/> (Accessed 1 September 2015). His other brother was Captain Wilfred Robert Whitson.

3

Back to the Front

This is a pretty rotten hell we are in just now.

WD: I think this first leave although the shortest was the best I had, partly I suppose owing to its novelty. The leave boat was not too crowded and the journey in a fast Pullman from Folkestone after travelling in the French trains seemed perfectly wonderful – like everything else. I returned on the 9th April and found the Battalion still in the same place.

10 April, 1915

My dear Dad,

Here we are again once more "dong La Belle Frongce" as people would say (who hadn't been there) or, as I would put it, I left the land of cakes and thistles, and reached the land of stinks and whistles. The whistling being done by Jack Johnston etc.

As you can imagine, there is not much by the way of news. We had a very comfortable crossing (at least some of us had) and then travelled up here last night. I don't go into the trenches till tomorrow morning. It is a fine bright day here with a warm sun and a cooling wind.

Math and three others left on leave today. I hope they dodge the submarines all right. Many thanks for the pile of letters which I found waiting for me, the news was not particularly interesting, but it would have been if I hadn't been home first.

13/04/15

My dear Mother,

Here we are again in the same old place at the same old job. I wrote you a postcard yesterday to say I was still flourishing but unfortunately forgot to post it last night so I shall not send it now.

There is really no news here except that I have become an expert at reaching Berlin with the silver bullet.[1]

I suppose you know Math is home on leave just now. He left the day I arrived.

I think I told you I had quite a comfortable journey up here. I arrived on Saturday, went into the trenches on Sunday and have been there since.

16 April, 1915

My dear Jean,

You will be interested to hear that we have all been instructed to cease shaving the upper lip and it is rather a nuisance but, if I clip it every second day or so, I will manage to keep it under control alright.

18 April, 1915

My dear Jenny,

I suppose you heard all our recent news from Math. I hope he has not been telling any tall stories about me. He said, I believe, that I extinguished the box of bombs with the tea which is, to say the least, not true as I didn't even know at the time that it was on fire. It certainly makes the story more interesting but there is quite enough excitement about this war without inventing any harrowing details. Wingate and I have just received a letter from Madame Mackereel asking how we are and saying they wrote my sister thanking her for the shawl and asking what sort of lace was wanted, but have not yet got any reply. They sent their best wishes and so on and have landed us with a reply on our hands. If anyone thinks of writing them again, would you mind sending out some British tobacco for the son? I will pay for it when I come back. We must have created quite an impression.

My upper lip is assuming quite a dirty appearance now so I expect I shall have to forget some morning and shave it accidentally.

I go back to the trenches again tomorrow for four days after which my movements are uncertain. I hope the weather keeps fine.

I suppose you will have heard that Sandy Reid got engaged when he was home just now to, I think, a Miss Law [Ina Law]. It seems to be the fashionable thing to do. Do

---

1   "Silver Bullet" or "The Road to Berlin" was a "British designed dexterity game: Anti-German propaganda of World War I. The player tries to manipulate a small metal ball on a course to a final objective while avoiding falling into one of many holes. ... The final objective ... is reaching Berlin. Along the way the player must elude holes labelled Cologne, Leipzig, Magdeburg, Dresden, Hanover, Potsdam, Hamburg and Spandau, all of these representing "fortresses"... Also holes are "Entrenchments", "Bridge Destroyed" and "Road Mined" etc." <http://www.whitefoxrarebooks.com/ci_384.html> (Accessed 10 January 2016).

you know how Chalmers is and if he is likely to be out here again? If you ever phone him, you can say I was asking for him. This is a funny wee billet we are in just now. Six of us live and sleep in a room about 2/3 the size of the parlour with a double bed, wardrobe, large cooking range sticking into the room, table, six chairs, six kits and six valises and about six square feet of clear floor space. Fortunately I have half of the bed. I expect that is why I get so sleepy at night after dinner. It is a change from my dugout in the trenches which is a sort of wind trap.

20/04/15 [Walter's birthday]

My dear Dad,
Many thanks for your and the family's good wishes which arrived last night also for the sweets and fish which also arrived. The sweets have been sampled and not found wanting in fact most of them can no longer be found at all. The fish gives its farewell performance at dinner tonight.

Today is another topping day though not so hot as it has been. Yesterday, the badges on my collar got so hot I could hardly put my face against them. It will be cheery when the hot weather comes.

I have a fairly good job here just now. I go into the trenches about seven or 8.00 PM and stay there till about 9.30 in the morning when I come out for breakfast. From 11 till 1.30, I supervise in a sort of way some digging which is being done. At three, I take a class of instruction till four when I knock off work for the day. I have absolutely no news as everything goes on as usual here. I have given up my kilt pro tem, and am swanking it like a Field Officer.

22/4/15

My dear Jean,
Many thanks for your and Jenny's present of the air cushion. I used it last night with very happy results. Please thank Mother for the salmon which arrived in splendid condition. It is a great improvement on the tinned stuff which we sometimes get here and which I generally avoid.

I leave this place tomorrow morning for another four days behind after which I rather think I shall come back here again but I don't know. We have been here for exactly a month now.

We are having the most beautiful weather here just now and I am writing this sitting outside at 4.00 PM. It starts to get light about 3.30 now and it does not get dark till between 7 and 8 PM.

Our aeroplanes are having a busy old time of it just now. Yesterday, we could see five of them up at once and not a German in sight.

WD: The whole Battalion was relieved and returned to Béthune on the 23rd. We got a good rest this time and did not go into the line again until the 3rd of May when we were sent in at Cuinchy.

26/4/15

My dear Dad,
I had a pretty cheery time of it on Saturday and Sunday when we were moving. I was awake from about 8.30 on Saturday morning till midday on Sunday. I was very sleepy as a result but I have often been more so. It was all in a good cause, however, as we are now resting for an indefinite period. I have got a most excellent billet as usual, with a bed to myself also a wash stand etc., which is unusual. We have also got a general Mess again for the first time since leaving Bailleul.

There is very little in the way of news here just now except that we are spending our time here getting into decent condition. It is fine getting some exercise again.

I met an officer the other day of a Territorial battalion that had not been out for long, who complained of being very tired as his battalion had now been in the trenches for a whole week and he thought it was about time he was relieved. I am afraid he didn't get much comfort from me as to when he might expect to be relieved. He left me as a wiser though, I am afraid, a much sadder man.

PS You should see my moustache. Just now, it looks like a Company in artillery formation. In a week or two, it should resemble a line of skirmishers at the beginning of an attack and in a month or so, a line of skirmishers massed for a charge.

28/4/15

My dear Doug,
Please note that this is a red letter day in the War. I have had a bath I could lie down in and cover myself with water. The first since I was home on leave. I took down about 100 men to get baths and while they were in, I hopped off and had a bath in a place reserved for officers. It is wonderful the way they manage the washing here. The man goes in at one end, leaves all his clothes behind, has a bath and when he comes out is handed a new or at any rate a clean shirt, socks and his uniform which has been disinfected by some heat method. He is then given a cup of coffee and finds when he goes to bed at night that his blankets have also been cleaned. The disinfecting machine I saw, was working at a temperature of 215° so they must have got an awful fright.

While I remember, please don't send out any more socks or clothes as we are now trying to lighten our kit as much as possible.

Today is another glorious day, bright sun with a cool wind. We are still resting, much to our surprise.

Walter (L) with an unidentified Glasgow Highlanders officer at Givenchy-lès-la-Bassée,
February 1915. Inserted in a letter home dated 28 April 1915. (WJJC collection)

PS There is so little doing here, please excuse me if I only send postcards for a day or
so. I enclose a picture of myself taken at Givenchy-lès-la-Bassée when we were there
last. The heap of earth on the right is a communication trench. The picture was taken
on our way up to the front trench.

30/4/15

My dear Mother,
The chief bit of news is that we are still resting and as Willie Graham would say "hope
to be". Do you know if he has got through his job at Ypres all right?

We gave a performance in the theatre here last night and it was a great success.
Each Battalion gives one when it is resting but ours was the star turn. There were some
fearfully funny turns. We had the Divisional General there.[2]

---

2   General Henry Sinclair Horne, 1st Baron Horne, GCB, KCMG, Commander, 2nd Division
January-November 1915; Lieutenant-General and GOC XV Corps 1916; General and
GOC First Army 1917-18. See Simon Robbins, 'Henry Horne as Divisional Commander'
in Spencer Jones (ed) *Courage Without Glory: The British Army on the Western Front 1915*
(Solihull: Helion & Company, 2015), pp. 103-24.

Talking of Generals, you will be pleased to hear that General Haig was along at our billets yesterday and was fearfully complimentary to our Colonel about the way the Battalion had done. The Colonel said he couldn't have been more complimentary, in fact he said so much, the Colonel began to grow quite embarrassed and didn't know what to do.

We are all very pleased out here that there is no chance of our going back to the Lowland Division if it ever comes out. I believe General Egerton was very keen to get us back, but our Brigade and Division took up the matter and refused to let us go.

I am afraid you will think this is rather a swelled head number but I know you are just about as keen on the Glasgow Highlanders as I am, so you will excuse me blowing our trumpet a bit.

Many thanks for your and Dad's daily letters. It is a great pleasure to get them and hear what is going on at home.

The weather here is absolutely blazing just now and, as we are out training all afternoon, we are all getting more or less sunburnt. This place, and the work we are doing, reminds me of Dunfermline. It is very hard to think we are at war. To add to the general home feeling, one of our men is a golf professional and has just laid out a golf course and one of our officers has just been sent a gramophone. Such is war.

No more news,
Your cheery son,
Walter

2 May, 1915

My dear Jean,
You will be interested to hear that we go back to the trenches again tomorrow. We have had a most splendid rest as it is exactly a week ago today that we left the last place. We had a most interesting day's work yesterday. We left our billets about 8.30 AM and spent the day training, arriving back about 5.00 at night. It was a blazing day but it was great sport. It was quite like Gailes [the Glasgow Highlanders' annual camp]. The men are all feeling the better of the exercise. The rest is not so much in the amounts of work done as in the change of work and relief from the bally bullet.

Please also thank Dad for the Faculty Roll Of Honour. The Faculty are certainly not very optimistic. Did Dad notice they had put "During the war 1914-19"? Another curious thing is that every man noted as killed or wounded is a G.H. man with one exception and that man was in Mc G D & Co.

Your about-to-censor-letters-and-therefore-somewhat-fed-up-brother,
Walter J.J. Coats

4 May, 1915

My dear Jenny,

There is not much news except that we are safely back to the trenches. I am back in the billet [Annequin] with the old Paris cook but I have got it to myself this time so I am living in great style. I am glad to say we are not inhabiting Park Lane this time, but another bit of the maze which is more comfortable.

Did Math ever tell you of the man he sent out one day to dig a refuse pit? He had just begun to dig when a shell landed near him, so he simply went and trimmed off the edges of the shell hole and had a beautiful pit in record time. Talking of records, some of our men are supposed to have created a digging record the other day. 100 of them filled 2000 sandbags and carried them to the place they wanted in 2½ hours. I don't know whether it is a record or not but it was jolly good digging considering it was done in the dark.

Please thank Mother for the chickens which arrived in splendid condition, and also for the rest of the food which is a very nice change.

[Cont.] 5/5/15

I began this yesterday but was stopped in the middle by a message which meant me going away up to the trenches to look at some new positions. I was considerably annoyed, as we were in the middle of a thunderstorm at the time, and I had already been up in the forenoon. We couldn't be the worse for several more thunderstorms now, as it is fearfully hot. I am more sunburnt already than I ever was at camp. It was funny how the rain yesterday stopped the war. Before it came on, both sides were popping off their guns but as soon as the rain started, everything calmed down.

Do you think someone could hunt out an old Glengarry among my kit and get a new one the same size? I think they take some time to get but I am in no particular hurry.

Things are very quiet here just now and everyone is in great spirits after their rest.

I expect to go into the trenches tomorrow for three days. We have a fine and soft job here.

WD: Much to our surprise we were relieved from Cuinchy on 5th May two days later and returned to Béthune. We were not however so pleased when we learnt on our return that we were to take part in a battle at Festubert [sic] next day.

We left Béthune about 2 a.m. on the 6th May and as all the Machine Guns were brigaded for the show we parted company with the Battalion for the time being. We spent most of the 6th in a field near Gorre waiting to join in but except for occasional rumours nothing happened till dark when we moved off. After passing through Essars we marched for several hours until we arrived at La Couture where we were halted for a few hours in a field. As we did not know what was going to happen most of us tried to get some sleep. As it was a bitterly cold night and the grass was very wet, I could not make up my mind whether to lie on my waterproof sheet, which was all the covering

I had, or whether to lie on the grass with the sheet over me. I started with the sheet under me but soon got so cold I had to change round but even then it was sometime before I managed to get to sleep.

I seemed to have been asleep about 10 minutes when we were all roused up again and, after falling over each other for a few minutes in the inky darkness, got straightened out and resumed our march. We arrived at Richebourg about dawn when we found the attack had been a complete failure, owing chiefly I think to uncut wire, and that any further attack had been postponed for the time being. Half the brigade was accordingly sent up to take over from the troops that had been attacking and we rejoined our Battalion in billets in Richebourg.

7 May, 1915

My dear Dad,
There is not much in the way of news just now except that we are pretty busy and I may not be able to write or even send a postcard for several days. However I shall write as often as possible.

I have sent a lot of surplus clothes etc. home today as in the first place we do not need as many clothes in summer and in the second place I had far more than my regulation allowance of weight.

I've got what I suspect is some more supplies from McG D & Co but I do not intend to open them just now. I shall simply put them on the Mess cart as they are. If you see any of McG D & Co, would you mind explaining the situation and thanking them from me. I shall write them when I get time to find out definitely if it is they who sent the stuff.

I should like to be able to give you more news but the Censor wouldn't like it, so I won't.

11/5/15

My dear Ellie,
I sent you a Field Service Post Card today as I thought I would not have time to write before the post went, however I find it is not going till tomorrow morning.

You will be interested to hear that we are in this performance that is going on just now, in fact as far as I can make out our bit of it comes off tomorrow. I hope we make a decent show as it is our first job of this kind.

There is not much in the way of news here just now. In fact, the first definite news we have had of what has been happening was in the Times of the 10th, which I saw this afternoon.

We are in the same place just now as we were in January, but the country has absolutely changed. In fact, it doesn't look half bad now with trees out etc.

11 May, 1915

My dear Dad,

As they would say in Glasgow, "We're fur it noo". In other words the Brigade is going to whoosh, or charge, tomorrow and as we are with the Brigade, we have to do it also. It is our first attempt so I hope we put up a decent show. I wouldn't tell you this just now, only the job will be taken over by someone else before you get this (i.e. after we break the line, other troops will carry on the work) and if there is any bad news, you will also have heard before you get this, so you will see there is no use worrying. I shall send a Field Service P.C. as soon as I can after the show is over, but you needn't worry if you don't get one for several days after this.

I suppose you will have seen from the papers about the performance that began on Sunday. We half expected to be in it and as a matter of fact we were moved about a lot behind the line but we didn't actually get into it. We are at present at the same part of the line as we were at in January.

We are having most beautiful weather here just now, only it is fearfully cold at night and as we have handed in our blankets and greatcoats, we are feeling it a bit. Sunday night, especially, we had it pretty cheery. We marched from nine till about quarter to 12, when we halted in a field for an indefinite period, so we all lay down with our waterproof sheets and tried to sleep. As a matter of fact, most of us succeeded all right, including myself, but it was the coldest bed I have ever had. As a matter of fact, we were only allowed to sleep till 2.30am, when we shifted again and we all thought we were for it, but we weren't.

I must stop now if I am to get this posted.

PS Please wish Jim many happy returns for his birthday, as I don't have time to write. Excuse scribble.

12 May, 1915

My dear Mother,

This is just a note to let you know that we were not pushed into the job today after all and are going up to the trenches tonight. At least that was the idea half an hour ago. I have heard a different idea since, so goodness knows what is going to happen. There is absolutely no other news, except that we are all flourishing exceedingly.

15 May, 1915

My dear Dad,

We have not been in it yet and goodness knows if we are going to be. Meantime we are waiting. I wish in a way, we could get into it, as I am tired of screwing up my courage and unscrewing it again. However, it's all in the game. There has been quite a bombardment going on here for several days now and I think most of us are getting a bit fed up with the noise.

PS Rumour has it we are for it tonight, so I shall have to start screwing up my courage again.

WD: We stayed in Richebourg waiting for our turn to come and getting to know the line as well as possible while the Artillery were cutting the German wire. This wait was rather trying as we all knew we were for it sooner or later and it was quite a relief when we heard we were to move on the 15th.

The orders for the attack were as follows:

1.   The 5th Brigade will attack the German trenches on their front from the bend in the German line exclusive between R6 and VI to the N.W. corner of the salient between V3 and V6.
     1st.Objective – The first and second line of German parapets from R7 inclusive to a point N.W. of V5 and to get in touch with the Meerut Division at that point. A further advance will not be made till after daylight.

2.   The detail of the attack will be as follows:-
     (A) Frontage – 570 yards to Bn's front.
     Inniskilling Fusiliers from communication trench W of cinder track exclusive to ditch 150 yards E. of cinder track. Frontage 250 yards.
     Worcesters from this point to ditch just E. of communication trench running through copse. Frontage 320 yards.
     (B) The attack is to be carried out by successive lines at intervals of about 100 yards. Especial care must be taken to ensure adequate support being given.
     (C) Working parties will be supplied by supporting Bns. Oxfords and Glasgows. The working parties for the first line will go as a third line. They will each consist of a platoon made up to 50 men with one N.C.O. and 4 men R.E. Details as to the method of attack by leading Bns. will be given later to officers. The Glasgows will be in support of the Worcesters in the left section of the attack. The Oxfords will be in support on the right.

3.   Forming up. The two Battalions allotted to the attack will form their men up on the front line and in the two cover trenches 50 and 100 yards in rear of the front line. The Oxfords and Glasgows will form up on B, C and D lines. Glasgows will have Nos.1 and 2 Companies in B; No.3 and half of No. 4 in C.
     The two front lines of the leading Battalions will be deployed in front of the British breastworks before the time for the assault. As they move forward their places at the breastworks will be taken by succeeding lines and as one

line goes forward the succeeding line will take its place. This applies equally to supporting Battalions. Watches must be accurately set.

4.   Bomb reserve depots & R.E. depots – Bomb depots each of 500 bombs are in front breastwork at exit of communication trenches 150 yards E. and 250 yards E. of cinder track. S.A.A. [small arms ammunition] stores each of 100 boxes exist at the same places. A further reserve of bombs and S.A.A. is at house S.9.A.9.1. and about house S.9.A.5.8. Depots of R.E. stores are near the bomb stores in front line. Reserve depot in house on the Rue du Bois next the factory.

5.   The Battalion will provide the following work parties which will be detailed by O.C. No. 4 Company: 1 platoon made up to 50 men for work in German first line – 1 platoon made up to 50 men for work in German second line. Both the above parties will report to O.C. Worcesters at S.3.C.5.5. at 5 p.m.

6.   Masks must be dipped in solution during the day and be carried by all men.

7.   Battalion H.Q. in B line till move to front line.

8.   Distinguishing marks – White patches back and front are being issued about 1000 to Worcesters and Inniskillings each. Sufficient must be given to working parties.

9.   Distinguishing marks of Divisions.
      2nd.   Division – yellow flags and screens.
      7th.   "   – red flags white bars.
      Meerut   "   – white diagonal cross, corners of flag red and black.

10. Communication's trench on left of cinder track is for wounded.

11. Send orderly when get in position to Battalion H.Q.

12. At 11.15 p.m. Battalion H.Q. move to front line on right of ditch.

13. Till 11.30 p.m. use communication trenches.

14. 1st. Aid post behind factory. Ambulances at cross roads behind.

15. Further advance will be at 2.45 a.m. if all is well.

Signals of 7th Div:

I. White starts. 2. Green smoke mixed with white stars. 3. Red smoke. 4. Red smoke and white stars. If seen, report when.[3]

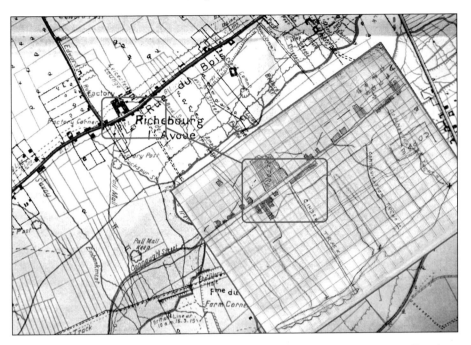

Battle of Festubert. Walter's hand-drawn map of the Richebourg L'Avoué sector, Rue du Bois, 16-17 May 1915 superimposed over issue trench map; British line "at 10 am 16-5-15" denoted. (G F Paterson records, Indian Corps Front Sheet 2 (Festubert), Sandhurst Collection).

My position was in line C until the attack started at 11.30 p.m. when I was ordered to push up to the front line. I accordingly left line C at this hour and after struggling through crowds of men reached the front line in time to see the Worcesters come tumbling back into the trench. They reported that they had met with very heavy machine gun fire as soon as they got out of our trenches and had then found the wire uncut, though some of them, including some men of our working party, had got into the German trench where they were killed or captured. The Battalion on the right had however got through

---

3   The Battle of Festubert (15-25 May) opened with a comparatively successful night assault followed by ten days of fierce fighting during which the attackers advanced 3 kilometres (1.9 miles) into the German defences. See Robert Williams, 'The Battle of Festubert' in Jones (ed), *Courage Without Glory*, pp. 258-81, Wyrall, *The History of the Second Division 1914-1918*, pp. 198-213 and Weir, *Come on Highlanders!*, pp. 82-101.

though with heavy losses. We accordingly prepared to have a second go at it but before we started, orders came through that we were to stay where we were and that the Worcesters were to be sent back to reserve.

We all waited here all next day wondering when we would be sent over and suffered very heavily partly from the German shelling but chiefly from our own which was hitting us very badly in the back. We spent the night of the 16th/17th getting in as many wounded as we could. The 17th was practically a repetition of the 16th, though to me it seemed much more miserable as I was not feeling particularly well. This I found afterwards was due to an attack of jaundice which must have started at this time.

Field Service Post Card (FSPC): 18/5/15

To John J. Coats: I am quite well. Walter J.J. Coats

WD: We were relieved on the night of the 17th/18th by the Indian Division, our two days in the line having cost us something over 200 casualties due very largely to our own shell fire.[4] On relief we moved back to a small village called Le Touret where we arrived on the 18th and after a night's rest moved back next day to Hurionville near Lillers. I was feeling so ill just now that I had to borrow a horse for the last mile or two of the march back and when I arrived was sent to bed.

Wednesday, 19th of May, 1915

My dear Dad,

You will be pleased to hear we have finished our job and are now well back behind even our biggest guns, having a rest. What is more, there is word of our going still further back, so I suppose we are at last for a long rest. I am not sorry, as I have had enough war for some time to come. The Brigade really got into the thick of the job on Saturday night when there was a night attack. We were very heavily shelled all Sunday, had a more or less quiet night on Sunday night, were very heavily shelled again on Monday, and were relieved on Tuesday morning just before daylight. We then marched back a short way, to temporary billets, where we stayed till 2.45 when we came on here arriving about 7.30pm. We have spent the day here trying to get cleaned up after a night of about the most solid sleep we ever have had.

---

4   Brigadier-General A.A. Chichester (GOC 5th Brigade) reported to 2nd Division HQ on the action of 15-17 May: "Artillery fire was often inaccurate ... I received constant and daily reports of this bad shooting, and there were besides a considerable number of prematures. I consider there is nothing that so adversely affects the morale of the troops as being shot by their own artillery and it is urgent that more care be taken." See TNA WO 95/1343-2: 5th Brigade War Diary.

Mathew Anderson is alright though I am sorry to say Carruthers has been killed.[5] He was hit in the head either by a bit of shell or a bullet, I don't know which.

You have no idea how thankful I am to get out of the job and absolutely clear of gunfire. We are now further back than we have ever been since Christmas.

PS If you write to Jim [serving in the Royal Field Artillery], please tell him for goodness sake to be careful and not drop shells into his own trenches as it is, to put it gently, very uncomfortable. Any talk of the lack of German shells is absolute bilge.

23/5/15

My dear Mother,
We had the G.O.C. Division [Gen Horne] along yesterday saying a few words of comfort. Among other details, he said he considered the fight we had been in was as hard a fight as any man had ever been in. I must say, I was glad to hear him say so as I haven't the slightest desire to be in a harder one.

24/5/15 Monday

My dear Mother,
Just a line to let you know I am still flourishing though the Doctor says that if I am not more flourishing tomorrow, he is going to send me to hospital. As I don't want to go, I am at present lying down trying to become more flourishing. I don't think there is very much the matter with me. I am off my feet, and feeling like a washed out dish cloth and periodically sick but these are all minor discomforts. The Doctor says he thinks it is jaundice. It is nothing to worry about at any rate.

We are having the most beautiful weather for our rest so we are all enjoying it to the full. I don't know when we will be sent back to work again.

Tuesday 25/ 5/15

My dear Dad,
I was so much better this morning the Doctor gave me my choice as to whether I would go to hospital or stay and let him treat me. He said if I went to hospital, I would probably be sent home and end up in the 3rd Battalion, so I said I would stay here. There is really not much wrong with me and I should hate to go home without a decent

---

5   Pte 2523 Frank Walter Carruthers, killed in action 17th May 1915. See letter 2 February 1915.

reason. Of course, if the Battalion is moved before I get better I shall have to go to hospital after all but that will be just bad luck.

28/5/15

My dear Dad,

Just a line to let you know the Battalion moved before I was quite cured, so I have been sent to hospital [in Lillers]. I arrived yesterday and it was like going to the dentist. I no sooner had got into the place, than I felt perfectly fit and I have felt rather a fraud ever since. I suppose there is something the matter however, as I have been put on a milk diet. My ticket says 'Catarrhal Jaundice', whatever that means. It sounds as if it might be exciting but as a matter of fact it is about the most uninteresting disease I have struck yet.

I am sorry I can't tell you what my address is, as I understand I shall probably be shifted from here by the first train. I shall however let you know my address as soon as I am more or less settled. Meantime, if you don't hear from me for a day or two you can take it that I am having the best rest of my life.

Sunday, 30th of May, 1915

My dear Dad,

My address is now No3 General Hospital, Treport, but for how long, goodness knows. I shall not be the least surprised if I am shipped across to England in a day or two as they like to keep the beds on this side free and I heard unofficially that I have been put down for a three week cure. This is a most beautiful place here, it reminds me of that place we were back in Devon, I forget its name. We are in a hotel perched on top of the cliffs, with the village below us.

It is rather funny, the nurse in charge of the room I am in is a Glasgow lady. I don't know her name but her face is not unlike Miss Thorn.

And as you can imagine, there is not much in the way of news at a hospital. Everything is delightfully clean and peaceful after the trenches. I shall let you know when my address becomes more or less permanent, in the meantime Cheer Oh.

Your ever cheerful son.

2nd of June, 1915

My dear Mother,

The rest of the occupants of this room were cleared out this morning for England so I have now got the place to myself. The people who were shifted were supposed to be suffering from nervous breakdown but I must say I have seldom seen such healthy looking people and the only trace of nerves that I could find was nervousness about not getting home. I was fearfully tickled at one of them who admitted there was nothing wrong with him (he was a fearful lout and fairly put my back up). The nurse came along one night with a large dose of oil which she insisted on his taking though he assured her it could not possibly be for him. The result was he looked miserable all next day. My private opinion is that the Doctor gave him the stuff for a joke.

I don't know whether I am supposed to be too bad to be sent home yet or whether I am not bad enough to be sent home at all. I feel all right, but I am still looking a more or less sickly yellow colour. I expect I shall be moved in a day or two.

I have just seen the Doctor and he is sending me to the base tomorrow, though I shall not be fit for duty for some time. He says I should apply for a fortnight's sick leave, so perhaps I shall be home in a day or two.

I must stop for the post.

3rd June 1915

My dear Mother,
I am at present at No1 Territorial Base Camp, Rouen. It is not a bad spot but I hope to shift before long. I go before a board on Monday, I think, and I shall ask for a fortnight's leave then. I have been told by the Adjutant here that it is impossible to get it, however the Doctor at Treport told me to ask for it so I shall have a jolly good try. If I don't get leave, I shall ask to be sent back to the Battalion, as this is a poor sort of existence.

8 June, 1915

My dear Dad,
I am sorry to say that all idea of sick leave is up the pole as they don't give it now. It is a pity, but it can't be helped. I believe I was passed by the Board yesterday as fit but I have not yet heard. If I am fit I expect I shall rejoin the Battalion tomorrow. I have been away for about a fortnight now, so I shall not be sorry to get back. This is an awful place here. It is a large plain surrounded by trees and the heat is something awful. I am at present sitting in a shirt and a pair of slippers and am absolutely boiling.

I am glad to say there is a thunderstorm coming along this way now, so it ought to clear the air a bit.

I shall be glad to get back to the Battalion and get some letters from you. I have received no letters since I left, and have never been long enough in one place to let people hear from me and get a reply. When I was in hospital, I told them to send home anything that came for me, so you will understand if anything arrives home.

I have just heard that the Board certified me as unfit, so I expect I shall be here for another week as I think the Board only sits on Mondays. I am not altogether surprised, as I am still pretty yellow. I have written Math asking him to send my letters on here.

I think I shall go and have a look at the cathedral tomorrow. I suppose it is worth a visit. I shall also try for a sail up the river someday.

I think I shall stop now as I still get very quickly tired.

11/6/15

My dear Mother

There is no news except that I am flourishing. I am still a bit yellow about the eyes but I am feeling absolutely fit and hope to be passed by the Board next Monday as I feel I am slacking here.

I went to the dentist in Rouen yesterday, and had 10 francs worth of the most lively excitement. I got him to pull the rear tooth in my upper jaw. I don't know whether it is usual in this country, but the silly old idiot brought in a man to hold me down. I was fearfully indignant but didn't know enough French to tell him I wasn't a Frenchman, added to which the tooth wasn't out by that time and I wasn't asking for an extra dig with his pincers. It makes you sick after a man has been trying to pull away your upper jaw for about 10 minutes to see him hold up a gory tooth and say "Bon". It sounds fearfully feeble.

PS You can tell Dad we are known as "The Glasgows" by everyone in our Brigade including the General and his staff.

13/6/15

My dear Dad,

There is no news except that I am still flourishing though I am getting a bit fed up with this place. I go before the Board again tomorrow so with any luck I shall be shifting in a day or so.

While I remember, could you find out if Hew Hedderwick is seriously wounded or not and let me know. I saw his name in the papers yesterday.

[Cont.] 14/6/15

I kept this over till today as I thought I might be able to let you know what the Board said. Unfortunately it has been put off till, I think, Wednesday. I received a great bundle of letters today dating back to about 24th of May. I spent quite a pleasant half hour reading them all.

The only thing to grumble about now is not having been sent back to the Battalion. I feel I am slacking here.

Carte Postale: 16/6/15 to John J Coats

Great news, I have just been passed as fit and hope to be out of here by the time you get this. Please address further letters etc. as of old. Please send my other pair of boots.
   W.J.J.C.

18th of June, 1915

My dear Dad,
I am off to rejoin the Battalion today and expect to reach them some time tomorrow. I can't say I am particularly sorry as I am about fed up with this place.

20/6/15

My dear Mother,
Here we are once more back in the trenches. I left Rouen on Friday night, arrived at
_____ [Noyelles-lès-Vermelles, S of Cuinchy] about midday on Saturday and was in the trenches on Saturday night [Vermelles]. This is a very quiet part of the line [Loos sector] and I have not heard more than about three bullets pass over me since I arrived.[6] I expect to be here for several days.

   Thanks for various letters I have received. Would you please send my new Glengarry, also some more of that thick milk chocolate? I should also like a small writing pad and a pocket "Primus" stove, if you can get one without too much trouble. I think they can be got in small tins about six inches long.

WD: The trenches here were all dug in chalk and as the weather was dry and we were about 1000 yards from the Germans we had a very pleasant time. Practically the only work we had to do was the digging of a new trench about 200 yards in front of us, which we worked on every night.

   We were relieved on the 25th and moved back to billets in Mazingarbe where we celebrated the Colonel's C.M.G.[7] and various other awards which we got out of the despatch that was published at this time. From here we moved back after about two days to Béthune where we stayed for a few days before returning to the trenches in front of Givenchy village on June 30th ("Windy Corner" Givenchy-lès-la-Bassée) [See map page 83].

---

6   2nd Division was now part of I Corps (GOC Lieutenant-General Monro); Lieutenant-General Sir Hubert Gough assumed this corps command in July 1915.
7   Companion of St Michael and St George.

25th June 1915

My dear Dad,

Please excuse my not writing for the last few days but we have been moving. We are now back resting, I think for eight days.

Many thanks for the cigars and boots which arrived all right, also for various letters.

I suppose you will have seen from the papers that our Colonel has the C.M.G., Sandy Reid the Military Cross, and that we have four mentions in despatches, not counting our Adjutant and Doctor.

There is a prospect of a new job for me which I hope I don't get, viz. training people at the Base. The authorities asked for the names of officers who required a month's rest and as they seem to think that I require more rest they sent on my name in spite of the fact that I assured them that I was all right. I believe the work will consist chiefly in lecturing. I sincerely hope I don't get it as I understand it will be regulars I have to train.

27 June, 1915

My dear Doug,

Many thanks for getting the pocket Primus etc. and sending them on here. They arrived safely this morning. I am sending back the Glengarry as it is at least half an inch longer than the one I last got from Andersons. If it is not too much trouble, do you think you could get it changed? There is no particular hurry as my present one is still wearable.

There is not much in the way of news here just now, except that things seem to be getting a bit easier for us. We are still resting and expect to go even further back tomorrow.

If you want to make your fortune quickly, invent a fly exterminator. They are something fearful out here.

29 June, 1915

My dear Dad,

Please congratulate Doug on his brilliant work. He will probably have plenty of ear work to do when this war is over.

WD: Trenches at "Windy Corner" Givenchy-lès-la-Bassée. My position here was in Givenchy Keep on the north side of the road leading to the Church[8] and I remember the

---

8   Givenchy Keep is marked as a square building on the map on page 83.

great excitement there was when it was discovered one day that a lot of the bombs in our store were liable to go off simply by a rise in temperature. As the weather was then very warm we were all glad when they were removed.

The reserve companies here were distributed in houses near "Windy Corner" and I remember on one occasion when I was back with them watching Wingate trying to shoot a pigeon. There was rather a scare on about this time about spies sending carrier pigeons over to the German lines and we had accordingly been issued with shot guns and cartridges to try and shoot them. On this occasion someone saw one sitting on the top of our house, so Wingate sallied forth with the gun and about half the men turned out to watch him. His first shot at a range of about 10 yards had no apparent effect so he loaded again and had another try. This time he managed to frighten the bird sufficiently to make it fly round a bit but it soon settled down again in its old place. A third shot drove it out of range but did not seem to have any bad effects. It was perhaps as well that a fourth shot was not possible as most of us were getting almost hysterical.

3rd July, 1915

My dear Mother,

I am afraid you will be disappointed to hear that I don't think there is any chance of my going to the base as instructor now or I would have heard before now. I am perfectly fit, so it is just as well that someone who needs the rest should get the job.

Shortly after I arrived up here today, the Germans started shelling an old church about 20 yards in front of us, so things were pretty lively for a bit as the slightest alteration of the range on their part would have landed one on top of us, however no damage was done. You can tell Dad, the rumour about us all going home has been running for several months now and is obviously not true, as you will see when Jack tells you the size of the draft that has been sent out. Very many thanks for the parcel of biscuits etc. which arrived today. I was fearfully glad to get it for various reasons. In the first place, I am in a position where I have to feed by myself, so any extras are very welcome. In the second place, I had been feeling the want of something sweet to eat. In the third place, this is a very quiet place and reading is the chief form of amusement, and in the last place it came as a complete surprise.

I may as well pad out the letter by telling you what I do here. I am afraid my letters recently have been rather scrappy. I relieve the other officer in the afternoon between lunch and tea time. I then take a walk up to the front line to see if some of my men who are up there are alright. This means walking up to the knee in mud etc. in some places. When I get back, I spend about half an hour scraping the mud off and then sit and read till dinner at about 8.00. After that, I sit and read etc. with periodical visits to sentries till sometime between 3.00 and 4.00 AM when it is daylight and I turn in for a sleep. I have breakfast about 9.00 am, after which I wash and shave etc. and then perhaps go visit the front line again. When I get back, I again read and write till lunch between 1.00 and 2.00, after which I hang around waiting to be relieved, which takes place about the same time as I came up, and then I go back to the billets for a day. And so it goes on, day in and day out, for an indefinite period. It is a funny life.

It is pretty warm here during the day but somewhat chilly at night. The flies and blue bottles are something awful. I don't think I ever saw so many before. They are especially disgusting when one thinks of the various places they may breed.

9/7/15

My dear Dad,

You will be interested to hear we have become such expert diggers and sandbaggers, there is some talk of our being turned into a Pioneer Battalion and used for nothing else.

10/7/15

My dear Ellie,

I shall let you know how the fly chips work in a day or two. As a matter of fact, I am not so much worried by the flies alighting on me as on my food etc. However, if it helps keep the flies off that would otherwise settle on me, it will be quite worthwhile using the stuff.

This is a pretty rotten hell we are in just now, in fact, barring the two days at Richebourg, yesterday was the worst day we have had as regards casualties since we came out. The Germans spent the morning, forenoon and afternoon blowing great holes in our parapets and then in the evening when we were burying those killed, they burst another shell over us and killed and wounded some more.[9] I am glad to say our guns got some of their own back today. I'm also glad to say we expect to get out of this place in another three or four days.

There is rather an amusing story going about just now about another part of the line where things have been very quiet for months past and where the lines are very close together. The story is that an engineer walked across to the Germans one night and borrowed a mallet to drive in some stakes with. The story is very like that of another part of the line where our engineers are reported to have put up part of a barbed wire entanglement only to find in the morning that the Germans had finished it off as it was as much use to them as to us.

---

9   The Battalion diarist observed on 9 July 1915: "8.15pm: Windy Corner shelled. One shell burst close to funeral party gathered at cemetery. Several serious casualties." See TNA WO 95/2431: 1/9th HLI War Diary.

WD: We were relieved on the 11th of July and moved back to Béthune where I got a very good billet with an old lady and her daughter not far from the church. They used to insist on my going in every night to have a chat with them or rather on my sitting with them while they chattered at me.

15/7/15

My dear Dad,

Just a line to let you know I am still flourishing. We are resting just now and I have got a most splendid billet as usual. My landlady roused me about 7.00 AM the morning I arrived and wanted me to have some tea. However, as I had no intention of getting up, I refused. When I did get up, my servant brought me some more tea and when I said I didn't want it, he informed me Madame was fearfully hurt at my not taking the first brew and he said if I would let him leave it in my room he would see it was disposed of. I tried a little of it, and judging by the taste it was the first brew recycled, however when I got downstairs, I told Madame how much I enjoyed it etc., or rather I tried to, and she was quite bucked. The only fault I have to find is that she and her daughter both talk about 15 to the dozen and at the same time, so I understand about one word in 30 instead of one in 12. However, a smile goes a long way even when it does get a bit fixed.

   I got some more parcels from McG D & Co today which I must acknowledge.

   I am rather busy just now as the other Machine Gun Officer is home on leave and we are training a lot of new men.

   I have no more news except that I am going to have tea with the Colonel this afternoon so must shut up.

   Please excuse rather scrappy letter.

16/7/15

To: Miss Coats, The Manse, Abington, Scotland [Edinburgh Rd, Abington]

My dear J.E., J.W. and D.H. [Jean, Jenny and Doug],

This is just a line to thank you for various letters etc. etc. which I have had from you. I hope you are having a decent time and hope to be with you within the month.

   I hear Doug is getting a bit uppish about his moustache etc. so I am prepared to bet him a birthday cake to a ham sandwich that my moustache will be superior, by the time I get home, to his moustache and imperial or whatever he calls the bit of his face he is too slack to shave. As a warning, I may say that mine already compares favourably with my toothbrush, which is only 3½ months old. In fact, if I liked, I could enclose a lock or cutting or whatever one calls surplus moustache-age but that might make him refuse the bet.

As you will perhaps guess from the above drivel, I am still resting. I think I said in my last letter that Madame and her daughter both talked about 15 or 30 to the dozen. Well, last night when I got in from Mess, they both tackled me and it took me ¾ hour before I could break away. They think me no end of a Knut at French but it is really my method that saves the situation.[10] The idea is to ask questions that you don't require to know the answer to and then sit and look interested till they run down, when I shove in another question and they start off again. As a rule, there is an element of risk in this, in that I may nod and say "Oui" where one should really shake one's head and say "nong". But I have got a soft job on here because the old ladies generally end up each paragraph by saying "N'est ce pas?", so I simply sit tight till they say "N'est ce pas?" when I nod and smile and say either "Oui", "Mais oui" or "Ah Oui" according as I can judge from their expression they want one or the other. When I gave absolutely stuck, I simply say "Oh" or "Ehm" which generally acts as a full stop to the question under discussion and leaves the boards clear for the next round. As an idea of the various things we talk about, last night I discussed their son for about 20 minutes (the most successful question), Did the Germans reach here? – 10 minutes – and the latest fashion in ladies' hats – 5 minutes. Total for 3 brainwaves, or "vagues du cerveau" – 35 minutes. I must stop now or you will think I am still suffering from "Hydrocephale" through a hole in the roof.

Your loving brother,

Walter J.J. Coats

17 July, 1915

My dear Dad,

Many thanks for your and Mother's letters which I got along with one from Jenny this morning. I was surprised to see you got the impression from my letter that there had been some hard fighting. As a matter of fact, there was no fighting at all unless you consider sitting down and letting people chuck things at you fighting. All that happened was that we sat in the trenches and the Germans had more luck with their shells than usual. We never fired a shot. Our artillery certainly let the Germans have it back afterwards but it didn't do us much good.

I am told it is a beastly thing seeing a shell coming straight for one. One of our officers said he saw one coming straight for him and thought he was in for it, however it landed several yards beyond him and he wasn't touched. The thing is, it is only the larger brand of shells that one can see coming and it is, I think, only when standing immediately behind or in front of the gun that one can do so. One can also see mortar bombs coming but they come comparatively slowly and can be dodged.

---

10 Knut: Edwardian slang – "An idle upper-class man-about-town". 'A Glossary of Slang', *Edwardian Promenade* <http://www.edwardianpromenade.com/resources/a-glossary-of-slang/#K (Accessed 2 September 2015).

We are giving a concert tonight. I hope it is as great a success as the last one. There is absolutely no news beyond the fact that we are still resting so Cheer Oh pro tem.

19/7/15

My dear Esda,

Very many thanks for your and Jack's birthday present which arrived partly yesterday and partly a day or two before. I don't think I ever saw chocolates disappear quite so quickly before. There are about seven of us in our Mess here and we all enjoyed them to the last chip. I am glad you forgot about my birthday before.

We are all rather sick here at the new officers that have been sent out. The authorities sent out one Captain and five 1st Lieutenants with the result that I have been done out of promotion by an officer who has only had about seven or eight months' training, and the 2nd Lieutenants are now nine places further from promotion and they were at the beginning of the war. The rotten thing is that four or five of those who are now 1st Lieutenants were privates at Dunfermline. We had a row about it last time and were told there was nothing to be done, so I don't suppose it is any good kicking up another row now, as it simply leads to ill-feeling. It is a dirty shame all the same, and was quite unnecessary as we are now, I think, five officers over strength.

We are still resting but I rather think we go back to the trenches on Wednesday. Rumour has it we are going to _____ which is about the best place we have ever been in, so I hope it is true. If it is, I expect I shall be billeted again with the Paris cook [Annequin].

It may interest Doug to know I saw Ian Hay in a tea shop the other day.[11] I believe he is the author of "The First Hundred Thousand".

I don't think there is anything else in the way of news except that I am still flourishing so I shall stop and get on with censoring.

WD: We returned to the trenches, this time at Cuinchy Keep, on the 22nd July, but had not been many days here before we moved into the line on the north bank of the canal where we stayed until the 7th of August. During this time the Machine Gunners were occupied making two deep dug-outs in the front line and another in the Spoil Bank some hundred yards behind. As we were unable to get the assistance of any tunnellers for this we had to do it by digging three enormous holes in the ground. We then built a framework inside with beams and pit-props over which we laid corrugated iron and then filled the hole in again on top with earth and bricks which we carried up from the houses behind.

---

11 Ian Hay (pseud. for John Hay Beith 1876-1952), pupil and subsequent master at Fettes College, soldier, and prolific author of 35 books including the acclaimed autobiographical active service narrative _The First Hundred Thousand "(K1)"_ (1915). As an officer in the Argyll & Sutherland Highlanders he was awarded the Military Cross (Loos 1915). Director of Public Relations during the Second World War (1938-45).

22/7/15

My dear Dad,
We are back in the trenches again at the place with the maze of trenches and as far as I can see we are going to have a good time.

While I remember, if I warn you when I expect to be home, could you fix up a meeting with some dentist, I don't care who? In the way of known repairs, I have lost a crown and some stopping and I expect there will be other work as well.

You will be interested to hear that we pretty well swept the board at some Brigade swimming sports that were held during our last rest. We won four events out of six and in the other two we got a second and a third. We won the 60 yards race, team race, fancy diving and polo and got second in the high diving and third in plunging.

I am feeling rather tired today as I was walking yesterday from about 9.30 AM till about 6.00 PM with about four rests lasting together about an hour and ½ and no food from breakfast yesterday till breakfast today, except half a stick of chocolate, a few redcurrants and about a dozen gooseberries and I have been walking through trenches again today for several hours. I expect to have a pretty soft job of it now however until we move again.

27/7/15

My dear Dad,
Please excuse my not writing for some time past. There has been absolutely nothing doing and therefore nothing to write about. We are at present in the trenches but things are very quiet. Thank goodness we are not in the Dardanelles.[12]

Talking about promotions, for goodness sake don't go and try to kick up a row about it at home as it will simply rebound on us here and get some poor chap who is not to blame into trouble. As regards Colonel Mackenzie's statement that it won't happen again, I simply don't believe it because we were told that the last time. However, what can one expect from a Liberal Government?

The flies here are as bad as ever and I am afraid the various remedies are not much use. Thank goodness I don't get bitten like other people.

Thanks for the Glengarry which arrived a few days ago and fits all right. I can think of absolutely nothing more to write about so Au Revoir soon I hope.

---

12 No doubt Walter was well aware that 52nd (Lowland) Division, to which 1/9th HLI had been attached until November 1914, was experiencing a gruelling time on the Gallipoli Peninsula. See Lieutenant-Colonel R.R. Thompson, *The Fifty-Second Lowland Division 1914–1918* (Glasgow: Maclehose, Jackson & Co., 1923).

28/7/15

My dear Mother,
I meant to write this to Ellie but it has just struck me that she may be with you, so I am writing you instead. We are moving tomorrow to another part of the line where we will be in the trenches, as far as I can see, for eight days. I am very sorry as the place we are at just now is about the nicest place we have been at.

I was told yesterday that I might expect to get leave about the 10th of next month, if not a little before then. I think I told you I wanted to see a dentist first thing. I shall let you know by telegram from London, if not sooner, when you may expect me. It is funny to think it is about four months since I was home last.

1 August, 1915

My dear Mother,
It is some time since I wrote last but there is not much news even yet. We moved into this place three days ago and to our surprise found it was quite a quiet place after all. As a matter of fact, we were very lucky moving here as the place we left was shelled for about an hour and a half with heavies shortly after we cleared out. I have got a very comfortable dugout here with a stretcher in it which makes a beautiful bed and altogether I am having quite a good time with enough work to keep things interesting.

I am afraid I am in need of a holiday as I have taken to contradicting everyone as the only means of keeping things lively. I know I talk a fearful lot of rot and the arguments generally end in everyone else trying to squash me, but I am in a sort of unsquashable mood just now and generally manage to hold my own. My family training together with a prolonged fit of periodic madness have stood me in good stead.

I am going to have a shot at any German aeroplanes that come across this way this afternoon. I hope one tries to come this way, as we have never done any shooting of this kind before and it should be rather interesting.

Cheer Oh.

4/8/15

Capt J.G. Coats, 27 Woodside Pl.

Dear Jack,
Wingate is at present buzzing round the trench like a wasp with a sore tail, so as you can imagine all the other officers are more or less sweet tempered, except yours truly who has now nothing to do with him and can keep smiling.

I think I mentioned in my letter to Dad yesterday that I had great hopes of getting a German work party last night with the gun. I noted the place where they had been heard the night before and when they were heard last night I loosed off a whole belt into the middle of them. Judging from the noises, the aim was pretty good and we bagged some. At any rate we gave them a nasty jar.

I was in great hopes of having a shot at an aeroplane several days ago, but unfortunately none turned up.

The weather is pretty beastly here just now, very hot with thundershowers every now and then, so that the men are kept busy clearing the mud out of the trench when not doing anything else. Things are fairly quiet however, so we could be worse off.

Cheer Oh till we meet in a few days I hope.

7/8/15

My dear Dad,

I expect to be relieved from this place in about an hour. We have been in it now for nine days, so I shall not be sorry to leave it especially as the weather is pretty beastly.

We had great fun with the guns again yesterday afternoon. We started off with two guns and sprinkled about 1500 rounds into a village behind the German Lines on the off-chance of doing some damage. We were eventually spotted by the Germans who started chucking across whizz bangs, so we thought discretion the better part of valour and cleared out.[13] Both guns were steaming like a locomotive by the time we had finished.

I expect I shall get home sometime on Wednesday but don't know yet for certain. I shall send a telegram from Folkestone if I can manage it.

I expect Math will arrive to stay the night with you by the time you get this, if not before.

The relief will be here in a few minutes now so I will dry up.

POST CARD 8/8/15 Sunday

To: John J. Coats: Expect to arrive in Glasgow by train leaving London early on Wednesday morning. W.J.J.C.

11/8/15 Wednesday

TELEGRAM: To: Coats c/o AJANDA GLW: LEAVING LONDON EUSTON THIS MORNING. WALTER

---

13 Whizz Bang: A high-velocity, flat-trajectory German field gun.

19th August, 1915

John J. Coats, The Manse, Abington

My dear Dad,
I arrived here safely this forenoon and go into the trenches tomorrow. Rumour is that we are going back for a long rest after four days. I hope it is true.

21/8/15

Mrs Coats, The Manse, Abington

My dear Mother,
Here we are once more back in the trenches. Unfortunately, we have struck a pretty rotten part of the line and as we are now told this is going to be a 16 day job, we have a pretty cheery prospect ahead. To add to the general cheeriness, it is at present raining. In fact all things considered, Abington is preferable to this as a place to stay in.

WD: Upon returning from leave on 19th August, I found the Battalion was now in the line in front of Givenchy and took up my quarters in Moat farm. This was an old square farm house with little but the walls left standing and which was being turned into a strong point. It was several hundred yards behind the front line and as the weather was very fine I used to take out my chair in the evening after tea and sit in the sun.[14]

23/8/15

My dear Dad,
Before I forget, my address is now simply "Glasgow Highlanders, BEF France". I came out of the trenches this afternoon but go back again tomorrow morning for either three or four days. Then I expect to get out again for two days, back in for two and then clear out for a week or so.
　　We had rather a cheery time of it when we were up just now, as the Germans where fearfully keen on chucking over great big mortar bombs.[15] It is a funny thing though, how little damage they do. After our first night in, they did us no damage at all except to blow in the trench in several places and give us extra work building it up again. Their bark is worse than their bite, for which I am devoutly thankful as the concussion of their bark is enough to blow you into your dug-out about 50 yards away.

---

14 A photograph of Moat Farm c. 1918 can be found in the IWM Collection Q 7848.
15 Minenwerfer: Trench mortar.

WD: Although the Battalion was relieved and went into billets at Le Preol on the canal bank, I was left behind with some Machine Gunners until the Battalion was moved back to Béthune on the 27th, when I rejoined them.

25 August, 1915

My dear Mother,

There is not much news except that I am sitting in a very comfortable cellar and the Germans are chucking over whizz bangs. Things are very quiet here just now and the weather beautiful, so I am quite enjoying myself.

I enclose a photo of myself which may interest you [see image opposite]. I can't tell you where it was taken just now but I will be able to tell you when I get home.

The news in the papers just now is very cheery. We threw the news about the sinking of the German ships across to their lines the night before last. I hope they could read it. We also had a gramophone set up to play them a few tunes but it didn't seem to rouse them much.

Someone set off a mine this morning, but I don't know whether it was ourselves or the Germans.

The rest of the Battalion is back for a few days just now but, as we are at present Brigaded, we are kept up here, with the result that I am alone just now with a few men. I must say I quite like it for a bit.

I have really nothing to talk about so must stop.

Your loving son,

Walter J.J. Coats

27/8/15

My dear Ellie,

Many thanks for your and Dad's letters, also the photos and cigars. I got them about 10 minutes ago and am in the middle of a cigar already.

I got some great good news today. We are being relieved tomorrow instead of in four days as I expected. I must say, I am very glad as except for 5 minutes when changing from my kilt into breeks, I have not had my boots or clothes off since I left home. I hope we get a decent rest.

The men are as cheery as crickets tonight with the thought of being relieved tomorrow. They are at present singing and making the most fearful noise. What they like is to get a sentimental song and sing it like a dead march. The more sentimental, the deader the march.

I have been fearfully tickled with them since I came here. There is only an open door between their cellar and mine, and I hear all that goes on. Three nights ago, I heard

Walter with an unidentified Glasgow Highlander officer, Herts Redoubt, between Windy Corner and Givenchy, 1915. (WJJC collection)

one team composing a French song and nearly died of laughter. The song seemed to consist chiefly of a list of different French foods strung together and put to music, with a "S'il vous plait" and "Mademoiselle" stuck in every here and there. They set it to rather a slow tune and it really sounded quite well. It was fearfully funny as they were quite serious about it. Last night, they had a violent political argument which was on the whole conducted in a very regular manner but occasionally developed into them all speaking out at once and at times became rather personal. I lay in bed and was highly entertained till I fell asleep about 11.30 and left them still arguing. I heard them at it again this morning. This afternoon, I heard them arguing about the origin of Genesis and Exodus. They are the most versatile lot. They are singing some ragtime now.

It is rather funny, I have just discovered my servant is an apprentice plater. Shaw was a plater too. The one I have just now is a most excellent kid and a good cook. He produced an old apricot tin this evening filled with some ripping tea roses he found in an old garden. The only unfortunate thing is that there is no window to my cellar so I have to light a candle to see them properly. However, they smell wonderful when there is no cooking going on next door. As the poet says "Many a flower is born to blush unseen and waste its sweetness on the desert air". The only difference is that these ones are wasting their sweetness fighting against the smell of ham and eggs etc. However, "C'est la guerre", as they say here.

I am afraid I am starting to drivel so I shall shut up for this evening. As our friends over the way say,
   "Auf Wiedersehen".
   Your loving brother,
   Walter J.J. Coats

PS Would they say that?

[Cont.] 29/8/15
I wrote this the day before yesterday but was so busy moving that I could not get it sent off. We had a fearfully hot march but fortunately stopped at the support billets half way back where we had lunch and then came on here. I am not with the two old talkative Mesdames this time but have got an excellent billet quite near without the necessity of a sort of dual monologue every evening.

29/8/15

My dear Doug,
Please excuse a rather belated many happy returns etc. etc. I rather think that I said I would give you 1/- for your birthday last year [letter 27 August 1914]. If you remind me when I get home, I will give you the interest on that shilling at the War Loan rate of 4½% and another 6d. I would make it 1/- again, but as you know the Government advises economy and you will now be able, I hope, to make 6d go as far as 1/- used to go, added to which I save 6d and the net gain is thus 1/-, viz 6d to you and 6d to me i.e. one birthday present, so you are getting something for nothing.[16]
   I am afraid I am drivelling somewhat, so I had better stop.

PS All my news is in a letter I started to write Ellie two days ago and finished today. In case he doesn't read letters between the lines, you can tell Dad I am super-flourishing.

---

16 By spring 1915 the British government was planning a second war loan. Unlike the first loan, it was to be marketed with small investors in mind. Prior to this, the minimum investment had been £100, but now participants could contribute as little as £5. This lower limit gave the government access to a much larger pool of potential investors. Moreover, drawing investments from the wider economy had the benefit of countering domestic inflation, thereby steadying international exchange. Programme details were announced to the public in June 1915.

30/8/15

My dear Dad,

I forgot to call in at Craddock's for a watch I was getting mended before I left home. Do you think, if it has not been sent to the house, someone could call in and hurry them up? The watch is not mine and I would not like it to get lost or anything like that.

There seems to be a proposal on foot that all subalterns of over four years' service should get promoted and I understand several of our names have been put forward but I don't know if it will come to anything.

We are all flourishing here and still resting though rumour has it we go in again in a few days.

WD: On the 3rd of September we returned to the line again on the north bank of the Canal.

3/9/15

My dear Dad,

We are back in the trenches again and have had a cheery day of it. I was wakened at 6.30 AM this morning and left for the trenches in pouring rain at 8.30. We arrived there about 11 AM and went slopping around in the mud and wet till about 1.00 when we got some lunch. It then poured steadily till about 9.00 PM, when the rain stopped and it is now 11.45 PM, a beautiful clear night. The only unfortunate thing is that the trenches are now in places ankle deep in water and one goes skidding about all over the place like a pat of butter on a hotplate. Added to this, I have been wet through my Burberry jacket and shirt and if I was at home I would change my socks. It quite reminds me of the dear old winter, only we have now got better dugouts. I have managed to get a stretcher again, so I am quite happy. I always feel it is one up for the Germans if I get depressed so I always look on the bright side just to score them off.

We had a most splendid concert last night in the theatre. One of the star turns was a son of Funny Frame. He was fearfully funny himself.[17] Another good turn was when we produced a beauty chorus for one of the songs. It consisted of Major Menzies, Carmichael Frame, Beattie and three subalterns.[18] The three subs made the most beautiful girls and I know a lot of people went away quite convinced that they <u>were</u> girls.

---

17 Either Pte 5467/331838 James Crawford Frame or his brother Pte 5468/332364 Adam Dickson Frame, both killed 27 May 1917 at Arras, and never identified. See Weir, *Come on Highlanders!*, p. 368.
18 Lieutenants William Fairlie Alexander, Terry Todd and Ted McCosh (Weir, *Come on Highlanders!*).

The man beside me could hardly believe they were not, and two Tommies went round to the stage door afterwards to meet them. The other three were the most awful looking old specimens. The performance was encored about three times. I don't think I ever laughed at a music hall anything like as much as I laughed at the whole show last night.

I must hop off for a moment to go and have a look at the sentries.

[Later] Here we are again. We have just spotted a German work party but I don't know whether we will strafe them or not as there are certain reasons why we shouldn't.

POST CARD 7/9/15

To: John J Coats
Having a very quiet time and still going strong. Hope to write soon. W.J.J.C.

9/9/15

My dear Dad,
Please excuse my not having written for some time. I have been fearfully busy for the last six days. In fact last night was the first since I came here that I have had more than 4 hours sleep. The result is I have had to get what sleep I could during the day and have not had much time to write. I meant to write before going to bed last night but I was rather in the dumps so I thought it better to wait till this morning.

Would you mind having the watch posted out to Captain Wingate? It is his, and if you sent it to me it might arrive at a time when I could not hand it over.

The weather here just now is fearfully hot and the trenches all nice and dry again so "everybody's happy here" as the song says (except those who have got to work).

I have absolutely nothing more to write about so may as well stop with love to all from,
   Your re-cheerfulated son
   Walter J.J. Coats
   Should it be cheerfulated or cheerfulised?

11/9/15

My dear Mother,
I enclose two photos which may be of interest to you. The funny one is of me and a man McLelland in smoke helmets.[19]

---

19 The Hypo (glycerin and sodium thiosulphate) anti-gas helmet with an oblong mica window was introduced in June 1915.

Walter and Lieutenant Robert
McLelland in issue Hypo
helmets. (WJJC collection)

We have had quite an interesting day of it here today. Early in the morning, we spotted a German work party in the mist and got it with one of the guns. In the afternoon, we first got news of the latest Russian success by phone from the 1st Army Corps and later on saw a German aeroplane brought down by one of our anti-aircraft guns. Early in the evening, the Germans sent up a mine on our left and we thought for a bit it might have got some of our men, but it didn't. It is now 2.00 AM and I am waiting to see what happens next. Meantime, everything is very quiet except for occasional shells and bombs which are being chucked at the people next to us. It is a beautiful clear starry night though somewhat chilly.

WD: On 13th September, we again returned to Béthune. This time I was billeted in the house of a French Notary who was serving as a private in the French Army on about 2d per day. While we were here he turned up one day in his private motor and, when he found I was going to be a lawyer, insisted on my telling him all about marriage according to the Law of Scotland. As I knew very little about it and less about French I don't think he was much wiser after it but we parted the best of friends. The chief attraction in his house was a pianola which was kept going most of the day.

16/9/15

My dear Mother,

We are at present resting but go back to the trenches again tomorrow. We have only had four days' rest this time, which is unfortunate as we have very good billets. The man who owns the house we Mess in is a corporal in the French army on between 2d and 2¼d per day. He has a lovely house and runs three motor cars. He is a lawyer by profession.

I don't know how long we are going to be in the trenches this time but I don't expect I shall be able to write you a decent letter for some days to come. I shall try to send as many PCs as I can manage. Don't however get worried if there are not very many.

We expect to relieve Murray Grierson's lot in the trenches this time, as they are now in our Division.[20]

When the General welcomed to them into the Division, he said he hoped they would emulate our example, which is one up for us.

I have really no more news except that I am what I believe the Muse of Melody would call going FF or, in other words, full blast.

Your loving son,
Walter J.J. Coats

PS There are a lot of interesting things I would like to tell you but non possum as I used to say in the days of my youth. I am going to have tea and a walk with Math. He is also FF.

WD: We returned to the same part of the line at Givenchy on the 17th and found that in our absence a lot of holes about 4 feet deep and one foot wide had been dug under the firesteps. We did not know what these were for at the time and no one would tell us but we learnt in a few days when fatigue parties arrived every night carrying very heavy iron cylinders which we found contained gas. These were put into the holes and covered up with sandbags except for the knob at the top which screwed off and disclosed a nozzle to which long metal pipes were attached so that the gas could be squirted over the parapet. We had all been expecting some sort of a show for some time past as Béthune was full of the 9th and 15th Divisions, and other troops of the New Army, but we had not suspected gas.

---

20 Captain J. Murray Grierson, 5th Scottish Rifles (and a Glasgow Academical).

POST CARD 18/9/15

To: Mrs Coats
We are back in the trenches again but things are very quiet and there is absolutely no news. I started a letter but had to stop as there was nothing to say.

WJJC

21/9/15

My dear Mother,
Wingate got his watch all right and also Dad's letter. He asked me to thank you and to say he will write as soon as he can find time. There are a couple of mice running about on the table I am writing on just now. They are very tame and have just been up smelling the book the man beside me is reading, which is only about a foot away from this pad.

There has been a bit of a bombardment on here today so we're all feeling more tired than usual but, except for whizz bangs and a very occasional heavy, things have quietened down for the night. I think some of the men have got pretty bad headaches though the shelling has not been very hard.

I had to break off for a bit and it is now about 11.00 PM. The Germans must be having an absolutely poisonous time of it as we have been worrying them all night.

From Capt George Wingate to John Jackson Coats:

France, 22 September, 1915

Dear Mr. Coats,
I got your kind letter of the 15th for which I am much obliged. The watch arrived the same day as your letter and I have to thank you for taking so much trouble in the matter. Would you kindly be good enough to ask Craddock to send the account to my wife: Mrs. Geo. Wingate, Mossyde, Kilmacolm.

Walter is with me just now in the front line with his machine guns and busy at night disturbing German work parties in front of their lines.

It has always been a matter of great regret to me losing him from my Company but I am glad to say that he is doing good work elsewhere. He is very fit and happy.

With kind regards
Believe me
Yours sincerely,
Geo Wingate, Capt.

24/9/15   [Battle of Loos start][21]

My dear Dad,

There is really no news today except that the bombardment is still going on. It is funny how we have all got accustomed to it. We eat and read and sleep and smoke and talk, and hardly notice that there is anything doing. The way it seems to affect us is that we all get very sleepy. I have been up all night for five nights now and am feeling perfectly fresh with a few hours' sleep during the day. I generally sleep from about 5.30am till breakfast at nine every morning and then I get another hour or two during the day. I expect I have told you all this before but at present there is really very little else worth talking about. The Germans over the way are having about as cheery a time as they can want but, as I said, we have got accustomed to that now. Thank goodness I am not a German. I think they have bitten off more than they can chew in Russia and their mouth is now full. It is funny, it reminds me of the times when Jean used to try how many grapes she could put into her mouth at once. I hope the results are the same. It is rather an unpleasant simile, but I have finished lunch and with any luck you will not be at a meal when you get this.

Excuse the drivel but I have really very little to talk about.

We had a pretty bad thunderstorm here last night and I got soaked through my Burberry jacket and shirt in about 10 minutes but it is dry again today so things are looking up a bit. By the way, I would suggest that if the Ladies' Committee of the Glasgow Highlanders have any spare cash for winter comforts for the men, they might buy Sou'westers. I have one myself and it keeps the rain from running down one's neck. You have no idea how much it adds to one's comfort on a wet night.

WD: After several days of very heavy bombardment the Battle of Loos began on the 25th, the instructions for letting off gas and smoke being as follows:

Time Table of Gas
Attacks North of La Bassée Canal
(Minutes)
0.0   Start the gas and run six cylinders one after the other at full blast until all are exhausted.
0.12-0.20   Start the smoke. The smoke is to run concurrently with the gas, if the gas is not exhausted by 0.12.

---

21 Launched in the operationally unpropitious Artois "Black Country", the Battle of Loos (25 September-19 October 1915) was Great Britain's contribution to a large-scale Anglo-French autumn offensive. Simultaneous French assaults occurred in Artois and Champagne. 2nd Division was attached to I Corps (GOC Lieutenant-General Sir Hubert Gough) throughout these operations. See Nick Lloyd, *Loos 1915* (Stroud: History Press, 2008), Wyrall, *The History of the Second Division 1914-1918*, pp. 218-41 and Weir, *Come on Highlanders!*, pp. 102-17.

0.20   Start the gas again and run six cylinders one after the other at full blast until all are exhausted.

0.30-0.40   Start the smoke again. The smoke is to run concurrently with the gas, if the gas is not exhausted by 0.32.

0.38   Turn all gas off punctually.
Thicken up smoke with triple candles.
Prepare for assault.

0.40   Assault.
On the 3 cylinder and no cylinder fronts, the smoke will be started at 0.60.

Note:- From 0 to 0.40 front system of hostile trenches will be kept under continuous shrapnel fire.

Defences further in rear under bombardment of H.E. shell of all calibre.

At 0.40 artillery fire will lift as required.

Unfortunately, the weather broke down at this time and the wind which was presumably in the right direction where the main attack was to take place, at our part of the line blew the gas from the South into our trenches and our own gas along the front without going near the Germans.[22] As we were relying on our part of the front almost entirely on the gas to cover the attack this might have been serious. Fortunately for us, our orders were to send out a patrol to see the result of the gas before we moved and not to attack unless the attacks of the troops on our immediate flanks, and who were nearer the Germans, were successful. We sent out a patrol as ordered, every man of which but one was promptly shot. The 6th Brigade on our right failed to get into the German line at all, and the other Battalions of our own Brigade on the left, after getting into the German lines successfully were soon bombed out again, so we were saved a very bad cutting up. The troops on our left were unable to hold the German trenches owing to the type of bomb they were supplied with. It consisted of a very heavy iron ball about the size of a cricket ball with about an inch of fuse projecting from it. The end of this fuse had a head like a safety match attached to it, and each man had a striker attached to his arm on which he struck the match head. Unfortunately, the weather was wet and the majority of fuses refused to light and moreover the bombs themselves were so heavy that the Germans who had a lighter and better type were able to outrange our men and clear them out without being touched. The new Mills Bombs which were better than the German ones arrived next day when of course they were too late.

---

22 The Loos offensive opened with the first British use of poison gas. See Sir J.E. Edmonds, *Military Operations France and Belgium 1915 Vol. II* (London: Macmillan, 1928), passim and Robert Graves, *Goodbye to All That* (1929) for a harrowing first-hand account of the asphyxiating gas cloud blowback as experienced by the neighbouring 19th Brigade.

25/9/15 [posted later]

My dear Mother,
What promises to be the biggest battle in history began exactly 24 minutes ago to be precise at 5.50 AM this morning. I knew there was going to be a show several weeks ago and would have liked to tell you but of course could not. Our Battalion is going to make for the Germans in about a quarter of an hour but I am in charge of two guns which are Brigaded, so I stay with the Battalion headquarters for the time being. I may of course be called on to go over at any minute but meantime I am sitting in a very comfortable dugout smoking a very fine cheroot.

The Germans opposite don't appear to have more than three or four guns which is all right for us.

So far we have had one officer wounded.

Our men have just started across and I am rather anxious to know how they're getting on. We cannot see them from where we are. It is beastly to have to sit and listen to the rifle fire and know that one's friends are up against it. I would rather go and take my chance with them but being the junior Machine Gun Officer I had no say in the matter. The rifle fire is now I think not quite so heavy so either we are across or are driven back. Which?

I must stop.

Later: I stopped this as I heard something which rather upset me and I thought I might be wanted any minute however I was not, so I can carry on. I have just sent off a Field Service PC to let you know I am still […] [sentence not finished]

WD: We stayed in this part of the line till the night of the 28/29th when we were relieved and moved back to Beuvry which is half way between the trenches and Béthune. Todd was sent to Brigade H.Q. at this time to take over as Brigade Machine Gun Officer and I was left in command of the section with a man called Wharrie as my second in command.[23]

28/9/15

My dear Mother,
I enclose a letter which I began some time ago but never got finished. We did not get across as it depended on the people next to us in the line as to whether we could or not and, as they did not manage, the result is we are still where we are. The rest of the Battalion went out for a rest but I have been left behind and have had a pretty cheery time of it. In the first place, I don't like living with a strange Battalion, and in

---

23 Lieutenant Robert Burns Wharrie, later Acting Major and awarded MC in 1917. See Supplement to *The London Gazette*, 1 January 1918.

the second place I have been soaked to the skin and my feet have been wet for about a week. The weather has been beastly and the trenches dreadful.

Please wish Jenny a belated many happy returns. When I get out, I shall send her the tip of a German shell which I picked up in the trench during the show today.[24] I have two other very good souvenirs which are too big to send home by post.

The Germans chucked some lachrymatory shells at us the other day.

Would you mind sending me another couple of pairs of socks? This weather makes an awful mess of them and we can't get them washed in the meantime so have to throw them away. The pair I took off yesterday had shrunk on to my feet so much with the wet that I could hardly get them off. My boots are simply saturated.

28/9/15

My dear Mother,

I am sorry I have not yet been able to get the enclosed letters off but I hope to do so tomorrow. I was relieved from the trenches tonight and had a pretty cheery job of it. It was pouring wet and the trenches were absolutely awful. I came on ahead and got here about an hour ago to arrange for the men to get something hot when they arrived and also to try and get them a drive back. I am glad to say I managed both but the men are not back yet and it is 11.30 PM. We go back to other trenches tomorrow. I must say, however, I quite enjoy this life and never felt fitter. I don't think being soaked does one the slightest harm if one has plenty to do to take one's thoughts away.

It is extraordinary how decent people are when one gets in late. Math no sooner heard what I wanted than he was away looking for the transport. The C.O. made me sit down and have something to eat, another man gave me a cigar and a third has gone away to bring the men back which I meant to do myself. It is almost worthwhile being late.

I am in charge of all the guns now, which means extra work etc. but it won't do me any harm.

What you think of the news? Isn't it splendid?[25]

WD: On the 29th after only a few hours in Beuvry, we moved into the line in front of Cambrin and relieved some of the Scottish Rifles of the 15th Division. Everything was in a great stage of confusion and it took us the greater part of the night trying to get up the communication trench (Lewis Alley) to the front line. Relieving troops were trying to go up one way and wounded and stragglers trying to get down, the trench was very muddy and slippery and if one was not being half strangled by a telephone wire catching

---

24 Visible in image on page xiii. Also mentioned in letter of 6 October 1915.
25 Possible reference to the neighbouring IV Corps' capture of Loos village and subsequent advance to Hill 70.

one round the neck one was tripped up by another wire catching one round the ankles. Blocks in the traffic lasting from a few minutes to half an hour at a time were frequent occurrences; guides lost their way and we had a merry time generally. How the men who were carrying the guns, each of which in addition to their equipment weighed over 60lbs, managed to carry them through this for hours on end was simply marvellous.

We stayed here for two or three days during which time we assisted an attack on the Hohenzollern Redoubt [S.E. of Cuinchy] on our right by covering fire and smoke. The state of chaos in which things were was brought home to us rather amusingly the night after the attack on the redoubt. One of our sergeants was sitting peacefully in his dug-out when the screen was suddenly thrown back and a British officer pointed his revolver at him and ordered him out. The sergeant was rather surprised but, thinking it advisable to obey, crawled out and was promptly made to put his hands up. He then discovered that the British officer was under the impression that he was in the German trenches and that he had just taken a prisoner. When he saw what the situation was the sergeant, being a wise man, led him along to H.Q. where the situation was cleared up.

After two or three days here we were moved back to Le Preol where we arrived about 6 o'clock in the morning. We hoped to get a few days rest here but that afternoon the Brigade again moved off and after about an hour's march halted in a field behind Vermelles. We were in full view of the German observation balloons here, and spent a very uneasy afternoon waiting to be shelled. We moved off again at dusk and had not been gone more than ten minutes when the shells started arriving and our transport had quite a lively time till they managed to get clear.

We marched from here into Vermelles which was simply crowded with troops and transport and, thanks to someone's transport pushing into the middle of the Battalion, I got hung up at a crossroads and lost touch with the rest of the Battalion. As I had only the very vaguest idea of their destination and no idea at all of my way through Vermelles, I had quite a merry time trying to find them again. Thanks however more to good luck than good guidance I made up on them about half an hour later on the Hulluch Road where I found them held up by the traffic. We spent about an hour here waiting to get on and a most uncomfortable hour it was. There was no cover of any sort except for the ditches at the side of the road which were already fully occupied and the bullets were whistling all round, through and over us so that we never knew when we would get in the way of one. Fortunately they did not shell us or we would have caught it very badly.

When once we started again it did not take us long to get into the trenches where we found we were in support in the old British front line. We had a very peaceful time of it here for three days although the 4th October was more strenuous.

4/10/15

My dear Doug,
Just a short note to wish you my heartiest congratulations on passing your exams. It is simply splendid and you must have worked very hard to do it.

I am afraid I can't write much just now as the candle is on its last legs and as I have just written Ellie and Jack I have no news that you won't see. I had to write however and congratulate you.

WD: October 4th was rather anxious. We knew we were to be relieved that night so did not worry at first when the Germans started landing some very heavy shells about 200 yards in front of us. As the day passed however the shells gradually drew nearer and nearer until for the last hour or two it was a toss-up whether the relief or the shells would reach us first. Fortunately for us the relief (Welsh Guards) arrived when the shells were still about 20 or 30 yards short and we did not lose much time in handing over.

As we had a good long way to go, I had ordered the Machine Gun limbers close up to the back of the trench and some of them had a very unpleasant time before they got clear though beyond being chipped by splinters no damage was done. There was now apparently an attack of some sort going on up in front and it was a wonderful sight to look back and see the whole place lit up with bursting bombs and shells with the men silhouetted against the flames.

I was very much struck here with the capacity of our men for "winning" things that they thought would be useful. On our way out we lay down beside a team of Guards Machine Gunners while I explained to the officer in charge exactly where he was and how he was to get on. We had not left them more than 10 minutes when one of my men came up and said he had found a spare Machine Gun barrel. I had a pretty good idea that he could only have found it beside one of the Guards but as there was no chance of finding out and they were always useful I told him to hang onto it and say nothing about it.

We got back to Béthune on the morning of the 5th after marching all night.

6/10/15

My dear Jean,
The best bit of news I have is that we are still resting though for how long goodness knows. The weather is not just what it might be so we are in luck.

I am going to send home my watch tomorrow. I should like it mended and sent out again. I bumped it against the side of a trench which seems to have somewhat upset its guts. I am sending a German button with it which you might add to your collection. I am also enclosing the tip of a shell for Jenny which is a souvenir of a most uncomfortable journey down a communication trench with the Germans chucking it and sundry other details into the trench. It was picked up about the third day of the battle.

Would you please ask Mother to send out a more or less constant supply of thick chocolate? It is extraordinary what a craving one gets in the trenches for something sweet and the thick chocolate also does for a meal when one gets landed.

8/10/15

My dear Dad,

Judging from the sound there is a pretty healthy battle going on not very far away. There has been a continual roar of guns all afternoon without a break in the sound. Fortunately, we are fairly far back just now so are not likely to be wanted. We are still resting and there is every prospect of our getting a day or two more yet.

The weather is getting quite wintry now, with a slight touch of frost at night.

There was rather a funny thing happened here the other day. The men were only given a half issue of rum, so half of one Company played the other half at football for its share. The match was a draw.

The artillery is still blazing away as cheerily as ever. I wonder what is on.

I think I told you I am now in charge of the Machine Gun Section, as Todd is now Brigade Machine Gun Officer. It means more work but it is rather nice to be entirely on one's own. It is rather complimentary to us to have one of our officers chosen to go on the staff. I am always very glad I took on the Machine Gun job.

[Cont.] 9/10/15

We spent rather an uncomfortable night last night as word came that we were to be ready to move on short notice. We had to sleep in boots and clothes. It is rumoured this morning that the Germans tried to counter attack and fairly got it in the eye for their trouble. Report here has it that three German Battalions were simply wiped off the face of the earth. I hope it is true.

There are sports going on here just now so I must stop.

PS You should see me swanking it on a horse now, especially when the horse is walking or standing still. I have got a very nice pony and a groom whom I am told is a bit of a ruffian though I don't believe it.

WD: On the 12th, we returned again to the trenches in front of Cambrin.

13/10/15

My dear Mother,

I rather think there is going to be another bit of a push on today but I am not yet quite sure. You will know however by the time this letter reaches you. There is really nothing else in the way of news except that I am still flourishing. I shall try and get off at least a PC tomorrow, but don't worry if I can't manage it.

Your loving son

Walter J.J. Coats

[Cont.] 14/10/15

I could not get this off yesterday so may as well continue now. I am glad to say I got through the show yesterday alright without a scratch. I was hit on the head by something but whether it was a small bit of shell or a lump of dirt I am not sure. At any rate, it did me less harm than when I bumped my head getting into a dug-out the night before. I am told our bombardment [of Hohenzollern Redoubt][26] for a bit was even worse than at Neuve Chapelle, which is looked upon as a sort of record, but the funny thing was I didn't notice anything extraordinary about it as I was very busy at the time. It is funny how one gets accustomed to the noise.

Would you mind asking Ellie for some more carriage candles? I only managed to bag three of the last lot for myself, as the Company I am messing with lives in a deep dug-out and we have to use artificial light all day. I am sorry to have to ask for some more of them so soon. I expect they are very expensive, but they are far and away the best candles for this job. I would also like a stick of shaving soap. We can buy British soap out here but the French charge about twice its value and I would rather the British Revenue got the price of postage than a Frenchman who is making his fortune by overcharging. If you can get it, I would rather have any British made soap than Colgate or any of those American ones.

With any luck the Battalion will get back for a short rest today but the best I can hope for is to get out of the front into some reserve line. However, we have on the whole had a very quiet though very busy time here so I have nothing to grouse about.

I had a new lining put into one of my jackets by the Regimental Tailor the other day for two Francs, which I should think is fairly cheap. I also got him to patch the one I have on, which was suffering somewhat from what we call the 'French walk' i.e. supporting ourselves down the trench with our elbows. It does not improve the jacket.

You will be pleased to hear that as far as I can gather Math did rather a fine thing yesterday.[27] He told me about it as if it was a mere nothing, when we were talking over things. So I told his captain and I hope he gets something for it. He has done some jolly good work here and he is at present running a Company.

I must switch off now as it is high time I wrote to thank Mc G D & Co. for their parcels.

Cheer Oh from your loving son,

Walter J J Coats

WD: We stayed in the front line without any undue excitement till the 17th when we returned to Beuvry

---

26   See Wyrall, *The History of the Second Division 1914-1918*, pp. 241-43 and Weir, *Come On Highlanders!*, p. 121.

27   It was during the bombardment of Hohenzollern Redoubt that Mathew Anderson managed to seal off a gas pipe fractured by a German shell. He was gassed himself in the process. See Weir, *Come On Highlanders!*, p. 121.

18/10/15

My dear Dad,

I am very sorry to be so long in writing or sending a PC but I have been fairly busy lately and as the Battalion has been back resting while I was in the line, I found it rather difficult getting any letters away. I came back for a short rest myself last night only to find this morning when I got to breakfast that we have to go in again this afternoon.

I am fearfully pleased I came back last night as I had a most beautiful bath this morning in a laundry nearby. It is the first decent bath I have had since I was home on leave. It is wonderful however how clean one can keep if one can get a change of clothes.

WD: We returned to the trenches again on the 18th and were put into trenches here just to the right of Cuinchy.

19/10/15

My dear Dad,

I got back to the trenches very comfortably again yesterday. I expect I told you I had a most splendid bath though I am still longing for one I can lie down in. I think it was the first hot bath I have had since I was home on leave though I have managed to have one or two cold ones.

It is getting very cold in the trenches now. In fact last night I was sleeping in a dugout with the two Majors and I think I was the only one who got anything like a decent sleep. Thanks to my being of a sleepy disposition and a copy of the Times shoved up my back, I managed to get an excellent sleep. I have shifted to a smaller dugout now, with only one wee hole to crawl in by, instead of two large doors, so I am feeling warmer tonight. I find the Times an excellent thing for keeping one warm. If Mother is not too busy, a few warmer clothes would be very much appreciated and comforting.

Please excuse the writing, as I am half lying down and I have nothing to rest the pad on.

I saw a rather amusing extract from a captured German's diary today. It went something like this:

"1st: Lieut. R. is drunk today
2nd: Lieut. R. is drunk again today
3rd: Lieut. R is reported sick this evening
4th: We attacked today and Lieut. R. was heard several times shouting "Vorwarts" from the 3rd line dugouts."

A later entry states that Lieut. R. has been awarded the Iron Cross. These are not the exact words but they are very nearly so and I believe the extract is a true one.

I must go and see that things are going on all right, so I shall shut up for now.

I have just got back after a fairly lengthy look around and I am glad to say everything is very quiet, not suspiciously quiet, but just comfortable.

Rumour has it that the Germans tried another counter-attack this evening and got it in the eye once again. I don't know whether it is true or not, but our guns were certainly giving them something to think about. I hope it is true.

I shall shut up for tonight, or rather this morning as it is now after 2am.

WD: Except for the usual discomforts of trench life, we had an easy time of it until we were again relieved on the 23rd. This time we moved back to Béthune. The Mess was in an old room over a smithy's shop close to the Fish Market.

23/10/15

My dear Jean,

I must tell you of a rather funny thing I saw in a letter the other day. The man was writing to thank someone for a shirt that had been issued to him with a ticket pinned inside saying who it was from. He wrote something like this – "I only discovered who it was from when I sat down. You really must be more careful where you stick pins in future".

We are back for a rest just now, in the same old place and as usual I have a splendid billet. I can read in bed at night, and when I am finished, I simply put out my hand and switch off the electric light. I expect I shall have a week of it this time but of course one can never be sure. I was jolly glad to get out yesterday as it poured all night.

I had a fine ride with Math this afternoon. He told me Allison has at last got through her exams with a 2nd Class Honours. Amy, he says, is very busy, sometimes doing 17 hours work a day. She has a lot to do in the Operating Theatre.

You would see from the papers that gas was used in these last attacks. It is abominable stuff and I wish it had never been invented. I got a few whiffs of it and to put it mildly it is not nice.

I saw a rather cute case of time saving the other day. A man wrote a great long letter of his experiences and took a carbon copy of it. He then simply filled in the beginning and the end of it and sent it off to two different people. He is a funny sort of a chap at any rate. When he went home on leave, I believe he wrote out various experiences he had had, and when people asked him to tell them about his war experiences, he first of all asked them whether they wanted it humorous, pathetic, horrible or otherwise and then simply reeled off the appropriate story.

We had a most violent argument in the Mess last night at which the Major talked the most awful rot I have ever heard. I left fairly late on in the evening but I am told he went on till all hours. As he was arguing against me, I flatter myself I was right.

WD: The violent discussion about the way in which the Mess was run ended up in a full blown mess meeting where it was decided that it would in future be carried on exactly as it had been before.

Sunday 24/10/15

My dear Jenny,

I was very pleased today, we had a Communion Service. It was awfully nice having one the same day you were having one at home. It was held in what I believe was once a Powder Magazine and is now a Cinema House. The man looking after us out here just now is called Pryde. He is a thoroughly good sort and I like him very much. I believe Boyd Scott is coming out. When Pryde heard of it, I believe he was rather sorry that he had not got the offer first, but as he is someone else's Chaplain I don't see how he could have become ours.

I am sorry to say that I think there is every prospect of a row between the Church of England and the Church of Scotland ministers. It arrives partly I believe from the fact that, while in some districts the majority of troops are Scots, when they ask for any building to have a service in they always find the Church of England people have got it first and the Scotsmen have to go into a field. I must say, I think it is a great pity they should start fighting about such a thing, especially as I am sure the troops themselves don't bear each other any ill will on the subject. In fact, as far as I can see, they would be quite willing to have a joint service.

PS With any luck we will not be in the trenches again this month.

26/10/15

My dear Jean,

Just a line to wish you many happy returns. I am afraid the wish is rather belated but "C'est la guerre" as people say out here when they can't find any other excuse, e.g. when they charge you about hundred times more for something than they paid for it.

I am glad to say we are still resting as the weather is simply beastly. My day here consists generally of: 9am till 12.00 or 12.30: Parade with Machine Gun. 1pm: Orderly Room. 1.30: Lunch. Afternoon: censoring letters, making up programme for next day's work, writing letters, reading, riding etc. 7.30: dinner. Bed around 9.30pm.

As I have already written to the mother of a man who wanted me to try and get her son home, any ideas I had have taken flight like butterflies on a summer evening. In other words, I am fed up and I am going to stop.

Your ... [dot puzzle, see next page] ... brother,
Walter J.J. Coats

PS The solver of the above picture puzzle will be rewarded by another proof (print) of my absolute insanity.

Dot puzzle in letter of 26 October 1915.[28] (WJJC collection)

28/10/15

My dear Jenny,
You will be pleased to hear we are still resting and that there is a prospect of our doing so for some time yet.

We left our billets today and came out here [Gonnehem, N.W. of Béthune]. We had a pretty cheery march as the weather is absolutely awful. It is somewhat chilly and lashing rain. Added to this, the country is once more turning into a huge mud puddle and is likely to remain so until next spring. Thank goodness we are not in the trenches.

I am glad to say that the men are gradually getting away on leave, though it is a slow business. There are a great many out here still who have been out for a year now without getting home. I drew lots for the order in which my men were to get leave and am sorry to say it will be some months before the last of them get home.

[Cont.] 30/10/15
I am glad to say we are back to the old billets and the weather is improving.

---

28 Answer: Flourishing.

1/11/15

My dear Doug,

Things are really looking cheery tonight. It has been raining off and on for several days, but tonight it is excelling itself. The unfortunate thing is that the Machine Guns have to go into the trenches again tomorrow morning, my senior sergeant has just gone for a Commission, Sandeman may be going any time now, one corporal is at a course of instruction and the other going on leave, and the other Officer is also going on leave. This of course means double work for us all which I am not looking forward to in the present state of the weather. If it wasn't that there is a certain amount of humour about it, I should have begun to feel a bit fed up. As it is, I am feeling perfectly cheery and unworried. It is funny how bad weather very often has that effect on me – the harder it rains the less I care.

Please tell Mother the chickens were excellent at lunch today. While I remember, would you please ask Mother to send me out some more thick chocolate, and also an occasional loaf of decent Scotch bread? It arrives out here quite fresh if sent off fairly new and it knocks spots off French bread any day.

I had tea with Math yesterday and dinner with him the night before. He was exceeding flourishing and I am glad to say does not go into the trenches for several days yet.

There is really no news except that it is raining so I may as well switch off.

Your prospectively drookit craw [Scots slg. "drenched crow"],

Walter J.J. Coats

WD: On 2nd November we again went into the line this time south of Cuinchy. The trenches here were very complicated to find one's way about and the communication trenches were very long but on the whole things were very comfortable. The Battalion was relieved on the 7th but as the Machine Guns were brigaded I remained behind until the 13th when the whole brigade was relieved. McCosh, who was trench mortar officer at this time, was also left behind and we messed together. I remember one excellent dinner we had off some cold grouse which had been sent him. When they were unpacked they were found to be green with mould but as the alternative was cold bully which we were both tired of we skinned the beasts and found they looked all right underneath so we each had one. No bad results followed.[29]

---

29 No "bad results followed" except for the enemy as recorded in the 5th Brigade War Diary for 8 November 1915: "8.30PM: Our trench mortars during last 24 hours were fired with good effect on German trenches. Hostile bomb attack on our saps in Z2 subsection was silenced by MG and Lewis Gun fire." See TNA WO 95/1343-2: 5th Brigade War Diary.

7/11/15

My dear Mother,
Many thanks for the parcel which I got yesterday. I am sorry to say the Germans have
been shelling this part of the line off and on all day, so things have been very uncomfortable, to put it mildly. They landed a 'Heavy' slap on top of the dugout we Mess in
this forenoon but fortunately the dugout was well made and no one was hurt.

By the way, I nearly became temporary Brigade Machine Gun Officer. I was sent
for late in the afternoon yesterday by the Brigade and when I got there I was told that
the Machine Gun Officer [Todd] was going to a course and then on leave and that
I was to carry on while he was away. I had actually taken over when a message came
to say he was not going after all so I lost the job. In a way, I was not altogether sorry,
though it would have been a fine job from the comfort point of view as I would not
have had to live in the trenches. As a matter of fact the trenches are not bad just now,
though they would be better if the Germans would stop shelling. As I said, however,
their shelling is not a patch on what we are giving them.

11/11/15

My dear Mother,
Many thanks for the last parcel with bread etc. The bread arrived in the most splendid
condition. As one man said, it reminded him of home more than anything he had ever
got. One gets fearfully tired of French ration bread.

There is not much news except that I am still in the trenches. The Battalion went
out of the line yesterday but I have another three days yet with the Machine Guns.
We had a fearfully wet night of it the night before last but I have managed to get hold
of a pair of long rubber boots that come right up well over the knee so I don't mind
the mud so much.

[Cont.] 12/11/15
I began this yesterday but could not get it away so I may as well carry on.

I was told yesterday that we were going to be relieved today, but last night I got a
message cancelling the order so here we are still in the trenches.

It is wet again today but, as I don't have to leave my dugout much, I don't care. We
have been doing some indirect firing from this place and it is great fun working out
bearings on the map and laying out lines to shoot on by day. We then put out lamps
to aim at by night and get an elevation by clinometer. I think we must have been
annoying them as they were searching for us with whizz bangs.[30]

---

30 "11.11.15, 5 AM: A machine gun sited near Arthur's Keep fired intermittently during the
    night on place S.W. of Auchy … Fire probably effective as hostile artillery retaliated." and

I had a very nice letter from Mrs Pyatt last night, thanking me for thanking her for the Punches etc she sent me.

I must stop now as I have to write to the sister of a man who was wounded the other day. It is very hard to know what to say on these occasions but it is only fair to write.

Walter's Uncle, Dr Walter Coats, wrote to Walter's mother, his sister, from Dundee:

12th November 1915

My dear Ellie,

I feel I ought to tell you that within the last few days, we have been receiving a good many men of the Glasgow Highlanders in the Hospitals here, and that when I ask about "Captain Coats", they are all so warm in his praise that I am proud to tell them he is my nephew and namesake. I am sure you and Jack will be glad to know your boy is appreciated, as I am sure he deserves.

I hope you continue to have good reports from him and all the others. Whether in these days it is harder to have <u>four</u> in it or an <u>only</u> son, I can't say.

Jock is now in the Machine Gun Corps. Of those who finished with him three weeks ago, 90 percent were overseas in a week. As he passed high, he was sent to Chipstone, where he now is.

Yours affectionately,

Walter W Coats.

WD: On 13th we got out and moved back to Annezin, behind Béthune

Sunday 14th November 1915

My dear Dad,

There is not much in the way of news except that we have got out for a rest. We expect to get 8 days, which is all right as I have got an excellent billet. It was originally intended for the senior Major but he got another one, so it must be one of the best in the place. We are billeted in a small village just now, near the same old place, and I intend going into it tomorrow to get my hair cut.

We had a Church Parade today in a building that is now being used as a Cinema house. Mr Pryde was preaching but I am afraid I was too sleepy to pay much attention. He usually gives us a good sermon but eleven days in the open air don't make it any easier to stay awake in Church.

"12.11.15, 5 AM: The indirect fire of our machine guns on road junction N W Corner of Auchy again drew hostile fire". See TNA WO 95/1343-2: 5th Brigade War Diary.

I hope you can read this writing. I just been out and I find my hand somewhat stiff with the cold.

The man McLeod you talk of in your letter is an awfully decent chap and is taking a commission in the 3rd Battalion. Sergeant Sandeman is doing the same, so if Jack has any room in his Company, he might do worse than snaffle them.[31] I don't know that either of them know much about Company drill as they have been Machine Gunners for some time now, but they are both good men with practical experience, and would probably pick up a new job very quickly.

It is just possible I may have to take on the job of Brigade Machine Gun Officer for a bit, but I rather hope not as it means living with the Brigade Staff and I would rather be with my own people.

WD: As Todd was sent off on a course, I was sent to Brigade H.Q. to act as Brigade Machine Gun Officer while he was away. The Brigade H.Q. was at Gonnehem, northwest of Béthune, and we expected to have a good long time out but had not been out more than three days when we were again sent into the line at the brickstacks[32] at Cuinchy with Brigade H.Q. on the Béthune-La Bassée road opposite the chemist's shop at Cambrin. The Brigade H.Q. at this time consisted of Brigadier General, General Corkran of the Grenadier Guards; Brigade Major, Captain Robertson, Indian Army; Staff Captain, Captain G. Blewitt, 2nd Ox. and Bucks L.I.; Intelligence Officer, Lieut. Wilde, 2nd Ox. and Bucks L.I.

Life here passed very pleasantly though it took a good deal of work to visit all the guns in the Brigade every day, and I had some trouble with one of the Battalion M.G. officers who was a captain and so senior to me. He rather objected to taking orders from me but was soon put in his place by the Brigade Major.

Apart from visiting the guns daily the work chiefly consisted of arranging for the relief of the various guns and for nightly harassing fire on cross roads etc. behind the German line. As this was all indirect fire the angle of elevation and deflection had to be worked out for each gun where the Battalion officer could not do it himself and checked in the case of those officers who could. On the whole I had a pretty busy time.

---

31 Sergeant 1466 Frank Watt Sandeman departed Battalion November 1915 and finished medical qualification MB at Glasgow University; commissioned RAMC 11 August 1917. See *Supplement to the London Gazette of 4 September 1917*, No. 30270, p. 9232 and TNA WO 339/95859.

32 The notorious Cuinchy Brickstacks were "a number of massive rectangular blocks of burnt brick near the La Bassée Canal. Some were in the British lines, some in the German. Many of them had concealed concrete machine-gun emplacements with shell-proof dug-outs beneath them. The Brickstacks had become well-known as a death trap, for not only had they been shaken by mines exploded beneath, but they were showered day and night with mortar bombs, 'flying pigs' and shells." See Alex Aiken, *Courage Past* (Glasgow: George Outram, 1971), p. 24, Graves, *Goodbye to All That* and Edmund Blunden, *Undertones of War* (London: Penguin, 2000).

Cuinchy Brickstacks. (RHF Collection)

As Todd went on leave after his course I was left on this job longer than I expected and was still on it when the Sportsmen's Battalion of the Royal Fusiliers,[33] the 99th Brigade H.Q. and some other Battalions of the 33rd Division were attached to us for training as they had just come out. The new Battalions were all armed with Lewis guns.

18/11/15

My dear Mother,

Here we are still resting and still going strong. So far, I have found the Brigade job about as slack as it is possible to imagine and I am rather sick about it as I want to go on instructing my own men while we are resting. My day at present consists of: Breakfast 8.30. After that I do anything I like till lunch at 1.30. After that, I do anything I like till dinner at 8.30pm, after which I go to bed. The only good point about it is the feeding, which is a bit of all right. We have fish, bacon and omelette and something cold for breakfast. Hot meat and some sort of pudding etc. for lunch, and soup, fish, meat, dessert and fruit for dinner, and the drinks are anything from port and champagne, to lemon squash and Perrier. The best of it is we have clean table cloths and clean knives and forks etc.

---

33 23rd Royal Fusiliers: Raised in London September 1914 by Mrs E. Cunliffe-Owen; transferred 99th Brigade, 33rd Division; disembarked Boulogne November 1915; transferred with entire Brigade to 2nd Division. See Fred W. Ward, *The 23rd (Service) Battalion Royal Fusiliers(First Sportsman's) During the First World War 1914-1918* (Driffield: Leonaur, 2010).

The weather here is simply extraordinary. It was very wet and showery till about 3 o'clock yesterday afternoon when it began to freeze. There was ice in the puddles by 9.00 at night and today it is very hard frost.

A "crump" is a shell that goes off with a sort of crumpy bang. The name is phonetic? It is anything from a 5 or 6 inch shell upwards.

25/11/15

My dear Dad,
It seems a long time since I wrote last but, since the Brigade came into the line, I have been too busy to do much except my own work. In addition to the usual Brigade work, we have had to arrange for training some of Kitchener's army and it is very hard to remember that they don't know as much as we do.

I expect to be on this job till about the 5th of next month.

27/11/15

My dear Mother,
The trenches are not all that could be desired but might be very much worse. We have learnt a lot in the last year about what we call 'house-wifing' the trenches (i.e. keeping them clean and dry and comfortable) and as a result I don't think we shall have nearly as bad a winter as we had last. One consolation is that we couldn't very well have a worse one.

30/11/15

My dear Dad,
My reason for sending Field Service PCs is not as you suggest that I am no longer in the lap of comfort, but rather that I am too busy. I get through one of the official telegraph pads in about three days now and generally spend the whole forenoon and most of the afternoon wandering around the trenches etc. I sleep in a bed every night, and feed like a king, but I think I would rather sleep in a dugout and feed like an ordinary mortal. Kitchener's people[34] increase the amount of work about three fold and it is just my luck being shoved onto this job at this time. As a matter of fact, I don't think I should care for the job at any time. I have already bumped up against two

---

34 A possible reference to the late 1915 influx of New Army divisions. See Peter Simkins, *Kitchener's Army: The Raising of the New Armies 1914-1916* (Barnsley: Pen & Sword, 2007), Chapter 12.

Colonels and I am in rather a funny position with one of the Machine Gun Officers who is a Captain and therefore my senior. I can tell him off on paper when I sign for the Brigade but I don't quite know my position when I meet him face to face. So far however, I don't think I have made any very glaring mistakes.

To turn to pleasanter subjects, rather an annoying thing happened today. A Colonel in the Gunners got some new glass put in his house yesterday afternoon, and this morning the Germans sent over a lot of heavy stuff and smashed them all again. I believe he is fearfully sick about it.

4/12/15

My dear Mother,

The weather here just now is the absolute limit and the trenches are awful. After seeing men stuck in the mud and being just about stuck myself, I have decided that it is a cruel thing to use fly-paper. You have no idea what a curious feeling it is to be absolutely stuck no matter how hard you pull. I heard of one Colonel today who went up to see about getting some of his men out and who had to have a fatigue party brought up to dig himself out.

What bucks me up chiefly just now is that I think I shall get rid of this job tomorrow and get back to my own people. I shall have to give up a bed at night etc. but I don't mind that in the least. I shall have one parting kick at several people that have been annoying me (chiefly Kitchener's) and then retire gracefully behind a thick curtain of mud.

We expect to be here for another three weeks yet, after which I hope I shall manage to snaffle a little leave.

I have absolutely no news except that I am still in a position to see the humorous side of the situation and am quite cheery.

Your fly from the paper,

Walter J.J. Coats

PS If Jim has any old gramophone records, one sometimes gets quite amusing results by boring another hole in it just beside the one in the centre and running it on that one. We tried it here with an old well known song and it was most amusing. It ruins the record of course for all other purposes.

6/12/15

My dear Dad,

Much to my relief I got back to my Battalion last night. I am going to live in the trenches tomorrow and expect to stay there till I go on leave which I hope will be on the 10th or 11th of this month. I shall let you know when I hear anything definite.

We are gradually getting the trenches cleaned up again here, but the work is fearfully hard. It is like digging in very stiff treacle and every shovel-full has to be lifted off the shovel by hand as it won't come off otherwise. I saw a party yesterday who gave up trying to use shovels and were using their hands only. As you can imagine, it is a slow job when you have several miles of trench to clear and I often wish I could get some of the slackers from home onto the job for even half an hour. The extraordinary thing is how cheery the men are in spite of it all.

Beyond the fact that I expect to be home in about a week's time, I have absolutely no news so I may as well shut up.

Your ever cheerful son

Walter J.J. Coats

WD: When Todd returned from leave on the 5th December, I rejoined Battalion H.Q. which was then in a small cottage about 150 yards in front of Harley Street. It was while we were in the line here that I had one of my narrow squeaks two rifle bullets hitting the bank within two inches of my head when I was returning from the line one day. I also learnt to have great sympathy for flies that get caught on fly paper as I got stuck one day in Coldstream Lane [just north of Givenchy Keep, see map on page 83]. The mud was particularly sticky and came within about half an inch of the top of my thigh boots. When I tried to get one leg out the other, just like a fly's, got stuck faster and it took me a long time before I managed to fight my way out.

WD: I got leave on 7th December and went home with Wingate, Cowie and Colonel Murray, who was giving up command of the Battalion.

7/12/15

TELEGRAM from J.Q. Rowett to J.J. Coats

MACTAGGART WILL BE WITH YOU FOR BREAKFAST TOMORROW. LEAVING BY NIGHT TRAIN TODAY.

4

Machine Guns and Nice

A mine went off outside about half an hour ago but it is a quite common thing here and no one worries except the patients who are suffering from nerves.

20/12/15[1]

TELEGRAM to J.J. COATS, GLASGOW from J.Q. ROWETT, LONDON

HAD BREAKFAST WITH WALTER AND COWIE AT EUSTON AND HAVE JUST SEEN WALTER OFF IN GOOD SPIRITS. ROWETT

WD: After the usual very pleasant leave, I rejoined the Battalion on the 22nd. They were just coming out of the line but as the guns were remaining in I went straight in and relieved Wharrie. Lieut. Col. Stormonth-Darling of the Cameronians was now in command of the Battalion.[2]

23/12/15

My dear Dad,
Here we are again once more back to work. I arrived back here about midday yesterday. In a way, I had rather bad luck. If I had only had one more day of leave, I should have been hung up in England, as they stopped all boats the day after I got across.

Things are very quiet here just now and the only news of interest is that the authorities have once more changed their minds about our getting out, so we will be in the

---

1 General, later Field Marshal, Sir Douglas Haig assumed command of the BEF from Field Marshal Sir John French the previous day (19 December 1915).
2 Lieutenant-Colonel John Collier Stormonth-Darling DSO (1878-1916). South Africa 1899-1902; commissioned Cameronians 1900; CO 1/9th HLI 9 December 1915.

trenches over Christmas after all. With any luck, I think we will be out before the New Year, unless they change their minds again.

I got the lamp and periscope all right when I got here, for which many thanks. The periscope is just what I wanted and so far, the lamp has been very satisfactory. It only remains to be seen how often I shall require a refill.

I suppose this will reach you too late to wish you a Merry Christmas but I can at any rate wish you all a Merry After Effects, or perhaps I should say it "quiet after effects", as to have one's inside "Merry" might not be altogether pleasant.

27/12/15

My dear Mother,

Things are pretty beastly here just now so far as the weather and trenches go. The only piece of news I have is that the General offered to put me in for command of a Machine Gun Company.[3] This is a fairly important job, as I would be entirely on my own with eight officers under me. It would have meant coming home for a bit to train them, but I might be sent to Greece or some such outlandish place afterwards and it would also have meant leaving all my friends here, so I thought it better to stick to the job I have. What amuses me most is that I have never been to a Machine Gun course in my life. It is quite possible that I may be put in charge of the Lewis guns of the Battalion, but I am not sure yet.

The only other bit of news is that we are sure to be out by the time you get this.

WD: We now moved back to St Hilaire-Cottes near Lillers where our Maxims[4] were taken from us and handed over to the Brigade Machine Gun Company which was now being formed. The Battalion was issued with Lewis guns in their place and though I hardly knew the inside of a Lewis gun from the outside I was given command of the Section. Lewis guns were then so scarce that the gunners were formed into sections similar to those for the Maxim guns but later when each battalion was issued with 36, each company was made responsible for its own with one officer in the battalion to supervise the training of the whole.

---

3   With the establishment of the Machine Gun Corps (MGC) that autumn, battalion machine-guns were reorganised into brigade machine-gun companies by an Army Order of 22 October 1915. Thus 1/9th HLI traded in their Maxim heavy machine-guns for Lewis guns, which were to be distributed 8 to 16 per battalion. See Sir J.E. Edmonds, *Military Operations France and Belgium 1916 Vol. I* (London: Macmillan, 1932), pp. 64-65.
4   Although the British Army had officially adopted the Vickers heavy machine-gun in 1912, large numbers of Maxim heavy machine-guns (adopted 1888) remained in service with some Regular and TF battalions at the start of the conflict.

30/12/15

My dear Jean,

A Happy New Year to you all. I must apologise for not writing for several days, but we have been moving, and are now settled down miles away from shells etc. I have got an excellent billet and the men are also pretty comfortable, so we ought to be all right. We expect to be out for several weeks.

If any of you want a New Year present for me, you might get a book called "In Kilt and Khaki" being "Glimpses of the Glasgow Highlanders in training and on foreign service" by Thomas M. Lyon (Private Leo). It is published by The Standard Press, Kilmarnock. Whoever gets it might order a copy to be kept at home for me and I will pay them when I get home on leave next time. The author was with us but lost the sight of one eye.

31/12/15

My dear Jenny,

The only news I have is that Madame has offered us the fois of her cochon, which we take to mean her pig's liver for dinner.

Somehow, Madame's offer has brought it home to me more than anything else that a pig has a liver. Somehow, I didn't seem to realise it before. I suppose it has a kidney too.

I enclose two banknotes which I should like kept for me as souvenirs. They have only recently been issued.[5]

I read the book "In Kilt etc." last night and found it quite interesting. I wish the author could have described the muddy trenches.

Please thank Mother for the bread which has just arrived. I have absolutely nothing to drivel about so Cheer Oh.

WD: We spent New Year at St. Hilaire-Cottes and had a great celebration on New Year's Eve. The C.O., who was not very sure of the Battalion yet, issued orders to the effect that the men were not to follow the pipe band when it turned out to welcome the New Year in. We were all therefore rather astonished when midnight came to find the whole Battalion out in the street in front of H.Q. with the band. On enquiring why they had not obeyed orders, we found that they had read them literally and had not followed the band but had made the band follow them.

---

5   One Franc and 50 Centimes banknotes issued 4 October 1915 by Béthune Chambre de Commerce.

1916

1st January, 1916

My dear Doug,

We have had today absolutely free without a single parade and I think the men have enjoyed it more than anything we could give them.

We had a tremendous dinner last night and set up to see the New Year in. Exactly at midnight, a full pipe band with drums etc. started to play through the village and about every man in the Battalion turned out. They were all both in and outside of pretty good spirits, and simply let themselves go. I expect the French inhabitants thought we were mad. One of them asked if the fête was going on again today. One of the Mess waiters nearly killed himself with a bottle of cherry brandy which he got hold of and was treating as whisky. Fortunately, he was stopped by another man who knew the strength of it. The men were allowed to have a good old blowout when they were at it and get it over and we settle down to the same old round again tomorrow. I think it has done them all a lot of good.

WD: On the 9th January I was sent to 2nd Division H.Q. to act as G.S.O.3[6] while they were waiting the arrival of a new one.

10/1/16

My dear Dad,

The only news I have today is that I have once again got a temporary staff job. I am answering for what is known as G.S.O.3. = General Staff Officer 3rd Grade. I got word yesterday afternoon that I was for the job and arrived here in the evening. I think the job will be extremely interesting as it is largely intelligence work.

Please go on addressing my letters to the Battalion as usual as I have not the slightest idea how long this job is going to last.

There was one rather funny thing that happened a few days ago, which I don't think I told you. We were having a concert and, just when we were going to start, the Major came in and took a seat which promptly collapsed under him amid loud cheers from the men. When he got settled down again, Reid, who was running the show got up and said "The second item on the programme is the song by _____". The men didn't quite see the point of it just at once but when they did they were fearfully tickled.

---

6   GSO3: General Staff Officer, Grade 3 belonging to the (I) Intelligence or (O) Operations branch of the staff.

11/1/16

My dear Mother,
I hope Ellie and the kid are both going strong.[7]

I should have been playing football for the Battalion today but I can't get away. I don't know that I am altogether sorry as I don't suppose I have run more than about 100 yards at any time since I came to France, and the trenches are not the best place to keep in training.

13/1/16

My dear Jean,
The only news today is that I expect to leave this job tomorrow as the proper man is coming back. I am rather sorry in a way as it is quite an interesting one and would get more so as time went on. One good thing about going back to the Battalion is that I shall get my letters which have been accumulating ever since I left.

Another good thing is that I shall get back among people I know and can talk to. You have no idea how a dull it is trying to make a conversation with a Major General or a S.G.S.O or A.A & Q.M.G. etc. etc. etc. One can't talk shop to them as their shop to mine is as the Western Club dining room is to a fish and chip cart in Argyle Street on a Saturday night. In other words, where we talk in platoons and companies they talk in Brigades and Divisions.

One can't talk of external affairs, as things that interest them don't interest me and vice versa and one can't, when there is nothing else to talk about, grouse at the staff as they ARE the staff. The result is that (except with the A.D.C's) conversation pretty well limits itself to a remark in the morning that it has been a very cold night and it is a beautiful morning, at lunchtime to the remark that it looks like rain, and at dinner to the remark that it has been a very cold day and that you are surprised it hasn't rained. Fortunately, we have our work to do between meals.

WD: I rejoined the Battalion at St.Hilaire on 15th.

16/1/16

My dear Dad
I got back yesterday from the Division job and got all my letters for the last week today. We move from here tomorrow up towards the line but it should be at least 10 days before we go back into the trenches.

---

7   Helen Graham Quiller Rowett (1915-2012) born to Ellie and John Rowett on 30 December 1915.

My face is in rather a mess just now as I had a bad shave several days ago and as the water I was using was not apparently of the cleanest, my face got a bit poisoned. It has been getting steadily worse for some time, and I have not been able to shave for two days, but the doctor is attending to it now so should be all right in a few days. I am going to bathe it now so I shall knock off for the night.

PS My face does not worry me in the least, though my beauty is temporarily marred. Did you notice we got two Military Crosses and six D.C.M's in the last list?

WD: We returned to Les Choquaux [Locon] on 17th.

19/1/16

My dear Mother,

Many thanks for the chickens, watch and collars which I got all right. The cakes also arrived all right, but when I got back from the Division, I found they had already been eaten. The tobacco had also been used up and the laces distributed. As a matter of fact, I arrived just in time to get my share of the chickens.

Please thank the girls for their sweets, which I am sorry to say went the way of the cakes, so I can't tell whether their selection was good or not.

My face has not improved in beauty since I wrote last but it is not so painful as it was. I should like to shave, but the doctor says if I do it will simply get worse. I don't think I shall be able to shave for about a week yet. I bet my beard is better than Doug's ever was, by that time.

The day I got back, I found the officers having great sport with a "spy hunt". The C.O. put them up to it. Three officers were sent out to a small village some way off and all the other officers who could raise horses were "hunters". The idea was that the three officers were to try to reach our Headquarters with a message, while the rest tried to catch them. The success of the show was one officer who had never been on a horse before and who got mine. He was one of the "hunters" and started off bumping down the street, returning all salutes in the most careful manner in spite of the danger of his hitting himself in the eye or the nose with the bumping. He was going along somehow when he suddenly vanished only to reappear as few minutes later, trotting down the street a little, and then vanish again and so on. The horse simply trotted into every lane, farmyard and open door that took his fancy, had a smell round and if possible a bite of hay. It then trotted down to its stable and had a drink and started all over again. By this time, every man, woman and child was out in the street watching him and of course the men were all very careful to salute him every time he passed just for the fun of seeing him salute back. After an hour of this sort of thing, he eventually managed to get out of the village which was only about 200 yards long, in the right direction. As luck would have it, he managed to find the Colonel a short way out, who asked him to ride back to Headquarters and see if any of the spies had got back yet, so away he went again. This time he was rather more successful but when he reached Headquarters he couldn't draw up and went straight past. He managed to turn his horse somehow a bit further down the road, but again his horse took him past Headquarters and he had to have another shot before he could come to a stop where he wanted. He didn't try to reach the Colonel again. I only arrived in time to see the finish of the show. Everyone I saw was absolutely weak with laughing and the C.O. nearly went into hysterics when he arrived back and was told about it. I am glad to say my horse was none the worse.

I am told my name is now up for promotion but I shall be sorry if it means me giving up the job I have. A great many of the old men went to the Machine Gun Company after all but I have got a good lot of new ones with the Lewis guns and I am more on my own with this job than I would be on any other.

I enclose the paper about the Exchequer Bonds which I nearly forgot about. Please thank Dad for all his trouble.

I have nothing more to say so will wind up.

Your loving son, Walter J.J. Coats

23/1/16

My dear Mother,

I see that Dad is going to give H.G.Q.R. [Ellie's new baby] a bowl that will do for porridge, sweets, sugar etc. I hope he gives it on condition that it is never used for porridge and sugar simultaneously.

One of our men who got a DCM in the last batch also got the Croix de Guerre from General Joffre two days ago. He jolly well deserves it too.[8]

My face, I am sorry to say, is not yet my fortune. The doctor has given me today a new sort of ointment of his own manufacture which I am to experiment with. I believe it burns some but that can't be helped. Meantime, I have got a magnificent beard as I have not shaved for over a week.

I have also successfully managed to lay out my forefinger. It is not bad enough to go and see the doctor about and I only mention it to explain the more than usually bad writing. I got it when I was leaping gaily over a trench and didn't notice that there was a branch of a tree in the way which got me on the head and knocked me into the bottom of the trench.

I think we go back to the trenches in two or three days now but unless the doctor's cure works, my face may be my fortune after all, as I may be kept out.

---

8   Pte 1791 James Robertson awarded DCM and *Croix de Guerre* for actions on 25 September 1915. See Weir, *Come on Highlanders!*, p. 388.

25/1/16

My dear Mother,

There is not much news today except that we go back to the trenches again tomorrow. It is funny we are going into a place we were in exactly a year ago. I believe this is the Kaiser's birthday. I certainly don't wish him many happy returns. This time, a year ago, we got a pretty heavy shelling but there doesn't appear to be much doing today.

Excuse writing as my finger is still a little tender. My face is not just what it might be yet, but it is getting better pretty quickly now.

WD: We went back into the line near Festubert on 26th.

27/1/16

My dear Jean,

There is no news here just now but as there is a prospect of our being busy for a few days, I may as well try and write a letter now.

We arrived here yesterday after a short march and find things are pretty quiet. I only hope they remain so.

My face is not quite better yet and the doctor said if it did not get better very shortly he would send me to hospital. Personally, I don't think it is necessary but if he sends me, I suppose I shall have to go. I also saw the doctor about my finger today. He cut it open and I have to have it dressed twice a day so it should be alright very soon now.

I am afraid this letter is rather full of my ailments but Dad asked me to write how I was getting on.

WD: We expected to be in the line for some time as we had had a good long rest but on the 28th we were pulled out and taken back to Essars. The next day, the Divisional Commander and his staff came to say farewell and on 30th we did not know what was going to happen to us when we were pushed into the train at Béthune.[9] We were not kept long in doubt however for after a few hours in the train we arrived at St.Omer where we detrained and found we had been detailed for a spell on Lines of Communication, while we were filled up with drafts (we were very much under strength) and to refit generally.

---

9   1/9th HLI were about to be reassigned from 2nd Division to the "Lines of Communication" as designated "GHQ Troops". The Battalion subsequently served in this capacity from 30 January to 29 May 1916. See Weir, *Come on Highlanders!*, pp. 129-52.

31/1/16

My dear Jenny,

I have a bit of news that will probably cheer you all up. We are miles out of reach of all shells and if they follow the precedent of the Battalion whose job we are taking over, we are likely to be so for several months to come. I am sorry I can't tell you either what the job we have got is or where we are but I don't suppose you mind so long as we are here. I expect we will get fearfully bored with the job before it is done but I would rather sit here than be shelled, any day. It will probably affect our leave, but that is only right. With regard to the £5.00 which Mr. McCallum gave you, would you mind keeping it aside a bit longer? I may want it if we are going to be here for a long time to buy things to amuse the men.

The only other bit of news I have now is that I am going to be sent to hospital either today or tomorrow. The doctor thinks my face will get better quicker there. I have been told to put hot formulations on my finger every four or five hours which is rather a fag.

WD: On the 1st of February I was sent off to No.10 Stationary Hospital in St. Omer, suffering from impetigo as a result of shaving in dirty water.[10] After two days here I was sent down on the 3rd February to No.14 General Hospital Wimereux, Boulogne.

3/2/16

TELEGRAM to J.J. COATS GLASGOW

Beg to inform you that Lieutenant W.J.J. Coats, 9th Highland Light Infantry, was admitted to 1st General Hospital, Boulogne, 1st February, suffering from Impetigo, severe. Further information when received will be notified as soon as possible.

Officer in Charge, Territorial Force Records, Hamilton

8/2/16

My dear Dad,

There is no news except that I am having a splendid time. They kept me in bed for two days when I arrived and today is the first time I have been allowed downstairs for

---

10 Impetigo is a bacterial skin infection transmitted via skin lesions. It is not particularly dangerous and can be treated, but it is highly contagious. Isolation is advisable to avoid spreading the infection. As it turned out, Walter also had a wound or other ailment of the foot.

meals. There is nothing really wrong with me but they seem to think I am run down and I believe my temperature is lower than it should be.

I must tell you the joke about my coming down here. There were four of us to come from the Stationary Hospital, all sitting cases and the only room on the train was for one sitting and three lying cases. They were determined to send us down, so they took us to the station in an ambulance with three stretchers, so to speak, 'under our arms'. When we got to the station we walked onto the platform, with the stretchers following after, and as soon as the train came in we lay down on the stretchers and were solemnly carried into the train and lifted into bed. When we got to our destination we all got up, explained what we were and walked out. The whole thing was due to red tape. There was heaps of room for lying cases in the train, but the Doctor in charge of the train would not have let us on if we had not been carried.

While I remember, would you mind sending out another box of cigars. We are not allowed to get food sent but we can smoke as much as we like.

When I left the Battalion, we had come back to Lines of Communication which is a fine soft job. The last people were on it for six months and the people before, for four, so we should be pretty safe for some time – the only trouble is that leave is harder to get.

Saturday, 12 February, 1916

My dear Mother,
While I remember, would you mind sending me out a new sponge and shaving brush as I intend to scrap the ones I have just now in case they infect me again?

I am getting better steadily now but I am not allowed downstairs yet. I think it is my foot that is keeping me up now. I am supposed to keep it off the ground as much as possible though I am allowed to walk about as much as I like.

18/2/16

My dear Jenny,
Many thanks for your letter which I got yesterday. I am getting on in great form here. My foot has got to the stage of a dry dressing and my face has finished with fomentations and got to the stage of lotions and ointment.

I hope Ellie is getting on all right and that she is out of danger now. I got a note this morning saying she was doing well.[11]

As a rule we get letters here the day after they are posted in London.

A mine went off outside about half an hour ago but it is a quite common thing here and no one worries except the patients who are suffering from nerves.

---

11 Walter's sister Ellie underwent major surgery at this time for a suspected cancer condition.

22/2/16

My dear Jenny,
Would it trouble you very much to send me my Gillette safety razor? Doug will probably be able to tell you which it is. The trouble is that when I started shaving here I have got to leave the razor in pure carbolic overnight every day, if you understand what I mean. The result is the edge is not improved and it struck me my Gillette would save my decent razors, not to mention my face.

24/2/16

To Mrs Coats at Perry Mount, Forest Hill

My dear Mother,
There is no news here except that I am getting along all right. I expect to be here for a week or 10 days yet at least.

I hope Ellie is getting along all right. Please give her my love and all good wishes. I hope the kid is still flourishing and that John is none the worse for his anxious time.

There is quite deep snow on the ground here just now and it is pretty cold but the place is very comfortable.

26/2/16

To J.J. Coats at Perry Mount, Forest Hill

My dear Dad,
Thanks for your and Mother's various letters. I hope Ellie is still getting on all right.

When you write to Jim next you might wish him good luck from me. I wonder where he is going?

I am getting on all right here but it is a slow business. I won't be the least surprised if I am kept here for another fortnight or three weeks. My foot is getting on all right but it is still tied up.

I am going to see a Colonel Lister today about my eyes. The doctor here seems to think they are not quite right, though I am inclined to disagree with him. I don't think they are used to eyes like mine in the Army.

1/3/16

My dear Dad,

I suppose you are home now or will be by the time you get this. I hope Ellie was all right when you saw her and still improving.

There is really no news to write about here but there is nothing else to do. I don't care much about going out as my head is still tied up in bandages and I am not the least bit keen on doing the wounded hero touch, up and down the street.

I am at present waiting to see if I can raise a barber anywhere as I have not had my hair cut since I was home on leave last. I was just about due a haircut when the imp laid hold on me about six weeks ago, so you can imagine what I am like now.

My foot is getting better pretty quick now, though it is still festering a bit.

I don't suppose you know yet where Jim has gone to. I should like to know his address when you find out.

[Cont.] 2nd March

I forgot to post this yesterday so may as well carry on. They are talking of sending me to Nice, but it is the last place on earth I want to go and I intend to tell them so. I am told there is no more infection about my face, so I don't see why I shouldn't get back to my job. I am sure it would do me far more good to get back to my Battalion than to go hanging round a place like Nice wondering when I could get away.

I am feeling in rather a bad temper over the prospect of Nice so better shut up.

9/3/16

My dear Mother,

Many thanks for the shirt and toothbrush which I got several days ago, also for the sponge and shaving brush which I got today.

There is no news here except that I have got a new doctor whom I shall have to convince that I don't require to go to Nice. I am getting on in great style now. My face has been pronounced clear of infection by a skin specialist and my foot has just about dried up, though it is still bandaged. While I remember, Col Lister said I had something that sounded like 'blitheritis' in my eyes.[12] Personally, I would call it sleepy marks but I suppose he knows what he's talking about. At any rate, he has given me a lotion and an ointment which I have to shove on.

Mr McCallum has just sent me an enormous box of sweets. It was very decent of him and I must write and thank him. I am going to make a present of most of them to the sisters here as I shall make myself sick if I don't. If you happen to see

---

12 Blepharitis is an inflammation of the eyelids that can result from a skin infection.

him, you can tell him I was fearfully bucked with them but don't tell him what I did with them.

PS I forgot to say that whoever said I should have got a mention instead of Todd was talking through his hat and you can tell him so with my kind regards.

Saturday, 11th March, 1916

My dear Mother,

I expect I shall leave very shortly now but I don't know where for. The new doctor we have here told me this morning that he thought I would probably have to go to Nice but I have not given up hope yet. It is just possible I shall hear definitely tonight and I shall keep this letter open until he has been round again. I hope Ellie is getting on alright, also Esda and kid minor.[13]

Sunday (cont)

Many thanks for your and Dad's letters. I was glad to hear that Ellie, Esda and what I understand may be called Emilie (hereafter referred to as the three E's) are all getting on so well.

I have seen the doctor today and they are not going to send me away till next Thursday at least, so there is still hope. It is all very well for Doug to say he would simply jump at the chance of going to Nice but there is no chance of him having to do the jumping. You have no idea of how fed up you get of five weeks' casual acquaintances some of whom are the most impossible specimens. I had the displeasure of sitting beside one of the most impossible cads I have ever met at lunch yesterday.

It is a most beautiful day here so I think I shall shut up and go for a walk.

Wednesday 15th March 1916

My dear Jenny,

Just a line to let you know that I am off to Nice tomorrow. I don't know what my address will be but I will let you know when I find out.

It will probably be some time before you hear from me again as it takes two days to get there.

I don't know why they are sending me to Nice, as I am perfectly well. I think it was the change of doctor that did me in. Whatever it was, I have got to go, so the next man to tackle is the doctor at the other end about getting away, as I don't suppose it will do

---

13 Emilie Coats, born to Jack and Esda Coats on 6 March 1916.

me the slightest good. As a matter of fact I feel more rundown now than I did a week ago and put the reason down to absolute boredom.

The rotten thing is that this will probably do me in the eye for leave when I get back, whereas if I went straight back now I might get leave any time.

I hope the three E's and also H.G.Q.R and yourself are all flourishing.

Your bored, stiff and fed up brother.

PS Excuse the tone of this letter but it is mild compared to what I feel.

Saturday, 18/3/16

The Michelham
Convalescent Home for British Officers[14]
A.P.O., S.7. B. E. Force

To: Miss J W Coats, Perry Mount

My dear Jenny,

Just a line to let you know my address.

I arrived here today about 2.00 PM. We went from Boulogne to Paris on Thursday, arriving at Paris about 5.00 PM. We spent Friday in Paris at the Hotel d'Iéna and left here about eight last night.

I didn't think much of what I saw of Paris. It is just a big town. I went to the theatre on Thursday night and could hardly keep my eyes open I got so bored. I stayed in bed most of Friday forenoon and only went out for an hour or two in the afternoon.

I haven't had much time to judge this place but so far as I can see I shall be mighty glad to get away from it.

I must stop for dinner.

---

14 The Michelham, Nice: "On the Riviera, philanthropic ladies and their husbands appropriated large houses and hotels to serve both as military convalescent homes and nurses' rest homes. The first convalescent home was in Cimiez. Funded by Lord Michelham, it was opened at the end of 1914 with Lady Michelham initially occupying herself personally with the running of the hospital. However, it was soon brought under the control of the British authorities, as reported in *The Journal of Nursing*, January 1915: The climate of Cimiez is an ideal one for patients on the road to recovery ... It is a happy arrangement, therefore, whereby the Grand Hotel has been opened as a Convalescent Home for British Officers, under the control of the Order of St John of Jerusalem and the British Red Cross Society, and with the approval of the King it is to be known as 'Queen Mary's Convalescent Home for British Officers' ... commands glorious views of Nice and the sweep of the coast border the Bay of Angels, those gardens, where the Bougainvillea will bloom ... the delight of Queen Victoria during her sojourns at the neighbouring Pavillon Victoria.'"<http://www.rivierareporter.com/features/805-fany-the-women-who-drove-to-world-war-1> (Accessed 1 September 2015).

Monday, 20 March, 1916

The Michelham

My dear Jenny,

I am fed up with this place already and goodness knows how much longer I shall have to stay here. It is one of those beastly fashionable places which I loathe. I went down to watch the crowd on the esplanade yesterday afternoon. It was quite amusing for an hour or so, but I have no desire to do it again.

I am going to motor to the Italian frontier tomorrow. It ought to be quite a nice run but all these trips are more or less spoilt by the people one has got to trip with. I suppose I may as well see what I can while I am here, as I shall certainly never come back if I can avoid it.

The hotel we are in here is pretty full with all sorts of people from full blown Generals downwards.

I have nothing to say except grouse so I may as well shut up.

I hope Ellie, Esda, Emilie, Helen and everyone else are getting on all right.

24/3/16

The Michelham

My dear Mother,

I am quite well and all that sort of thing but I am fearfully fed up with this place. Judging from what the doctor said today, it looks as if they mean to keep me here till all the marks have left my face. I hope not however, as it will probably be weeks yet before they have quite gone and I have no desire to stay longer than I can help.

I hope Doug is getting on all right with his exams. I suppose he is in the thick of them just now. Thank goodness I got most of mine over before I came out here. I hope Ellie, Esda, Emilie, Helen and everyone else are getting on all right.

There is going to be some sort of commemoration service in the Russian Church here tomorrow which we are all requested to attend. If I go, I shall let you know later what it was like.

Saturday 1 April, 1916

The Michelham

My dear Dad,

Just a line to let you know I am leaving here tomorrow.

I shall be in Paris on Monday morning and will probably leave there the same day for the Base at Rouen. With any luck, I shall not be there more than two or three days before I rejoin.

I have been away now for more than eight weeks so I shall not be sorry to get back.

I shall let you know my address as soon as there is any chance of it being more or less permanent.

I am very glad I'm leaving here as I don't care for this sort of life.

6 April, 1916

No. 1 Territorial Base Depôt, Rouen

My dear Dad,

Just a line to let you know I have arrived at the base. I told the Adjutant at Nice that my Base was here but being a superior class of idiot he told me he knew better so he sent me to another base. When I arrived at the other base, they told me I should have come here and sent me on the next day. The result was I had about a 4 hour journey from Paris to the other place, stayed there one night and then had about a 16 hour journey here, instead of having about a 3 hour journey from Paris to here. The Government, of course, have to pay the extra. Another silly thing is that at the other base, I was only about 4 hours away from the Battalion but to get there I have to come here and may possibly leave here for the Battalion (about a 24 hour journey) tomorrow or the next day. The only good point about the whole show is that I got a day in Paris on the way back which I would not otherwise have got. I spent the forenoon in the Bois de Boulogne and in the afternoon went to see some of the decent shops. I tried to get into the Louvre but it was shut for the day.

Friday 14/4/16

My dear Dad,

Please excuse my being so long in writing. I have been kept pretty busy since I came here. As soon as I arrived, I was sent up with a draft of another Battalion. When I got back, I was made Censor one day and Orderly Officer the next, and they have parade every day from 8.15 till about 12.30 and again from 2.15 till about 4.30. I may say that, so far as I am concerned, the parades are an absolute farce. I am being lectured to by people who have joined since the war started and who have about half the practical experience that I have had myself. Fortunately, they have the sense to let me do as I please.

16/4/16

No. 1 Territorial Base Depôt, Rouen

My dear Doug,

Heartiest congrats on your passing your exams. I was looking casually through an old Herald yesterday and came across a list of people who had graduated in Medicine. I don't know why I read the list as I never thought your results would be out so soon but, as luck would have it, I did. You must be quite a brainy sort of specimen to get slap through without a stop.

As you will see from the address, I am still stuck here. It is a fearfully boring place and the lectures we have to attend are the absolute limit. The man who was lecturing on Field Sketching yesterday had the nerve to say that 6,000 yards was equal to six kilometres. When I heard that, I got up and went for a walk.

I am living in hopes of getting away from here any day but so far it has not come off.

I hope Ellie is still getting on all right, also the Kid and John. What is your private opinion of the Kid? You are the first of its Uncles to have a squint at it her.

21/4/16

No. 1 Territorial Base Depôt, Rouen

My dear Dad,
You will be pleased to hear I am at last getting away from here. It is 10 or 11 weeks since I left the Battalion so it is about time I got back. I am going up with a draft today and hope to stay there this time.

We have still got the same soft job, so there is no cause for worry.

WD: When I rejoined them on 22nd, the Battalion was still on Lines of Communication work with detachments out at various places guarding ammunition dumps, stations etc. I spent my time here trying to reorganise the Lewis Gun section which was rather uphill work as nine of my best men had been taken while I was away and promoted to sergeants in their Companies.

9 May, 1916

My dear Mother,
I got my kit back alright several days ago. I was very glad to see it again, now that I have settled down.

It has been pretty wet here for several days now so I have not been able to go out riding. I am rather sorry as there is not much else to do here.

I got a note last night from Math asking me to stay with him for a day or two. I think I shall manage it all right as I am doing nothing here. I have not seen him since the beginning of February.

15/5/16

My dear Dad,
I have just been staying for about four days with Math. When he got back from leave, he wrote asking me to pay him a visit, so I went to the CO and got permission to go.

He has a very nice billet in a hotel but I would very much rather have my job than his. We spent a good deal of the time I was with him riding, as he had to go round various places and I went with him.

The letter you enclosed was from Mr. Pyatt. He and Mrs. P. are always very decent about writing to me.

I expect to be more or less busy for a bit now but it is work I like, so I don't mind, in fact I am very glad.

I have got to go and see someone just now so I must hop off.

PS Young Raeburn knows about as much about our future arrangements as the rest of us but, as the rest of us know absolutely nothing, I would not worry about what he has been writing home.[15]

20/5/16

My dear Mother,
The weather here just now is absolutely perfect. The sun is shining all day but there is generally a bit of a breeze to keep it from being too hot.

While I remember, please don't worry sending out any more tobacco unless I ask for it. As long as I am within reach of what are called the Expeditionary Force Canteens, which are really stores run by the Government, I find I can get things much cheaper here than one can do at home. I can get two ounces of Chairman Tobacco out here for about 7½d, while I believe it costs about 1s/4d at home. I believe the French people hate these canteens as it rather knocks their show on the head but they are jolly good things.

I am playing cricket this afternoon. The game should be rather exciting as we play on the parade ground which is absolutely devoid of grass and is considerably rougher than a good main road in England. The pitch is made by brushing aside the loose stones.

We had a most extraordinary Chaplain preaching to us today. He is the sort of person who can't resist the temptation to raise a laugh, even in his sermon. He informed us that he was going to inflict himself on us again next Sunday, so I shall try and get off parade.

24/5/16

My dear Mother,
I have at last got my promotion [to Captain] and it has been dated back for about six months, so I should have quite a decent amount of money in the bank again. I am in

---

15 Lieutenant Alfred Anthony Douglas Raeburn, 1/9th HLI; killed in action at High Wood 15 July 1916.

great hopes of keeping my present job in spite of the promotion. I hope I do, as it is the best job there is.

Saturday, 27 May 1916

My dear Dad,

Many thanks for the various congratulations. As a matter of fact, I am a very much less important person as a Captain than I was as a senior subaltern. I am glad to say, I am being allowed to keep my job as Officer Commanding Lewis Guns, instead of being shoved onto a company as a second in command. Among other details, I remain a mounted officer and so can carry 20lbs more kit besides having a horse to amuse me.

The Battalion was photographed yesterday, and all mounted officers had to be mounted. I was rather afraid I would not appear in the photo as my beast is distinctly restive. As a matter of fact he stood like a lamb for the first time in his existence. I think he must have been impressed with my third 'wart' [Captain's pip].

I believe we are leaving here the day after tomorrow. I am quite sorry anyway but after all, this is not helping on the war very much.

WD: On the 29th we were sent up to join the 100th Brigade, 33rd Division at Annezin, near Béthune.[16] This Brigade we found was commanded by General Baird,[17] his staff being: Bde. Major, Captain O C Downes; Staff Captain, Captain Ward Brown; Intelligence Officer, Lieut. Edwards and Interpreter, Etchats. The G.O.C. Division was Major-General H J S Landon[18] with Col. Symonds as his G.S.O.1 and Col. Commings as his A.A.& Q.M.G [Assistant Adjutant and Quarter Master-General].

---

16 The 1/9th HLI, as part of an on-going leavening programme of attaching experienced Regular/Territorial battalions to inexperienced New Army divisions, was assigned to the recently arrived 33rd Division. This formation, organised in December 1914 as part of 'Fifth New Army', embarked for France in November 1915. Consisting of 19th, 98th and 100th infantry brigades by December 1915, the latter's component battalions as of May 1916 were as follows: 1st Queen's, 2nd Worcestershire Regiment, 1/9th HLI and 16th (Church Lads Brigade) K.R.R.C. See Lieutenant-Colonel Graham Seton Hutchison, *The Thirty-Third Division in France and Flanders 1915-1919* (London: Warlow & Sons, 1921) and Major A.F. Becke, *Order of Battle Divisions: Part 3B. New Army Divisions (30-41); & 63rd (RN) Division)* (London: HMSO, 1945).

17 Brigadier-General Alexander Walter Frederick Baird, CB, CMG, DSO (1876-1931). Educated Eton College, Oxford University and the RMC Sandhurst; commissioned Gordon Highlanders 1897; South Africa 1899-1901; ADC District Commander India (November 1902); DAAG Mohmand Field Force 1908; GSO2 Mauritius October 1908-May 1911; SC War Office May 1911-October 1913; CO 1st Battalion Gordon Highlanders 1 November 1914 to 8 April 1915; GSO2 BEF (July 1915-February 1916); GOC 100th Brigade from 19 February 1916.

18 Major-General Herman James Shelly Landon (1859-1948). GOC 33rd Division September 1915-September 1916.

Glasgow Highlanders' parade, St Omer, 26 May 1916. This photograph was taken from the top of a London bus requisitioned for troop transport. (WJJC collection)

Monday 29/5/16

My dear Jean and Jenny,
Many thanks for your congratulations. It seems very funny being a Captain after being a First Lieutenant for 5½ years. As a matter of fact, the person that seems most impressed at my new dignity is my horse. Ever since I was gazetted he has behaved in a most beautiful manner, whereas before I never knew what he was going to do next. I think I told someone in my last letter that we had a Battalion photo taken the other day, and as my horse was duly impressed, I appear in the photo instead of being last seen galloping over the horizon. We are back in the same old spot now, and expect to be in the trenches any day. My leave is due, however so unless I hear from you soon that you want me to wait till July, I may be home in a very short time.

30/5/16 Tuesday

My dear Mother,
It is rather funny Doug being sent to India. I am really rather glad he is not coming out here. India ought to suit him rather well as he used to have a sort of hankering after tropical work. We will be a pretty well scattered family by the time he arrives there.

The cricket match went off alright without anyone being seriously damaged. I skilfully managed to field in a place where I had no running to do and, as a matter of fact, I never had to stop a ball the whole game.

I am going to dine in the hotel with Math and Cowie tonight. I would very much rather eat decent British food but I couldn't very well refuse.

I spoke to my men some time ago about Mr McCallum's £5. I believe they are sending home for a football and some other things. I think the best way to run the show is for me to send one of my cheques to whoever has to be paid and then I can get repaid whenever it is convenient.

Friday, 2nd June, 1916

My dear Dad,

I think the best way to work my leave will be to take it when it is offered to me. I told them some time ago that I could not take it till I had got an understudy trained to do my job. They said alright and asked me who I thought should take the job. I told them who, and the next thing I knew they had sent him on leave, so I expect I shall have to wait till he comes back and give him a little instruction before I can get away.

We were inspected by our new General today. He seems quite a decent sort and I believe was quite pleased with the turnout.

We are still out of the trenches and I am flourishing.

WD: We were inspected by General Baird on the 2nd June and the C.O. told us afterwards that he had been very pleased with the turn out. As a matter of fact General Baird told me afterwards when I got to know him that he had never seen a smarter Battalion in his life not excepting his own.

Sunday 4th June, 1916

My dear Ellie,

Things are very much as usual here and the weather is splendid so we are alright. I was playing football yesterday and am a bit stiff today as a result.

I am getting into training just now to tackle my niece, my sparring partners being two kids in my billet aged about 2 and 3. Our conversation consists chiefly of "Pour quoi" and "Comme ça" but it seems to work all right. I shall try them on my niece when I get home.

I am sorry to say my horse met with a slight accident yesterday. He will be all right again in a few days but in the meantime I have to foot it to get anywhere. I have got quite keen on riding recently.

I dined with Math in the hotel last night. It is quite nice dining out occasionally but I do not like the French food.

I don't have anything more to say except as the song says "Everyone's happy here".
Cheer Oh,
Your loving brother
Walter J.J. Coats

WD: The Brigade was kept in reserve round Béthune until about the 9th as the authorities were rather expecting a German attack but as this did not come off we were moved up to Annequin. I went on leave from here on the 12th.

From Douglas Coats, on his way to India:

At sea, 6th June 1916

My dear Wat,

You have probably heard from home where I am off to and when I left etc., so I need not bore you with all that. As a matter of fact, I have really no news to give you but thought I would like to write you before I land anywhere – wherever that may be!

The sea here is just like glass, without so much as a ripple and so no one is sick. A good few men were sick on our first and second days out, but why, I cannot think. There certainly was a slight swell but nothing to speak of.

The heat so far is nothing to shout about, though of course it is already far warmer than it is at home. I believe it begins to get really oppressive in a few days from now. I don't know at all how I will stick it later on. I am sure I will look sweet in my helmet, etc.[19] I must get my photo taken and let you have one.

I expect you may be home on leave when this letter reaches you as I believe you are going to try for it when Ellie is up north. I hope you get it when you want it.

What I miss most at present, is the Home News. I have not been away long yet and yet I miss it horribly. Also I don't think there is any prospect of getting any letters for two or three months yet. I am thankful however that all was going on well when I left and not as when Jim left.

It is just lunch time, so I will stop.

Wishing you the very best of luck,

I am,

Your loving brother,

Douglas H. Coats

WD: When I returned from leave on 24th June, I found the Battalion just coming out of the trenches after a pretty lively time chiefly through mines.[20] The mining round this part of the line had always been particularly active and I remember being in one spell when five went off in three days. No one thought this particularly unusual.

On the night of 27th June, D Company under Captain Frame raided the German lines at Mad Point, Cuinchy, with great success. Great care had been taken in preparing this raid and exact copy to scale of the German lines being marked out in tape close to our

---

19 A reference to the Wolseley pattern tropical sun helmet.
20 1/9th HLI had been holding the line just south of Cuinchy.

Walter with Helen Rowett
at Perry Mount, June 1916.
(WJJC collection)

Walter relaxing
with a book in the
conservatory at Perry
Mount, June 1916.
(WJJC collection)

Walter and Nibs at Perry Mount, June 1916. He returned to the front shortly afterwards. (WJJC collection)

billets in Annequin where the raid was practised first in daylight and then at night. In addition, the wire was cut as much as possible beforehand by the gunners and kept open by machine gun fire all night; mines were driven under this wire, and also under a saphead where there was known to be a German machine gun. In order to keep the Germans from guessing the actual night that the raid was going to happen, machine guns were kept playing on the German parapet for several nights before and right up to the time when the raiding party crawled out and lined up ready to go. An artillery box barrage was also arranged, to isolate the part of the trench to be raided from the rest of the German line. R.E. parties armed with great boxes of explosives made especially for the purpose were told off to go over with the infantry; other parties were sent off some to clear the trenches, some to attend to dug-outs, some to look after prisoners and some to block the trenches at the furthest points reached. And arrangements were made to run over a telephone line so that we would know how things were going on, and a recall signal decided on.

On the night of the raid, the men crawled out in three parties as near the German wire as they dared and when the time came the mines were blown, the barrage came down and the men went in. The result was complete success. 42 prisoners, 1 machine gun and parts of a second were taken and various mine shafts and dug-outs were blown in. After staying in the German trenches for an hour and doing as much damage as they could the men were recalled and got back to our lines without trouble, the only casualties being a few men slightly wounded.[21]

The Battalion got a special wire of congratulation from the C. in C. [General Haig] for this raid and also many similar wires from other people including some from our old friends in the 2nd Division.

28/6/16

My dear Ellie,
The weather is again absolutely beastly but otherwise all is merry and bright. I am living in a dugout with Math and a brace of Warrens.[22]

When I arrived back from leave, I found a whole heap of letters waiting for me, one or two being from you. It is always rather an anti-climax getting back from leave and finding letters saying how pleased the writers are that you are going to get home soon etc.

Give my love and kind regards to my niece, and if a kiss through the post is sufficiently sanitary to meet with your and the nurse's approval you might give her half a dozen from me.

30/6/16

My dear Dad,
The chief news today is that we have been congratulated by all the generals above us right up to the Commander in Chief, himself. You would see our performance mentioned in the communique of the 29th.

I don't think there is much other news except that we are all flourishing.

Did you see in the papers that Sandy Reid has been wounded? I think he is fairly bad but not dangerous.[23]

I may be sending home some clothes soon, as my kit is too heavy. I intend, if possible, to send home my kilt and greatcoat, which should help to lighten my valise by the necessary amount.

---

21 See Weir, *Come on Highlanders!*, pp. 142-50.
22 Probably 2nd Lieutenant George Howden Warren (a Glasgow Academical, wounded near Ypres April 1918) and Captain Timothy Henry Hamilton Warren (lost an eye at High Wood 14-15 July 1916), both 1/9th HLI.
23 Captain Alexander Reid was wounded by shrapnel on 22 June 1915. He returned to service with the Glasgow Highlanders on 20 July 1918, as Major. See TNA WO 95/2431: 1/9th HLI War Diary.

The weather here is gradually improving but we have had it pretty filthy for some time. About two days ago we had over half an inch of rain, and just before that we had just under half an inch. It doesn't improve the trenches.

7/7/16

My dear Dad,

There is not much news here except that we are rather unsettled. There is going to be a presentation of medals here this afternoon and this Battalion is getting 10 Military Medals which is not bad going considering we only got back to work about two months ago. I expect we will get something more out of the raid as it seems to have been about the most successful there has ever been.

Two of the men who are getting medals are Buglers who went across to act as Orderlies and I believe it was fearfully funny to see them. Whenever there was a job to be done one would say "I'll go etc.", then the other would say "No, it's my turn", and then the first one would say "Let's toss for it". I don't know whether they actually did toss a coin or not but they were quite capable of it.[24]

Another funny thing that happened is that one German who was captured gave the man who bagged him an electric torch so that he could find his way back to our lines.[25]

Did I tell you that Math has gone to a school of instruction? I had a letter from him the other day and he says he thinks it is a five week course.

I have got into a most ripping Mess just now, as we have started a sort of junior headquarters Mess. It is rather a relief after messing with whatever Company happens to be handy. Our Mess is known as the Junior Carlton, so you can imagine how we do ourselves.

WD: On the 7th July, there was a presentation of medal ribbons in the Grande Place at Béthune. General Sir Charles Monro[26] who was then commanding the 1st Army presented them, the Guard of Honour for the occasion being supplied by half the Battalion under Major Menzies.

---

24 Bugler 1480/330103 Andrew Johnston and Bugler 1616/330161 George Kerr both received the Military Medal (MM) for their actions during the Mad Point raid (*Supp. to the London Gazette*, 10 August 1916, p. 7888). Instituted on 25 March 1916, the MM was awarded to those below commissioned rank for bravery on land.

25 German pocket torches/lamps of this type could be affixed to tunic button/buttons by means of component steel hanger or leather tabs.

26 GOC First Army February-August 1916.

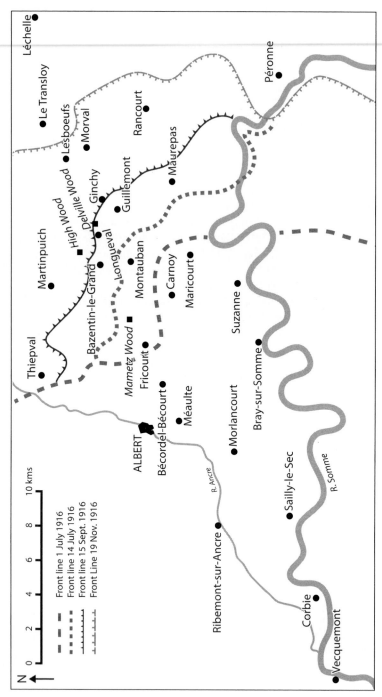

Map 3 Somme, 1916.

5

Battle of the Somme – High Wood

The country round here would be quite pretty if it wasn't for the war.

WD: We left Béthune on the 7th of July for billets close to Lillers and entrained there on the next morning. On the morning of the 9th, we detrained somewhere E. of Amiens and after marching for about 25 miles arrived that night at a village called Vecquemont, south of the Amiens-Albert Road. As it was a very hot day and the marching was for long stretches over pavée we were rather pleased to find that only one man had fallen out.

We stayed here on the 10th and on 11th the Battalion marched to billets at Morlancourt, south of Albert. Shortly before moving off were issued with the new Lewis Gun Handcart instead of Limbers. These looked very handy sort of things but we soon found out that they were by no means a blessing. In fact, the very mention of one to anyone with practical experience generally drew forth a flow of very unparliamentary language.

On the 12th we moved up to Bécordel-Bécourt which we reached after dark and as there were no houses standing spent the night in a field. We remained here on the 13th and I took the opportunity of taking a party of men up in the afternoon to the battlefield round Fricourt to look for Lewis Gun magazines, as were very short of them. That night we held a conference in an old gun pit which was used as Battalion H.Q., and we were told what was likely to happen. As Donald our Adjutant had been taken to Brigade H.Q. to act as assistant Brigade Major, McLelland was appointed acting adjutant in his place.

On the 14th July, we moved up towards the line.[1] We halted for several hours about mid-day beside some 8 in. Howitzers which were bombarding the Germans and in the

---

1 The great Anglo-French offensive opened in Picardy on 1 July 1916. Relatively fresh and fit for the next major phase of the "Big Push", 33rd Division had been dispatched south to Fourth Army (GOC General Sir Henry Rawlinson) in order to participate in the impending 'Battle of Bazentin Ridge' (14-17 July 1916). Launched in the early hours of 14 July, five assault divisions successfully stormed the German second line. Subsequent attempts to seize the enemy defences beyond, including Delville Wood and High Wood, continued with enormous losses from mid-July until the next great push (Battle of Flers-Courcelette 15-22 September 1916). See Captain Wilfred Miles, *Military Operations France and Belgium 1916 Vol. II* (London: Macmillan, 1938) and Andrew Rawson,

Crucifix Corner, situated
at the road junction just
north of Bazentin-le-Grand,
15 July 2016. (JC)

afternoon moved on into Mametz Valley which we reached at dusk. We stopped here for about quarter of an hour while the C.O. received final instructions from Brigade, and the Lewis guns, except for two which were kept in reserve with Battalion H.Q., were allotted out to Companies. Shortly after starting again, however, I found that, thanks to the new handcarts, they were not able to keep up with the rest of the Battalion and we had not gone more than half a mile before I found them all on my hands again and the rest of the Battalion disappearing into the dark. The only thing to do was to abandon the handcarts and carry the guns on by hand but, by the time we had got them unloaded, the Battalion had completely vanished and I had rather an anxious time before I found them again. When we eventually did find them, they were lying beside the road at Crucifix Corner in front of Bazentin-le-Grand waiting till the C.O. got back from reconnoitring the position we were to take up.

The Somme Campaign (Barnsley: Pen & Sword, 2014) for a recent day-by-day chronology of military operations from 1 July to 19 November 1916.

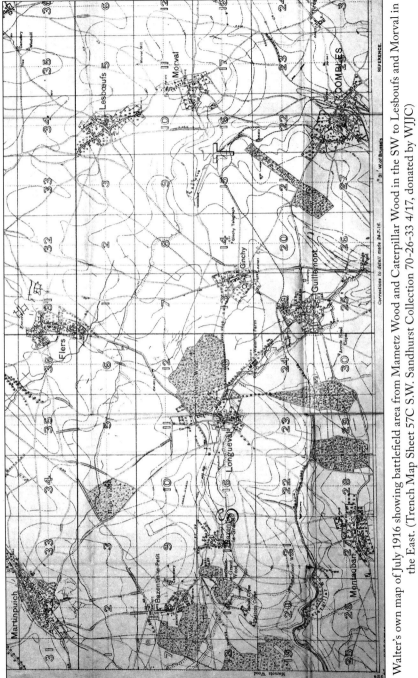

Walter's own map of July 1916 showing battlefield area from Mametz Wood and Caterpillar Wood in the SW to Lesboufs and Morval in the East. (Trench Map Sheet 57C S.W. Sandhurst Collection 70-26-33 4/17, donated by WJJC)

After waiting some time, the C.O. came back and took off A & B Companies to the N.W. corner of High Wood.[2] We had been told that the wood itself was in the hands of the British and the intention was that we were to dig in on the left front of it ready to advance next morning. The C.O. then came back and led up the other two Companies.

I followed after the last Company with all the guns. When we got up we found the two front Companies having a very bad time of it from the Germans in the wood on their right rear in spite of the fact that it was supposed to be held by the 7th Division.

The first thing to do was to get the guns again distributed with the Companies. This I found to be a most unpleasant job as the air was thick with bullets and men were being knocked out on every side. "A" Company had already lost practically all its officers and a large number of its men and, among other officers lying around, I found McLelland the Adjutant lying in a shell hole with his thigh broken.[3] As I was alone, however, I could do nothing for him and he told me someone had already gone for stretcher bearers, so I left him. When I got the guns distributed, I returned to Battalion H.Q. which was established in a slit in the ground about 200 yards from the wood and reported to the C.O. how thing were going. Everyone was in the dark as to the situation and things were very uncomfortable generally. Our left flank was completely in the air and our right flank was gradually being turned by the Germans who were working down through the wood. The C.O. accordingly sent "C" Company to extend through the wood and prolong our right flank.

Things remained in this state for the rest of the night and at dawn, to add to the discomfort, we were shelled out of Battalion H.Q. which we found was in front of our front line. We accordingly moved back to a position about 50 yards behind our left flank and took up our abode in a couple of shell holes behind a low ridge.

15/7/16

FSPC to J.J. Coats Braidwood House
I am quite well.
   W.J.J.C.

WD: Shortly after arriving here we got orders to attack at 9 a.m. This seemed a pretty hopeless job as there was no artillery support, no one on our right flank to get in touch with and the nearest troops on our left flank (the 1st Queen's) were about 600 yards off. We had however to make the attempt. We found, when we started, that we were

---

2   See Aiken, *Courage Past* and Weir, *Come on Highlanders!*, pp. 153-76 for accounts of 1/9th HLI's gruelling and costly ordeal; also Terry Norman, *The Hell They Called High Wood: The Somme 1916* (Barnsley: Pen & Sword, 2009).

3   Lieutenant Robert Carrick McLelland, 1/9th HLI died on 17 August 1916 from wounds received in action at High Wood 14/15 July 1916. See image on page 145.

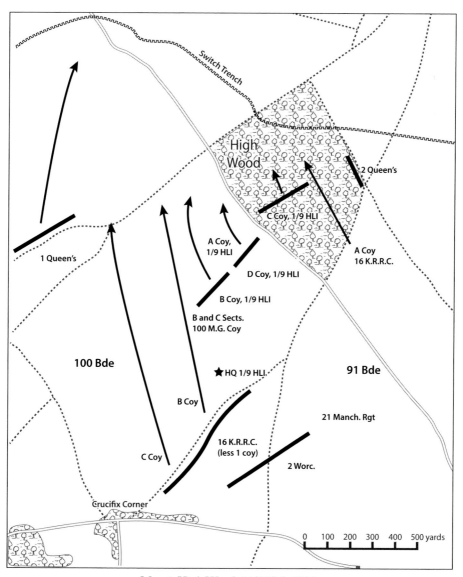

Switch Trench

High
Wood

2 Queen's

1 Queen's

C Coy, 1/9 HLI

A Coy,
1/9 HLI

A Coy
16 K.R.R.C.

D Coy, 1/9 HLI

B Coy, 1/9 HLI

B and C Sects.
100 M.G. Coy

★ HQ 1/9 HLI.

100 Bde

91 Bde

B Coy

21 Manch. Rgt

C Coy

16 K.R.R.C.
(less 1 coy)

2 Worc.

Crucifix Corner

0   100   200   300   400   500 yards

Map 4 High Wood, 14/15 July 1916.

up against several machine guns and the attack was simply wiped out before it had gone more than about 100 yards. We could see that the Queen's on our left had also been held up and the whole show came to a standstill. How anyone though we were going to reach Martinpuich which was our objective and hold it when we got there has always struck me as rather strange.

The rest of the day was occupied fighting in the wood, the Germans and ourselves attacking and counter-attacking all day long. Mixed up in the wood with our men were, I believe, some of the 7th Division and half a Battalion of the King's Royal Rifle Corps [K.R.R.C.], but the brunt of it fell on our men.

Meantime the hollow in the ground around Battalion H.Q. had been steadily filling up with wounded as our M.O., Captain Charles, seemed to be the only one available. Both he and the stretcher bearers were wonderful. In the course of the afternoon the Germans apparently spotted that something was going on round this place as they started to shell it. The place at the time was crowded with wounded and as there was no cover it soon became a perfect shambles. We now moved our H.Q. back to a point several hundred yards south of the S.W. corner of the wood where we sat down in the open. The C.O. now grew rather anxious in case the Germans should attack between us and the Queen's and sent me round to collect what men I could and get them put in position to stop them. Men were certainly pretty scarce by now but after searching round a bit I managed to collect 57 and distribute them in shell holes facing the right direction. At this time, this was the total number of men in the whole Battalion that we actually knew to be still alive.

We stayed here about two hours and as nothing happened the C.O. decided to move back to our old position, which we did. I was then sent off with the last two Lewis guns to try and cover the gap of 600 yards between us and the Queen's. I had hardly left with these two guns when a shell from a field gun landed at my feet and ricocheted away without bursting. If I had been a step further forward I would have had my leg taken off and if the shell had burst I would have been blown to pieces. As it was I had not even time to be frightened before I knew I was safe.

After I had posted the guns, I returned to H.Q. Things remained in this state until dark. Shortly after dark a message came in that there were a lot of wounded lying about in front. The stretcher bearers by this time were absolutely done, so the M.O. and I went out to see what we could do. Fortunately the night was fairly quiet so we were able to do some good until the M.O. got a piece of shall in his leg which necessitated his return to H.Q. His leg must have been pretty painful but he refused to go further back and after he had bandaged himself carried on doing what he could for the wounded that were brought to him.

It was getting towards dawn on 16th now and we were making up our minds for another day of it when some of the 19th Brigade suddenly turned up and told us much to our joy that they had come to take over from us. We just managed to get clear before dawn. Our casualties for this show amounted to 21 officers and about 400 or 500 men which was pretty heavy for 24 hours fighting.

Vicinity of Mametz Wood, July 1916. Walter slept in excavated funk holes similar to those depicted in the photograph. (IWM C.407, WJJC collection)

We now moved back to Mametz Valley and bivouacked beside Mametz Wood, just south of Bazentin. There were no shelters of any sort here but we found a lot of sort of graves about 2 or 3 feet deep which made excellent beds and kept the wind off.

16/7/16

My dear Mother,

We are sitting on the roadside just now so I have not got much time for a letter.

I am still flourishing though we have been having as cheery a time recently as we have had since I came out. I am not the least bit keen to have any more like it.

I am glad to say the weather here is pretty fine, though it gets very cold at night. I hope you are having better weather now there and that the kid is able to admire the scenery of Scotland. I shouldn't mind admiring it myself for a change, though the scenery around here is more or less similar.

I had a fearful time of it this morning trying to get a four days' beard off. The implements I started with were: a blunt safety razor, a cake of Pears soap, and some cold water from the water cart which is purified with chloride of lime and refuses to lather. I found that not only was the performance extremely painful but I was making no headway, so I held on a bit and borrowed a brush and another razor and managed more or less to expose the outline of my face to daylight again. My face stood the strain remarkably well.

I don't suppose however that my face is of much interest to you, so I will shut up as I have no more to talk about.

Your loving son,

Walter J.J. Coats

WD: On the night of the 16th, I stretched my waterproof sheet over my hole and went to sleep quite comfortably but woke up in the middle of the night to find I was lying in about half an inch of water as it was raining hard. As it was too cold to sleep in the open and I was too tired to look for shelter elsewhere I simply dug a slightly deeper hole at the foot of the one I was in to drain the water into and went to sleep again. I was already wet through and the mud was a minor consideration.

17/7/16

My dear Mother,

There is really no news since I wrote yesterday and this is only to let you know I am still flourishing.

We slept at the side of the road here last night in holes scooped out of the ground. I stretched my waterproof sheet over the hole as a sort of roof with a slope on towards the feet so that the rain would drain off into a deeper hole I had dug at my feet. Unfortunately, I did not dig this hole deep enough and when I woke up in the middle of the night I found I was lying from the waist down in about half an inch of water. The funny part of it was that I hardly even felt annoyed. I got up and drained the water off as well as I could and then lay down and slept soundly the rest of the night. My clothes are more or less dry now but you can imagine the mess they are in.

The men have been simply splendid and I am especially pleased with the machine gunners. It must be awful to belong to a poor Battalion.

Please thank Ellie for her very cheery letter which I got yesterday. It is fine getting letters from home after living in the mud. You can tell her I carry the picture of Billikins round with me for luck.

While I remember, please don't send anything in the way of parcels that can't be carried easily in my haversack. I am not even carrying shaving stuff just now, so chocolate is about the only thing I can take.

PS We have just heard that Car. Frame [Alexander Carmichael Frame] has got the DSO and 2 other of our officers the Military Cross.

WD: On the 18th we took over the defences of Mametz Wood and moved our H.Q. into it. We stayed here for three days and were fairly comfortable as there were some good German dug-outs in it. While here we had our first experience of German gas shells. They made a peculiar sort of fluttering noise in the air and landed in the ground with a sort of pop. We thought at first they were duds until our eyes began to nip and water.

German observation post, Mametz Wood, July 1916. (IWM C.142, WJJC collection)

Several drafts arrived to join us at this time but they were a very mixed lot, one draft in particular of 35 men consisting of men from, I think, seven different regiments. The whole system of sending up drafts at this time was in a state of chaos and if we complained the only reply we got was that drafts had to be sent to the Battalions that most needed them without consideration of what units they belonged to. The Brigade rather caught them out once, however, when they found that a draft of about 100 men of the Queen's had been sent to the Hants and a draft of about 100 of the Hants sent to the Queen's, the two Battalions at that time occupying opposite sides of the same road.[4]

---

4   Commenting on consequent casualties amongst assault divisions during this phase of the Somme fighting and the reinforcements dispatched to replace them, the British official historian observed: "In the infantry a great proportion of the best and most experienced officers and men had become casualties in the previous actions, and the loss of their enterprise and resource was severely felt. The desire of the War Office to cultivate an 'Army Spirit' at the expense of regimental 'esprit de corps' had resulted in the deliberate posting of reinforcement drafts to regiments other than their own. The result was unhappy, since the drafts, containing many wounded men who had recovered, felt a proper pride in their own regiments, and often deeply resented the transfer. A heavy price had to be paid for the consequent, if temporary, deterioration in the fighting efficiency of many battalions." See Miles, *Military Operations France and Belgium 1916 Vol. II*, p. 147.

19/7/16

My dear Dad,

There is really no news except that I am still flourishing. I am suffering from a bit of a cold in the head but that is about the least I could expect.

I got a dose of gas the other day from German gas shells and I felt pretty well washed out yesterday, but whether it was gas or lack of sleep I don't know. I got a splendid sleep last night and am perfectly all right again now.

At present, I have only got a two-day beard on just now but I don't know what it will be like by the time I get another shave. I have no intention of trying another shave like the last one, if it can possibly be avoided.

I am at present sitting in a most splendid, deep German dug-out and writing by the light of an electric searchlight which we souvenir-ed yesterday. It gives a splendid light and saves candles.

Please excuse writing as I am in rather an uncomfortable position.

WD: We left Mametz Wood on the 20th and moved up via Caterpillar Valley to a position behind High Wood. Just before starting, we saw a German aeroplane forced to land just in front of the wood which cheered us considerably.

It was pitch dark when we arrived in Caterpillar Valley and I was standing with the Battalion waiting for guides when there was a blinding flash and a bang just beside me. I thought I had just been missed by another shell but a few minutes later when I was able to see and hear again I found I was standing within a few feet of an 8in. Howitzer that had just gone off.

When we got our guides we climbed out of the Valley and down into trenches on the forward slope just east of Bazentin-le-Grand. After distributing guns along this trench, the guide eventually led us with the two last guns out of the trench, over the wire in front, over a road and into another very shallow trench about 20 yards in front of the road. This was a most uncomfortable spot as shells were falling round it at the rate of about three per minute, however there was nothing for it but to put the men in and tell them to dig, though I don't think they needed much telling. As it was not my job to stay with these guns, I cleared off as soon as I saw them decently in and returned to H.Q. I found them all asleep in a sort of sandbag shack on top of the hill and as there was no room inside had to make the best of it in the open. Fortunately, the weather was fine and I soon got to sleep.

Next day, 21st July, in visiting the guns I found that the two guns that had been put in last were just in front of Crucifix Corner where we had stopped a few days before. I had not recognised the place in the dark the night before.

We spent the day in this position and from Battalion H.Q. got a beautiful view of the German shells landing in Caterpillar Valley and Wood which were shelled all day.

21/7/16

To Miss J Coats, Braidwood House

My dear Jean,
I saw a most splendid fight in the air yesterday, in which our man drove the German down. It was most exciting as it took place only about 500 feet above us. I thought at one time the German was going to land on top of us.

The weather here just now is absolutely perfect for lying about, though too hot to do much work. I am longing for a bath and some clean clothes but see no prospect of either. Water even for drinking has to be carried a long way and my servant has quite enough to do without carrying water for washing.

The Germans must be having a pretty thin time of it just now as our ammunition supply seems to be absolutely unlimited. It is simply splendid to sit and listen to one of our full dress bombardments. I wish some of the munition workers could come out and see the show. It is a fine sight, especially at night.

There are any number of fine souvenirs to be picked up around here if one could only carry them but that is absolutely impossible. I picked up a small book of German marching songs for Jenny the other day and then it struck me that goodness knows what dirty beast of a German had owned it so I threw it away again. Metal souvenirs are more or less clean but the paper souvenirs are more likely to be dirty.

The country round here would be quite pretty if it wasn't for the war. As it is, it is ugly and likely to be so for some time to come. I should think it will be years and years before the country is anything like normal again.

WD: We were relieved on the night of 22nd, but as it always took longer to get out the guns, I found when I got them together that the Battalion had gone. I sent the men down to the Valley to get the guns packed on the handcarts and went to report to the new Battalion H.Q. that I had handed over. While I was here I saw what looked like a display of fireworks in the valley below but did not think much about it until I got down to the men and found that five or six of them had just been removed on stretchers including my servant, Crews.[5] I found that a German shell had apparently landed the day before in a dump of Mills grenades close to the handcarts and smothered them with the grenades many of which had had the safety pins broken and only required a slight touch to send them off. When the men got down to the carts they had started to clear away the grenades and they had started going off all round the place. This accounted for the firework display I had seen and I considered I was lucky to have so few casualties.

After examining the carts to see if there was any way of getting them clear I decided it would be too dangerous to try and that they would have to be left. The trouble now was that we had an 8 or 9 mile march ahead of us and had very few men left to carry the

---

5   Pte 2151/330435 William Crews.

guns and equipment. There was no use sitting and looking at it however so we tipped all the ammunition out of the magazines, loaded up as best we could and set off. It was now broad daylight.

Progress was not very fast and it had taken us about an hour to do the first mile when we saw a couple of lorries coming up behind us which we promptly stopped and asked for a lift. We found the lorries already full up almost to the top cover but the drivers were good fellows and said that if we could squash in they were passing the place our Battalion was to halt and would willingly take us there. This was an additional stroke of luck because I had no map and only a very vague idea of the road.

After one or two efforts we all got squashed into the lorries somehow and after about an hour's journey were dumped at the side of the road close to our destination which we reached shortly afterwards and found everyone asleep except the sentry. They were bivouacked in a field between Bécordel-Bécourt and Méaulte.

After searching round a bit we managed to find a Lewis gun sergeant who had been left with the transport to look after our supplies etc. He showed the men where to go and when I had got them off my hands I skirmished around until I found my valise which I unrolled and got into without worrying to do more than take my boots off.

I had a splendid sleep and when I awoke found a man looking at me who came over as soon as he saw I was awake and said he understood my servant had been knocked out and asked if I would take him on as his officer had also been knocked out. I knew he was a good servant so I took him at once. He was a sort of Cockney-Scot and rejoiced

Lewis Gun handcarts, August 1916. (IWM D.144, WJJC collection)

in the name of Fosh but he did for me very well and I kept him until he went home for munitions in February 1917.[6]

We stayed at Méaulte for some time but did not get very much rest as we were under orders to be ready to move on short notice. Physically of course we got a good rest but mentally I think most of us had the "just before the battle feeling" which is not pleasant. The men built bivouacs for themselves out of some old munition boxes and their waterproof sheets and the officers had a couple of tents to live in. The Mess consisted of a trench about 18 inches deep cut round in the form of a square. We sat with our feet in the trench and used the middle piece as a table. At first this was all we had but latterly we managed to get some wood and put a roof over it and put some canvas round on the windward side.

25/7/16

My dear Dad,

Please excuse my not having written for some time but I have been fearfully busy recently and have had no time.

I hope Jack's demonstration came off alright the other day. You can tell him I know of one Machine Gun Officer who is not given to flashing lamps, or whatever his one did, when there is any chance of his being potted for his trouble. I didn't know Jack had such a vivid imagination. I am sure he hadn't before the kid arrived.

Talking of kids, please thank Jenny for her letters and the photo of the other 'It'. The photo is not very big but as far as I can see it appears to be quite a decent wee specimen and not the least like either of its parents, for which, I hope, it is duly thankful.

WD: We stayed about a fortnight here, the forenoons being spent getting the new men into shape and training new Lewis gunners, and the afternoons either going for a short ride (we were not allowed away for more than an hour at a time) or simply lying about trying to keep cool. We were very short of trained gunners by now but fortunately I had two most excellent sergeants called Diamond and Hannah who were splendid instructors.[7] Diamond in particular was a perfect marvel. He was under age when we came out but managed to get across and before the war was over was a Company Sergeant Major with the M.M. and D.C.M. and should also have had the V.C. for his work during the retreat in April 1918.

In addition to being short of men, we were also very short of guns as a good many had been knocked out and others lost through their teams all being killed or wounded. It was some time before we could get new guns and when they did arrived they were so badly made that most of them would not fire. Fortunately we had an excellent armourer

---

6   Pte 2790/330708 Jack Fosh from Leytonstone.
7   CSM 1834/330271 James Diamond and Sergeant 1905/3303305 Arthur Brown Hannah.

sergeant attached to the Battalion and I used to spend most of the evenings with him and the two Lewis gun sergeants tinkering at the new guns. In some cases we had to file off more than an eighth of an inch before they would work but before we moved we had as many of them in working order as we had men to work. The amusing part of it was that an order came round from G.H.Q. at this time that on no account were Lewis guns to be filed. Needless to say this order was promptly put in the waste paper basket.

While we were here, the absence of German aeroplanes was very noticeable and during the fortnight we only saw three very high up and far behind the German lines. This was very fortunate as the country round about was simply thick with troops, horses, guns, lorries and every sort of transport all of which was within easy reach of the German guns if they had only known it.

30/7/16

Sunday

My dear Dad,
As usual, I have absolutely no news except that I am very flourishing.

The weather here is absolutely boiling, so we do nothing in the afternoon but slope about in our shirt sleeves and, if one feels sufficiently energetic, bathe in the river.

You will be pleased to hear we have just been given another 14 Military Medals.

We are going to have Church Parade in about half an hour. It is the first one I have been able to get to since I was on leave last. The unfortunate thing is that I have very little respect for our new Chaplain.

I shall keep this open till the mail arrives in case there is anything to answer.

Later: Many thanks for your and Mother's letters with copies of Doug's which I have just got.

I have just heard that one of my men who has been missing has rolled up in hospital in Glasgow.[8] News like that fairly bucks one up.

I must shut up now as the heat is absolutely awful.

31/7/16

POST CARD to J.J. Coats, Braidwood

Still flourishing. The weather very hot. Thanks for the chocolate and letters.
W.J.J.C.

---

8   Pte 3962 G Young.

2/8/16

My dear Mother,

Many thanks for your various letters which I have been receiving. We are having it most fearfully hot here just now from about breakfast time to tea time. We feed out in the open here and at lunchtime we have to be careful when we pick up our knives and forks as they are often too hot to hold. Fortunately, there is a small stream near us where we can bathe. We have parades up until about midday and after that we have the day to ourselves. I must say it rather upsets the theory that heavy bombardments cause rain. I don't suppose there ever were heavier bombardments than now and there is not a drop of rain.

Talking of theories, I have just knocked one on the head today that the Lewis Gun will fire without an ejector. It won't. This will not interest you but it may interest Jack, though I don't know if he has anything to do with guns. Has he got the job of Instructor in Chief that he thought he might get?

Please excuse the smudges on the paper as it is impossible to keep dry here i.e. externally. Internally, it is the easiest thing in the world.

I had a letter from Mathew Anderson today. He expects to be back with us in a day or two. I shall be glad to see him.

WD: We moved into the trenches again on the 7th of August and took over in High Wood from the 51st Division which at that time was a very second rate one though it afterwards became one of the finest we had.[9] Their idea of working a relief was to take us all up into the open on the south west side of the wood and then take us in from there by companies. As we were in full view of the Germans here, we were lucky not to be badly shelled.

When we got into the wood we found the trenches were very shallow and badly made and very uncomfortable from the number of dead lying about. Fortunately, the undergrowth was very thick so we were not much troubled by snipers. Battalion H.Q. was in a small dug-out in the side of a trench running down the south west edge of the wood.

To add to the general discomfort, our artillery was shooting very short and I remember one occasion when we got a very good example of this. It was arranged that the artillery would bombard the German lines in front of us and as they were rather close all our men were taken back to the second line to avoid the risk of shorts. When the bombardment started, all our men in the second line had to lie flat on the bottom of their trenches to avoid being hit in the back by our shrapnel. In the middle of it one of the men remembered he had left something up in front which he particularly wanted so he went up to get it. When he got there he found it so much safer than the second line that he decided

---

9   The 51st Division was much criticized for perceived poor battlefield performance during this time.

to remain instead of coming back. He told us afterwards that no shells landed anywhere near him or the German line.

Another great discomfort about this position was the fact that there were only two communication trenches leading up to it, viz High Alley and Thistle Walk [see Map 5]. As both of these could be clearly seen by the Germans who were on the higher ground they were kept under a constant and very accurate shell fire and it was very difficult to get up food and ammunition.

9/8/16

FSPC to J.J. Coats Braidwood House
I am quite well. I received your letters.
    W.J.J.C.

WD: After a few days in the wood we were relieved by the 2nd Argyll & Sutherland Highlanders and moved back, two companies being put into trenches along the side of the roads running north and east from Crucifix Corner and two companies and Battalion H.Q. in trenches running along the forward slope of the hill east of Bazentin-le-Grand. We now knew that we were to make another effort to take the wood and that the 2nd Argyll & Sutherland Highlanders were getting things ready for us.

One of the schemes this time was an arrangement for throwing drums of paraffin into the German trenches. These drums before being loaded into the machines that were to fire them were wound round with cloth dipped in petrol which was supposed to catch fire when the drums were fired towards the Germans. The idea was that on landing the drums would burst, the paraffin would catch fire and the Germans would be burnt out. This idea was dropped without being used which was probably fortunate.

When things were ready we took over the wood again all wound up and ready to go but after waiting in suspense for a few days the attack was put off. We were relieved on the 13th and taken back close to our old bivouacs near Méaulte. Math rejoined us here and was given command of a Company as he was now pretty senior. He had been away on a course since about the first week in July.

13/8/16

My dear Dad,
Excuse my not writing for some time as I had no envelopes till I got the parcel today.

Many thanks for the two parcels which I got and which were exactly what I wanted, especially as we have been living rather poorly for a week past. I also got a parcel consisting of a tinned ham from Gibson the Grocer in Edinburgh. I haven't the foggiest idea who it came from as there was no card inside.

You may be interested to hear we have two more Military Crosses and a DCM in the Battalion. McCosh has got a MC and had a pretty thin time in the getting of it.

The name of the man who rolled up in hospital in Glasgow is Pte 3962 G Young. When he wrote me, he said he thought his spine was affected. He is in Merryflatts Hospital.

The weather is still pretty hot here and the worst of it is that it gets so cold at night one has to carry about warm clothes.

I wonder if Jim had anything to do in the show against the Turks. I rather hope that he had, as he must be longing to get a biff at them.

I am afraid I must switch off now as I have a good deal of writing to do and am a wee bit tired.

[Cont.] 14/8/16

I could not get my letter away yesterday so I am going to open it and shove this in just to let you know I am still flourishing and more or less enjoying life, especially the sleeping part of it.

We are having it very wet here today but it is still hot. I went for a ride with Math this afternoon on my animal. I am getting to like the beast (not Math) better every day. We had a most splendid gallop. I was most fearfully bucked when it jumped a ditch about 2 inches wide and I didn't fall off.

Talking of falling off, an inlay fell off one of my teeth the other day, I expect from shell shock. I suppose it is now strolling about in my guts and chumming up with various bits of almost equally indigestible dog biscuit.

Your ever cheerful son.

WD: We moved into the line again to the left of Delville Wood on the 19th going up via Mametz and Montauban to Green Dump where we picked up extra ammunition etc. before going in.

Late in the afternoon of the 21st we got orders to attack along with two companies of the Worcesters and take the trench in front.[10] Unfortunately, very short notice was given with the result that, thanks to our C.O. being an especially quick man, our orders were got out and the men were ready to go over in time whereas, the C.O. of the Worcesters being an exceptionally useless man, the Worcesters did not get their orders in time to act. Our men accordingly went over unsupported, without knowing that the Worcesters were not ready, and got very badly cut up the two Companies that went over losing six officers including both Company Commanders of whom Mathew Anderson was one.

On 21st August a night attack was ordered on very short notice. The brigade order reached the battalion at 9 p.m. – the attack to be launched at midnight.

---

10 The 1/9th HLI's objective, 'Orchard Trench', was situated between High Wood and Delville Wood. See Rawson, *The Somme Campaign*, p. 149 and Weir, *Come on Highlanders!*, pp. 179–84.

The Worcesters and the Highlanders were to take the enemy front line from the Delville Wood-Flers Road on the right to Wood Lane on the left [Orchard Trench] ... B Company under Captain Mathew Anderson was given the right next the Worcesters. D Company under 2nd Lieutenant Duckett the left. ....Shortly before midnight they were ready. Whether it was the Worcesters that got the order later than we did, or they had greater difficulties to contend with, is not clear, but they were not ready at zero hour, and just before midnight Capt Anderson received a message informing him that they would not attack. He immediately sent a message to Lieut. Duckett ordering him to stand fast. It was now midnight.

The order was too late. D Company was advancing. Anderson had to make a quick decision. He probably knew that the attack was now a forlorn hope. Should he stand fast with his company and cut the loss? A lot could be argued in favour of this, but such a decision was one that all who knew Mathew Anderson knew him incapable of taking. The other company had started, he must back it up. The enemy was now thoroughly awake, and Anderson led his company forward through a storm of shot. He advanced erect – not stooping as one instinctively does – and was last seen by the light of flares and bursting shells at the enemy's wire, where he was killed. His company did its best to follow him but the leading line was simply withered away.[11]

As all the officers of Math's Company were knocked out, I was sent up to collect his Company and take it out of the action. I knew the way up as far as the support trench and was told that after going along it for a bit I would find a communication trench leading off to the front line. I accordingly set off and, after wandering about a bit, I found what I took to be the entrance to the communication trench. I had been told it only went out a short distance so I was not surprised when I came to the end of it and had to climb out into the open. In accordance with instructions, I now cut straight ahead for about 50 yards till I came to a trench which I presumed was our font line so I climbed into it. I was rather surprised to find no one in it but decided to have a look at it before going further. The question was which way to go first? As it did not seem to matter much and I thought I was more likely to meet some of our own men if I tried the right, I turned off that way. I had not gone more than 10 yards however before I was challenged by some of our men from the other side of a sandbag barricade across the trench. When I told them who I was they pulled me over and I then discovered that I was in our front line all right but further to the left than I had expected. The extreme left end of this trench was held by the Germans and I had landed in the bit of empty trench between the two blocks. It was lucky I had not turned to the left or I would have walked into the Germans. The officer at our block told me afterwards that his men thought I was a German and nearly shot

---

11 Colonel A.K. Reid, 'Shoulder to Shoulder'.

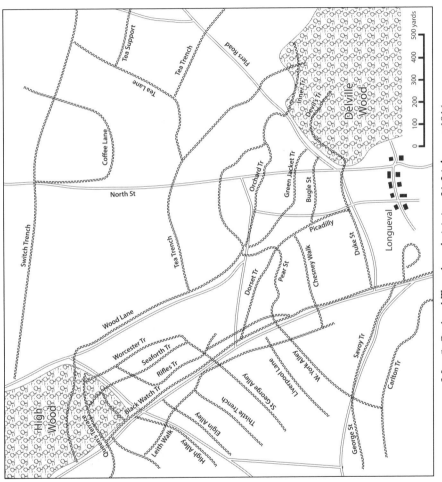

Map 5 Orchard Trench and vicinity, 21-24 August 1916.

me but decided to challenge first. He also told me the Germans had been sniping down the trench all night and that I was lucky not to have been hit by them.

I found that the senior sergeant of Math's company had already collected the men, so I told him where to lead them to and, after a look round to see if there were any stray ones, I followed on and got the Company stowed away in a trench behind. I then went back to Battalion H.Q. which was in Carlton Trench.

22/8/16

FSPC to J.J. Coats Braidwood House

I am quite well.
  W.J.J.C.

WD: We were relieved on the night of the 23rd and moved back to Montauban-de-Picardie. The men were put into some old trenches here and Battalion H.Q. was put in an old German dug-out.

23/8/16

My dear Dad,
Please excuse my not writing you for some time as we have been fairly busy. As a matter of fact, things are still busy but I happen to have nothing to do pro tem except sit still.

You will be sorry to hear that Mathew Anderson was killed two days ago.[12] He got right up to the edge of the German trench and was killed, I believe, when he was practically stepping into it. I expect his people will have heard about it by now, but in case not please don't say anything about it till you are sure they know. I am going to write them and shall try and get the letter away with this one.

I am feeling rather seedy today as the result, I think, of eating green apples. Fortunately, as I said, I have nothing to do of much importance and I am sure I will be alright tomorrow.

Many thanks for the parcel of chocolate which I got today.

I think I shall shut up now as I must write Mr Anderson.

WD: We hoped to be left in peace for a few days here but early next morning (24th) we heard that the Brigade was to attack again that night and that we were to move up that afternoon.

---

12 Mathew Anderson is buried at Delville Wood Cemetery.

As the attack was to be carried out by three battalions this time, the question then arose of where our men, who were to be in support, were to be stowed away and I was accordingly sent off at once to try and find some spare trenches to put them in. Thanks to having supped not wisely but too well the night before I was feeling very seedy and I found it rather an effort scouting round in the sun for hours on end looking for unoccupied trenches. When I did find room, I then had to go back and pick up guides from the companies and show them where to go. As a result I was pretty well done up by the time I got back to Battalion H.Q. which had now arrived in the trench. I was hoping for a stand easy here but had no sooner reported myself than I found I had been detailed to act as liaison officer with Brigade H.Q. and had to push off there at once. Fortunately, when I got there I found I would not be wanted till the attack began so I was able to sit down for a bit.

The objective of the attack this time was Tea Trench to the left of Delville Wood and was in conjunction with an attack through the wood by troops on our right.[13] The attack was quite successful this time but shortly after the objectives were taken the attacking battalions all reported very heavy losses and asked for support, and my Battalion was accordingly sent up to take over the captured trenches. When they got up they found that there were already far more men in the line than were required but as their orders were to take over they had to do so and the other battalions except the 16th K.R.R.C., who had entirely vanished, went back to support.

When things got straightened out a bit, it was found that the K.R.R.C. had gone six or seven hundred yards past their objective and were well out in the blue. This caused a lot of trouble before we were able to get in touch with them.

25/8/16

I am sorry I could not get this away on the 23rd and I was too busy yesterday. I am still flourishing, but as we have had another rather super strenuous time I am rather tired and I shall not write much.

Please thank Mother for the sweets and mag, and various people for various letters. Cheer Oh.

Your loving son.

WD: After spending another night and day in this position the Brigade was relieved on the 26th and moved back to Fricourt Wood and I believe that all our work was undone a few days later when the Germans counter-attacked and recaptured all we had taken.

As Brigade H.Q. always had to wait until the relief was reported complete, we were always very late in getting away and I remember that night in particular trying to get down the communication trenches which were a perfect tangle of telephone

---

13 See Rawson, *The Somme Campaign*, pp. 150-51 and Weir, *Come on Highlanders!*, pp. 182-84.

wires stretched across heights so that one would be caught round the ankle one step and across the eyes the next. We struggled through this for more than an hour before the C.O. got tired of it and we climbed out of the trench and went back over the top.

We stayed the night in some old dug-outs and trenches close to Montauban and next afternoon moved into Fricourt Wood where we spent another night.

CONFIDENTIAL   Headquarters,
                                                  100th Infantry Brigade
                                                    27th August, 1916

33rd Division

1. Since the completion of the relief of the Brigade under my command and more especially in view of the very serious representations made to me by the only Battalion Commander now left, I have carefully considered the present fighting value of my Battalions and feel it is my duty to forward for the information of the Major General Commanding, the conclusions at which I have arrived and the grounds on which they are based.

2. The Brigade has been taking part in the present operations since the evening of July 14th up till early morning 26th instant, a period of 43 days, which have been passed as follows: [Front Line – 21 days; Divisional Reserve – 6 days; Out of the Line (Corps Reserve) – 16 days]. It has fought two Brigade engagements (July 15th and August 24th) as well as the unsuccessful enterprise of the night of August 21st/22nd, and has been constantly employed in the construction of offensive or defensive works under conditions entailing the severest strain on the endurance of all ranks.

3. It has also incurred heavy casualties during this period. They include: 3 Commanding Officers, 1 Second in Command, 24 Company Commanders, 1 Adjutant and many senior Non-commissioned Officers. [655 1st Queen's, 568 2nd Worcesters, 783 16th KRRC, 762 9th HLI, 73 Brigade MG Coy and 7 Brigade Trench Mortar Battery – in total 123 officers and 2725 other ranks]

4. These casualties, the bulk of which were incurred on July 15th have never been adequately, or even nearly so, made good... The present serious deficiency of capable Company Commanders and N.C.O.s coupled with the continual bombardment by the enemy's heavy artillery, to which troops in the line are now increasingly exposed with little or no cover, have undoubtedly resulted in a general loss in "morale" to which it would be foolish to blind one's eyes.

5.   Under these circumstances I feel it my duty to report that there is now not a single unit in the Brigade that is not in urgent need of an immediate period of rest and reorganisation prior to taking any further part in active operations

6.   I am very reluctant to have to forward this report but, in the interests of the fighting efficiency of the Brigade and in justice to the units of which it is composed, (two of whom have been in the Field since the opening of the campaign and had already done several consecutive months in the trenches prior to coming down here), I feel bound to make these representations before they are called upon for further effort, which in their present state I know them to be unfit to make in a manner consistent with their previous distinguished records.

> AWF Baird, Brigadier General
> Commanding 100th Infantry Brigade[14]

29/8/16

My dear Jean,

It is ages since I wrote you but I expect you have seen all my letters.

We are in the middle of a thunder storm just now but as I am under cover and there is no immediate prospect of my having to go out, I am quite happy.

You will be interested to hear that at the present moment (barring an attached man) I am second in command of the Battalion, as the Major has gone sick.

The storm is now over and the pipe band is playing outside so everything is merry and bright once more.

WD: Next day, 30th August, much to our joy we started to march back right out of the area. As we had been in it since the middle of July during which time we had lost over 800 men and had never been out of range of the guns we found it a great relief when we at last got out of the sound of the guns.

31/8/16

POST CARD to J.J. Coats, Braidwood

Am still flourishing. Thanks for letters. Had a bed to sleep in last night.
W.J.J.C.

---

14 See TNA WO 95/2428-3: 100th Brigade War Diary.

WD: We marched steadily north for seven days after this, being told each afternoon when we got to our destination that we would not be moving next day only to receive orders about 2 a.m. next morning that we were to move about 7 or 8am.[15]

3/9/16 Sunday [Prouville]

My dear Dad,
This is Sunday and the first really peaceful day we have had for a long time. We can hardly hear the guns at all. I have got an almost perfect billet and slept between sheets last night for the first time in about six weeks. I had a warm bath last night before dinner. It is the first warm one I have had since my last leave, so I fairly enjoyed it. We have got a fine day so things are almost perfect. One good thing about being shelled, is that one appreciates absolute quiet more than ever.

There is some chance of our getting a few days leave to Paris someday soon. I don't know that I am particularly keen on it myself but I suppose if I get the offer I shall probably take it. It depends who I get the chance of going with.

WD: On 6th September, after marching for 7 days we at last reached a small village several miles behind the Vimy Ridge front [Maiziéres, S.E. of St-Pol-sur-Ternoise] where we were told definitely we would be staying for a fortnight at least before moving into the line in front.

7/9/16

My dear Jint,
This is just a line to let you know that I am still going strong. Everything goes on here as usual except that we have got a new Mess cook who is rather an acquisition. One sits down to dinner now wondering what one is going to get instead of knowing the menu for weeks before.

I am having a very easy time of it just now as we are moving so much. It is all right in its way but I would rather get settled down and get some work done.

WD: In the middle of the night along came an order that we were to move, I think it was at about 5 am on the morning of 8th, and embus at a point on the main road some miles away. We accordingly moved off as ordered, climbed into the waiting buses and

---

15 "At Querrieu [the] battalion marched past Commander of 4th Army, Lt General [sic] Rawlinson who, when he heard what the Battalion's casualties had been, said 'what have they been since you came to the Somme, not since the beginning of the War'." See 31 August 1916 entry in TNA WO 95/2431: 1/9th HLI War Diary.

that afternoon found ourselves back in the Somme area not very far from where we had started. We stayed in a village here for the night and next day moved off via Souastre for the trenches at Foncquevillers where we took over support trenches, Battalion H.Q. being in a cellar in the village.

10/9/16

My dear Dad,

The chief item of news today, which I expect will please you, is that McCosh and I are being sent off tomorrow for a week's holiday. We are going somewhere near the coast. I am not particularly keen to go as I think a lot of the men deserve to get away before me, but so many officers who have been through the battle here have been detailed to go and I have been chosen. We ought to have quite a good time and at any rate we will get away from all parades and things of that sort.

The only other news is that I am at present acting as Adjutant and 2nd in Command of the Battalion. It is quite an interesting job but is of course only temporary.

I don't know what my address will be when on holiday but if you send letters here as usual I expect they will reach me.

I'll let you know how I get on.

WD: The Battalion moved into the front line trenches opposite Gommecourt on the following night 11/12th but McCosh, the M.O. and I were sent off to the Army Rest Camp near Boulogne instead of getting leave as all leave for the Army was stopped.

14/9/16

BRITISH OFFICERS' CLUB
Boulogne

My dear Mother,

Just a line to let you know I am flourishing. Our rest camp is about an hour and a half's journey from here but as there is absolutely nothing to do there we always come in here after breakfast and spend the day here. This is quite a good place and we can at any rate get a decent meal and a hot bath. We are spending a good part of our rest in the bath to make up for lost time.

We are having what I believe they call battle leave just now. It sounds very swanky but I would much sooner have ordinary leave, which apparently other people are getting as we see them going for the boat every morning.

WD: When we arrived at the Camp we found it was situated on top of a hill 5 or 6 miles outside of Boulogne. As it was just being started everything was very uncomfortable. There was no furniture in any of the tents, the messing was hopeless e.g. the first night at dinner one of the officers covered his helping of fish plus bones with his slice of lemon. There were no books or papers, no form of amusement and no fires and as the weather was getting cold we were pretty miserable. Fortunately they allowed us out of camp so after breakfast every morning we cleared off to Boulogne where we lunched, tea-ed and dined returning to camp about 11 p.m. Even in Boulogne there was nothing to do, so we used to spend most of the morning having a bath in the Officers Club which was a great treat. The annoying thing was that while we were here leave opened again and we saw officers going off who were below us on the leave list.

It was while we were here that tanks were first tried and I remember reading great accounts of them in the Continental "Daily Mail". Knowing the amount of lies the papers always told we did not of course believe half we read but we were very much delighted to see that thanks to their help High Wood had at last been taken.

Fortunately our rest here was cut short and we left on the 17th.

17/9/16

My dear Dad,
We are leaving here two days earlier than we expected. Personally, I don't care much as I am about fed up with it but I am sorry for the men as I think they were enjoying themselves. We leave here tonight and expect to go back to the Battalion some time tomorrow.

The chief piece of news I have for you just now is that there is every chance of my getting home on leave within the next two or three weeks. It does not seem very long since I was home last but I think I am keener to get home now but I have been for a long time.

[Cont.] 18th
Back with the Bn. and going strong.
    W.J.J.C.

WD: We arrived at Mondicourt [N. of Souastre] on the 18th in a regular thunderstorm and I found a cyclist waiting with instructions for me to report at once as a member of a Court Martial assembling at Humbercamps in an hour's time.[16] I had no idea where the place was but after some inquiry found the direction it lay in and pushed off hoping that I would be too late. My luck was out however and I arrived in time and spent most of

---

16 Courts Martial of 2nd Lieutenant Harrison. Harrison, of 31st Division Cyclist Company, joined the Glasgow Highlanders from England on 12 August 1916 and was transferred to 4th Gloucester Regiment on 9 October 1916. See TNA WO 95/2431: 1/9th HLI War Diary.

the rest of the day on this job. When it was over, I managed to borrow a horse and rode over to our transport lines at Gaudieupre and got a lift from there up to the trenches after dark that night. I found the Battalion still in the line at Foncquevillers where I had left them and expecting to attack. This attack would have been utter madness so we were greatly pleased next day when we were told it was cancelled and that we would be relieved that night by the 16th K.R.R.C.[17]

19/9/16

My dear Mother,

I think I told you in my last letter that I had got back to the Battalion. As soon as I got out of the train, I was met by a cyclist who gave me a message saying I had been detailed as a member of a Court Martial at some unheard of place at 10 am. It was then 9am. Fortunately, I had a map so I started off at once and just got there in time. I spent the rest of the forenoon there and then started off for our transport and got there about 3.00 PM. I changed into my trench clothes there and after dinner started off for the trenches. I had about 8 miles to do and didn't know the road, but fortunately got a lift up in a motor which passed me soon after I had started. The beauty of this country is that if one wants a lift, one simply stops the first empty car that passes. I got a very good dugout here for the night and we are being relieved tonight, when I hope to get back to a decent billet.

We had an absolutely beastly day yesterday, heavy rain and a high wind but it has cleared up again today.

Isn't the news from all quarters absolutely splendid just now? I only hope the weather keeps fine so that we can get on a bit further before the winter sets in. I am not looking forward with much pleasure to a third winter in the trenches.

I heard rather a good story today about one of our officers. The General was up in our line and wanted to see the Officer. He couldn't be found for a long time and the story goes that he was eventually discovered trying to bag some pheasant behind our line with a bomb. I don't know if the story is true or not but it might well be. History does not say what the General said.

Many thanks for the tie which I got yesterday.

WD: We moved back that night into billets in Souastre a few miles behind the line, where we stayed about a week and had a very pleasant time.

---

17   See Weir, *Come on Highlanders!*, pp. 189-90.

20/9/16

My dear Dad,

I am sorry to trouble you but one of my men has just brought me a wire saying that his brother has been killed.[18] His father is already dead and he wanted to get home to make arrangements about the funeral etc. And also to fix things up as his mother is left alone. I am trying to get him leave but it is quite possible he will not get it, at any rate not for some time, so I told him I would write you and ask you to help her. Her name etc. is Mrs. McLaren 33, Clarendon Street, Partick. Do you think it would trouble Jenny very much to call on her? I would be awfully grateful if she could as the man jumped at the idea when I offered to write and I think it unlikely that he will get home for some time, as there are several men waiting in much the same position.

WD: The authorities at this time were very worried with the lack of training of some of the junior officers who had recently joined the Brigade so our Regimental Sergeant-Major,[19] who was a Scots Guardsman, was sent up to Foncquevillers every morning where he held a class for young officers under cover of the trees. He had a very powerful voice and the men in the front line told us that they could hear all his words of command quite clearly. We used to wonder what the Germans thought of it.

26/9/16

My dear Dad,

Many thanks for various letters. I will sign the papers and get them sent off tomorrow.

I am sorry to say that I believe all leave is going to be stopped before I can get away. I don't know for certain if this is the case but if it is, I am afraid it can't be helped.

I am going to the Brigade tomorrow to act as Staff Captain while the other man is on leave. I would very much rather stay with the Bn. though it is something to be chosen for the job. With any luck, it may help me to get leave.

I must shut up now as I have no more to say and I want to go and listen to the band.

Your ever cheerful son,

Walter J.J. Coats

PS I have just got hold of a rather good poem written by one of the men, which I made a copy of as I think it may amuse you.

---

18 Private 4376 331588 Alexander Baird McLaren.
19 RSM, later Major, Frank Ernest Lewis, MC, DCM, grandfather of Alec Weir (author of *Come on Highlanders!*).

To a Sodger's Louse[20]

Wee scamperin' irritatin' scunner,
How dair ye worry me, I wunner,
As if I hadna' lots tae dae,
Blockin' the road tae Auld Calais
Wi'out ye.

Ye'll hardly let me hae a doss,
For you paradin' richt across
Ma back, ma neck and doon ma spine,
Thinking, na doot, ye'r dain' fine
Sookin' ma bluid.

When at ma country's call I came,
Tae fecht for beauty, King and hame,
I read ma yellow form thro' twice
But it said nought 'bout fechtin' lice,
Or I'd hae gibbet.

When "Little Willie" skips ma heid,
An' me about tae draw a bead,
I fain would stop to scart ma back
Tae shift ye off the beaten track,
Afore I fire.

When through the shirt o' Sister Sue,
I search maist carefully for you,
I smile tae think the busy wench,
Ne'er dreams her seams mak' sic a trench,
Tae give ye cover.

What labyrinthine dugout too,
Ye're makin' in our kilts the noo,
Ye're reinforcements tak' the bun,
Encouraged by the Flanders sun,
Tae keep us lively.

---

20 The poem, attributed to a private of the Royal Scots Regiment, also appeared in Abraham
Kingdon (ed), *Patriotic Poems* (Winnipeg: Kingdon Printing Co., 1916).

Gott strafe ye little kittlin' beast,
Ye maybe think ye'll mak' a feast
O' me, but no, ye'll hae a had
When next ye try tae promenade
Across ma kist [chest]

The mixture in the bottle here
Is bound to mak' ye disappear
Nae man I'll need tae mak' ye click
Yin dose, they say, will dae the trick,
As shair as daith.

"Click" is the noise made when they are squashed. You may not see the humour of it so much as we do but I hope it will amuse you.

WD: We left Souastre on the 27th for a back area [Humbercourt] and, as the Staff Captain (Bushell) was on leave, the Brigade borrowed me to help with the billeting on the way back. This was my first experience of this sort of work from a Brigade point of view and I found it a most disagreeable one.

After about three days marching we arrived at Bouquemaison and as the Staff Captain was still on leave I was kept at Brigade H.Q. to help the Assistant Staff Captain, a man, White of the 1st Middlesex. As I had absolutely no responsibility, I used to amuse myself giving him suggestions about the efficient running of his job and enjoying myself generally. General Landon was sent to command a Division of Bantams[21] at this time and General Pinney[22] took over command of the Division.

5/10/16

My dear Dad,
I am quite liking the job of Staff Captain but expect the other man back in about two days now, when I shall retire to my own job again. One thing this job has taught me, if nothing else, is the reason for the shortage of paper. In this connection, did I ever tell you of McCosh's experience when he went to the Ordinance Stores to buy a pair of bootlaces? He had to sign six sheets of foolscap before he could get them, and then they could not supply him with a bit of paper to wrap them up in. The trouble

---

21 35th (Bantam) Division. See Becke, *Order of Battle Divisions: Part 3B.*, pp. 51-59.
22 Major-General Reginald John Pinney (1863-1943). Sandhurst 1882; commissioned Royal Fusiliers 1884; Staff College 1889-90; DAAG Quetta 1896-1901; South Africa 1901-02; Colonel 1906; AAG Egypt 1909-13; GOC Devon & Cornwall Brigade TF 1913-14; GOC 23rd Brigade 1914-15; GOC 35th Division July 1915-September 1916; GOC 33rd Division 1916-18.

here, so far as I can see, is lack of foresight. Things are sent round simply shouting for an obvious question in reply which means another letter answering it, instead of the question being answered when the original is sent off.

I have not yet made up my mind what to do about leave. There is a chance if I applied for special leave that I might get it, but I rather think I would get less than if I wait till ordinary leave opens, so I think I shall wait.

As far as suggestions for parcels go, I should like any of the following anytime: black and white puddings; oatcake; plain cake; scones; biscuits; sausages; tinned ham.

[Cont.] 6/10/16

I should also like a new khaki shirt when you can be bothered as the one I have is absolutely done in.

I was on another Court Martial yesterday which was rather a waste of half a day. I always feel fearfully sorry for the prisoners because at the worst I consider them better than all the slackers who are still going about at home with badges on their coats. I wish they would start Court Martialling them when they strike for extra pay.

I was fearfully pleased to see Hedderwick got another mention. I expect very few people have got a record like his now.

WD: Bushell got back about the 5th of October and White and I got off on leave on the 10th. Thanks to White I got a lift to Boulogne in one of the Divisional cars and we had a very pleasant run down.

20/10/16

My dear Dad,
I arrived back safely this morning about 7 o'clock.

In spite of what the man told me at Victoria, the boat did not sail until well on in the afternoon and it was dark when we got to this side. There was no motor waiting at Boulogne so we got a train at 1.00 am which got us to a certain station about 4.30 am, where we got the car and arrived in time for breakfast. The only sleep I have had since I got up at Perry Mount yesterday morning was about two hours in the train, so I shall sleep well tonight.

We rolled a bit coming across the Channel and at one time I half expected we would roll over as the wind was blowing hard on one side. The chairs etc. were fairly scooting about the deck.

While I remember, I left a toothbrush in the tumbler above the basin in my room. It was a brand new one, so I would be much obliged if someone would send it on.

It has been absolutely ripping day here but fearfully cold, especially in the morning before the sun rose.

I hope you can read this as I am writing almost in the dark.

WD: I rejoined my Battalion on the 20th at Corbie, east of Amiens, and on the 21st we moved up to Méaulte where we spent the night, moving on the next day to Mansel Camp [Mametz] which consisted of a few tents and shelters in a very muddy field. The only incidents of any interest here were my first sight of a tank, a visit of the Prince of Wales to Brigade H.Q. and a large tear in a new pair of riding breeches while reconnoitring a road for our move to a new position.

23/10/16

My dear Mother,
It is warmer today as the wind has died down. The mud in some places at present takes you up to about the knees so it should be pretty cheery if it starts raining.
I nearly rode into a shell hole full of water today. But fortunately one of the men I was with did it first. He was covered with mud up to the knees even on his horse.

[Cont.] 24/10/16
It has been pouring all night and for most of today, and things are pretty cheery as a result. I expect we are going to have a pretty thin time of it for some time to come.

WD: After three nights in Mansel Camp we moved up across country to a camp called "Carnoy Huts", close to Montauban, where we spent two days, one of which was very fully occupied reconnoitring the road up to Lesboeufs.

26/10/16

My dear Jean,
I don't know whether you are home again or not but I know this letter will be opened by the first down for breakfast (Dad or Mother) so it doesn't matter who I write to.
I am still going strong, likewise the mud. I have never seen anything like it out of the trench before. I am sorry for the men and almost sorrier for the horses but thank goodness I have not yet reached the stage of being sorry for myself and I don't think the men have reached that stage either. I don't know what the world was like before it was mud, but I know what it was like when it <u>was</u> mud and, like Doug, I can now understand why Adam and Eve had no clothes, as I don't suppose they had any knives to scrape them with and they would be unwearable otherwise.

WD: On 29th October, we moved up from Carnoy Huts to Bernafay Wood where we were told we would find sufficient shelter for the Battalion but when we arrived were unable to find cover for more than about 50 men. As it was pouring wet and very cold things were not looking very bright when General Baird turned up to see how we were getting on. When he saw the mess we were in he was very angry and at once rode off to Division H.Q. where he apparently stirred things up so effectively that it was not long before we had a supply of canvas trench shelters to make bivouacs with, not to mention a supply of Divisional Staff Officers to see if they could help in any other way. Battalion H.Q. here consisted of a small hut about 6 feet by 4 built against the side of what looked like a small concrete shelter. As it was only built of Artillery ammunition boxes laid one on top of another with a bit of canvas for a roof, it was very uncomfortable and cold but, except when the roof blew off, it was fairly dry. The C.O. spent the night in the concrete shelter which was certainly warmer but was so small that when he sat upon the floor he could not stretch his legs.

Early next morning, the C.O. went off to reconnoitre the line and when he got back about mid-day he was very depressed and told us we were in for the most uncomfortable time we had ever had. He brought back orders with him that we were to take over that night and, as it always took longer to get the Lewis Guns relieved, I set off immediately after lunch in order to get them out of the way before the rest of the Battalion came up.

We moved up past the side of Trones Wood, through Guillemont, which consisted of a few bricks, a notice board and the stumps of a few trees and then up to Ginchy where we picked up our guide.

So far the road had not been too bad but the guide now proceeded to lead us off across country by a narrow and very slippery duckboard track which wound in and out

Main road into Guillemont, 11 September 1916. Walter passed through here the following month. (IWM C.684, WJJC collection)

Remains of Guillemont railway station, autumn 1916. (IWM C.691, WJJC collection)

Ginchy: Wounded awaiting evacuation, autumn 1916. (IWM D.735, WJJC collection)

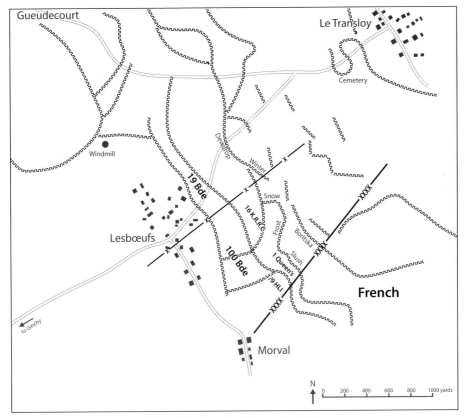

Map 6 Lesboeufs, 1 November 1916.

among the shell holes. If one slipped off this track it was pure luck if one did not go more than up to the knees in mud. To add to the general cheerfulness, it was lashing with wind and rain and very cold and we were all soaked to the skin. In fact I was beginning to wonder if things could be much more uncomfortable when a shell came along and knocked out one of my men. This rather upset things but fortunately he was able to go back on his feet with the help of another man. If he had been a stretcher case it would have been very awkward as we were a long way from anywhere and I could not very well have left him lying.

Shortly after this, the track came to an end and we started to flounder on through the mud and, this being the first opportunity of doing so, the guide promptly lost his way. As the whole place was simply a sea of mud in which all tracks were obliterated, I could not blame him but I was considerably annoyed and rather worried till another man turned up who put us on the right way. After this we floundered on for some distance until we struck a sunken road leading from Morval to Les Boeufs and the guide proceeded to lead down into a trench running alongside of it. As this trench was about six feet deep with

Top: View of Morval, 1916, possibly from Lesboeufs. (IWM D.336, WJJC Collection)
Bottom: View of Morval from Lesboeufs, 15 July 2016. (JC)

about 18 inches of water in the bottom of it, it did not look very tempting but, as the guide said that it was the proper way, we had to get into it. As it was full of men and very narrow we had an awful job getting along it with the guns and I was wondering how much further we would have to go when the guide proceeded to climb out again. As we had only gone about 50 yards I was rather relieved to see this as I thought he had decided to go along the top, but when I got out and found that we had now arrived at Battalion H.Q. of the Battalion we were to relieve, which we might just as easily have got to by walking down the road, I was distinctly annoyed and let him know it.

As the guns were all going in different directions from here, I handed them over to their respective guides who were waiting for them and went to report my arrival to the Battalion we were relieving (The Cameronians). I found the Battalion H.Q. in a deep dug-out on the side of the road. When I got into it, I found that it would have held four comfortably but was now packed full with men sitting on the stair. In addition there was a fire going in it on which dinner was being prepared the only outlet for the smoke being up the stair over which a waterproof sheet was hung. As a result the atmosphere was so thick that I could see nothing for about ten minutes and reported to a glimmer of candle light shining through the smoke. As there was nothing more to be done for the moment, I then found a place on the floor where I could sit down and wait for the relief to be completed.

The rest of the Battalion rolled up in due course and the relief was finally completed about midnight. As soon as this was reported, the C.O. sent me off with a couple of runners to try and find the H.Q. of a French battalion that was on our right in order to get into liaison with them. I was told I would find these H.Q. by going straight along the sunken road we were in, so I set off quite cheerfully expecting to be back in about half an hour. After splashing along the road for about 300 yards, however, it ceased to be sunken and, as it was pitch dark, could hardly be distinguished at all and after going a bit further it seemed to cease entirely. This was rather awkward as I had been distinctly told the H.Q. were on this road and I was quite certain we had not passed them. While I was wondering what to do, a flare went up from the front line and I saw a track leading straight on so decided to follow it. Progress now became very slow as it was only when a flare went up that we were able to see the track and we did not dare to risk losing it.

After about an hour of this sort of thing we eventually ran into a couple of Frenchmen who said they had come from the French H.Q. but that it was some way off and very hard to find. They advised us to go with them to some place behind to which they were taking a message and that they would hand us over to a party that would be going up to the H.Q. from there. This seemed quite a reasonable idea and I agreed to go with them, but I began to doubt of its wisdom when we had gone about a mile without any sign of reaching their destination. There was nothing for it now however but to go on and after going a bit further we arrived at a position with a lot of Frenchmen in it.

I was handed over to the officer in charge here who told me that there was a relief going up shortly which would pass close to the H.Q. and who would take us on to it. Shortly after this, we started off behind the relief and I thought my troubles were at an end. My luck however was out for I was just thinking we must be near our destination when a Frenchman loomed up out of the dark and started to talk to me. I thought he must be my guide so stopped to hear what he had to say while the people in front vanished into the darkness. After talking about five minutes I found that my supposed guide was a stray Frenchman who had lost his way and wanted me to put him right. I am afraid I was no in a position at the time to see the humour of his having hit on me of all people in the area to put him right.

Except for a general idea of direction, I was now completely lost and as it was pouring wet and pitch dark with the ground all round a sea of mud and shell holes, not to mention the fact that the Germans were shelling the area, I was beginning to get a bit fed up. However, we had not yet found the French H.Q., so I started off again in the direction I thought they should lie. We had not gone far on this line when we ran into another Frenchman who said he knew the place I wanted and pointed out the direction to me. This bucked us up a bit but when the next Frenchman told us it lay in a totally different direction we began to calm down a bit and when the next half dozen Frenchmen all pointed in different directions I decided we had better go home and start again. This decision was rather helped by the fact that we now found ourselves in the middle of a heavy German barrage which was rather uncomfortable though not so dangerous as it appeared owing to the softness of the ground.

The question now was which direction we should go in to get back. I was fairly certain we should go one way while the men with me were equally certain we should go the opposite way and by way of proof pointed out some flares that were going up in the opposite direction to what I thought they should be. While I was trying to reconcile their idea of the direction with my own however I spotted a flare going up where I thought it should be which settled the matter as far as I was concerned and the men had to come with me.

We were all pretty tired by now, so were not sorry, after falling about in shell holes and mud for another half hour or so, when we struck the sunken road again and got back to H.Q. I reported to the C.O. that I had not yet found the French H.Q. and offered to go out again with a couple of fresh runners but fortunately he decided it could wait till daylight so I lay down and went to sleep.

I was roused at dawn on 31st by the C.O. getting up to go out and when I found he was going round the line I decided to go with him and see how my gunners were getting on. After going forward for two or three hundred yards we struck a second sunken road in which, as we then guessed the French had put their H.Q. We did not, however, go along to see as we were in rather a hurry but went straight on to the front line. When we got to the trenches, we found them waterlogged and all the men in them nearly frozen with cold and wet. We got into the trench here but soon found that if we wanted to get along at all we would have to go along the top. As it was very quiet at the time we proceeded to do so and after visiting all the men, got back to Battalion H.Q. in time for breakfast. As I had found everything all right with the guns, I had no further worries for the rest of the day and spent a quiet day in the dug-out.

During the night we heard that we were to attack next day, so Colonel Darling wrote out his orders and at dawn next day, 1st November, I started out again with him to see how the men were.[23] We found them, if it was possible, even more miserable than they had been the day before as in addition to the cold and mud and wet they had been heavily shelled during the night. I remember coming across the remains of one Lewis gun team that had been completely wiped out by a shell that must have landed right on top of them. As we had done the day before, we walked round on top of the trenches with occasional stops while the C.O. was speaking to someone in the trench. At one of these stops while the C.O. was talking to Whitson[24] in the trench below him I heard a sort of metallic click and saw the C.O. stumble and fall on his face. I thought he had tripped on an old piece of metal and stooped down to help him up when I found he had been shot through the head, the click being the bullet hitting his helmet. We could of course do nothing for him and he died a minute later. This was the worst blow the Battalion ever had as he was the life and soul of the Battalion and the finest soldier I ever met.

As the sniper who had killed the C.O. was meantime trying to get Lamberton[25] and myself who were with him, we got down into the trench for a bit and then Whitson, who was the senior officer left with the Battalion, went back with me to H.Q. to take over command until Major Menzies should arrive from the transport lines behind.

The first thing Whitson did when we got back was to write to Brigade H.Q. and point out to them the utter futility of trying to attack with men who were too frozen to move. I imagine the Brigade knew this pretty well already and had reported it to Division but nothing came of it and orders were issued for the attack, which was timed to take place shortly before dark.

Shortly before the attack came off, I was again sent to Brigade H.Q. to act as liaison officer. I found them all very much cut up about Colonel Darling's death.

In due course, the attack started but, as everyone who had seen the condition of the men knew it would be, it was a ghastly failure. Most of the men were so cold and stiff they could hardly claw their way out of our trenches and were simply shot down on our parapet before they could get on their feet and those who did get out were unable to advance quicker than a slow walk and were shot down without a chance of getting near the Germans.

---

23 This attack, launched by XIV Corps (GOC Lieutenant-General Earl of Cavan) during the latter stages of the Somme offensive, was part of 'The Battle of the Ancre Heights' (1-11 November 1916). Carried out over some of the worst ground conditions encountered by 33rd Division thus far, the operations against 'Boritska Trench' commenced on 29 October. 19th Brigade having failed to seize the objective on the 29 October and 1 November respectively, 100th Brigade was tasked with resuming the assault on the afternoon of the 1st. See Rawson, *The Somme Campaign*, pp. 265, 267-68 and Weir, *Come on Highlanders!*, pp. 191-98.

24 Captain Wilfred Robert Whitson b. 30 May 1888. Educated Glasgow Academy and University of Glasgow BSc 1910; 1/9th HLI; brother of Ernest J Whitson and Harold Whitson.

25 Captain, later Major, John Robertson Lamberton DSO, MC, b. 1889. Fettes College (Carrington House, 1901-06), Glasgow University BSc (1910); 1/9th HLI (Glasgow Highlanders); Acting CO 16th KRRC for short spell during 1918. His brother Andrew was also educated at Fettes (Carrington, 1910-14) and served with 1/9th HLI.

Information of the situation in front generally reaches Brigade H.Q. between one and two hours after the attack starts but in this case we could get absolutely no information at all so after waiting several hours the Brigadier General sent for me and told me to go up to the front line and find out what the situation was, so off I started. I hoped with any luck to get back in a couple of hours but it was so dark when I got outside that I could not see my hand in front of my face and promptly lost myself and it took me about half an hour to reach Battalion H.Q. about 400 yards away. Incidentally, I was very frightened as I knew the whole place was thick with guns and I did not fancy the idea of walking in front of one just as it went off.

When I got to Battalion H.Q., I borrowed a runner to go up with me in case of accidents and set off again. We found the going very heavy as we each had about six inches of mud clinging to our boots but after ploughing along for some time we got up as far as the support trench which we found was empty. We were both so tired by now that we did not dare to risk trying to jump over the trench but climbed down into it with the intention of climbing out again on the other side. We found however, when we got into it, that it was full of mud and the runner stuck fast. In his efforts to struggle out he managed to strain his back and I had a terrible job trying to get him out. I managed however to get him out by pulling up one leg at a time and then I found I was nearly stuck myself as pulling him out had pushed me in. Eventually when we did both get out I found he was suffering so much that I had to help him back almost to Battalion H.Q. before he thought he would be able to get back the rest of the way himself.

I now turned back again for the line and after nearly sticking in the mud in the support trench again, managed to reach it. My job now was to get hold of someone who knew what had been happening, so I proceeded to look for an officer or responsible N.C.O. and after hunting round a bit was lucky enough to fall in with Lamberton. As usual he was perfectly calm and collected, though he was about the only officer left. When I told him of the feverish state of excitement behind for lack of news he simply laughed and said "So that's what all this bumf is about" and held up a great handful of messages he had. We were both hugely tickled when I told him that that was what it was all about and he then explained that he had no light to read them by, and that anyway he had hurt his hand and could not have replied to them. He told me what the situation was and I started off again.

The journey back was even worse than the journey up as the Germans had started throwing over gas shells. The gas helmets at this time were of the old bag type[26] and I found when I put mine on that I could not see an inch in front of me and as a result simply fell from one shell hole into another. As this was no good I tried with it off and though the gas made me feel a bit seedy I was able to get along a bit. Even now, however, it was so dark that I fell into a shell hole about every 6 or 7 yards and the more often I fell the less inclined I was to go on again. Fortunately, there was a group of burning houses on my right which enabled me to keep my direction.

---

26 The PH (Phenate Hexamine) anti-gas helmet was first introduced in October 1915.

I got back to Battalion H.Q., with my inside almost shaken out of me and full of gas, just before dawn and was lucky enough to find an officer from Brigade who took on my report with him and saved me going further. I then had breakfast and went to sleep.

2/11/16

FSPC to J.J. Coats, 27 Woodside Place

I am quite well.
 W.J.J.C.

WD: That afternoon we heard we were to be relieved and shortly after dark two other battalion H.Q.s rolled up to take over our H.Q. As it was small for one H.Q., we were like sardines with three and spent a very uncomfortable night till the relief was complete and we got clear. On my way back my feet nearly gave out for the first and only time during the war. This was partly due to the fact that I had had a good deal of walking to do, but chiefly I think to the fact that my feet had been soaking in mud and water for so long that the leather of my boots had gone quite soft and I could feel the nails through the sole. To add to my troubles, the C.O. who was leading kept flashing his electric torch to see where the duck-boards were with the result that everyone except himself was quite dazzled and kept skidding off the boards into the mud. We got back in due course to a camp near Guillemont which consisted partly of huts and partly of tents and dug-outs and after getting something to eat turned in for a sleep.

3/11/16

My dear Dad,
Please excuse my not having written for some time as I have not been able to do more than send a Field Service Post Card.

We have just been having about the thinnest time we have had since coming out. The result is that I have a slight cold in the head. I have also got a pretty healthy cough but I think that is the result of being gassed a bit about two days ago. I must say I felt pretty seedy for a day or so after it but I am perfectly all right now.

While I remember, would you please send out my oilskin coat and a new pair of boots (usual size)? An oilskin is the only thing that will keep out the rain here and it is not comfortable being soaked to the skin without any prospect of a dry change for about a week ahead.

I have not been getting any of your letters for several days now, but I understand that is because the Channel is closed or something like that. I hope you have been getting my PCs all right as you must be more worried about not hearing than I am.

I suppose you will have seen from the papers that our C.O. was killed the other day. I was standing beside him at the time and got a fearful shock. We are all fearfully cut up about it, as apart from being a magnificent soldier, he was one of the finest men I ever knew. Personally, I came in contact with him more than most people and I was very fond of him. It was a privilege to serve under him.

They are wanting this table to set dinner on, so I shall have to shut up.

Later: I have just had an excellent dinner.

While I remember, please send me another two pairs of socks. I had to cut my last pair off my feet as they had been saturated in mud and water for three days and were too stiff to pull off.

WD: We spent the day of 3rd here and, at dark, a party went off to bring back Colonel Darling's body.[27] When they got back, they reported that there were a lot of wounded lying about asking for help so, as I was the only officer available who was not quite done, I volunteered to take a party up to find them and see if we could tie them up a bit. The C.O. agreed to this so, while the men were getting ready, I went over with one or two of them to a dressing station close by and got them to fill some water bottles with hot tea etc. in the hope that it would still be warm when we got up. When the rest of the men were ready, we set off but, as it took as a good two hours hard going to get up, it was nearly dawn before we arrived. Our guide, who had been up with the party for the Colonel's body, was by now absolutely done and had unfortunately lost his bearings and we wasted some more time looking round for the wounded. We managed to find one man, eventually, but as he was shot through the stomach we could not do much for him except try to make him more comfortable and, as it was now broad daylight, I decided it was not safe to look any longer so we came back intending to have another try next night. When we got back to camp, however, we found that the whole Battalion was ordered to go up again that afternoon for an attack which was to take place next morning.

We moved in again that afternoon as ordered and found that we were to be in support and to supply carrying and work parties for the attacking Battalions. Battalion H.Q. this time was in a hole dug in the side of a trench, so as it was very small, I took up my abode in a derelict tank which was quite close. It certainly kept the rain off but was too draughty and cold to allow much sleep.

The attack next day was carried out by the 16th K.R.R.C. and the 2nd Worcesters, who attacked through the French on our right flank, and it was quite successful.[28] One amusing incident which occurred in the middle of the attack was the delivery of a message from Brigade addressed to an officer who was then, so far as we knew, in the thick of it with a carrying party. As it was marked urgent, it was opened and was found to be a request by the Ordnance for payment of £1 for a pair of boots.

---

27 Lieutenant-Colonel John Collier Stormonth-Darling DSO is buried in Guillemont Road Cemetery.
28 See Rawson, *The Somme Campaign*, p. 268.

6/11/16

My dear Mother,

We have just come through another bit of a battle and as result I am somewhat tired. Apart from the actual physical exertion which is pretty considerable, I suppose there is a certain amount of excitement which takes it out of one and of course, at a time like this, one does not have the usual comforts of a dugout.

Personally, I spent the last two nights in a broken down 'tank'. It was not particularly safe and was beastly draughty but it was out of the rain. I am at present sitting on the stair which is the beginning of a deep dug-out, but as it also is dry I am quite happy.

As I am now out of the battle, I am open to receive parcels etc. I should very much like some chocolate and sweets, also cigars as I have not had any for a long time.

I got one or two letters yesterday, which I was delighted to get as I had not heard for some time. Please thank Jenny for the trouble she has taken about McLaren [Letter 20 September 1916]. I have not been able to see him since I got the letter, but I shall see if I can get hold of him when we get properly out.

While I remember, you might tell Dad that our Messing here costs us £3 per month i.e. £36 per year. This includes drinks. I don't know what a 2nd Lieut's pay is, but it must be considerably more than £36. Of course, it all depends on what Battalion one is in, but I should say 75 francs per week for any Battalion would be excessive.

Please excuse dirty paper as it is impossible to keep clean.

WD: We were relieved during the afternoon of the 6th and moved back to Guillemont where we found the cookers waiting for us with hot soup and, after a short rest, we moved on again. After marching for another 4 or 5 hours along very crowded and very bad roads, with nothing to cheer us except a splendid view of a large dump which the Germans had managed to set on fire and which lit up the sky for miles around with the most wonderful colours, we made up on our transport which had gone ahead and, after having something more to eat, pushed on for our destination, a few huts and tents not far from Fricourt, which we reached after daylight next morning.

After sleeping for the rest of the forenoon Whitson and I started off to see if we could find Col. Darling's grave near Trones Wood, but after getting bogged right up to our horses' bellies about three times we decided, as it was getting dark, that we had better give it up so we returned to camp.

9/11/16

My dear Dad,

Today has been fine for a change, so we have had a chance of cleaning up. We are at present sleeping under canvas, which is somewhat chilly at this time of year, but it is better than nothing. I expect to get back to a comfortable bed in a few days now.

I wonder if Jenny would mind calling on the mother of one of my men who has just been killed as I am afraid she will not be too well off.[29] The man has served with me ever since we came out and was one of the best men I had. He was a pretty rough diamond and that is why am afraid his mother is not well off. I am going to write to her tonight and would like if Jenny would call on her in a day or two. Her name is Mrs. Bilton, and I think her address is 4, Greenwell Place, Govan. If that is wrong, it is 802, Govan Rd, Govan. Perhaps both addresses are the same place.

I must dry up now as I have one or two letters still to write.

WD: We left here on 10th before dawn and marched through Méaulte to Morlancourt where we were put in a train and, after travelling all day, arrived after dark at Airaines, where we detrained. From here we marched to Sorel-en-Vimeu and Wanel, where we were to rest.

Colonel John Collier Stormonth-Darling DSO (1878-1916), Commanding Officer 1/9th HLI (Glasgow Highlanders), 1915-1916. September 1916 at Lednathie, the family holiday home in Glen Prosen, Kirriemuir, during a brief spell of leave taken to attend his father's funeral. (Stormonth-Darling family collection)

---

29 L. Cpl 1810 Robert Bilton was killed on 31 October 1916 and is buried at Caterpillar Valley Cemetery, Longueval.

6

Brigade Staff and the Battle of Arras

I shall be very sorry to leave the Battalion, as it is just possible it may be for good. I feel that I am deserting them.

12/11/16

My dear Dad,

I have got a bit of news which may cheer you up a bit. Four officers from the Brigade have been detailed to attend a Course for Instruction in Staff Duties and I have been chosen as one of them.[1]

It does not of course mean that I shall at once become a Staff Officer or anything of that sort, but it is a step towards a staff job of some sort. The course only lasts a week, so it is not worthwhile changing my address, as it is being held quite close to where we are just now.

Please thank Ellie for the turkey which we are having tonight. It was a bit mouldy after its journey, but, like its human brother, will no doubt brisk up a bit after a wash. At any rate, it is going to enjoy a personally conducted tour of my internal workshop before the world is much older.

We have got a <u>most</u> comfortable Mess here, with a fire going and a table cloth and all sorts of comforts, and I have got a ripping billet so I shall be quite glad when the course is over and I can get back to it.

I believe we really are going to get a decent rest now and there is every prospect of my getting three days in Paris, so things are looking up.

I must stop now as the turkey is about to make its bow.

Your supremely cheerful son,

Walter J.J. Coats

---

1   Walter had been chosen to take part in an established staff duties training programme. See Paul Harris, *The Men Who Planned the War: A Study of the Staff of the British Army on the Western Front, 1914-1918* (Farnham: Ashgate, 2015), pp. 97-122.

WD: After I was informed on 12th that I had been chosen by the Brigade to attend a Divisional course for instruction, I accordingly reported at Div. H.Q. at Hallencourt next day. I found the class consisted of 4 officers from each Brigade, the other three from the 100th Brigade being Donald who was acting as Brigade Major's assistant, White, who was acting as Staff Captain's assistant, and an officer from the 16th K.R.R.C. We were kept working pretty hard on this job until the end of the month when the class broke up and I rejoined my Battalion.

14/11/16

My dear Mother,

I am now at the Divisional Staff School and having a good though pretty strenuous time. We start work at 9am and are out till any time between 12.00 and 1.00. We then have lunch and write out our reports which have got to be in by three o'clock. At three, we have a lecture which lasts till about 4.30, when we have tea and from 5 till 7 or 7.30 we do some sort of indoor scheme. We dine at 7.30 and then spend the evening writing out Operation Orders etc. for next day. If we are lucky, this does not take too long but last night it took me till 10.30 PM. In our spare time we are supposed to do a lot of reading.

The course is going to last for at least four weeks and maybe longer. It is interesting and I am rather keen on it.

17/11/16

My dear Dad,

Please excuse my not having written for some time as I have been too busy with the Staff Class.

I am finding it fearfully interesting though it is hard work. I have not used my brain so hard since I left the University.

It is freezing hard here just now, but I have got a warm billet.

I see from the papers, they are going to start food tickets at home. I should like to hear all about that when you have time. The only serious objection to them that I can see is that it will rather buck up the Germans. I expect he needs bucking up after the last smack in the eye that he has got.

22/11/16

My dear Jenny,

Just a line to let you know that I am still flourishing. Please thank Mother for the chickens which arrived yesterday. There are four of us in the Mess I am in just now and we had one for dinner last night, with mashed potatoes and another for lunch today with beans and pommes sautées. I am not quite sure if they were sautées or not, but I am told they were. The chickens were in great form and some of them at least are still in great form (see above).

[Cont.] 23/11/16
I did not get this letter posted yesterday so I may as well carry on.

Very many thanks indeed for the trouble you have taken about Mrs. Bilton. I don't want you to use any money from your own pocket for these people. If they need it, please remember that I have heaps, and I would only be too glad to give it.

I spent till 12 o'clock last night writing orders and was at them again before break-fast but I have, at present, got a couple of hours to myself as this morning's work did not need any report. We had great fun this morning running around seeing how business is carried out at railhead and refilling points. It took us from 9am till 1.00 in a motor bus. Among other details, we got bogged in a cross country track when we were coming home. This periodically happens, as there are about 12 of us in the bus and it is no one's special job to see that we keep in the right direction. The driver, of course, has no idea where we are going, so can't help much. I thought we were going to be completely stuck today as a great enormous bus to hold about 25 is not the ideal thing for a cross country cart track.

30/11/16

My dear Mother,
This course finishes tonight and I shall be going back to the Battalion tomorrow forenoon.

I am going to try and send home some of my surplus clothes which have been stored out here for some time now and are rather getting in the way. There is absolutely no news so Cheer Oh.

PS I have just got a bit of news for you. When I was leaving the class tonight, the instructor who is the G.S.G.I. on the Division Staff called me back and asked whether I would care to be attached to a Brigade for instruction. I said it depended whether the Brigade wanted me or not. He then told me the Divisional General wanted me to see some of the actual workings of a Brigade, so I said I was quite willing. The result is that I will probably be going in a few days as assistant to a Brigade Major or something of that sort. It is another step in the direction of a staff job and I am rather pleased about it. It may not of course lead to anything but it is a jolly good chance at any rate. I know you are very keen that I should get a staff job so I hope I manage all right.

I am afraid the PS is longer than the letter but the letter was finished before I had any news.

2/12/16

My dear Dad,

I am rather in a fix just now and would rather like to know what you think of it.

When I got back to the Battalion yesterday, I told the CO that there was every chance of my leaving him soon to be attached to a Brigade. He did not seem overly pleased at the time and asked me to come and see him in his room. When I went there, he explained that he had intended going to see the General and asking for me to be made 2nd in Command of the Battalion, but that he would not stand in my way if I wanted to do the other thing. I explained to him that I had promised you I would take a Staff job if I could get it, but I said I would write and ask you again.

From a personal point of view, I rather fancy a Staff job if I could get one but, as things stand at present, I think I <u>ought</u> to take the second in command job if it was not for my promise to you.

If I took the second in command job, it would probably mean my becoming a Major but I have no ambition in that line and it simply comes down to the question of which I ought to do. It is possible of course that I may not be allowed any say in the matter but it looks at present as if I would.

I know this is a question I have really got to decide for myself, as I know you will not hold up my promise against me if my duty is the other way but I would rather like to have your opinion on the subject if I have given you enough information to base your opinion on. If I haven't given you enough information please say so and I will worry the thing out for myself and I am afraid I can't put full reasons down on paper because of the censor regulations.

I am afraid I have put rather an unfair question to you, but I don't expect you to say yes or no, I would simply like your general views on the subject.

Your loving son,
Walter J.J. Coats

WD: We moved off on 4th December before daylight and after a short march to Pont Remy entrained there for Morlancourt. From Morlancourt, we marched to Sailly-le-Sec where we spent a couple of nights, my billet being in the summer house in the garden of the H.Q. house. While here, the Staff Captain of the 98th Brigade, a man called Clarke of the 4th Suffolks, turned up and said he had been told he could take me as his assistant but as I had no definite orders from our own Brigade I refused to move.

4/12/16

My dear Jenny,

I expect to be leaving the Battalion tomorrow to be attached to the 98th Brigade Headquarters but I am not absolutely sure of the date yet. I saw our Staff Captain today and he told me a message has arrived saying I am to go there but it has not been sent on here yet and may not arrive in time for me to go tomorrow. I shall be very sorry to leave the Battalion, as it is just possible it may be for good. I feel that I am deserting them. However, so far I have had no choice in the matter. I believe our Brigadier is trying to get me on to his own Brigade Headquarters which would mean that I would see more of the Battalion, but I don't know whether he will manage it or not.

McCosh went home on leave today. It must be months since he was home last.

We moved down here today and had a pretty early start which is not the least bit nice in this weather. Breakfast was at 4.00 AM and fortunately I managed to waken myself as my servant slept in and he just managed to catch the Battalion by the skin of his teeth as we moved off. In fact, if I had not sent someone to waken him he would probably be sleeping still.

I was sorry to see Doug has had jaundice. I know how beastly it is in this climate but I should think it would be a good deal worse in India. I hope he is better by now. Jim seems to be going strong alright and more or less enjoying life though he must be a bit bored.

My quarters for tonight are in a summer house and may be somewhat chilly but I expect I shall sleep all right as I have got back my sleeping bag. I put it aside with my other surplus kit such as my kilt and greatcoat when we started scrapping in July, and it rolled up again a few days ago. I think I shall keep it now until the winter is over. I think I told you I am sending home my coat and other surplus kit and I hope they will turn up alright, though goodness knows how long they will take.

Have you started living on standard bread yet? I should think it ought to be jolly good, though I suppose some people will treat it like a holiday task and dislike it because they have got to eat it.

I think I have let off sufficient gas for this attack so will switch off.

WD: On 6th, we moved from Sailly-le-Sec into some large French huts, I think they were called "Adrian" huts, just north of Bray-sur-Somme where we spent a very cold night. On the 7th we moved to a camp some miles due east of Bray.

7/12/16

My dear Jenny,

As we have recently been moving, I have not received any letters for the last three days and it is doubtful if we will receive any today. It will be a fine mail when it does arrive.

I am told now that I am not to go to the Brigade until the 15th. The 98th Brigade say I should have gone to them on the 3rd and my own Brigade say I am not to go until the 15th, so meantime I am rather unsettled and may be cleared off any day. In a way, the sooner I go the better as I may manage to dodge a spell in the trenches.

The weather is very cold here just now but I have plenty clothes and it is better than rain and we have got a good stove going in the hut.

I tell you what I would like from someone for Christmas – a good, strong oilskin jacket as mine is done. I don't want anything fancy about it. The plainest and strongest is the only kind that is any use out here. I am finding my oilskin coat most beautifully warm and it is a great deal more satisfactory than all these patent trench coats with oil-silk lining etc. etc. etc. which to my mind are far too heavy and are more use outside than inside a trench.

I must shut up now so Cheer Oh,

Your flourishing brother.

WD: On 8th December, we moved into dug-outs near Maurepas. We spent another night here and the following afternoon moved up into the line in front of Le Priez farm north of Le Forest, halfway between Combles and Rancourt. We relieved a battalion of French troops here who informed us that they had just done three weeks in the line after having had a three months rest and that they were now going back for another rest.[2]

We found the trenches here in the usual filthy condition and to make things worse the French insisted on our going in by the communication trench instead of over the top so that the men were all soaked before they got in. We presumed at the time that there must be some reason for this but when the French calmly walked out over the top when they had been relieved we were considerably annoyed.

11/12/16

My dear Dad,

Please thank whoever sent the parcel of biscuits and puddings. The CO bagged the paper off it before I got up this morning, as he wanted something dry to sit on, so I did not see who had addressed it. It will come in very useful here.

As regards Christmas presents, I don't want anything. You keep me supplied all year round with necessaries and out here anything that is not necessary has to go. I sent home a red chamois vest with the last lot of superfluous kit and I sent home the long woolly gloves with leather palms which I think I got last Christmas, a good long time ago.

If you are staying with Ellie just now, you might please thank her for the offer of a coat for Christmas and tell her on no account to send one out. I am afraid this is not very politely put but if you knew my opinion about these coats for anything but swanking about in, you would understand.

---

2   Fourth Army, as per a previous agreement between British GHQ and French GQG, extended its right flank south as far as Bouchavesnes (neighbouring French Sixth Army sector) on 12 December 1916. See Cyril Falls, *Military Operations France Belgium 1917 Vol. I* (London: Macmillan, 1940), pp. 19-20.

I think you know alright not to send me anything that has to be carried about until I ask for it but Christmas is a dangerous time so I hope you will excuse my repeating it.

Please thank Ellie for her last letter including two photos of "It". I am glad its lonely tooth has now got a partner. With any luck I shall be home to see it in January. I am afraid I have nothing to send it for a Christmas present except a clod of mud which I am afraid it would not appreciate.

PS I hope you can read this. I am sitting on the floor of an old German dug-out and have no table.

I have just received orders to report to the 98th Brigade for attachment so I shall be going there tomorrow. With any luck therefore this is my last night in a trench as regimental officer. In a way I am very sorry as I should like to have seen the show through with the Battalion.

My address there will be: Headquarters 98th Infantry Brigade, B.E.F.

WD: On the 11th, I was peacefully sitting in the Battalion H.Q. dug-out which was a narrow shaft dug into the chalk with a small hole in the bottom when I got orders to report at once to the 98th Brigade H.Q. as a Staff learner, so I pushed off next morning and after wandering round a bit found them in a palatial dug-out just outside Le Forest. It was built on the French type in the side of a hill with windows facing out to the back, with a deeper dug-out below in case of heavy shelling. The Mess and officers were in the top part and the lower part was divided into a lot of small rooms for sleeping in.

I found the trenches here were just as bad as the ones I had left. Some idea of the state they were in may be got from the case of one man of the 2nd Argyll and Sutherland Highlanders. This man got stuck in an isolated part of the trench and could not get out and was found by a patrol with a dead man on either side of him, one of whom had been shot through the head and the other of whom had died of exposure. The patrol tried to pull him out but were unsuccessful and had to leave him. Next night they went out with shovels but were unable to find him and it was not till the third night that they were able to dig him out. He then calmly walked down to the dressing station as if nothing had happened.

13/12/16

My dear Dad,

I am now with Brigade Headquarters and having quite a good time. I am at present assisting the Staff Captain but the Brigade Major told me tonight he would show me how things were run as soon as he had time. They all seem a very decent lot and I expect I shall learn quite a lot.

One thing that I have got is a more comfortable time than one can get in the trenches. I am living in one of the safest dugouts that I have ever seen and added to this it is dry, warm and comfortable, so altogether things are looking very bright.

I am glad to say I don't think I am going to be troubled about deciding whether to take the job of 2nd in Command of the Battalion or not. Our CO spoke to the Brigade Major about it and was told that he might try and get me but that there was very little hope he would manage now that I had been spotted for this job. It only remains to wait and see.

I am out of touch with the battalion just now so I am not getting any letters but I expect they will all turn up in time.

WD: We stayed in this part of the line till the 18th when we were relieved by the 800th Brigade and moved back in buses to billets in Bray.

19/12/16

My dear Dad,
I am liking my job very much now and it is certainly far more comfortable than regimental work though I can't help feeling I am rather shirking.

I don't think I shall start work today for some time yet as I had a job last night which left me awake all night. I am going to try and get one or two letters written as I can't be bothered going to bed.

This should reach you about Christmas, so many happy returns etc. etc. to you all.

WD: After four days here we again returned to the line this time a little north of our last place with the 100th Brigade on our right and the Union Brigade, composed of dismounted cavalry on our left. This time however I was left behind near Maurepas to look after what was known as "B" Echelon i.e. transport, Q.M. Stores etc. and to arrange for sending up food, ammunition and R.E. material as required. I spent a very pleasant time here living with a man, Richards, the transport officer of the 4th Suffolks who at the time was in charge of the pack animal transport of the whole Brigade.

22/12/16

My dear Dad,
I have struck it lucky this time. The Brigade is the line but I have been left out at what we call 'B Echelon'. I have got a very comfortable dugout with another officer that I only met a few days ago but I like very much. I expect I shall be here over Christmas.

I don't know why, but I am feeling particularly cheery tonight. I think it is the pleasant surprise at finding such a good dugout when I half thought I might have to use a tent. I must say, I have no desire to spend Christmas in a tent.

I have only had the one batch of letters since I came to the Brigade, so I don't know whether there is anything you want answered or not. With any luck, I may be able to get my letters tomorrow, as I am at present not far off from the Battalion.

Christmas cards 1916: XV Corps, 33rd Division and Glasgow Highlanders.
(WJJC collection)

I am afraid the proposals for the distribution of the Regimental Christmas cards came too late to be much use. I got a dozen dumped on me one night just before going into the trenches so I had to send them off to any one I could think of and I have not been able to get any more. What do you think of the Divisional Christmas card? It looks to me like a stationer's Christmas advertisement. That funny-looking thing at the top is the Divisional sign.

I must go to bed now so Cheer Oh pro tem.

23/12/16

I have had a fairly strenuous day of it today but nothing compared to what I am used to with the Battalion and one of the chief things is that I have got comfortable quarters and I'm pretty sure of getting to bed at night.

One of my jobs today took me for a ride and as I left my own horse with the Battalion I got a sort of Comic Opera horse from the Brigade. I bore with him for a long time but eventually he got the best of it and I had to climb off and get a stick. We got on better after that and I came spanking (literally) home at the rate of about 2 miles per hour.

I have just got your letter of the 20th, which is pretty good going.

I must shut up now so Cheer Oh and a Happy New Year.

23/12/16

Dear Mrs. Stuart,

Please thank the Women of Sandyford for their kindness in sending me a Christmas present. I got it some time ago and must apologise for not writing sooner but I have been too busy. The socks are most acceptable just now as we are living in the mud and one's feet are constantly wet. I am glad to say I have now got a job with the Brigade Staff as a learner which may eventually lead to a real staff billet. I feel rather a slacker when I see the Battalion going into the trenches without me but I am very glad to have the job for my people at home's sake as I believe they have a worse time of it than we have. Out here, the hardships are to a great extent physical while at home they are mental, which is worse.

Please excuse the blot at the top of the page. I knocked over the candle and paper is too precious here to rewrite the letter.

With best wishes for a good New Year.

Yours very sincerely,

Walter J.J. Coats

WD: On the 27th we were relieved and after spending the whole night on the road superintending the embussing of the Brigade, I arrived back in Bray about 10 a.m. next day with the last bus load of stragglers.

Early next morning we marched to Morlancourt and the whole Brigade was entrained for Longpré-les-Corps-Saints, where we arrived that night. Clarke had already gone on ahead to arrange for billets, so on our arrival all I had to do was to get into a car with the General and Brigade Major and we were driven to Brigade H.Q. which was in the Château de Vauchelles at Vauchelles-lès-Domart [5km south of Gorenflos, about half way between Amiens and Abbeville].

30/12/16

My dear Dad,

You will be pleased to hear I am once more out of the sound of guns and may be for some time. I have struck a splendid billet in a château and there is every prospect of my having a good time.

I am open to receive food of any kind at any time now that I am on this job. I would like some Nairn's oat cakes if they can still be got.

I have just received a letter of season's greetings from Jack which rather put me in my place as I forgot to send him one.

The name of my new General is Maitland.[3] I think he is a Rifle Brigade man.

---

3   Brigadier-General James Dagleish Heriot-Maitland (1874-1958). GOC 98th Brigade 1916-18.

I had a rather lengthy job the other night seeing people into buses. It took me from 5.00 PM till 12.30 next day hanging about the road, doing nothing most of the time except being there. I didn't think it was going to take me more than about five hours, so I took nothing with me to eat and I found when I had started that I had forgotten my gloves. My hands were all swollen with the cold as a result, and are just beginning to look normal again now. However it is better than the trenches so I have nothing to grouse about.

With best wishes for the New Year.

WD: On the night of the 31st I walked over and spent the evening with my Battalion at Gorenflos where we brought in the New Year with the usual celebrations.

1917

1/1/17

My dear Dad,

I have an afternoon off so I shall try and write a letter. As we are out on rest, the Staff Captain takes half the day off and I take the other half.

I went over and saw the New Year in with the Battalion last night. They are quite near and I walked across. I was glad to see them all again.

I am having a splendid time of it here and like the work, so there is some prospect of 1917 being a more comfortable one than 1916 especially as regards the last six months.

I am glad to say my servant is going on leave soon. It is 13 months since his last one. I always seem to strike it lucky with my servants. Shaw was the first. The next one I had [Crews] got wounded about five months ago, and with any luck I shall keep this one [Fosh] till the end of the war. They have all been about the best servants in the Battalion, and have brains enough to do things for themselves, so I don't have to worry about them. As a rule, I would far rather they did a thing without coming and worrying me about it, even if they do it wrong, than that I should be perpetually chasing them.

Talking of bringing in the New Year, I was bagged by some of the Sergeants yesterday and simply had to drink their healths. The only thing available to drink it in was whisky which one of them poured out for me. Fortunately, I managed to stop him by the time he had poured out half a glass. I am glad to say the room was very badly lit, as I took it like a medicine in two large gulps. I thought I was going to be sick for about 5 minutes after, and it took several bits of chocolate, some crystallised fruit and some almonds and nuts before I got rid of the taste sufficiently to be able to enjoy life once more.

WD: I was just settling down with the 98th Brigade and beginning to get to know the various units, when I suddenly received a message on the 4th to report as soon as possible to the H.Q. of the 100th Brigade at Gorenflos to act as Staff Captain there. As it was getting on in the afternoon, I at once packed up and rode over to Gorenflos which I reached about 5 pm. I found that the Brigadier General was on leave and that the Brigade was temporarily under the command of Colonel Storr of the 18th Middlesex. The Staff Captain told me he had been appointed to command a battalion and was leaving at 8 next morning, so after tea I went with him to his office and took over from him. Fortunately, he had everything in excellent order or I would have been rather lost.

When I arrived the Brigade H.Q. consisted of G.O.C. Brig. Gen. A.W.F. Baird; Brigade Major Capt. O.C. Downes, Rifle Brigade (in hospital); acting B.M. Lieut. A.W.F. Donald, 9th H.L.I.; Intelligence Officer Lieut. W.B. Edwards, 2nd Worcester Regiment; Signalling Officer Lieut. P. Baillie, 14th Battalion (London Scottish) London Regiment; Bombing Officer Lieut. E.J. Whitson, 9th H.L.I.; French Interpreter Sgt. Major Etchats; Captain H.W.M. Paul MC, 1st Middlesex Regt. was appointed Brigade Major a few days later in place of Downes, who went home.

My duties as Staff Captain included the following:-

Appointments – Burials – Casualties – Cemeteries – Ceremonial – Courts Martial – Courts of Inquiry – Discipline – Interpreters – Law – Leave – Medical Service – Pay – Personal Service – Police – Promotions – Prisoners of War – Spiritual Welfare – Supply of Personnel – Traffic Control – War Diary – Reinforcements – Moves – Supplies (R.E. material, ammunition, food, fodder and ordnance) – Remounts – Labour – Veterinary Service – Postal Service – Salvage – By-products – Cookery – Entertainments – Billeting – Claims – Baths – Laundry – Lorries – Canteens – Fires – A.D.C. to the B.G. and any other odd jobs that turned up except operations, training, signalling and intelligence.

5/1/17

My dear Jean,

Many thanks for your last two letters.

I don't know that I have much news except that I am now acting Staff Captain on the 100th Brigade. I must say, it came as rather a shock to me to be so suddenly pushed into the job, and I wish I could have had a longer spell as assistant. I don't know whether this job will eventually become permanent or whether someone else will be sent to take over. I hope in a way I get sticking to it. I shall have to do a tremendous lot of reading etc. before I can get into the swing of things, so don't be surprised if my letters don't come quite as often as usual. I must shut up now and get a move on, so Cheer Oh.

7/1/17

My dear Jenny,
Please excuse paper as I can't be bothered going upstairs for decent stuff.

I am still liking my job very much but as we are having an easy time of it just now it is hard to say how I shall get on when things get busy. Today being Sunday, I have had a fairly slack day. In the forenoon I went over several commission papers and other odds and ends and in the afternoon I made arrangements for a funeral. It meant a ride of between 15 and 20 miles, but I had a good horse and quite enjoyed the ride.

All my Christmas parcels have rolled up in the last three days including my oilskin jacket which I thought had got lost. Many thanks to everyone for everything. I am afraid my chances of leave are not quite so good as they were when I was assistant. It will take me some time to get into the swing of things here and I am not at all keen on going home until I do.

I don't know that I have very much news that I can give you except that I am extremely flourishing and enjoying life.

15/1/17

My dear Dad,
Just a scribble to let you know I am flourishing. Many thanks for the last parcel with black pudding, oat cake etc.

The reading up I have to do just now consists to a great extent in reading back orders for months past so as to have them more or less at my finger tips and also Military Law as I am to a great extent responsible for seeing that Court Martials are carried out properly etc.

I have got the length now of sticking a blue band on my arm as a sign of office. I told the person who told me to put it on that I could work quite as well without it but he insisted on my sticking it on.

I don't see any prospect of leave for a good long time but I am perfectly happy and don't feel that I need it. The system I worked on with the Battalion – that I was due leave when my razors began to get dull, i.e. once every four or five months – will probably have to do here too.

WD: My actual appointment as Staff Captain came through on the 17th.

17/1/17

My dear Dad,
The weather is absolutely beastly. There is about 4 inches of snow on the ground now and I rather think it is beginning to freeze. I do hate snow.

Many thanks for various letters I have received recently. I am afraid I have less than ever to write about now that I am on this job. For the last several days it has been almost entirely office work and that would be about as interesting to write about as your day's work to a person who is not a lawyer.

You may be interested to hear that I am now a full blown Staff Captain. I may stick on red tabs someday but I understand it is not necessary to put on a red hat, so I shall probably stick to my own old one. I must have something to show that I am a Scotsman.

I must go to bed now so Cheer Oh.

WD: After several days at Gorenflos, during which the only excitements were an aeroplane which fell to bits as it flew over the village and the burning down of a house by the 9th H.L.I., we again moved up to the line, entraining at Longpré and detraining as usual at Morlancourt from where we marched to billets at Bray. I went on early the day before, 19th, to arrange for billets and on arrival at Bray found that one of the battalions whose huts we were to take over had several cases of measles. This rather upset my arrangements for a bit but fortunately I managed to get a wire through to Division H.Q. before the brigade we were to relieve moved out and next day I got authority to billet one battalion in the town proper.

We spent one night here and moved up the following day to camps round Suzanne with Brigade H.Q. in the Château along with half the Division H.Q. and another Brigade H.Q. The Château was, I think, about the coldest place I ever lived in. The Mess room had three outside walls which consisted chiefly of doors and windows and to keep the draught out we rigged a canvas screen right round the table. Even then, however, we had to sit with our coats on and could hardly read as the screens kept out the daylight and the candles kept flickering in the wind. The weather outside at this time was so cold the Somme was frozen over and it was always a considerable effort to leave the comparative warmth of the Mess to go to bed.

We spent several days here, the only excitement being caused by people trying to shoot ducks on the Somme [marshes] with rifles and revolvers which made things rather uncomfortable as the bullets used to ricochet off the ice.

2/2/17

My dear Mother,

Very many thanks for the parcel of cake and sweets which I have just received.

Congratulations to Doug on his getting into the RAMC proper.

I don't think there is much in the way of news except that I am going very strong and having an easier time than I expected. My hardest work appears to be when I am out of the trenches. I expect too that I am getting more into the swing of things and don't take so long in dealing with them. The trouble, to a great extent, is knowing what the procedure is in various places. I used sometimes to take about half a day reading Military Law and King's Regulations etc. to find out what should be done, only to find that it is done "according to the practice of the service", which rather puts me in the soup. So far, I have been lucky enough not to put my foot into it very badly and everyone is extraordinarily decent.

I manage to get on very well with the General, thanks, I think, to the fact that I have done my share of the trenches. He can't stick people who have never been in trenches. I did a great piece of work too, the other day, with the D.A.Q.M.G. with a glass of whisky and a piece of cake when he was nearly starving. He took a job off my hands which would have meant hours of work and pages of correspondence. As it was, I simply wrote to the people that had been worrying me "Please refer to _____" and the job was done.

WD: On the 6th, we moved into the line just north east of Cléry-sur-Somme, SE of Maurepas, with Brigade H.Q. in a French dug-out which was known as P.C. Ouvrage or as the British called it P.C. Earthworks. The trenches here were dug on top of a hill about 1000 yards in front of Brigade H.Q. and there was a light railway running up the valley between which was used to take up ammunition and R.E. material when it was not being blown up by shells. On the night of 7th, the Glasgow Highlanders brought off a very successful raid taking several prisoners and a machine gun with the loss of one officer[4] and one man killed.

8/2/17[5]

My dear Mother,

I expect I shall be very busy for the next eight or nine days but at the present moment things are very quiet in my line of business.

I was very amused at Jim being so pleased at getting a tent to sleep in. Personally, I prefer a dugout every time. I have no fancy for that life in the middle of winter. I have got an enormous dugout just now and am fearfully comfortable. I have got a table about 5 feet by 2½ feet in my office. I share a bedroom with two other officers. The General and Brigade Major each have a room to themselves and we have a mess for 8 officers comfortably at table.

The frost here is still as hard as ever but it is so dry, I am not even wearing a woolly waistcoat.

---

4   2nd Lieutenant Conrad Blackadder Wilson. See Weir, *Come on Highlanders!*, pp. 207-10.
5   The German retirement to the Hindenburg Line (*Operation Alberich*, 9 February-20 March 1917), during which the *Westheer* conducted a scorched earth policy, commenced the following day. 33rd Division, in preparation for the forthcoming spring offensive following a harsh winter on the Somme, did not participate in the subsequent Anglo-French follow-up to the new enemy defences. See Falls, *Military Operations France and Belgium 1917 Vol. I.*

There is no apparent prospect of my getting leave but I am trusting to luck that the General will send me off next time we come into the line. He does not like us to ask him for leave.

WD: We were relieved after 8 days in the line and taken back to reserve at Suzanne where we spent about six days and after arranging for the Brigade's return to the line on the 21st, I went on leave from the 20th.

On my return, the train up from Boulogne was so slow I eventually decided to drop off it outside Amiens and see if I could not get along quicker by road. I was fortunate enough to get a lift in a car as far as Corbie, which I reached just after dark, and after walking on about half way from there managed to get a lift in a lorry to my destination at Suzanne. I reported here to Division H.Q. and found much to my delight that the Brigade was being relieved that night so I waited out for them.

When the Brigade got back I found that they had, on the night of 27th/28th February, again brought off a good raid on entirely novel lines which had been thought out by the Brigadier. He had noticed that, after a raid, things were generally abnormally quiet while both sides were apparently getting reorganised and he accordingly decided that it might be a good idea to have a second raid an hour or two after the first one in the hope that they would not be expecting it. He therefore arranged for a party of about 50 of the Worcesters to raid the Germans in the ordinary way and organised a second party of 100 to go over two hours later. The first raid was quite successful and the prisoners from it were sent down at once to his H.Q. where he examined them and immediately sent the information he got up to the second party which was just about to start. The second party then went over and took the Germans completely by surprise capturing quite a lot of them. The best part of it was that the Germans raided were the Prussian Guards.

We stayed in Suzanne until the rest of the Division was relieved a few days later on 4th March and were then taken out of the area and moved back to Corbie for a rest.

I now began to get really busy as in addition to the ordinary routine work which was always very heavy when we were resting, orders began to come out for the spring offensive[6] which was to start in the beginning of April, i.e. about three weeks head. The general idea for the attack was, so far as we were concerned, that we were to be formed into a Corps along with the 29th [sic] and two other Divisions[7] and, when the initial attack broke the German line, we were to go through and seize a certain objective well behind the German line where we were to hold on until the rest of the army made up on us. This meant that we were to be entirely isolated from the remainder of the army

---

6   The Battle of Arras (9 April-16 May 1917) was the British component of the projected Anglo-French spring offensive. French assaults in the Aisne and Champagne sectors would commence on 16 April. See Falls, *Military Operations France and Belgium 1917 Vol. I* and David Murphy, *Breaking Point of the French Army: The Nivelle Offensive of 1917* (Barnsley: Pen & Sword, 2015).

7   VII Corps (GOC Lieutenant-General Sir Thomas D'Oyly Snow) consisted of 14th, 21st, 30th, 33rd and 50th divisions prior to the opening of the Battle of Arras.

for several days and required very careful preparation and organisation especially as regards the supply of food, water, ammunition etc. which was to be taken with us. First of all, it had to be decided how many days we would be cut off and, when this was fixed, questions arose as to what could be dispensed with, what articles were essential, what proportion of transport was to be given to ammunition and how much to food, water, tools etc., what kind of food and ammunition was to be carried etc. etc. Arrangements then had to be made to store all surplus kit etc. at the last possible moment and to draw the extra food etc. which was to be taken forward.

As the concentration area was around Pommier, several days' march away, and as we only expected to be in it for a day at the outside, very careful orders had to be issued to ensure that there should be no hitch when we got there. As we did not know the exact date on which we should start all these orders were made out on the basis of the battle starting on "Z" day, and "Z-1" day was accordingly the day on which all final arrangements were to be completed. The Division told me that if I got through it without grey hairs I would be lucky! As a result of all this we had a pile of orders about an inch and a half thick before we left Corbie.

12 March, 1917

My dear Dad,

Many apologies for not writing for so long but I have been fearfully busy. All the people I had attached to me as sort of assistants have been taken away for a sort of staff class and the result is I often ought to be in two places at once.

The Brigade Major's job lies outside a great deal, and the result is that I am left in charge of the office with very important business outside at the same time. Among other details, I had to dine out tonight with one of the Battalions. As a Staff Officer, of course I have to be very polite and civil etc. to all sorts of people and when I am invited out to dinner, I simply can't refuse although I would very much rather dine at home. After dinner, I had to take part in a sort of musical evening which the French people in my billet had got up. Fortunately, I had too much work to be able to spend very long at it.

You will be pleased to hear I am feeling very much the better of my leave. I must say I was feeling a bit washed out before I got it but I am very flourishing now.

Thank goodness the General does not mind us getting up late in the morning. I came down to breakfast this morning at 20 minutes to 10.00 and he never said a word. It is midnight now, so I must shut up and get to bed.

Your loving son,

Walter J.J. Coats

18/3/17

My dear Mother,

I am very sorry not to have written you sooner but I have been very busy recently and I do get sick of the sight of paper. I am still in the same comfortable billet, miles from shells and may be for some time yet.

I have absolutely nothing in the way of news for you except that I am exceedingly flourishing and am beginning to know a little more about Courts Martial etc., so I don't have to do so much reading.

Did I ever tell you my servant disappeared on munitions when I was on leave and I arrived back to find someone else running my kit?[8] The man I have now is quite a good sort. He has been out since 1914 and has about half a dozen brothers serving, so he is more or less entitled to a soft job. I must shut up now as I have to get on with some work.

Your loving son,
Walter J.J. Coats

22/3/17

My dear Jean,

Just a line to let you know that I am still going strong. I am still in the same old spot and more or less enjoying life.

I don't think I have much to say except that at the present moment business is fairly slack. I am dining Chez McCosh tonight. I like dining with people of my own Battalion, but I do hate when I am invited to dinner by other Battalions.

[Cont.] 24/3/17

I did not manage to get this away the other day so may as well let you know I am still flourishing before I close it. We had a presentation of medal ribbons today and as it is my job to arrange for all the ceremonial parades, I was rather worried till it was all over. Fortunately, everything went alright. Among other details that had to be provided was a flagpole and Union Jack. I got a sort of handy man to rig up the pole and borrowed a flag from the ambulance but the next difficulty was arranging for the flag to be run up when the Inspecting General rolls up. The idea is that it is run up to the top of the pole in a ball before he turns up and just at the critical moment you pull the string and the thing flies out. The man who had put up the pole was the only man I could get for the job and as he had no idea how it was done I rolled the thing up myself and pulled it to the top of the pole and told him to pull the string at the critical moment. I was not at all sure how the thing was done myself, but I climbed on to my

---

8   Pte 2306/330369 Joseph McDonagh.

horse to receive the old buck and trusted to luck. As a matter of fact, when he did turn up I was so interested in watching the flag to see if it would work alright that I quite forgot to salute him until I suddenly realised that everyone else was standing at the salute. I don't know if he spotted it or not. I am glad to say that after pulling for about a minute the flag worked all right. Everything went swimmingly after this.

27/3/17

My dear Jenny,
Just a line to let you know I am still going strong.

I wonder where I shall spend my next birthday. I don't suppose it will be in as good a billet as I have at present. I am working just now with an orchestra playing next door. It is quite pleasant and I find I can work with any old row going on.

I am sorry to say I have got to dine out tomorrow. It is not half as good fun as dining at home. The General is in great form and keeps me very amused.

4/4/17

My dear Mother,
I have no news and this is just to let you know that I am still going strong. The weather here just now is absolutely beastly and it is very poor fun being out. It is rather unfortunate that my job just now consists to a great extent of billeting. This morning, I got up about 4.30 and had to ride to the billeting place, which I got to at about 7 AM and it took me till about 1.00 PM before I had finished with it. Billeting is one of those jobs where your best thanks is no complaints.

WD: We eventually left Corbie about the 3rd or 4th of April and after moving north by easy stages arrived at Bienvillers on "Z-I" day, the 8th April. We arrived at Bienvillers-au- Bois early in the morning and the fun began by our finding it full of other troops who refused to move out. As a result it was well on towards mid-day before I managed to get these other people out and our own battalions in. Fortunately however everything else worked smoothly, though it was well after dark before I was able to get back to Brigade H.Q. and report everything ready.

The battle began early on the 9th. We were all up before dawn and got ready to move but thanks, as we learnt afterwards, to the fact that the Germans had forestalled us and moved back, all our plans were upset and we did not move for another two or three days, though we were kept ready to move at half an hour's notice and the horses were kept harnessed.

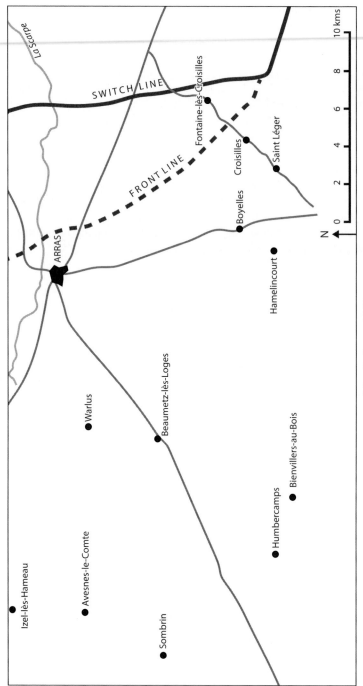

Map 7 Arras, 1917.

9/4/17[9] [Battle of Arras]

My dear Dad,

Just a line to let you know I am going strong. I think yesterday was one of the busiest days I have had for a long time. I got up about 5.30, left on my horse at 6.30, arrived at my destination at 7.00 AM, and was hard at it until 8.00 PM, with about 10 minutes off for lunch. After dinner I had a few papers to do and then cleared off to bed. As a matter of fact, I had been looking forward with dread to that date for the last three or four weeks and thank goodness it is over. The Division warned me some time ago I would be lucky if I got through the day with all my hair on my head.

What you think of the news? You will see now what I have been busy about. You will be pleased to hear the General is going to keep me to run the show behind while he goes up with the Brigade Major, so I should be fairly safe, though I expect to have my work cut out for a bit.

Many thanks for the various letters, I always look forward to them however busy I am. I must buzz off again so Cheer Oh.

11/4/17

My dear Dad,

Many thanks for the map case, chocolate etc. which I got yesterday. The case is exactly what I wanted.

What I would like now, if you would not mind, is a map measurer i.e. one of those things you run along the map and it tells you how far you have to go. I am very busy just now, but very flourishing. The news is good.

WD: The weather all this time was very wet and cold and when we eventually moved up to a position close to Boisleux-au-Mont [5km S of Arras] about the 11th, things did not look bright as the area was full of troops and there was absolutely no shelter until the Division managed to find us a few trench shelters, i.e. large canvas sheets, which the men made into bivouacs. Even then half of them were left in the open.

After a day or two here we were moved forward again to an area round Hamelincourt with Brigade H.Q. in a broken down house in the village where we were fairly comfortable. Unfortunately, this was the only place for miles around where there was anything like decent shelter so we had hardly got in before the Division informed us they were going to

---

9   The 33rd Division remained in corps reserve throughout the opening day of the Arras offensive. For accounts of its subsequent participation in the First Battle of the Scarpe (14 April 1917), Second Battle of the Scarpe (23-24 April 1917) and Actions on the Hindenburg Line (20-30 May 1917), see Falls, *Military Operations France and Belgium 1917 Vol. I* and Hutchison, *The Thirty-Third Division in France and Flanders 1915-1919.*

take it for their H.Q. and ordered us to be out at daylight next morning. We pointed out to them that with the amount of paper work they were expecting us to do, it would be almost impossible to carry on in the open but they insisted on our moving, though they gave us a few hours' grace in which to do it. As we could not carry on entirely in the open, the B.G. accordingly chose a spot in the railway cutting between Judas Farm and St Léger and ordered the Field Co. R.E. to build us a H.Q. by next morning. This was a pretty stiff proposition as we had no material to give them but when we turned up next morning we found they had managed to rig up a couple of rooms sufficiently strong to keep the rain out. As there was no means of keeping this place warm, we pinched the stove from the H.Q. at Hamelincourt before we moved. We were nearly caught doing this as we were just covering up the hole we had made with some canvas when two officers turned up from the Division but we managed to keep them occupied looking round outside until the job was done and then calmly loaded the stove onto our waggon under their very noses as if it belonged to us.

Shortly after this, we took over the front line which consisted of a few outposts about 800 yards short of the Hindenburg line where the Germans had now taken up their position. Brigade H.Q. did not have to move.

It was now about the 15th of April, so we had to start at once to make arrangements for an attack on the Hindenburg line which was to take place about the 20th. The artillery started cutting the German wire and all other arrangements were made for the attack, including the formation of an ammunition dump in a quarry in front of Croisilles. This latter job was rather a ticklish bit of work as the quarry was right up in our front line and time was so short we had to take the ammunition limbers right up to it.

16/4/17

My dear Mother,

I don't think I have much news except that I am going strong and for the time being have practically nothing to do. I am thankful to say that, as far as my arrangements are concerned, everything has gone smoothly. I had time to sit down and read a book last night for the first time since I was on leave.

The country we are in just now is the absolute limit. The German swine have cut down every tree in sight and have even cut down the shrubs in the gardens. They have, of course, blown up what they couldn't cut down. We spent a pretty cheery day yesterday waiting for our house to be built. We arrived at a spot on the map where we had sent some men ahead to start building our happy house, and found they had not got much more than the foundations levelled off. It was raining hard and life presented a more or less doleful picture. However, we all got under cover before dark and are more or less happy now.

[Cont.] 17/4/17

Things are still pretty quiet from my point of view and I am having a very slack time. The weather is the only trouble. It is absolutely beastly cold and very wet.

Many thanks for various letters I have received. You might tell Dad I know Colonel Harris very well by sight, he is one of our Divisional Artillery Colonels.

WD: On the night of the 22nd/23rd April, the Brigade moved up for the attack which was carried out next morning. The scheme of the attack was as follows:- The 98th Brigade who were astride the Hindenburg line 500 or 600 yards north of the Sensée River were to bomb down this line to about the Croisilles-Fontaine Road where they were to join hands with us. Our Brigade (100th) was to attack the line from the direction of Croisilles with our left about on the Croisilles-Fontaine Road and our right several hundred yards further south. As no one was attacking to the south of us, it was quite obvious that if we got into the line we could not stay there for very long unless the 98th Brigade joined hands with us. The 98th Brigade accordingly undertook to reach us in three hours' time from the start off and we undertook to hold on till then.

During the night, the rest of Brigade H.Q. moved up to a position on top of a hill about 800 yards N.W. of Croisilles from where they could get a view of the battle and I was left behind at the old H.Q. to arrange for any further supplies of ammunition or other material which might be required and also for the sending up of rations when this was considered possible.

The attack was carried out by the 1st Queen's and half the 16th K.R.R.C., the 2nd Worcesters and the 9th H.L.I. being in support and the other half of the K.R.R.C. being used as a carrying party for ammunition etc. They started at dawn under cover of a creeping artillery barrage and got into the German trench quite successfully without much loss. Shortly after this, I got an urgent telephone message from the Brigade Major in front to the effect that ammunition was beginning to run short. I was rather surprised at this as I thought I had arranged an ample supply up in front, however I ordered up several more limber loads at once and telephoned to Brigade Major that they had started. Sometime later I got another message asking when the ammunition would arrive and I replied that it ought to be up any time now, though I was beginning to get rather worried as I was told that unless it arrived soon our men would be driven out of the trenches they were in and would have to retire back over the open ground for several hundred yards. I heard no more after this for about half an hour and was just beginning to hope that everything was all right when the limbers turned up at my office and reported that they had not been able to get through as one of the tanks which was supposed to be co-operating with us had stuck in the cutting through a railway embankment and it was impossible to get the limbers past. This was rather a blow but I at once telephoned Division H.Q. and asked for all the pack animals they could lay hands on to be sent up at once and they promised me fifty. I then telephoned the Brigade Major explaining what had happened and got the cheery reply that I need not worry now as it was too late as our men had been bombed out of the German line and lost very heavily getting back. I was now thoroughly worried as I imagined the failure of the whole show was due entirely to my not having arranged for a sufficient supply of ammunition, so my relief can be imagined when the General came back that night and told me it was not my fault as the Brigade Bombing Officer had gone up in the middle of the show to find out why the ammunition had been used up so quickly and had found several thousand grenades and any amount of small arms ammunition within a few yards of the H.Q. of the battalion that had been complaining of the shortage. The reason our men had been bombed out was that it had been impossible to get the ammunition up to them as the intervening ground was swept with machine gun fire from the flanks and though we had held on for seven hours the 98th Brigade had not joined hands with us.

Shortly after this the Division was relieved and the 100th Brigade moved back to bivouacs round Moyenneville where we stayed a few days and then moved up to bivouacs round Boyelles.

26/4/17

My dear Dad,

It is some time since I last wrote you but I have had a pretty strenuous time. I think the 23rd was one of the most worrying days I have had for a long time. I was under the impression all day that everything had failed through my not having made suffi-cient arrangements and you have no idea what a relief it was when the man who was assisting me came back about 7.00 PM and told me that I had got more than enough stuff up.

Yesterday, too, was a very strenuous day billeting. Altogether I managed to cover 33 miles. Six of these I did on a horse and the remainder on a bicycle and on foot. The worst of it was the wind was so strong I had to pedal downhill and walk up and the roads were in many places so bad I had to walk. I am fairly tired today as a result but as the weather is fairly fine and I have a good billet, I am perfectly contented.

Please thank the girls for their birthday present which arrived safely.

7

Another Summer in France and Flanders

The only matters of interest while we were here were a Brigade Shooting Tournament, a Brigade Boxing Competition and the Half-yearly Despatch in which I found I had been given the Military Cross.

WD: On 7th, the Division held a Race Meeting on a strip of ground between Ayette and Moyenneville which was a great success.[1] I entered one of my horses for a race but unfortunately it bolted twice with the Brigade Signalling Officer, who offered to ride it to the course, before he got there so it was not in the best of condition. The rest of Brigade H.Q. drove to the meeting in a four-in-hand which consisted of a General Service wagon with four of the Brigade H.Q. horses hitched in, which the General drove himself.[2]

7/5/17

My dear Mother,

I have just spent a most enjoyable afternoon at a Divisional race meeting. To start with, we drove to the show in a four-in-hand G. S. Wagon with the General himself driving with one of my cigars sticking out of the corner of his mouth to complete the picture. As a matter of fact, he drove jolly well, though I generally took care when rounding a corner to stick my legs over the side so I could make a simple jump for it if we upset. The meeting itself was a huge success. The races themselves were all very good and between whiles we had the Divisional Band and the Divisional Concert Party in full blast not to mention free tea and drinks for everyone. The mule race was one of the funniest. Altogether there were about 150 mules in it but the field soon

---

1   Captain Bernard Law Montgomery (GSO2 33rd Division), the future Field Marshal Montgomery of Alamein, was one of the race meeting organisers.
2   See Hutchison, *The Thirty-Third Division in France and Flanders 1915-1919*, pp. 50-59 for a facsimile reprint of a humorous, contemporary *Illustrated Sporting and Dramatic News* (20 June 1917) article chronicling this wartime equestrian event.

Artist's depiction of Brigadier-General A.W.F. Baird enjoying one of Walter's cigars
whilst driving 100th Brigade staff officers to the "Arras Spring Meeting".
(*Illustrated Sporting and Dramatic News* of 20 June 1917)

got thinned out a bit by several of them running the wrong way. You could hear the
whack, whack of the sticks about ¼ mile down the course. One mule kicked its rider
clean over its head in front of the whole crowd, much to everyone's delight. To add to
the general interest of the performance, there was an aeroplane overhead looping the
loop and doing all sorts of tricks.

Did I ever tell you of the gas alarm we had a few nights ago? About 11 o'clock at
night there was suddenly the most violent ringing of gas alarms and everyone started
putting on their masks. It was eventually discovered that it was a false alarm. The
next morning at breakfast we were all discussing what could have been the cause of it
and had more or less given it up as useless when the General casually remarked that
he had received a present of some plovers' eggs the day before which had gone bad in
the post. I at once suggested that the cause of the gas alarm had been discovered, and
curiously enough it was found that the parcel had been opened a few minutes before
the alarm went.

Another funny thing about it was that the sender of the eggs had enclosed a note
saying that he hoped this would be the last lot of eggs he would be sending out. We
all agreed. The alarm, of course, had nothing to do with the eggs but it is funny how
they should have been opened just at the right time.

WD: After about ten days out we again moved into the line at the same place to prepare for a second attack on the Hindenburg line and after getting things ready moved back to Moyenneville on the 16th.

17/5/17

My dear Dad,

I am afraid it is some time since I wrote last but I have not really had time. When one is told to do a thing by a certain time and arranges accordingly, and is then told that instead of having seven days one has only three do the job in, it doesn't leave much time for letter writing.

The weather for the last two days has been absolutely beastly but it is better again today.

I had rather an interesting walk the other night. I was walking across country to try and get to a place for something. The night was as black as they are made and one could hardly see an inch. We were going along quite gaily, when the man with me suddenly vanished. Fortunately, he was a step in front of me so I stopped and looked and listened, as George Robey would say, and I found he had gone plop over a bank about 4 feet high. No damage was done, so we carried on. The next thing that happened was that we were brought up with a bump against a wire fence. We got our job done all right and started back and as luck would have it, the man I was with was again nearly winded on the fence. He was quite annoyed but, as I had remembered the fence, I was fearfully pleased. We decided to go by the road after this but after walking a bit, as I knew the road doubled back, I suggested cutting off the corner and he agreed. We both climbed up a small bank about 3 feet high, took one step forward and fell straight into a hole. When I had got safely to the bottom and found the other man wasn't hurt, I simply lay back and roared. The other man didn't seem the least bit amused, which tickled me more than ever. I have been chuckling about it ever since. We had fallen into a trench about 6 feet deep which I remembered, after reaching the bottom, had been dug along the side of the road. After that, we went home by the road.

It is just possible there will be a presentation of medal ribbons tomorrow. Personally, I hope not, as it means I shall have to sit up tonight and write the orders. One of the Staff Captain's jobs is arranging all ceremonial parades and rot of that sort. In a way, these shows always amuse me. The inspecting officer comes on and is received with a general salute and a tootle from the band. He then walks around and everyone who thinks he is anyone seizes the opportunity to walk around behind him. Very often, no one looks at the troops that <u>are</u> being inspected and it has always struck me that it is in many cases an inspection <u>by</u> the troops of the people walking round them rather than the other way around.

I must shut up as is time for dinner.

WD: On the night of the 19th/20th May, we moved up for the attack. The Divisional scheme of attack this time was the same as before i.e. the 98th Brigade was to bomb down from the north and join hands with us who were again to attack from the west. The Brigadier however decided that his best hope of success was to advance over the 800 yards between us and the Germans by night and try to surprise them just at dawn. This meant that the advance would not be covered by the artillery barrage and though the higher authorities wished him to have one he declined, though he asked them to bring down a barrage on the German second line the moment our men got into the first one.

The attack this time was carried out by three battalions, the 2nd Worcesters on the right with their right flank on the Croisilles-Hendecourt Road, the 9th H.L.I. in the centre and the 16th K.R.R.C. on the left with their flank on the Croisilles-Fontaine Road. The 1st Queen's were held in support.

As the roads on the right and left diverged as they went east, and the number of men to attack was based on the length of the German line between the roads, it was obvious that if we were to use these roads as guides, and this was essential in the dark, that the men must be crowded into the space between the roads at the starting point. In order to avoid crowding as much as possible, a semi-circular line was accordingly taped out

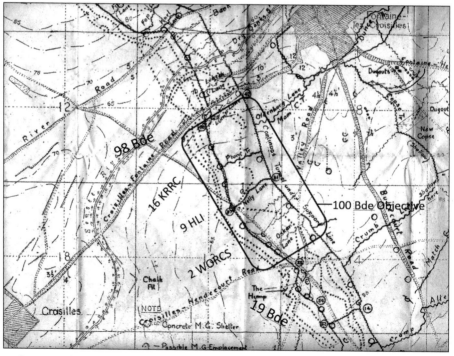

Issue trench map: Fontaine-lez-Croisilles, 20 May 1917. Annotated to show position of British units. (WJJC collection)

round the quarry or chalk pit from which they were to start. Each battalion's frontage was then marked out on this with more white tape and finally a white tape line was run out from the front of each battalion on compass bearings taken by the R.E.s in order that each battalion should get a good start in the right direction.

In case it got light a little too early, arrangements were also made for aeroplanes to do tricks such as looping the loop etc. behind the German lines in order to keep the German sentries amused and distract their attention. To ensure against further trouble with ammunition, limbers were sent well forward with extra ammunition ready to take up to the dump, and 3 or 4 half limbers in the charge of volunteers were also pushed up ready to gallop right into the German trench if required. This was rather a desperate expedient but it was decided that some at least might get up and it was a minor detail whether they got back or not.

Finally, the time for starting was arranged. This required very careful calculation as it would be fatal to our chance of surprise if the artillery barrage on the second line came down too soon and on the other hand it would not be safe to arrive too long before it, as our second and third lines were not to stop in the front German line but were to pass over it and attack the second line under cover of the barrage. It was decided eventually, as the advance was to be in the dark, to allow 1½ minutes per hundred yards and orders were accordingly given to start 12 minutes before zero, i.e. the hour at which the barrage was to start, the 98th Brigade was to advance.

A new Brigade H.Q. was built on top of the hill N.W. of Croisilles overlooking the valley between it and the Hindenburg line and on the morning of the attack we all collected up there to see how things went off.

As luck would have it, it was a very misty morning and we could see nothing but we got a telephone message through from Battalion H.Q. in the quarry saying the men had started and as the 12 minutes gradually passed it was most exciting waiting to hear if they would be spotted before they got in or not. Just on time, we heard a Machine Gun start followed at once by the explosion of a hand grenade and then the barrage came down. Shortly afterwards we got a telephone message to say that the front line was taken and that the men were advancing on the second line.

Fighting went on all day and though we were unable to capture the second line as the wire had not been properly cut, when darkness came we had consolidated our position in the front line. The 98th Brigade had again failed to reach us and the 19th Brigade, which was sent up in the afternoon for a second attempt to take the second line, also failed but on the whole it was a very successful show and we were able to congratulate ourselves on being the only Brigade that had up till then captured a part of the Hindenburg line by direct assault.

The limbers to take up ammunition to the front line were not required but twice during the day ammunition was sent up to the dump by the other limbers and it was a fine sight to see the four of them going over the open to the dump in the quarry at full gallop with shells bursting all round them. On one of the trips, one of the horses came down and we thought he had been hit but the driver managed to get it on its legs again and go on, and on the second trip half of one of the limbers came off. The driver stopped

Message, with muddy
fingerprints, signed by
Walter Coats as acting
Brigade Major, 26 May
1917. (TNA WO 95/2428:
100th Brigade War Diary)

and turned back to pick it up but the officer in charge ordered him to leave it so he came back. Otherwise there were no casualties among horses or drivers.

We were relieved that night and moved back to the railway cutting north-west of St Léger and next day returned to our bivouacs at Moyenneville. As we did not expect to go in again for some time the Brigade Major [Captain Paul] now went on leave and I took over his duties while Whitson the Brigade Bombing Officer took over mine.

27/5/17

My dear Dad,

I am still flourishing and for the moment not very busy. The Brigade Major is at present on leave so I am doing his job. It was rather a strain the first day I took it on, as I had to do my own job as well but I have now handed my job to someone else and am having an easier time.

We had Beach Thomas and Philip Gibbs lunching with us about three days ago.[3] Thomas is not so bad but I did not like the other man. 'Gilip Phibbs' would have been a better name for him. He tried to get out of me what my views were on the War in

---

3   William Beach Thomas (1868-1957) and Philip Armand Hamilton Gibbs (1877-1962), two of the five official British War Correspondents.

general, but I am afraid he didn't get much information. I find the War in particular gives me quite enough to think about.

I am very glad the Brigade Major is on leave, as it considerably brightens my own prospect of leave. I could not hope to get away till after he had been. The chances are I shall get some time in June.

30/5/17

My dear Mother,

I am still going strong and more or less enjoying life. I do about half or even quarter the work as Brigade Major that I used to do as Staff Captain. It is great fun watching the fellow who is Acting Staff Captain for me struggling with water supply, food and ammunition, R.E. material supply, cover for the troops, blankets, baths etc. etc. while I have nothing to do but sit and watch him.

I read the result of Beach Thomas's lunch with us in the Daily Mail of the 26th. It remains to be seen what 'Gilip Phibbs' has to say.

While I remember, I have lost my knife and scissors, could you please get me replacements some time. I would also like you to send out my Glengarry again, if you can find it.

WD: A few days after the Brigade Major had gone, we got orders to move into the line again and, after issuing orders for the relief, I was enjoying myself watching Whitson struggling with the food and ammunition arrangements etc. and feeling very pleased with myself when an order suddenly arrived from Division that we were to carry out another attack during our next turn in the line. This gave me rather a jar as I had been expecting an easy time, but after reading the order through more carefully I brisked up again as it was perfectly obvious that the proposed scheme was utterly impossible to carry out. It meant doing with the remnants of our Brigade considerably more than we had already failed to do with the Brigade when fresh. Fortunately for us, the Corps saw that it was a mad scheme and put their foot on it.

After a few very peaceful days in the Hindenburg line we were relieved on 31st May and moved back to billets in Bienvillers, Pommier and Berles-au-Bois with Brigade H.Q. at Pommier, where we remained for several weeks. The only matters of interest while we were here were a Brigade Shooting Tournament, a Brigade Boxing Competition and the Half-yearly Despatch in which I found I had been given the Military Cross.[4]

---

4   Walter's award was announced in the King's Birthday Honours List (June 1917) "for distinguished service in the field." See *London Gazette*, No. 30111, 1 June 1917, p. 5478. Instituted on 28 December 1914, the Military Cross (MC) is a third-level military decoration awarded for gallantry to officers with the substantive rank of captain and below, warrant officers inclusive, and (since 1993) other ranks of the British Armed Forces.

8/6/17

My dear Dad,

Many thanks for your and Mother's congratulations, which I got this morning. I also got congratulations from John and Mrs. Pyatt.

As regards being entitled to MC after my name, I believe under the new regulations that I actually am entitled to it. I may say however that I don't want it any more than I want "B.L." It doesn't do anyone the slightest bit of good and is therefore a pure waste of energy and ink.

I must shut up now as it is time to wash for dinner.

11/6/17

My dear Mother,

Many thanks for your, Jean and Jenny's congratulations. Many thanks also for the knife, scissors and Glengarry which are all exactly what I wanted.

I have absolutely no news as usual except that I am flourishing. Everyone has been extraordinarily decent about my getting the M.C., even people who might have got it if I hadn't.

I am glad you all seem to like 'Longcroft'. I am quite keen to have a squint at the place.

16/6/17

My dear Dad,

I have no news except that I am still flourishing. I am in the same old billet and having a very quiet time. I am hoping to get leave to cross on the 18th but it may be the 19th before I can get away. At any rate, I should be home inside the week. I am not sorry, as I have had a fairly strenuous time since I was on leave last and am getting a bit fed up with the life of a soldier. How anyone could take it up as a profession, I don't know. It is bad enough when there is a war on, but it must be too awful for words in peacetime.

WD: I left here on the 19th of June for a spell of leave and on arriving back on 30th, I found the Brigade bivouacked in a field not far from Hamelincourt and on their way out for another rest. I spent the night with them here and on the 1st of July we started moving.

1/7/17

To: John J Coats, Longcroft, Thornton Hall, Lanarkshire

My dear Dad,

I got back here safely about midday yesterday. The journey was not quite as bad as usual and would have been all right if they hadn't pulled me out of the train at the wrong station at about 5.00 AM in the morning. I got a lift from there on a lorry that was going my way with a load of coal and finished the journey on foot. The weather here just now is very cold and I got pretty well soaked yesterday by the time I arrived as it was pouring wet.

I hope Ellie, John, It and baggage arrived all right.

I am back much to my surprise in the same old billet that I started from and expect to be pretty busy for the next three or four days. After that, I expect we shall slack off a bit as far as I am concerned.

I must shut up now as it is time for tea.

WD: After several days' marching, we arrived on the 7th July in the Picquigny area behind Amiens, with the 1st Queen's and 2nd Worcesters billeting in Picquigny, Brigade H.Q. and our Company of the Division Train at Saint Pierre à Gouy, the 9th H.L.I. at Crouy-Saint-Pierre, and the K.R.R.C., the Machine Gun Company and T.M. Battery also nearby.

8/7/17

My dear Dad,

I am still very busy so won't have time to write a long letter. My work for the last few days has been chiefly billeting, with the result that I have now several days' accumulation of paper. However, I am still going strong and the exercise of billeting has done me a lot of good. The other day, when I was billeting, I had to walk over 20 miles on my flat feet. It reconciles one to an office again.

I have struck a very fine billet for myself just now. It is stuck on top of a hill overlooking a river whose name does not begin with X or Z but one of the other letters of the alphabet. The censor won't allow me to say more.

WD: We spent about three very good weeks in this place, the only drawbacks being the tremendous amount of office work and a Staff Ride which was organised by the Division. The latter promised to be rather a bore but fortunately the Brigadier treated it as a joke and as it took place close to our H.Q. allowed me to disappear quietly and get on with my proper work.

11/7/17

My dear Mother,

I don't know that I have very much to write about except that I am still going strong.

I am glad Ellie and It are with you just now during all this raiding business in London. I hope John will not be in too great a hurry to get back.

I have got an extraordinary good billet here just now. The house is almost surrounded by a park with about a dozen deer in it. They are fairly tame and come and feed out of one's hand after meals.

We are having a Divisional Horse Show here in about a week's time and I have entered one of my horses. It is a very nice looking beast and stands quite a good chance. I shall let you know the result later.

15/7/17

My dear Dad,

This is the anniversary of our show at High Wood. Thank goodness it is not today a year ago.

Many thanks for various letters which I have been receiving. Jim seems to be in great form, judging from his last effort.

We are having a Horse Show on the 17th and 18th. I have put in my horse as an 'Officer's Charger over 15 hands'. I hope the judges don't discover that if it charges more than 100 yards it would probably blow up, judging by the noises it makes (like an engine letting off steam). I shall have to suggest that it is one of those modern chargers especially designed for a modern charge i.e. a walk. I don't quite know what 15 hands' is, but I believe it is a considerable height. My beast is over it, at any rate. I am thinking of inventing an elastic stirrup leather for mounting by. I shall send you a programme when the show is over.

The cigars and razors have not rolled up yet but there is no hurry for them. I will always let you know when I am in a hurry for anything and at other times there is no need for the girls going off "ventre a terre", as they say in this country, in order to get things which would do just as well a week later. Talking of "ventre a terre" how is "It" getting on?

Talking of "It", our A.A.& Q.M.G. [Assistant Adjutant and Quarter Master General][5] has a he 'it' for whom he is trying to collect foreign stamps. I know you occasionally get them in the office and I would be much obliged, if you get any, if you would tear them off the envelope and send them to me. He is the head of my branch of the job at the Division and has been extraordinarily decent to me ever since I became Staff Captain.

---

5   Possibly Colonel Percy R.C. Commings DSO, South Staffordshire Regiment. See War Diary entry 16 November 1917.

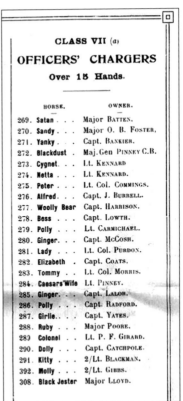

CLASS VII (a)

OFFICERS' CHARGERS

Over 15 Hands.

HORSE.	OWNER.
269. Satan	Major BATTEN.
270. Sandy	Major O. B. FOSTER,
271. Yanky	Capt. BANKIER.
272. Blackdust	Maj.Gen PINNEY C.B.
273. Cygnet	Lt. KENNARD
274. Netta	Lt. KENNARD.
275. Peter	Lt. Col. COMMINGS.
276. Alfred	Capt. J. BURRELL.
277. Woolly Bear	Capt. HARRISON.
278. Boss	Capt. LOWTH.
279. Polly	Lt. CARMICHAEL.
280. Ginger	Capt. McCOSH.
281. Lady	Lt. Col. PURDON.
282. Elizabeth	Capt. COATS.
283. Tommy	Lt. Col. MORRIS.
284. Caesars'Wife	Lt. PINNEY.
285. Ginger	Capt. LALOH.
286. Polly	Capt. RADFORD.
287. Girlie	Capt. YATES.
288. Ruby	Major POORE.
289. Colonel	Lt. P. F. GIRARD.
290. Dolly	Capt. CATCHPOLE.
291. Kitty	2/Lt. BLACKMAN.
392. Molly	2/Lt. GIBBS.
308. Black Jester	Major LLOYD.

Walter's copy of 33rd Division Horse
Show programme. (WJJC collection)

18/7/17

My dear Mother,
I have no news except that my horse did not win in the horse show. The judges were
too good. The show itself was quite a success though I can't say I enjoyed it. I went for
an hour or two yesterday, which was the first day, and got so thoroughly bored with the
whole thing that I didn't bother to go today. There was a fair amount of jumping but all
I saw wasn't worth watching. I could have done better than some of the horses myself
with one eye shut and a blister on my left foot, so you can imagine what it was like.

27/7/17

My dear Jean,
Very many thanks for your letter and the stamps. I hope I haven't entirely cleared you
out of the stock that you must have been collecting for some time.
    I was very interested to hear about [cousin] Jock being in the 98th Machine Gun
Company. I am afraid he is too far away just now for me to spare the time to ride over

and see him but I am sure to meet him sometime soon. I was also interested to hear about [cousin] Pat. Please convey my sincerest sympathy to him. It looks as if I would be the only eligible Best Man when the war is over. I think I shall set up as a professional. Tell Pat that if he still wants to walk the plank when the war is over, I shall be very pleased to blindfold him and shove him off at the deep end.

We are still where we are, the weather is still hot and the mosquitoes still bite. I seldom have less than about three bites, each about the size of a Half Crown, either on my hands or face. However they don't worry me, I don't care.

You may be interested to hear that the Gazette which brings Jack out as a full blown Major, brings me seven places further down the list and I think five, if not six, of those who are pushed over me have never been out of the country and know about as much about shells as the hair of my head, which springs to attention whenever one comes within 100 yards of it. However, as I have no intention of staying in the Army when the war is over and as I should probably get acting rank over their heads if they came out here, I am not worrying.

WD: On the 29th we got orders to move up to the coast sector of the line so on the 30th I pushed off by motor with the D.A.A.G. and arrived at Dunkirk in time for lunch.[6] After lunch, we went on to Corps H.Q. at Bray Dunes where we were given our areas for billeting and I spent the rest of the day going through our area and deciding where I would put the various units when they arrived. Early next morning the billeting parties turned up on bicycles and were given their areas and a few hours later the battalions themselves turned up.

As orders had now come through that we were to move again next day, I rode over that afternoon to Ghyvelde to arrange billets there for the next day. Fortunately, I found an excellent area Commandant in the place who said he would have everything ready next morning, all he asked for being the strengths of the units and the order in which they would arrive, so I was able to get back in time to get some of the arrears of office work cleared up. Next morning we moved to Ghyvelde and found everything in order as promised so I had a very easy job.

We stayed here a few days during which, on 6th August, the official photographer [Lieutenant Ernest Brooks (Source: IWM)] turned up and took a photo of Brigade H.Q.

---

6   The 33rd Division, now attached to XV Corps (GOC Lieutenant-General Sir John Philip DuCane), was part of a force poised for an eastward drive along the Flanders Coast, the second and penultimate phase of the projected summer advance from Ypres. It was to be supported by a hazardous amphibious landing, unofficially known as "Operation Hush", behind enemy lines at Middlekirke. The successive coastal advance from Nieuport on Ostend and Zeebrugge would follow in due course. Subsequent failure to obtain objectives farther south and consequent diminishing strategic expectations during the summer and autumn led to the shelving of this part of the Flanders offensive design. See Andrew Weist, 'The Planned Amphibious Assault' in Peter Liddle (ed), *Passchendaele in Perspective: The Third Battle of Ypres* (London: Leo Cooper, 1997), pp. 201-12.

100th Brigade HQ Staff at Ghyvelde, 6 August 1917. L to R: Sergeant Major Etchats, French Interpreter; 2Lt WB Edwards, 2nd Worcester, Intelligence Officer; Bde Major Captain Paul, 1st Middx ; Brig Gen AWF Baird; Captain WJJ Coats, Staff Captain; Captain EJ Whitson 9th HLI; Lt. GA Pilleau, 1st Queen's. Taken by the "King's photographer", see WD entry 6th August and letter 11 August 1917. (WJJC collection)

100th Brigade HQ Staff, date unknown. Standing L to R: Sergeant Major Etchats, French Interpreter; Lt. GA Pilleau (1st Queen's); Captain EJ Whitson 9th HLI; 2Lt. WB Edwards, 2nd Worcester, Intelligence Officer. Seated L to R: Brigade Major, Capt. HWM Paul MC, 1st Middx; Brig Gen AWF Baird; Captain WJJ Coats, Staff Captain. (WJJC collection)

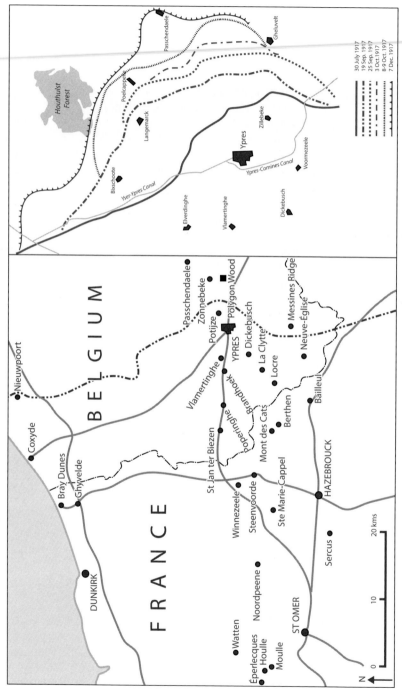

Map 8 France and Flanders and stages of the Third Battle of Ypres, 1917-18.

11/8/17

My dear Dad,

I am afraid it is some time since I have written last but I have been pretty busy.

To begin with, I may as well say McCosh is extremely flourishing. I saw him at his lunch about 5 minutes ago. He is, at present, acting as second in command.

I believe Chalmers is out here again but I have not seen him yet.

We had the King's photographer here the other day and he took a group of Brigade HQ so you will perhaps see your son appearing in the Daily Mirror or some other rag. He told us, among other things, that he had been in the Belgian lines some time before and had seen one of the Belgian soldiers fishing over the front line parapet. It gives one rather a good idea of how hard they are fighting.

Another interesting thing that happened here the other day is that young McGeorge crashed in his aeroplane about 300 yards from our front door. His engine stopped when he was up in the air and he came down with a bit of a bump as he could not find a decent landing place. As luck would have it, he came into our HQ to use a telephone, so we gave him a drink. He didn't seem to be much the worse of it. If you happen to be telling his people that I met him, don't say he had just come a bit of a bump.

Rather a funny thing happened in our billets here. The old lady we are billeted on had a bit of a hole in the floor of our room so we removed about a dozen of the boards and put in new ones for her. The General, when speaking to her after, told her he had had the floor mended but that it didn't look very good, as he had no paint to paint it for her. The old lady, instead of thanking him for it, simply said "Oh, but you can buy paint in the village". The paint, I may say, has not been bought.

14/8/17

My dear Dad,

I gave the AA&QMG the stamps that were sent me some time ago and he was fearfully pleased with them. When I said I had some stamps for him, he expected about three or four, and was fearfully bucked when I produced my bundle.

I went out for a gallop on the sands two days ago and have repented it ever since. I have been sitting in the office so much lately but I have got into rather bad training and the result of the ride is that I can hardly move, I am so stiff. However, I suppose it will do me good.

I have no other news except that the cigars are fine so Cheer Oh.

WD: At this time, the new Brigade Major, Capt J I Muirhead of the King's Own Yorkshire Light Infantry, turned up to replace Paul who had been ordered to take over the job of G.S.O.II Flying Corps.

The day after Muirhead arrived, I moved off to Coxyde to arrange billets for the Brigade which was under orders to move next day. While I was interviewing the area

Commandant there, as luck would have it an officer turned up from Division and waited while the arrangements were being made and took me back in his car. As the area Commandant had promised to have everything ready for the troops arriving next day, my work was soon done.

Next day I arrived early with the billeting parties as arranged, and found the area Commandant still in bed. He had apparently arranged everything with his clerk the night before, however, for his clerk handed me out a list of the billets allotted to us and I was able to get the billeting parties started. After giving them a bit of a start, I then went round to see how they were getting on but had not got far before I met them all coming back as practically all the billets allotted were already occupied. I at once went back with them to the area Commandant's office and got an order from him in writing that the other people were to turn out. All this of course took time with the result that the Brigade turned up before billets were ready for them and had to wait by the road side.

As some of the other troops still refused to move, I started off again to rout out the area Commandant in order to get him to come and clear up the mess he had made but had not gone far before I saw him tearing past in a motor car which drew up at Brigade H.Q. about 200 yards down the road, so I turned back. When I arrived at Brigade H.Q., I found him simply stamping with rage and demanding to see the General at once. When he saw me he became even more excited and was quite unapproachable until the Colonel who was in command of the Brigade for the time being turned up, when he at once let out and started accusing me of having done all sorts of things and demanding that I should be court martialled. He was assisted by an Assistant Area Commandant, an old Major, and a broken-down looking billet warden, and between the three of them it was almost impossible for the Colonel to get a word in and, when I tried, it seemed to excite them more than ever. Fortunately, in the middle of the whole show the officer from Division H.Q. who had been with me the day before turned up and as his presence did not seem to anger the others quite so much, he at last managed to get them quietened sufficiently to find out what the trouble was. We then took their statements against me one by one and as the Divisional officer was able to back up all my answers, we at last managed to prove to the area Commandant that he himself was entirely to blame for the mess that had been made and he was informed that he would be reported to Division H.Q. for incompetence and that meantime he was to get a move on and straighten things out. As he was a full blown colonel he did not quite like this, but he had the grace to apologise for his behaviour though he rather blamed it on his juniors.

Next day, I had occasion to visit him again and found him holding an indignation meeting with his assistant and a neighbouring area Commandant who had also apparently been badly jumped on by Division. When I arrived, they were talking very loudly about their not going to stand it but when I walked in on top of them they were most polite and, thanks to a good Divisional Staff, were kept in that state till we left the area.

18/8/17

My dear Jean,
I don't think I have any news today except that I had the most fearful row with an old dugout Colonel who was acting as Area Commandant. I was just going up to see him about his having made rather a mess of his job, when he passed me in a motor which I saw draw up at our HQ. I went back to see him and found him stamping up and down asking to see the Brigadier and saying he wouldn't stand it etc. etc. After about a quarter of an hour, I found it was my scalp he was after. We had a long sort of court of inquiry after that which ended in his apologising to me.

[Cont.] 20/8/17
I did not get this posted yesterday, so shall carry on.

I have just had another set to with the old Colonel. I wanted a bit of ground to put some people on, so went to ask him for some and he gave me a rotten bit that wasn't fit to use, so I went chasing round and eventually found a most excellent piece he had been holding back. I went to him to see if I could have it and was most polite to him. We discussed aeroplanes and weather and even the question of the number of blankets he slept in at night, and after about an hour he consented to give us the ground. So far, so good but even a lively interest in his blankets would not make him give me some other room he had. I thought I was done, but then but fortunately an officer from the Division came round and found out what was happening and, I believe, the old man has been told exactly what is thought of him and ordered to give us what we wanted. I don't know what he will say when I call on him tomorrow and am rather wondering what to talk to him about. I think I shall try moustache wax and digestion or something of that sort.

WD: The billets in this area were huts built among the sand dunes and at first we thought we were going to have a very pleasant time but had not been there long before we found out our mistake. The Germans had got the exact range of our camp with long range guns and shelled us every night. These guns were a long way off and we had time after hearing them going off to wonder where the shells would land, then there would be a shriek followed by a bang and we knew that they had missed us, whoever else they might have got. As there was no cover to be had, there was of course no use worrying about it but I could not help being in a blue funk from the time the gun went off till the shell arrived and my sleep was consequently rather disturbed.

28/8/17

My dear Dad,
I enclose some papers which may surprise you. The fact of the matter is that one of our chaplains came to me the other day about one of his men and asked if I could give

him any advice on a point of law. I told him I was too rusty on the subject to justify his taking my advice but that I knew you would be very willing to do anything in that line. He fairly jumped at the idea, so I said if he sent me the papers I would send them to you. The trouble is that the man the chaplain told me about does not like to sign and hand over a receipt to his customer for £42.7s.7d without first being sure the money has indeed been paid to his firm and he also does not know whether he is letting himself in for anything in the way of very heavy expenses.

I don't know if there is much in the thing but as the man's firm may be rather a poor one, I should be much obliged if you could get the money for him from the customer and hand over the receipt if things are alright, or let me know what you think should be done. If you know the customer's firm is a good one etc., the best thing then might be to send the papers out here again when we could send them home in the ordinary way as if nothing had happened, though I should think a really good firm would not be particularly offended by a man taking whatever precautions he thought fit. I hope this will not be a fearful trouble to you if it is, please let me know and I will take care not to let you in for any more cares.

I was inoculated the other day for typhoid. It is three years at least since I was last done, so I walked round to one of the M.O.s and got him to squirt some stuff into me. I believe he repeats the performance in about a week's time.

Personally, I am extremely flourishing and hope you are ditto.

Your loving son,

Walter J.J. Coats

WD: We stayed here about a week with the uncomfortable prospect of a tour in the line at Nieuwpoort where the Germans had just started using mustard gas but fortunately for us on the very day before we were to move in it was decided that the operations for which we had come up, viz. a frontal attack by us in conjunction with an attack by a Division which was to be taken out to sea and landed behind the German lines, were off and the Division was accordingly taken back to our former billets in La Panne, Bray Dunes and Ghyvelde. After about two days here on the 31st of August I went off with the D.A.A.G. to billet in the Éperlecques area just north of St Omer and the rest of the Brigade followed by train to Watten on the 1st September. The billets in this area were exceedingly good Brigade H.Q. being in the Château du Gandspette.

We spent our time here training for the battle (3rd Battle of Ypres) which we now knew we were in for and before we moved I managed to get into St Omer and visit Elsie [Graham].[7]

---

7   The Third Battle of Ypres, popularly known as "Passchendaele", opened on 31 July 1917. For full campaign narratives see Sir J.E. Edmonds, *Military Operations France and Belgium 1917 Vol. II* (London: HMSO, 1948), Robin Prior & Trevor Wilson, *Passchendaele: The Untold Story* (New Haven: Yale Nota Bene, 2002) and Chris McCarthy, *Passchendaele: The Day-by-Day Account* (London: Arms & Armour Press, 1995).

4/9/17

My dear Mother,

I am afraid my last letter was a bit scrimpy but in the first place I was in a hurry and in the second place I had no news. I haven't had any news even yet, but as business is slack I may as well let you know that I am very flourishing.

We are at present living in a very nice Château with tennis and all sorts of things for those who have time. We are having the Count and his family to dinner on Thursday night, so I foresee I shall have to get my second dose of inoculation that day and kill two birds with one stone. If the day is going to be spoilt, it may as well be spoiled thoroughly and it is just possible I may be feeling too seedy to go to dinner at all.

I hope Esda and the son and heir are flourishing.[8] Who is it supposed to be like?

7/9/17

My dear Dad,

I am enclosing the papers in connection with the man the Chaplain brought to me. It seems to me too much trouble over nothing and I hope it has not worried you much. From the man's point of view however it was, I suppose, very important, and it is at any rate good for morale to let them know that you are prepared to help them if possible.

I am getting quite a lot of riding now as things have slackened off a bit in the office and I am getting to like it better every day. There is not so much of the cup and ball sort of performance now when the beast canters. The first day out after a long spell in the office is a sort of diabolo performance when I start off, and I am glad to say that so far the horse has always managed to catch me when I come down. After a day or two, the game quietens down to one of cup and ball in which I never rise further than the length of the stirrup leathers. Things then quieten down for a bit, until I get stuck in the office for several days on end, when the game starts all over again.

We are getting letters out here very quickly now. Your letter of the 3rd I got on the evening of the 5th, which is not bad going from Glasgow, and I believe we now get letters from London on the day they are posted.

I was inoculated for the second time after dinner last night and my arm isn't even stiff today.

I must shut up and get a move on.

---

8   John Reddie Coats born to Jack and Esda Coats on 26 August 1917.

Glasgow Highlanders concert programme, 12 September 1917. (WJJC collection)

Third Battle of Ypres and 1918 Spring Offensives

There have been moments during the last week or so when I had grave doubts as to whether I should see tomorrow.

WD: About the middle of September we were on the move again and after marching through Oost Houck, Steenvoorde and Berthen at each of which places we spent a night, we arrived in camp at La Clytte, south west of Ypres. Here we got our final orders and arranged our plan of attack.

We moved from La Clytte on the 24th to the front line east of Ypres around Polygon Wood.

> Night of 24/9/17. The ground is unrecognisable owing to huge shell holes. But for a regularity of a number of tree stumps the MENIN road is a mass of huge holes. Coys have great difficulty in getting over the ground with guides and some sections are detached for a time. The hostile barrage is still intense.[1]

WD: On the 25th, while getting into position for the attack on the 26th, we were ourselves attacked by the Germans.[2] This attack was carried out at 5.45 a.m. and was supported by a very heavy concentration of artillery with bombardment commencing at 5.15 by 27 Batteries of Field Artillery (of two Divisions) 17 Field Howitzer Batteries, 15 Heavy Howitzer Batteries and 5 Batteries of H.V. long range guns. In addition, the neighbouring German Divisions were to support by counter battery work and subsidiary bombardment. We thus had against our Divisional front alone over 200 guns or one

---

1 Extract from TNA WO 95/2431: 1/9th HLI War Diary.
2 The unexpected German riposte was launched the day before the commencement of the Battle of Polygon Wood (26-27 September), the second in a series of three measurably successful offensives launched by General Sir Herbert Plumer's Second Army during the Third Battle of Ypres. The hard-hit 33rd Division suffered 2,905 casualties killed, wounded and missing during three days' subsequent fighting. See Edmonds, *Military Operations France and Belgium 1917 Vol. II*, pp. 282-84, 293 and Prior & Wilson, *Passchendaele: The Untold Story*, p. 127.

gun to about every 6 yards of front. As well as this, the neighbouring German Divisions shelled our artillery in order to prevent them backing us up and they then sent forward their storm-troops into the attack. In spite of this, however, by the end of the day we had broken up the German attack at the cost of a short stretch of our first line and when we attacked on the 26th, we re-took the lost ground and managed to advance a considerable bit on our left. The shell and rifle fire was so heavy during the German attack that one of our men Corporal Hamilton was given the V.C. for distributing ammunition among the men in the front line.[3]

As a result of our heavy casualties, we were withdrawn from the line on the night of the 26/27th and billeted for the night in Dickebusch, moving back next day to Sercus near Hazebrouck. We stayed in Sercus for about a week and on 3rd October were inspected by the C. in C.

4/10/17

My dear Jean,

I have at last got a little time to myself after one of the most strenuous times I have had for quite a while. The division has however had a great show and everyone is fearfully bucked. I have got copies of the C-in-C's, the Army Commander's and Corps Commander's[4] wires of congratulations and also copies of some captured German orders which will make very good souvenirs. All of the Officers got copies. The C-in-C himself came and inspected us yesterday and for the moment we are more or less the blue-eyed boys of the Army.

I don't know that there is very much I can write about as, barring work which one can't talk about, there has been nothing doing.

I heard rather a good definition of Jack's job today – "Teaching young officers to eat peas without a knife". I suppose that is more or less what he is doing. I can imagine him at it.

---

3   L. Cpl 4876/331958 John Brown Hamilton (1896-1973) 1/9th HLI. Awarded Victoria Cross during the Battle of Polygon Wood: On 25/26 September 1917, north of the Menin Road, great difficulty was experienced in keeping the front and support lines supplied with small arms ammunition owing to intense hostile artillery fire. At a time when this supply had reached a seriously low level, Hamilton on several occasions and on his own initiative, carried forward rifle cartridge bandoliers through severe shellfire and then, in full view of snipers and machine-guns lying out in the front of the British frontline at close range, distributed the much-needed ammunition.
4   Field Marshal Sir Douglas Haig, General Sir Herbert Plumer and Lieutenant-General Sir Thomas Morland (GOC X Corps) respectively.

WD: On the 4th, we moved back to billets behind St Omer where we were told we would be kept for some time in order to reorganise.[5] We were just sitting down to dinner, however, when we got orders to entrain early next morning at St Omer as we were being sent to take over the line at Messines. This of course meant sitting down at once to make arrangements for the move and it was well into the night before we got our orders out. Early next morning, I left with the D.A.A.G. by car for Ravelsberg near Bailleul where the H.Q. of the Division we were to relieve was situated. Here we made arrangements for billeting the men and then returned to Bailleul where they were to detrain.

7/10/17

My dear Jean,

Things have been fairly strenuous recently but as I have today got a march ahead of the transport and consequently of the office, I am having rather a slack.

The weather, I am sorry to say, is absolutely the limit. It is wet and windy and fearfully cold.

I saw Elsie the day before yesterday. She told me they were starting leave in her hospital but that she did not expect to get away for a good long time yet. I passed [cousin] Jock's people [Black Watch] on the road about two days ago, but did not see him. Do you know if he is on leave?

I am next but one on the list for leave, so I am hoping.

13/10/17

My dear Dad,

Things are very quiet so far as I'm concerned just now and prospects of leave fairly bright. I was introduced to General Hunter-Weston yesterday.[6] I don't remember having seen him since he was more or less running the show at the manoeuvres the

---

5 Relieved near Polygon Wood by 23rd Division on the night of 27/28 September, 33rd Division was sent south to VIII Corps, which was responsible for the line in the vicinity of Ploegsteert Wood; a relatively quiet sector when compared with the offensive activity farther north.

6 Lieutenant-General Sir Aylmer Gould Hunter-Weston (1864-1940). Commissioned Royal Engineers 1884; Miranzai Expedition 1891; Waziristan Delimitation Escort and Night Action of Wana 1894; Acting CRE Waziristan Field Force 1894-95; Dongola Expedition 1896; Staff College 1898-99; South Africa 1899-1901; CO RE Field Company Shorncliffe 1902-04; DAAG IV Army Corps 1904; General Staff Eastern Command 1904-08; General Staff Scottish Command 1908-11; ADMT 1911; GOC 11th Brigade 1914; Major-General and GOC 29th Division February 1915; Gallipoli campaign April-July 1915; promoted temporary Lieutenant-General and GOC VIII Corps May 1915; GOC VIII Corps Western Front 1916-18; MP for Ayrshire North 1916-18, MP for Bute and Northern 1918-35.

first year I joined. I didn't tell him who I was, as I was in a blue funk in case he would ask me to dinner or something of that sort. As it was, he walked off with our intelligence officer to lunch and has bagged our Brigade Major for dinner tonight. Such is war. He looks a much older man than I thought.

I went in and saw Elsie a few days ago as we are living comparatively near to her. Unfortunately, she was on duty and I only saw her for about 10 minutes. I shall try to get in to see her again before we move.

I am afraid my leave may not come off as soon as I expected as my regular understudy has fallen off his horse and gone to hospital. We hope he will be alright in about 10 days.

WD: Our Brigade stayed in camps between Neuve Église and Ravelsberg until about the 14th October when we moved into the line which the Division at that time was holding on a one Brigade front. The trenches here were situated well down the forward slope of the Messines Ridge and we found the communication trenches the most curious articles of their kind that we had ever seen. They were dug about three feet deep and as the ground was very wet what were called "A" frames i.e. wooden frames shaped like an upside down 'A' were let into the trenches and duckboards were laid above the top cross-piece. There were miles of this sort of trench which must have taken thousands of feet of good timber to make and the result was quite useless as one was practically never covered more than a little above the knee and often not even as much. Incidentally, they took a tremendous amount of labour to make as all the wood had to be carried for miles by hand and one well-placed shell knocked yards of it to pieces. As General Hunter-Weston was commanding the [VIII] Corps, however, the waste of labour did not worry him. Fortunately, the Germans did not shell the forward slopes much unless we sent large parties of men down it in daylight, but confined themselves to shelling the dumps and batteries on the rear slope of the hill. This made the visiting of dumps and Battalion H.Q. rather an unhealthy job but was better than if they had shelled the trenches in front.

The chief events of interest in this time were a successful raid by the 1st Queen's and a visit from General Hunter-Weston who came round with the intention of visiting the trenches but got so excited about Brigade H.Q. that he never reached the trenches at all.

Brigade H.Q here occupied a large and very deep dug-out with about 120 yards of passages, all about 30 feet below the surface. It was lit by electric light from a dynamo run by a small petrol engine installed in it and was kept dry by means of a hand pump which was kept going by a few men detailed for that purpose. We knew that Hunter-Weston was rather a crank about tidiness etc. so before he turned up we had the place put in order as well as we could with the labour at our disposal.

This however was not good enough for H-W who gave us an exhibition of the German bully at his worst for about two hours and then departed in a flood of absolutely impossible orders and left us so exhausted listening to him that we could hardly get on with our proper work.[7]

I went on leave the day we came out, 23rd October.

24/10/17

TELEGRAM to COATS, 27 Woodside Place. From Euston Station

TRAVELLING NORTH 8.50 TONIGHT. WALTER

WD: When I returned from leave on 4th November, found that the Division were still in the same sector. After another spell in the line at Messines, we got orders to move into the Ypres sector. This we did on 16th by marching to Locre and bussing from there to near Ouderdom from where we marched to camps round Brandhoek, a small village between Poperinghe and Vlamertinghe. Here we took over from the Canadian Corps who had just completed the capture of the Passchendaele Ridge.

16/11/17

My dear Dad,
I have as usual no news and this is only to let you know I am very flourishing.

I see from your last letter, Elsie is at Treport. That is where I went when I had jaundice in 1915. It is a great improvement on the last place she was at.

One of our officers is there now. I must write and let her know.

WD: About this time we lost Colonel Commings, our A.A. & Q.M.G., who was sent to G.H.Q. and his place was taken by a Colonel Pack. This was a great loss to the Division as Col. Commings was one of the best Staff Officers I ever met and Col. Pack about the worst, but after I had had a good deal of trouble with Col. Pack, who kept me

---

7   Hunter-Weston had, given his myriad command responsibilities, the contemporary reputation for excessive devotion to seemingly unimportant aspects of military minutia. Still viewed by many as the archetype "Donkey" general officer, Major Cuthbert Headlam (GSO1 VIII Corps) observed: "H[unter]-B[unter] is getting wilder and wilder ... Men like HB who consider themselves tin Gods and lay down the law about everything never can get the best out of their underlings ... My plan with HB is to let him have his say, and then, if what he says is too ridiculous, simply not carry it out! So far the plan has worked well – but probably someday I shall be discovered and then the fat may be in the fire ..." Durham County Record Office: D/He/168/10, Letter to Beatrice, 8 December 1917. See MacFarland, *A Slashing Man of Action* for a balanced biography of this controversial mid-level commander.

doing his work at the expense of my own, the B.G. managed to get him sent away and his place was taken by Colonel Ramsay, who was another good man.

19/11/17

My dear Mother,

Many thanks for the chickens and ham which have just arrived. I have not opened them yet but I have no doubt they will be alright. The weather here just now is behaving itself as well as can be expected. As long as it doesn't rain, we have nothing to grouse about.

Please also thank Dad for the cigars which arrived all right with the mags etc. last night. Fortunately, we are at present in a very nice camp in which we can enjoy them and the chickens.

22/11/17

My dear Mother,

The chickens and ham are no more. They were in excellent condition and were a splendid change from the ordinary food. Many thanks for them.

WD: As our Brigade had been last in the line at Messines, we were kept in reserve at Brandhoek for several days and then moved up to Ypres on about the 25th. Brigade H.Q. was put into the Convent at Ypres, which had at that time about two rooms which could be occupied, though the walls collapsed a few days later on the Brigade that took our place and killed one or two men.

28/11/17

My dear Dad,

Many thanks for various letters I have been receiving.

Things are going very well with me just now and I see from the papers that I shall be getting the 1914 Star sooner or later. I am rather keen to see the ribbon. It sounds as if it would be striking but ugly.

29/11/17

We got great news yesterday. We have at last got a V.C. in the battalion, a man called L/Cpl Hamilton. He jolly well deserves it too, from what I can hear.

If "My Four years in Germany"[8] is not very huge, I should rather like a copy. By the time it would get out here, things ought to be a bit slacker.

WD: After a few days in Ypres, we moved up to the front line and found it particularly beastly. There were no roads at this time nearer than about three miles from the front line and everything had to be carried up by hand along duckboard tracks which wound among and sometimes over shell holes. As these holes were often very deep and were all full of water, it was quite an unpleasant business walking along the tracks in the dark, especially as the Germans knew their position to an inch and used to shell them off and on all day and night. As it was quite impossible to move except by the tracks, one's nerves were kept on the stretch from the time one left the road till one got up to the trenches or got back to the road again.[9]

Brigade H.Q. here [Potijze area] were at first in a broken down pill box, but as a large lump of concrete fell off the inside one day when it was hit by a shell and brained the Brigade Major of another Brigade, we moved back about quarter of a mile to one which had not been quite so badly smashed. As there was no room for me in the pill box, I was left down behind in a broken down shed about half a mile in front of Ypres, where I dealt with the paper work and saw to the supply of ammunition and rations. As this latter was a particularly difficult job owing to the nature of the country, I was not sorry when we were relieved about the 8th of December and moved back to Winnezeele some miles north of Steenvoorde.

8/12/17

My dear Mother,

Please thank Dad for his letter enclosing a copy of Doug's Kashmiri Love Log. I am glad he has got such a decent place to go for a holiday. That is one of the bright spots about this place; one can always get home for leave.

We have got an artist on the Brigade Staff now, with all sorts of funny letters after his name. He is painting a Brigade Christmas card and I hope to get one to send home. He will only be able to turn out a few but I shall get at least one.

---

8   James Watson Gerard (1867-1951). US Ambassador to Germany 1913-17; assumed custo-
dial care of British interests there from summer 1914; author of the best-selling *My Four
Years in Germany* (1917). See letters 29 November, 15 and 20 December 1917.

9   The 33rd Division was, as a component formation of Hunter-Weston's VIII Corps, deployed
in the ghastly "Passchendaele Salient" from mid-November 1917 to April 1918. It was during
this period that 100th Brigade carried out a so-called "Chinese Attack" diversion – unmen-
tioned in Walter's diary and correspondence – to assist an ultimately barren two-division
night assault in the vicinity of Passchendaele village. See Michael LoCicero, *A Moonlight
Massacre: The Night Operation on the Passchendaele Ridge, 2 December 1917* (Solihull: Helion &
Company, 2014) for a full account of this almost forgotten coda to the Third Battle of Ypres.

Cheer Oh pro tem, as I must rush or for dinner.

[Cont.] 9/12/17

I did not get this finished last night as I had a lot to do after dinner. I am now quite a long way from where I started this letter and I do not expect the others to make up on me till tomorrow afternoon.

It always amuses me the cool nerve with which one walks into the best house in the village when one goes on ahead to billets and calmly says "I expect the others will be along tomorrow. Can I stay here tonight?" It is surprising how well the French people take it. For instance, I have just done that where I am just now and they have shown me up to a very nice bedroom and are going to give me sheets to sleep in.

The weather, I am sorry to say, has broken down. It always seems to do that when I have to move.

While I remember, Collins is a Captain in the 1st Battalion, 9th H.L.I.[10] He is a very good fellow and very amusing. He is the sort of man whom bursts into a roar of laughter at about midnight and when you ask what the matter is, he tells you that he has just at last seen the joke you told him at breakfast and when you ask him to explain it, you find he has not really seen the point of it even then.

WD: The intention was that we were to stay in Winnezeele for about a month but after a few days we got orders to move up Brigade H.Q. and 2 battalions to Poperinghe and 2 battalions into camps between there and Ypres. This was pretty hard on the battalions, as they had to go out on fatigue up to the forward area every day but as far as Brigade H.Q. was concerned it was very pleasant, as Poperinghe was at that time quite a lively spot with lots of concert parties who performed every night.

15/12/17

My dear Mother,

The Brigadier got hold of the book Dad sent me for Christmas and I did not see it until he had finished with it. I am now in the middle of it and find it extremely interesting.

The Brigadier is at present on leave. He was wounded the other day but it doesn't seem to worry him much.

My ex-assistant Whitson has been made Staff Captain of another Brigade and I expect I shall miss him. I don't think anyone is coming in his place. I am sorry to say,

---

10 Captain, later Major, J W Collins *Croix de Guerre*; Assistant Brigade Major 100th Brigade (see WD entry 15 April 1918).

his brother who used to be in our Battalion was killed the other day. It is the second brother he has lost this war.[11]

I got a most beautiful full length hot bath yesterday. It was glorious.

20/12/17

My dear Mother,
This will probably reach you about Christmas, so I may as well wish you a Merry Christmas and a Happy New Year.

Will Jack be with you for Christmas or does he sail before then? Please wish him the best of luck for me if he has not gone before you get this. I am glad it is Egypt and not here that he is going to. The climate ought to suit him better. Thanks for various letters of Christmas wishes which I got yesterday. I have just finished reading Gerard's book. It is fearfully interesting. Someone else is in the middle of it now.

We have not had any snow here so far but it is very hard frost and my bedroom is like an icehouse. However, it is not so bad when I get under the blankets. The trouble comes when I have to get up in the morning. I do not have a cold bath.

I am having a very easy time just now and quite enjoying life.

25/12/17

My dear Dad,
I have sent Mother today the only New Year card I have so far been able to get as the artist had not time to do as many as we wanted. The flag, in case you do not know, is the brigade flag. All brigades have them.

Today is what one would call "seasonable" i.e. snowing and beastly cold. I am glad I am not in the trenches.

I don't think there is anything else to write except to wish you the compliments of the season.

---

11 Having taken temporary command of 1/9th HLI following the tragic death of Lieutenant-Colonel Stormonth-Darling, Ernest Whitson's brother (Captain Wilfred Robert Whitson) was subsequently attached to 9th Suffolk Regiment in August 1917. He was killed in action during the Battle of Cambrai on 30 November 1917. See <http://www.glasgownecropolis.org/profiles/wilfred-robert-whitson/> (Accessed 4 December 2015).

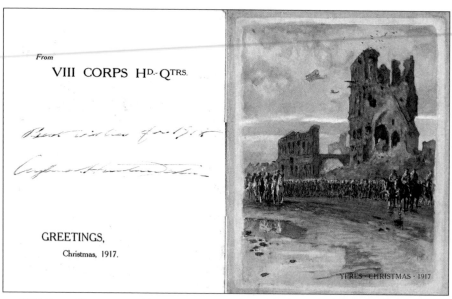

VIII Corps Christmas card bearing Lieutenant-General Hunter-Weston's signature (here juxtaposed with card front). Designed by the artist Captain Gilbert Holiday (1879-1937) of VIII Corps staff, the watercolour depicts Hunter-Weston on horseback during an awards parade held at the Ypres Grote Markt on Christmas Eve 1917. This imaginative watercolour had to be rendered prior to the event on the express orders of the corps commander. (WJJC collection)

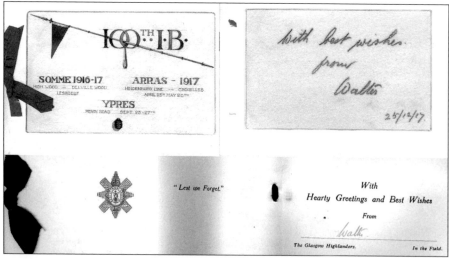

Composite image of Christmas cards 1917: 100th Brigade, with red pennant brigade flag and ladybird, and Glasgow Highlanders. See letter of 25 December 1917. (WJJC collection)

26/12/17

My dear Jean,
The only news today is that the weather is beastly. It started to snow yesterday afternoon and has been snowing off and on ever since. It does not make things any more comfortable.

I am at present acting as Brigade Major, Staff Captain and Brigade Intelligence Officer. So I am more or less busy. Fortunately, there is not much doing so I can manage them all for a few days, after which the BM's assistant comes back from leave and can take on that job. The BM himself has gone off for three months for a course. I am afraid it knocks on the head any chance I had of getting a month's leave, at least until he comes back. With any luck, I should get my ordinary leave sometime in the early part of February.

WD: After a week or ten days in this area, we were relieved by one of the other Brigades and returned to Winnizeele where we brought in the New Year. The Brigade Major [Muirhead] left us at this time for a three months course in England and his place was taken by his assistant Pilleau of the 1st Queen's.[12]

1918

1/1/18

My dear Dad,
I brought in the New Year with the Battalion last night. I dined with McCosh and the rest of the Battalion HQ and then went to the Sergeants' Concert [see image on page 293] which I enjoyed alright till I saw that the Sergeant Major who was running the show was out for my blood, in other words, a speech. He thought he had me when he proposed "the gaests" but I diddled him by getting up and drinking the toast. I had pointed out to him that I did not consider myself a guest in my own Battalion. He got me however when he proposed "the Brigade Staff" as I was the only one present. I am always afraid of getting up to speak now, as I once got up to propose someone's health and quite unintentionally insulted him so much that he didn't thank me.

The worst of these shows is the way they thrust drinks on one. They always feel insulted if one refuses and never have anything decent to drink e.g. water. Last night, they started me off on whisky (about ¾ neat). I managed to avoid most of this by changing glasses with the fellow next to me. He was pretty cheery and did not notice it. His glass was empty. They next filled my glass up with beer but I again managed to

---

12 Lieutenant Gerald Arthur Pilleau, 1st Queen's (Royal West Surrey) Regiment. See p. 275.

Glasgow Highlanders Sergeants' Mess Supper and Smoking Concert Menu, 31 December 1917. Designed by Sgt 761/330015 John Gilbert Hamilton. (McCosh family collection)

dodge most of this by changing my seat and forgetting to take my glass with me. They then gave me a glass of port. This lasted me through most of the toasts and was then providentially upset during the singing of "He's a jolly good fellow" or something of that sort. I thought I might get away without any more after that but they again thrust a very strong whisky on me. I managed to leave a large part of this behind.

Best Wishes for 1918.

WD: A few days after the New Year we again returned to the Passchendaele sector. We found things here much as we had left them, the only change being in the Brigade H.Q. which had moved to another pill box which was even smaller than the one before and was known as the Bear's Cage. I remained in the old place in front of Ypres.

6/1/18

My dear Jenny,

Many thanks for the sweets you and Jean sent to me for Christmas and New Year.

The Divisional Commander is at present reading the book Dad sent me for Christmas. Practically everyone in Brigade Headquarters has had a read and when the Divisional bloke dined with us the other night he said he would like to read it too.

I must shut up to catch the post.

24/1/18

My dear Mother,

Many thanks for various letters. I see you have been having pretty brutal weather at home, and a lot of trouble with frozen pipes. That is one of the worries we are to a great extent, though not entirely, saved from out here. The beauty of life out here is that if the place does leak, one simply removes anything of value from under the leak and lets it leak.

I am getting very hot on the leave track just now and am hoping to get home in three or four weeks' time for 14 days. I believe the extra four days makes quite a bit of difference. I hope to bring you home some real butter and a sugar ticket.

We are rather short-handed here just now as the Division have bagged one of our officers for a job and another has gone sick. I believe oysters were the cause of his downfall. He was in one of the towns round here last time we were out of the line and had about a dozen, so I am not surprised.

27/1/18

My dear Jean,

As usual, no news except that I am exceeding flourishing.

I have just been out and found Charlie MacPherson's grave.[13] It is between ¼ and ½ a mile out of Vlamertinghe. It is in the extreme south east corner of the cemetery and has a small black cross with an inscription in silver letters:

In Memory

Of

Lieut. Chas Kenneth

MacPherson

42nd Bn

The Royal Highlanders of Canada

Killed in Action

October 25th

1917

WD: We spent the rest of the month dodging between Ypres and the front line and on the 28th were relieved by 50th Division. Just before we were relieved the B.G. got wounded in the leg but as it was not serious he refused to go to hospital.

On the 30th we were taken back by rail to Wizernes and marched from there to Hallines [near St Omer] with Battalions at Esquerdes, Setques, Quelmes and Leulinghem.

30/1/18

My dear Jenny,

Many thanks for your letter which I got yesterday.

The letters arrive here very quickly now. Last night at dinner I got a letter from Mother posted in Glasgow at 5.00 PM on the 28th. I must have got it within about 30 hours of it being written, which is pretty good going from Scotland.

The weather here just now is simply perfect, bright sun all day and bright moonlight with just a slight touch of frost.

As usual, I have no news. I hope that the family are as fit as I am. They could not be fitter.

I am glad to say business is fairly slack in my line just now and is a great deal out of door work. I have shifted my billet since last writing. The old woman whose billet I was in cut up rough about the length of time my servant spent in my room cleaning

---

13 Lieutenant Charles McPherson, 42nd Bn. The Royal Highlanders of Canada, was a cousin of Walter, being the grandson of Walter's great uncle, Robert Coats. He was killed in action at Ypres 25 October 1917 by shellfire whilst on duty in California Trench, a position situated in the immediate rear of the British frontline and is buried in Vlamertinghe New Military Cemetery.

up, and nearly collapsed when I told her I was going to have a bath in my room and expected my servant to bring the water every night to wash for dinner, so I cleared out. I have got another equally good billet elsewhere.

WD: While we were here the B.G. [Brigadier-General Baird] was ordered to go to G.H.Q. to collaborate with two other Generals in the writing of a pamphlet on "The Division in Defence". Colonel Johnson [CO 16th KRRC] took over command of the Brigade while the B.G. was away.

1/2/18

My dear Mother,
Many thanks for your letter of 29th which I got last night.
   I put up my 1914 Star ribbon today.[14] It goes quite well with the other one. The Brigadier and myself are the only officers on Brigade HQ that got it.

5/2/18

My dear Dad,
Just a line to let you know the Brigadier has approved of my going on leave as soon as I can get away. I am going along to Divisional HQ in a few minutes to see when they can give me a vacancy on the leave board. With any luck, I shall cross on Friday or Saturday. I shall let you know before I close this letter. The fellow I am handing over to knows nothing about A&Q so I will take longer to hand over and explain things to him before I can get away. I should be home sometime this week at any rate.
   I am extremely flourishing just now and businesses fairly slack.

WD: I got away on leave on 7th February. On my return on the 21st February, I was turned out of the train at Poperinghe. On finding that the Brigade was up beyond Ypres, I decided, as it was then well on in the afternoon that I would stay there for the night and rejoin next day. I accordingly went round to the Officer's Club and booked a bed but after having a look at it I decided that it would be better to walk all night if needs be, rather than sleep in it. As it was now dark, I decided not to wait for dinner but to push on at once and I was lucky enough to find a lorry that was going that way before I

---

14 The 1914 Star medal was authorised by Special Army Order No. 350 in November 1917 and by an Admiralty Fleet Order in 1918. Awarded to BEF officers and men who served in France and/or Belgium between 5 August and midnight of 22-23 November 1914, the former date corresponds with Great Britain's declaration of war; the latter with the end of the First Battle of Ypres.

had even got out of Poperinghe. I accordingly climbed in and arrived at Brigade H.Q. in time for dinner.

When I had left to go on leave, I had handed over my job to the assistant Brigade Major, Pilleau, so when I walked into Brigade H.Q. and found an officer of the Glasgow Highlanders there whom I had never seen before I concluded I must have come to the wrong place. But on asking where Brigade H.Q. was, I was told I was right enough. The officer then explained that his name was Brown[15] and informed me that in my absence Pilleau had gone off to another Brigade as Staff Captain and that he was running my job for the time being. He also told me that he was thankful to see me as he had not the least idea what to do and I found out afterwards that, when the B.G. had asked for him, they had made it clear that he did not care much whether he knew the work or not, provided he could eat decently at table.

28/2/18

My dear Dad,

Please excuse my not writing sooner to say I had got safely back.

When I got back, I found the man I had left in charge had gone off to be Staff Captain to another Brigade and another officer was trying to carry on who knew absolutely nothing about it as he had only been in the country about 10 days so did not know anything. The result is I have been most fearfully busy ever since I got back. Fortunately, I do on average about 12 miles walking every day which helps me to keep fit.

2/3/18

My dear Dad,

I am glad to say I have got things straightened up a bit now so I am not quite so busy, though I still have enough to keep me from wearying.

The weather here just now is bitterly cold and I can hardly hold my pencil even in the shack which I have for an office so please excuse the writing.

You will be pleased to hear there is an off chance of my being sent to England at the end of this month for a three month's course. I should prefer to be out here getting on with the War but I know you would prefer if I went home, so I did not refuse to let them send in my name.

WD: I then started on about the hardest six weeks work I ever did. Rear Brigade H.Q. this time was in a shack built against the side of an old tank near the Potijze Cross

---

15 Lieutenant T W L Brown, 1/9th HLI.

Roads about a mile in front of Ypres. Advanced Brigade H.Q. was in a large pill box just behind Zonnebeke, a good three quarters of an hour's hard walk up the Zonnebeke Road, and from there getting round the battalions in the line taking anything from another hour and a half or two hours walk. As I had to go round the battalions every day, this meant that if I left immediately after breakfast I got back pretty tired in time for a late lunch about 2p.m. I then spent the rest of the day struggling with paper and making arrangements for rations etc. being sent up to the line, which took me till 11 or 12 at night and in addition I sometimes had to go up to Advanced Brigade H.Q. a second time to get urgent papers signed.

In the middle of all this work, the Corps started a mad scheme of having a huge supply of emergency rations and ammunition taken up to the front line in case of attack. As some of this consisted of water in tins which had to be renewed every week to keep it from getting stale, and as odd tins of bully beef etc. were always going astray when battalions relieved each other, and as an explanation had to be sent to the Division when any of it was lost, this scheme proved about the last straw. Fortunately, however, I had Brown still with me as assistant, so after struggling for some time with the problem I turned it over to him and by working on practically nothing else all day he managed to keep it fairly straight.

In addition to all this work, arrangements had to be made for a supply of dry socks to be sent up to the men every night; when battalions were relieved, train arrangements had to be made to bring them back by light railway and send the relieving battalions

Ypres-Zonnebeke Road, autumn 1917. (IWM C.143, WJJC collection)

up, and when a battalion was out of the line, arrangements had to be made for it to be bathed and receive anti-trench-foot treatment before it went in again.

The Brigade stayed in the front line here for six weeks and by the time we were relieved I was feeling more done up than I had ever felt before.

4/3/18

My dear Mother,

Many thanks for your letter which I got yesterday.

I have not got much by the way of news, except that I am still fearfully busy though not quite so bad as when I came back. It is rather amusing, the man I have got assisting me now is a writer in Glasgow called Thomas W Brown of Hill Brown & Co. He is most fearfully keen, in fact, I might almost say painfully so.

It has been most awfully cold out here for the last day or two, a mixture of hard frost, sleet, hail and a biting easterly wind. However, I have plenty of warm clothes even if I am reduced to sitting in the office with my coat on.

St Julien, 13 March 1918. (IWM NR.10, WJJC collection)

27/3/18

My dear Dad,

I am still going very strong though as usual I am very busy. I am going to try and get a stock of Field Service Post Cards and will try and get one off daily as I have so little time for writing.

It is rather cold again today but as I have now got an oil stove in my little hovel, I am not so badly off. My servant [Joseph McDonagh] has turned out to be the most splendid cook. Brown and I are living away from the rest of Battalion HQ, as there is no room up in front and I can carry on just as well behind. They of course kept the cook, so we had to do our best here. As a matter of fact, my servant is a better cook than the proper one. He gives us pies, tarts and all sorts of good things. I don't know where he learnt to cook, as he is a carter by profession.

29/3/18

My dear Dad,

Just a line to let you know I am still flourishing.

The weather has broken down here which is perhaps a good thing. The men's letters are all extraordinarily cheery in spite of what the Germans have done.[16] They at least appear to have absolutely no doubt about the result.

WD: The German offensive began down in the south towards the end of March and much to our relief we were taken out about the 3rd or 4th of April to go down and help. We moved back the first day to Red Rose and some other camps just north of Brandhoek.

On 5th, I went off to billet in the 17th Corps area round Duisans behind Arras, the advanced parties from Battalions following by motor bus and the remainder of the troops by rail. I spent the night with the advanced party of the K.R.R.C. in Penin, and next morning the Brigade arrived and detrained at Tincques and were billeted in Penin, Villers sur Simon and Izel-lès-Hameau, Brigade H.Q. being at Izel.

On 9th, I went off to arrange for billets in Sus St Léger and Warluzel and the next morning the Brigade started to march to these places. We got about half way there when

---

16 A reference to the current state of morale resulting from the early success of the great German spring offensive (*Kaiserschlacht*) that opened against the British Third and Fifth armies on 21 March 1918. See Sir J.E. Edmonds, *Military Operations France and Belgium 1918 Vol I* (London: Macmillan, 1935), David Zabecki, *The German 1918 Offensives: A Case Study in the Operational Level of War* (London: Routledge, 2006) and Martin Middlebrook, *The Kaiser's Battle* (Barnsley: Pen & Sword, 2007).

orders were received that we were to return at once to the billets we had just left and be ready to move at short notice so we turned about and marched back.[17]

Nothing further happened on 10th, until about 7p.m. when orders came that we were to entrain at Aubigny at 8p.m. As the Brigade was scattered round a large area with no signal communication and as it would take well over an hour to get from Brigade H.Q. to the station, it was quite obvious that this could not be done, however we ordered everyone to move at once and trusted to luck that they would not meet on the road. The Brigade Major (Muirhead), who had returned a few days before) then cleared off to get things straightened out at the station and to push the men into the trains as they arrived, while I made out more detailed orders for the move of the transport which, except for the cookers, water carts and mess carts, was to follow by road starting early next morning. As they would have to march for about three days, and as the orders had to detail the roads they were to move by, times of moving, places for billeting at night, and feeding arrangements on the way, I did not get this job finished and receive the acknowledgements back until about 11p.m. when a car turned up from Division to take me off to make arrangements for billeting at the other end. In the rush to get off, I left behind all the necessaries of life such as toothbrush, razor etc. which I had put in my haversack, which made the next few days even more uncomfortable than they might have been.

After a very cold journey of several hours in the car, we arrived at Caëstre and found a sort of advanced Brigade H.Q. After waiting for some time here, we were told to go and make arrangements for the troops to billet in Méteren and that they would be sent on to us by bus as soon as they arrived, so we pushed on to the Town Major's office there and sent the car back.[18]

We found the Town Major knew practically nothing about his area, so things did not get on very fast until the A.A. & Q.M.G. turned up and took things into his own hands. I found that my area was a mile or two out of Méteren on the Méteren-Bailleul Road, so pushed off at once to get it divided up before the battalions arrived. I found it consisted of about three farm houses and a few fields, so after deciding where I would put the men, I returned to Méteren and, after hunting around, I found a house for Brigade H.Q. and then hung around waiting for the billeting parties.

While waiting, I had time to look around and see how things were going on. The roads were crowded with lorries taking back machinery, stores, guns, R.E. material etc. and

---

17 Deployed south near Arras to reinforce the hard-pressed Third Army, 100th Brigade was recalled to Second Army following the opening of the Battle of the Lys (9-29 April), the second in a series of German offensives that continued well into summer 1918 before the worn-out attackers went on the defensive. Second Army bore the brunt of the northern assault with subsequent French assistance before the enemy drive was halted. See Chris Baker, *The Battle for Flanders: German Defeat on the Lys 1918* (Barnsley: Pen & Sword, 2011).

18 By this time, 100th Brigade had been placed in immediate reserve to 25th (New Army) Division, the latter formation tasked by IX Corps with the defence of Hill 63 (west of Messines Ridge) before it was lost to the seemingly relentless German advance on 11 April 1918.

there was also a constant stream of refugees; waggons drawn by oxen and piled up with household goods with the old grandmothers and children perched on top, old women staggering along under bundles of as much of their belongings as they could carry, men with wheelbarrows piled with their possessions, women pushing prams with babies almost buried under a pile of goods and chattels, women with babies in their arms and whole families with bundles on their backs tied up in old sheets, tablecloths etc. even the small boys carrying bundles of some sort. One old woman had to be carried out in her chair and put in a lorry that was going back. All the inhabitants of the place were out in the streets gazing anxiously down the road and wondering what was going to happen and there was a constant rattle of musketry and machine gun fire going on all the time in the distance. Everyone seemed uneasy and unsettled.

After waiting an hour or two, the billeting parties turned up and I pushed off with them at once to show them their billets. When I returned, I found the Battalions just arriving so I directed them where to go and then went to Brigade H.Q. where I found they had managed to raise something to eat. As I had had practically nothing to eat since lunch the day before I was not sorry to get a bite and a seat but I had hardly finished when orders came that we were to picket the roads to the south of us and put out outposts. As no one else in the Brigade knew exactly where the Battalions were to be found, I was again sent off to see this done and to see that the outposts were properly put out.

When I had got this done and returned to H.Q., I found that we had been put under the orders of the 19th Division and that they had ordered us to move up at once to a position in front of Neuve Église. The rest of the Brigade H.Q. moved off at once and, after arranging for the move of the transport, I followed on and found Brigade H.Q. had taken up their position in the old Divisional Camp at Ravelsberg between Bailleul and Neuve Église. I learnt here which Brigade we were taking over from, and went on at once to find the Staff Captain in order to learn where the ammunition dumps were etc. I was told he was in Neuve Église but wandered all through the village without finding any trace of him. Fortunately, I met a man in the village who told me Brigade H.Q. was about a mile out the other side and I eventually ran them to earth in an old hut by the side of the road. My labour however was useless as the Staff Captain knew nothing.

When I left here it was quite dark and I had a very uncomfortable walk back to my own H.Q. as the Germans were shelling the road with very heavy stuff and I had to take refuge in the ditch several times.

When I got back, I found that some of the Battalions were already asking for ammunition and it was a piece of pure luck that someone found a dump close beside us and by emptying the Mess Carts we were able to send some up. As things were fairly quiet, the cookers were also sent up with the rations.

Early next morning, I went round the Battalions to see how they were getting on and if they wanted anything. I found the Glasgow Highlanders in support in a camp between Ravelsberg and Neuve Église and then went on to see the Worcesters who were holding the line in our left front. I had a pretty fair idea of where to find them as I knew the district well but it was a very lonely walk as there was not a soul in sight and I was beginning to wonder if I had walked through our front line by mistake when I found a small party of Worcesters who directed me to their H.Q. I found they were in a camp which we had occupied as a rest billets when in the line at Messines.

When I had finished with the Worcesters, I set off to find the K.R.R.C. who were on the right, making a big detour towards the rear as I went, as I had no idea how the front line ran. I had got about half way back towards Brigade H.Q. when I met the Adjutant (Malcolm) of the 101st Field Ambulance who told me that if I turned left down the next road and kept straight on until I was stopped I would then be quite close to the K.R.R.C. H.Q. I accordingly set off quite gaily down the road, which as usual was deserted and I was just beginning to think I must be about there when the Germans began to snipe at me. I at once got into the ditch beside the road to think about it and after a minute or two decided that I must have walked right through our front line and that it would be advisable to get back especially as I was unarmed. I accordingly got up and, after a most uncomfortable walk down the road with the Germans sniping all the way, I at last reached a house about 150 yards down the road and got under cover. Here I found a sentry who advised me that the road was not safe, so I told him what I thought of him for letting me past and as he could not tell me where the K.R.R.C. H.Q. were, I went on again to look for them. After one or two more visits to the ditch to avoid the sniper, who was very persistent and seemed to have got my range, I at last found the H.Q. I wanted in a small cottage beside the road. I found there was nothing they wanted but, as the cottage they were in had been a sort of shop, they were able to supply me with a piece of soap. I suppose this was looting to a certain extent but as the Germans captured the place a few hours later together with all the officers in it except the C.O. and Adjutant who were both badly wounded but managed to get away, I do not suppose it mattered.

I then made my way back to Brigade H.Q. and, after getting something to eat, started out to look for another Brigade H.Q. on the reverse side of the hill, as the camp we then occupied was in full view of the Germans.

When I got back to Brigade H.Q., I found the attack had begun and that things were not looking too well.[19] The troops on the right of the K.R.R.C. had given way and the K.R.R.C. H.Q. was already surrounded and captured. The men however were holding out, though their flank was in the air and the Glasgow Highlanders were sent up to fill up a gap which had been driven between the Worcesters and the K.R.R.C.

To add to the trouble, our transport had not yet turned up and the men were very short of tools but fortunately a lorry load of picks and shovels and another of S.A.A., which we had asked for some time before, now turned up and were sent straight on without being unloaded. We did not expect to see these lorries again but after an exciting time they managed to get back all right.

Lewis Gun magazines were also short as most of them were on the transport but here again our luck held firm and we managed to lift some off a dump which some other Division, whose troops had now vanished, had left behind.

---

19 Officially known as the "Defence of Neuve Église" (13-14 April 1918), the British formations involved were 100th Brigade and 148th Brigade of 49th (West Riding) Division (TF).

During the afternoon things grew rather critical and the B.G. [Baird] sent up the Minimum Reserves to reinforce the line. These reserves were normally kept out to form a nucleus on which Battalions might be built up if they suffered very heavily and there were strict orders against their being used but it could not be helped as there were no other troops to send up. We were still holding out when night fell.

A few hours after dark, as our camp was being shelled pretty freely, the B.G. decided that we had better move our H.Q. back a bit so we cleared at once and it was fortunate we did so as a shell arrived in the hut some of us had been sleeping in shortly after we had gone. We had rather a job finding a place in which to set up our new H.Q. but eventually found a room in a house where we stayed till daylight and then moved into a cottage about half a mile further back.

The fighting meantime was very heavy especially round Neuve Église, which changed hands several times. The Worcester H.Q. very foolishly allowed themselves to be surrounded in the village where they were bottled up for some considerable time and completely out of touch with their men who were left to carry on as best they could without them. On the other flank there was also considerable chaos as the Battalion H.Q. had been completely wiped out and it was only in the centre, which was held by the Glasgow Highlanders, that we had the position properly under control.

During the day, we were again shelled out of our H.Q. but after sitting in an open field for an hour or so moved in again and were not further disturbed.

I was getting rather anxious by now about our transport which had not yet turned up, as the horses of the little we had were almost completely done up and could not last much longer so it was a considerable relief when I got word that it would arrive in a few hours. I at once went off on my horse to meet it and tell it where to go and when it turned up I put them into what seemed to be a quiet field some distance behind Bailleul and, after ordering some ammunition to be sent up, at once returned to Brigade H.Q.

When I got back, I found the fighting was still very heavy and that we had been pushed back to the road between Ravelsberg and Neuve Église and that we were going to move our H.Q. after dark to a larger farm house several hundred yards behind us.

Shortly before dark it was decided that things were now sufficiently settled to send up rations and, as there was no one to spare at Brigade H.Q., I set off again for the transport lines. On the way back I passed through Bailleul which I found completely deserted but on the way out past the Asylum I was stopped by a picket on the road and it took me some time before I could establish my identity and get past. The trouble was that the remainder of the Division was fighting in another area around Méteren and the picket who knew this could not understand what I was doing there.

When I got back to where I had left the transport, I found that it had moved and as it was now quite dark it took me nearly an hour before I found them. I was rather annoyed at their having moved without letting me know but it turned out that they had been shelled out of one place after another all afternoon and had just settled down when I found them.

When I had arranged for rations to be sent up and for a better system of communication between Brigade H.Q. and the transport, I returned to Brigade H.Q. and found them on the point of moving but, as I had arranged to meet the ration limbers at that point and tell them where to go, it was some hours later before I was able to join them. When I did get back, I found the officer on duty dozing in his chair and everyone else sound asleep so as I was pretty well fagged out I followed their example.

An hour or so later, I was shaken up by the Intelligence Officer and told to clear out at once as the Germans were coming over the hill in front. This was a bit of a shock and roused me fairly effectively but it was not till I found that everyone else had already cleared out that I really woke up and got a move on. As a matter of fact it was a false alarm.

Apparently, however, orders had come through during the night that our men were to be relieved by a scratch lot that had been sent up to take their place and when I reached the B.G. I found him riding round with the Brigade Major looking for new positions to take up, though no orders had been received where we were to go or what we were to do. As I was not wanted for anything special at the moment, I started skirmishing round for ammunition while another officer went off to look for a place for H.Q. When I got back, after rather an unsuccessful search, I found the B.G. had collected all the men of the Brigade that could be found (they were all Glasgow Highlanders) and was explaining the situation to them. He told them straight out that the situation was pretty desperate as there were no troops behind, that they were the only men in the Brigade that he could find, and that he did not expect that the troops in front would be able to hold out for long. He then told them he would allow them 4 hours sleep, as they had had none for three days, and that after that they were to dig a new line of trenches where the Germans were to be held up at all costs.

While they were resting, I got up all the tools we had with the Brigade transport and about 100,000 rounds of S.A.A. so that when they started work we were ready for them. The empty tool waggons were then sent off to a dump I had heard of at Dranoutre to see if they could find more tools and the ammunition waggons were returned to the Brigade Transport Officer with orders to beg, borrow or steal enough ammunition to refill them and to be ready to send up more when called on. I then had time to look round.

Our Brigade H.Q. was now in a place called Hille [just south of Dranoutre] on the side of a road running along the bottom of a small hill and on the same road within 300 yards were six other Brigade H.Q.s, none of which belonged to the same Division as any other and several of which had no troops. None of them seemed to have any orders and, until the B.G. called on them and suggested that they should prolong his line, none of them seemed to be doing anything. As a matter of fact this line which the B.G. initiated was the place on which the attack was eventually held up.

We spent the rest of the day digging in and getting things in order and when dinner time came we were all so sleepy that we kept dropping off to sleep between courses. I was just thinking of getting to bed after dinner when the Worcester H.Q. turned up after fighting its way out of Neuve Église and I spent most of the night finding billets for them and odd groups of Worcesters and K.R.R.C. that now came straggling in. I managed however to get an hour or two's sleep or I would not have been able to carry on.

14/4/18

My dear Mother,

I am sorry I have not been able to write for some days. As a matter of fact, I have been fearfully busy and have only had something like a total of 7 hours sleep for the last five days or, rather, 4½ days. I find if I shut my eyes after my soup at dinner that I can take a very comfortable 40 winks before the meat course arrives. The life seems to suit me, however, as I am extremely flourishing.

There is a most fearful cold wind blowing today which does not add to the comfort of life.

15/4/18

My dear Dad,

I am still going strong and managed to get quite a good sleep last night. I don't know how much longer I could have gone on without one but I am now ready for another four or five days. Dinner last night was the most amusing meal. I had to rest my elbows on the table and prop up my eyelids to keep from going to sleep between courses. Collins, who was opposite me, was just about going to sleep between bites and only woke up when a stranger came into the Mess. Everyone else was quite satisfied about him but Collins seemed to think he was a spy and asked him the most ridiculous questions. Dinner, incidentally, was not till between 11 o'clock and midnight. It is a curious sort of existence, but there is always a certain amount of interest and excitement about it. All the same, I would rather have the sort of curious feeling one has in the stomach after a good dinner (sometimes) than the curious feeling one has in the stomach when one is in a blue funk. It is like a prolongation of the feeling one has in a lift for the first foot or two of its descent.

While I remember, would you mind sending me out a razor, shaving brush, tooth-brush, soapbox, sponge and a small folding mirror, and a comb? I have lost all mine pro tem but expect to find them later on.

WD: On the 15th, the Brigade was in the thick of it again but managed to hold up the Germans on their outpost positions on the forward slope of the hill, while the main position was being further strengthened behind the crest. There were of course all sorts of wild rumours floating about that the Germans had broken through on our flanks etc. and except on our own particular bit of front no one really knew what was happening. Even we ourselves could not tell for a time what Division we were supposed to be fighting under. Fortunately about this time the 49th Division took over command of the front and though there were still no troops behind us things began to improve as they had a broader view of the situation and were able to organise some sort of system out of the previous chaos.

Things went very satisfactorily during the day but that evening, shortly after we had sent back the mess cart to join the rest of the transport behind, we got such definite information that the Germans had taken Bailleul on our right and were already across the road by which we could get back that

the B.G. decided that Hille was no place for us. We accordingly got on our horses which had been left saddled at the door and cleared off across country to the Locre Château which we reached after a rather unpleasant canter over the fields and ditches in the dark. While the Brigade Major went to bring in the rest of the H.Q. that were following on foot, the B.G. and I went round the Château grounds to see how it could best be defended and, when the H.Q. turned up, all the spare servants etc. were pushed out under the Intelligence Officer to picket the road and hold up any Germans that might come down it during the night.

After sending word to the Brigade Transport Officer to let him know what the situation was and ordering up more ammunition and the Battalions rations, I found I had some spare time on my hands so, as we had had no dinner and did not expect to see the mess cart again, I went skirmishing around to try and find something for us to eat. Fortunately, there was a dressing station near us and I managed to borrow a loaf of bread and some biscuits, cocoa and jam and fixed up a meal of sorts in one of the cellars of the Château where we had established our H.Q.

Shortly after this, the men with the rations for the Battalions and the ammunition reported to me and, as things seemed fairly quiet up in front I sent them across country to the Battalions on the pack animals and formed a dump of the S.A.A., which had come up on limbers, at Brigade H.Q.

Fighting went on all that night and next day (16th). As the Germans had now got up a lot of trench mortars, things were beginning to look serious as we had no artillery, when we suddenly heard some guns firing behind us. As they sounded very like French guns, the B.G. at once sent off an officer [Assistant Brigade Major J W Collins] and interpreter to look for them and after searching for some time they came back to tell us that they had found them on a hill behind us.[20] They had apparently been sent up by motor lorries from the south with orders to support the British but had no idea what the situation was and had no definite orders whom to support so the B.G. had a telephone run out to them and sent back the officer and interpreter to keep them posted as to the situation and they agreed to support our Brigade. This was a considerable help as they had thirty six 75mm guns with them.

We held out for the whole of that day and the night following, though how the men managed to do it without any sleep surprised everyone.

Next day, the fighting continued as hard as ever and, as the men were now practically exhausted, things were getting really exciting when the Germans suddenly started to

---

20 The French artillery (59th Regiment) was commanded by Lieutenant-Colonel P. Marty. See TNA WO 95/2429: 'Brigadier- Gen AWF Baird report to 33rd Division HQ, 28 April 1918', 100th Brigade War Diary.

shell our H.Q. with gas and H.E. and managed to cut the telephone to Battalion H.Q. which increased the excitement still more. Fortunately, however, some more troops were now arriving and we were told that, if we could hold out till night, they would relieve us. I accordingly started out at once to arrange for billets at Westoutre where we were told we would be sent and was lucky enough to find, when I got back, that Brown, who had been doing great work together with the Transport Officer in keeping up the supply of ammunition, had already made all arrangements. This was a great relief as I was pretty tired.

The Brigade managed to hold out until they were relieved and got back to their billets during the night where they had a well-earned rest.

As we were moving again on 18th, I went off early in order to get ahead of them and arrange billets. Here again my luck held as I found, when I reached the Monastery on the Mont des Cats where we were to billet, that the rest of the Division had already concentrated there and that all arrangements had been made for us.

19/4/18

My dear Dad,

Tomorrow is, I believe, my birthday and the best present I expect to get is to get out for a rest. There have been moments during the last week or so when I had grave doubts as to whether I should see tomorrow. You will be sorry to hear Chalmers has been killed.[21] I don't know how it happened. Our men, as usual, were absolutely magnificent.[22]

WD: On 20th, we moved back to Noordpeene where we found splendid billets for everyone and spent six very pleasant days the only trouble being an inspection of the Division by the French Prime Minister, Clemenceau,[23] which we had to prepare for but fortunately we were left out as the Division decided we were too far off.

---

21 Major John Stuart Chalmers DSO was killed by shellfire on battalion headquarters during 17 April 1918. He has no known grave and is commemorated on the Ploegsteert Memorial to the Missing. Jack Lamberton's brother, Lieutenant Andrew Robertson Lamberton, was also injured in the same incident but returned to the Battalion on 2 May 1918. See TNA WO 95/2431: 1/9th HLI War Diary.
22 Still attached to IX Corps, 33rd Division had been involved in the subsequent "First Battle of Kemmel Ridge" (17-19 April 1918), during which the British line was stabilised prior to relief by French divisions.
23 Georges Benjamin Clemenceau (1841-1929).

9

Endgame

Thank God!

22/4/18

My dear Dad,

Many thanks for various birthday letters and cigars which I got yesterday.

I managed to get a bath last night and all I want now is a haircut, which I hope to get after tea.

I am still going very strong and hope you are all ditto.

25/4/18

My dear Dad,

I am still very flourishing but as usual newsless. I hope [Cousin] Pat's wound is not bad. Do you know if it was done by a shell or a bullet?

We are feeding like fighting cocks here just now. Porridge and <u>cream</u> for breakfast, eggs and bacon, fish, liver, as much butter as one wants, scones and cakes baked by the cook, red and white wine, whisky and soda, and quite reasonably decent plain water.

I wonder if leave will be open again by the time I am due for it.

WD: We were just getting comfortably settled down here when we suddenly got orders to move to an old aerodrome near St Marie-Cappel. The order was so sudden and unexpected that one of the officers of the Glasgow Highlanders, who had gone to bed feeling quite settled, found when he woke in the morning that the whole Brigade had moved and that his servant had cleared off with them without taking time to wake him or let him know where we had gone.

On our arrival at the aerodrome, we found that practically all the accommodation had been taken by the 19th Brigade and we had rather a job to get our men in. The men, however, made the best of it and that afternoon every unit in our Brigade played its corresponding unit in the 19th Brigade, all our teams winning except the Brigade H.Q. officers.

As we were not at all comfortable in the aerodrome, and were rather afraid of what might happen if the Germans chose to bomb us, we got permission to move next day to Ste Marie-Cappel. Even here, there was not much room but everyone felt happier away from the crowd.

Next day I spent trying to find Jack who was reported to be somewhere near. I was not successful though I had a very pleasant ride.

28/4/18

My dear Mother,

I am still having quite an easy time, comparatively speaking, though I am still struggling with about 10 days' accumulation of paper.

Many thanks for the razor, mirror etc. etc. which arrived safely, also for the last bundle of socks. I'm pretty well equipped now. I have not absolutely given up hope of finding the razor etc. that I lost. At any rate the Germans have not got them, which is one consolation.

WD: Next day we started to move to Wardrecques but, after marching about half way there, we were turned back.

3/5/18

My dear Dad,

The only news I have today is that I nearly found Jack yesterday. I found some of his Division, but found from them that he was another four or five miles further on. As I had already ridden about nine miles and had another nine to go to get home, I decided it could not be done. The only other news I have is that we have had a message of congratulation from Haig.

WD: In the afternoon of May 3rd, we were moved by bus to some fields near Steenvoorde. As I was getting a bit tired of billeting by now, and in any event I wanted to superintend the embussing and make arrangements for the blankets and stores being brought on later, I sent Brown off to do the billeting and came on myself with the last Battalion. We got off the buses on the road between Cassel and Steenvoorde, where guides were waiting to take on the Battalion and, after seeing it off, I sat down to wait the arrival of the lorries with the blankets etc. which were to report to me there. After waiting an hour or two, the lorries turned up and, as it was some miles from there to the bivouacs, I got authority from the D.A.A.G., who had turned up at the same time, to take the lorries right on.

We had quite an exciting time reaching the bivouacs as we had to leave the main road and take to tracks, which were so bad that the lorries were constantly getting bogged down and running into the ditches in the dark, as we were not allowed any lights. To add to the general discomfort, the guide who had gone on the first lorry had apparently gone straight through and left us to find our own way.

When we eventually got to the bivouacs, we found the place a regular blaze of lights from camp fires etc. but fortunately no German aeroplanes came over and after an hour or two everyone was completely settled in.

4/5/18

My dear Mother,
I am still very flourishing, though for the moment living in a tent.

I saw McCosh today who told me he saw Jack two days ago looking very fit.

The weather here, I am glad to say, has turned warmer so it is not so chilly sleeping out.

WD: Next morning (4th) we got things properly straightened out and in the afternoon I rode over to see about billets some distance behind Poperinghe. I found when I got there that the best fields were already occupied and all the woods full of French transport, and as great care had to be taken to keep the troops out of sight of Kemmel to the south, which was now in the hands of the Germans, it took me the best part of the afternoon to find places for our men. After arranging for the troops, I was looking round for a place for Brigade H.Q. when I was lucky enough to meet the D.A.Q.M.G. who had served in South Africa and could speak a little Dutch and with his help I was able to arrange for a room in an estaminet where they only spoke Flemish.

7/5/18

My dear Dad,
The weather here last night and today has been absolutely beastly but it is a little better now. One good thing is that wet weather is worse for the Germans than for us. Concentrating and attacking in wet weather is no joke. There is quite a lot of gunning going on just now but it doesn't sound like a full blown battle.

WD: Around the 8th, we got orders to move forward at once as the Germans had attacked and driven in our line in front.[1] As I happened to be visiting the Battalion at the

---

1   "Fighting for and recapture of Ridge Wood (with Comp[osite] Bde., 30th Division attached) [XXII Corps, Second Army] (8 May 1918)." See Becke, *Order of Battle Divisions: Part 3B.*, p. 38, Sir J.E. Edmonds, *Military Operations France and Belgium 1918 Vol. III* (London: Macmillan, 1939) and Hutchison, *The Thirty-Third Division on France and Flanders 1915-1919.*

time, I was much relieved when I got back to Brigade H.Q. to find that the Brigade Major had gone on to arrange billets and I was able to make the necessary arrangements for transport and Q.M. stores and follow on at my leisure. As we expected to be fighting in a few hours, I also left Brown behind to deal with the routine paperwork at rear Brigade H.Q.

When I made up on the rest of the Brigade, I found that they had been put into some old huts between Poperinghe and Reninghelst and that thanks to some fine work by the 5th Scottish Rifles, under Spens, the situation in front had been restored.

Next day, as we were still in the same place, we were asked if we would put up a French Divisional H.Q. in the farm house with our Brigade H.Q. which we agreed to do. We found however that they had spread themselves so much that we were left with no room to work so we left them in possession and moved into an old Red Cross camp which was quite close and turned out to be much more comfortable.

12/5/18

My dear Mother,
I am as usual very fit and I am having a more or less easy time.

I had an enormous lunch which lasted about an hour and a half with a French Colonel and his staff today and am slowly recovering from the effects.[2] I must say, it was a very good lunch but the mental strain of listening to nothing but French rather took the edge off any pleasure there might have otherwise been.

I am getting quite good at understanding what they say but when it comes to talking I rather fail through knowing too much. I know that what I am saying is very bad French but don't quite know how to make it correct. People who know less simply go at it bald-headed and don't care how many mistakes they make. Their French is bad enough to make even my hair stand on end but they seem to be understood. To return to the lunch – I got on all right until some things that looked like apple fritters appeared. As it was about time for the sweet, this did not strike me as unusual until the Colonel offered me salt. Even then, I thought that this was probably only a French custom but when the next course turned out to be veal it struck me that something must be wrong. On enquiring afterwards, I discovered that the apple fritters were camouflaged potatoes.

Some more of us have got to dine there tonight but I am glad to say I am not one.

[Cont.] 13/5/18

Still going strong. The French are dining with us tonight.

---

2   Officers of French 14th Infantry Division: "Divisional Commander visited Bde HQs with General Officers Commanding 14th French Division. Command of Sector handed over to 14th French Div. and Bde with remainder of Div. in reserve to II Corps." See TNA WO 95/2429: 100th Brigade War Diary.

14/5/18

My dear Ellie,
It is ages since I wrote you last and as it may quite possibly be ages before I write you again, I would recommend you to read this letter very carefully on the off chance of finding a little news in it.

To begin with, I am very flourishing (news). We gave a tremendous dinner last night to the French Colonel and four of his staff. It was rather a joke because we knew from experience that their cook was better than ours, so sent our interpreter over early in the morning and engaged their cook to cook our dinner, without letting them know about it. We put up a very fine dinner and when they praised the cooking, they offered to exchange our cook for theirs. When we told them, after the port, that it was their cook who had done the show they were very tickled. As a matter of fact, the Brigadier got rather a shock when he thought for a time, wrongly, that we had not only pinched their cook but their food also.

16/5/18

My dear Mother,
The weather here for the last few days has been absolutely glorious.

I was rather amused the other day at a remark made by one of our officers. We had just moved into a hut that had some glass in the windows. When he saw it he remarked "Well, at any rate we will know when any shells land near us". We asked what he meant and he said quite solemnly "The glass will break". He didn't realise he had said anything silly for a long time.

It is just on three months since I was last on leave, but I don't see any immediate prospect of it for a bit yet.

WD: After a few days in the Red Cross camp, we decided that it was not a particularly healthy place to live in as it was in full view of Kemmel, so we got permission to move to the cellars of a large house on the southern outskirts of Poperinghe, which we called Elizabeth Château. This house had formerly been a hospital run, I believe, by the Queen of the Belgians, until the Germans landed a large shell through the roof and killed some of the nurses and patients.

The cellars here were eventually occupied by the H.Q. of the reserve Brigade while the other Brigades were in the line and, as we spent about three months in the district, they were very comfortable by the time we left as each Brigade made a point of adding something to the safety or decoration of the place while they were resting.

18/5/18

My dear Mother,
The weather here is almost uncomfortably hot. Thank goodness I am not stationed in India. Fortunately, I am not living in a tent at the moment but have struck a fairly cool cellar. I think a tent is about the hottest place one can find when there is much of a sun.

I hope Dad is none the worse of his hard work at the Term.

I am looking forward very much to going to Kirkland Park when I get home on leave. Jenny can sit up the tree in front and watch the station for when I arrive. Are the old guns still in front of the place? Do you require a meat coupon for crow pie?

I am going off to have a bath now. I shall have to walk about a mile to the bathroom but it is worth it.

21/5/18

My dear Jean,
There is no news, as usual, except that one of our officers left us this afternoon to go up in observation balloon and we are rather keen to know if he went up, as we have just seen the balloon come down with considerable greater speed than is usual.

22/5/18

My dear Jenny,
It is a long time since I addressed a letter to you because I knew it would be opened by Dad or Mother. Now that summer is come, however, and knowing how you like to get up early in summer, I feel sure that you will open this yourself. I have spent the whole morning on an inspection parade. As I think I have told you before, these sort of performances are Staff Captain's jobs and I find them about the most disagreeable he has. First of all, a ground has to be found. It has then to be marked off with flags and spots etc. where people have to turn and wheel etc. etc. Detailed orders then have to be written saying exactly what various people have to do, and when and where they have to do it. In fact, I have been a sort of glorified stage manager.

The weather here is still glorious and the only question is when are the Germans going to attack again?

WD: During the days we spent in the château in Poperinghe, the French took over the whole line and General Plumer, in whose army we now were, took the opportunity of inspecting the Division one Brigade at a time. Our Brigade was inspected on the 25th. We had considerable trouble in finding a piece of ground suitable for the purpose as the whole country was overlooked from Kemmel but eventually we got a place north of the

Ypres – Poperinghe road which was screened by the trees and camouflage along the side of the road.

The Brigade at this time was billeted in camp near Brandhoek where the reserve Brigade had been when we were holding the Passchendaele Ridge some months earlier but things were very much changed. The line had been withdrawn from the Ridge to a short distance outside of Ypres and the Germans were in possession of the ridges overlooking the country for miles around. As a result no movement of any size was possible by daylight and all the roads were hung with camouflage screens to a height of about 10 feet from the ground. Poperinghe was evacuated and there were very few civilians to be seen for a considerable distance around except a few who still remained in their farm houses north of the Ypres-Poperinghe road.

28/5/18

My dear Dad,
I have no news and no wants so may as well get to the point of the letter (i.e. I am still super-flourishing) and shut up.
   Your loving son,
   Walter J.J. Coats

WD: A few days after General Plumer's inspection we moved to Dirty Bucket Camp in the woods north of Brandhoek and after a day here moved up and took over from a Brigade of the 6th Division which was holding trenches on the Voormezeele Ridge with Bde.H.Q. about a mile south of the Ypres-Vlamertinghe road and about equidistant from either place.

When we took over we had some French Chasseurs Alpine on our right but they were shortly afterwards relieved by the 6th Division who much to our delight proceeded to capture and hold some ground overlooking Dickebusch Lake which the French had lost and failed to recover.

We spent the next three months in this part of the line doing an average of about eight days in the front line and four days in support. For most of this time, we were constantly under the threat of a heavy German attack and line after line of trenches was dug behind us, between us and Poperinghe. These trenches were dug almost entirely by the Labour Corps and must have looked very formidable from the air, the wiring of them was also very well done and the only weak point about them was that there were no troops available to man them as the scheme of defence, as laid down by the higher authorities, placed all out troops up in front. Later on, however, this scheme was altered and it was laid down that, on the night before an expected German attack, all the troops would be withdrawn 12 or 15 hundred yards in order to avoid the preliminary bombardment, except for a few who were to be left in strong points in front to break up the attack as much as possible.

As all these plans depended on our getting information as early as possible of the German intentions, raids and reconnaissances by large fighting patrols were every night occurrences and as the Germans seemed equally anxious to get prisoners there was seldom a night in which some sort of skirmish did not take place. The men as a result had a very hard time of it but kept very cheery.

8/6/18

My dear Mother,
I am still going very strong but as usual I have absolutely nothing in the way of news. Everything goes on here in the same more or less monotonous fashion. The worst of this war is that it is either very monotonous or too exciting. Personally, I rather prefer it when it is very monotonous.

I stopped smoking yesterday for lack of anything better to do so you can imagine how busy I am. I think I shall have to start again this evening to relieve the monotony.

21/6/18

My dear Mother,
I am glad to see Jack has got a good safe job, or at any rate that there is a prospect of his getting one. I suppose Jim is still in Edinburgh. If he is ever feeling bored, there is or was a few days ago a very good fellow in the Leith War Hospital called Wilkins who was Adjutant to one of the Battalions of this Brigade until he was wounded last April. He is an Englishman and I think he's probably rather lonely. I told Mrs. Pyatt about him some time ago and she went and saw him, but I don't know if he knows many people.

Have you read the skit in Punch on Hunter Weston called "The sincerest form of flattery"? Everyone over here who knows him is roaring over it. It is very true.

WD: When we first took over the line here, we found that the H.Q. of the two Brigades in the line were living side by side in some huts and shelters in full view of Kemmel. After we had been occupying them for about a month, the B.G. one day took it into his head that it was not a particularly healthy spot to live in. He was so convinced of this that he insisted on our moving at once to some other huts about half a mile away in spite of the fact that it was still broad daylight. I don't know whether he had a sort of premonition of evil or not but it was certainly a most fortunate move for us, for we had hardly been gone two hours when the Germans started to plaster the place with 8 inch shells and kept it up for the remainder of the afternoon while we stood in safety and watched them and wondered how the H.Q. we had left were getting on. Fortunately no one was hurt, though one of the huts we had just left was blown to bits and a barn in which we were building a concrete block house was set on fire and burnt down.

25/6/18

My dear Mother,

As usual there is no news here and I am only writing to let you know I am still very flourishing.

The news from Italy seems to be improving daily. It would be a great thing if Austria had to chuck in the sponge. I hope our people don't make peace until the Germans are absolutely done in. I would rather go on for another two or three years and get the job done thoroughly than chuck it now.

I am sorry Mr. Stevenson-Stewart's son has been killed. Was he in the infantry?

1/7/18

My dear Mother,

I am as usual still flourishing but newsless. The only news is that, according to the Brigadier, I am getting old and grey. As I am neither old nor grey enough to get leave I do not think there is any cause for alarm.

18/7/18

My dear Dad,

I am afraid my chances of leave while you are at Kirkland Park are gone as there is a rule that no officer is to get leave under a certain number of months and I am nowhere near it. I might get a month's leave if I asked for it but with things in their present state of unrest, I cannot very well ask. I would feel rather a beast if the Brigade found itself in a battle while I was away. I am not by any means a fire eater and do not consider myself indispensable but I don't like to be out of it. Perhaps I shall get a month in the winter.

Do you think you could send me out a pot of zinc ointment? There are a lot of mosquitoes and horse flies round here, which are rather a bother. I know this will be a good joke for Doug. I often thank my lucky stars that I am here and not in India.

Curiously enough, I am at present living within 20 yards of Charlie MacPherson's grave. It is not a particularly cheery spot.

WD: Around the middle of July, a Division of Americans (the 30th) were attached to our Division for training.[3] We started by having some of the Generals and their Staffs

---

3   The 30th (Old Hickory) Division, American Expeditionary Force was composed of Army National Guard units hailing from North Carolina, South Carolina, Georgia and Tennessee. Attached to the BEF along with the 27th (New York) Division, it went on to participate in the Second Battle of the Somme (21 August-2 September 1918) and the Ypres-Lys offensive

attached to our H.Q. and went on from that to sending some of their troops into the line scattered among our own men. After this we sent them in by platoons, then by companies and finally by battalions. We found that the men were good, I think they were Virginians [sic], but they had a very vague idea of soldiering and their staff work and organisation was hopeless. We heard afterwards that when we eventually handed over the line to them that their men starved for three days as they were unable to organise the supply of rations for them.

When we had finished training one Battalion of Americans, it was sent back to rest and another sent up for us to carry on with. As the Division from which they came was encamped near Watten the finished Battalions were always sent back by light railway and as a rule the entraining, being run by the British, went pretty smoothly. I remember once, however, when I was superintending the entraining of one of their Battalions, an American subaltern arrived with his platoon and wanted to get onto the train. As it was already pretty full, I asked him what Battalion he belonged to and found that he belonged to a different Battalion so I advised him to join his own unit. He told me that he had no idea where they were and when I suggested that if he knew where they were going, I might help him, he answered that he could not remember. I then asked him if he knew at what place he was to entrain and after thinking for a bit he replied that he did not know but that he thought it had a French sounding name, which I thought not a particularly bright answer. Fortunately, someone then came to our assistance who said he thought the particular Battalion was entraining at the next station so I sent him off and told him to follow the railway line.

19/7/18

My dear Mother,

I am sorry poor old Sandy [the dog] has gone. He can't have had much pleasure in life since the rationing started.

I suppose by the time you get this you will have heard about the French taking 200 guns and 17,000 prisoners.[4] I wish we could do something up here to give the Germans another knock.

(19 August–11 November 1918). See Mitchell A. Yockelson, *Borrowed Soldiers: Americans Under British Command, 1918* (Norman, Oklahoma: University of Oklahoma Press, 2008).

4   A reference to a French counter-offensive that occurred (18 July) in the immediate aftermath of the so-called *Friedensturm* ("Peace Offensive") that opened on 15 July 1918. The last German offensive before the *Westheer's* adoption of a theatre-wide defensive stance, its strategic design was a three-army assault in the vicinity of Rheims in order to draw Allied reserves away from Flanders where another offensive (*Operation Hagen*) was contemplated. The latter scheme was shelved following the Champagne front reverse. See Zabecki, *The German 1918 Offensives.*

Walter's parents with granddaughter Helen at Kirkland Park, Strathaven, July 1918. (WJJC collection)

27/7/18

My dear Dad,

As usual there is no news except that I am super-flourishing. I am glad Kirkland Park seems to be suiting mother so well. I hope it suits the Ellie, John and It equally well.

McCosh has gone home on a month's leave which leaves me, I think, with the longest service out here of any officer in the Battalion. I remember wondering when we came over on the boat who would last longest. McCosh, as a matter of fact, has already done three months at home on some duty which hardly counts.

11/8/18

My dear Dad,

Still merry and bright as usual. Isn't the news splendid?

I am going over to dine with the Glasgow Highlanders tonight. It is about an hour's walk to get there, in other words I shall have to walk about 7 miles, in all, for my dinner, but as one doesn't lock up the house here at night it won't matter when I get back. As a matter of fact, if they did lock the door, I could walk through any of the windows without breaking any glass.

I suppose it is too late to wish Doug many happy returns of his birthday. It takes a letter something like six weeks to get to him, I suppose. However, next time you write, you can tell him that if I remember, I will drink his health in water and chloride of lime, seeing he is a medical man and also (though you needn't tell them this) because there will be no other water to drink it with.

I am glad to hear Kirkland Park is suiting everyone so well.

I have taken to smoking again now and would be very glad to receive the box of cigars you spoke about some time ago, if you still have it.

I must dry up for the day.

Your loving son,

Walter J.J. Coats

12/8/18

My dear Dad,

I am going off for a jaunt in a motor this afternoon, so I am writing a short note to let you know I am very flourishing. I am quite looking forward to the run in the car, as it will be a pleasant change to be out of reach of shells for a few hours. I have really got no news and as I want to get things straightened up before going I must stop.

Your loving son,

Walter J.J. Coats

14/8/18

My dear Mother,

There is just the faintest of faint chances that I may get leave a little sooner than expected. I believe the Division want to send someone to run my job for a bit for the sake of experience. If they are sufficiently keen on the idea, they might with any luck push me off on leave meantime. It sounds quite a good idea and it has my heartiest support.

WD: After about three months in this place we were beginning to think we would never get away when orders suddenly came through about the 15th of August that we were to hand over to the Americans and move out which we did on 17th and then moved back to St Jan ter Biezin between Poperinghe and Watou.[5]

---

5   The camp here was known as "Mendinghem", a name jocularly coined by the troops for one of the casualty clearing stations, as were nearby "Dozinghem" and "Bandagehem". See TNA WO 95/2431: 1/9th HLI War Diary.

16/8/18

My dear Dad,

I have just received a pleasant surprise but I can't tell you anything about it except that it is pleasant.

Otherwise I have the usual lack of news to tell you.

I'm expecting someone to call me any minute now so as I shall have no time to finish this once he comes, I shall dry up.

Your loving son,

Walter J.J. Coats

WD: After a few days, we entrained at Proven for Watten and were billeted round Houlle and Moulle, northwest of St Omer. The chief event at this time was an inspection, on 24th, by the Divisional Commander, Major General Sir RJ Pinney, KCB. As I was pretty busy at the time, our new Brigade Major, Innes, offered to run the show for me and thanks to his effort we had the finest ceremonial parade I ever saw, the only hitch in the performance being that I forgot to salute at the right time as I was so interested watching the man with the flag trying to get it up. Around 27th, we were suddenly moved off by train to Sus St Léger where we stayed for some days.

29/8/18

My dear Dad,

The news for the last day or two has been quite good. I certainly didn't think in March that the situation would be like this in August.

I have just been speaking to Jack on the phone. He is about 9 miles away and I am going over to see him today.

30/8/18

My dear Mother,

I saw Jack for a few hours yesterday. He was looking very fit. I had tea and an early dinner with him.

Things still seem to be going pretty well and the question now is where are we going to set down and spend the winter? I hope it is well clear of the old mud.

11/9/18

My dear Dad,

I become top of the leave list and due to go on the 18th but I don't know if I shall be able to get away then. Unless there is anything particular doing, I ought to at least be able to get away when Brown returns about the 23rd.

WD: On 15th, after staying here long enough to give us the impression that we were in for a decent rest we again got sudden orders to move. I at once went off with the other Staff Captains to the 5th Corps H.Q. in whose area we were to billet. When we got there we found that they knew nothing about accommodation but they gave us each an area and pushed us off again. As chance would have it the area allotted to the 100th Brigade was round High Wood where we had seen such heavy fighting in July 1916. As the area was about 8 miles square I spent the remainder of the day trying to divide it up so that each unit would have a fair share of the various dug-outs in it and next morning returned early with the advanced parties in order to get things finally divided up. Fortunately the Battalions did not arrive till well on in the afternoon when everything was ready for them.

Next day, I again when on ahead to billet in Léchelle and as it was not too far away was able to take billeting parties with me which saved a lot of trouble next day as the Brigade started moving about 2 a.m. As it was pouring wet and pitch dark when we moved we had a pretty miserable march but we found the billets when we arrived were pretty good which cheered us up a bit.

On the 18th, we again moved forward, to Mesnil [Mesnil-en-Arrouaise] but as outpost positions had now to be taken up, the disposal of the troops was a matter for the Brigade Major to deal with and I only had to find accommodation for Brigade H.Q., Trench Mortar Battery, Transport and Q.M. Stores which was a comparatively simple matter.

18/9/18

My dear Dad,

I have been too busy to write you for the last few days and life is still a bit unsettled. One satisfaction, however, is that it is probably more so for the Germans.

There is absolutely no news here except what you get quicker from the papers, so I shall not try to rack my brains for something to say.

WD: It was now the 19th of September and when I arrived at Brigade H.Q. after getting the transport etc. in, I found that orders had come through for me to report to the 3rd Division H.Q. to officiate as D.A.A.G.[6] I was rather annoyed at this but there was

---

6   The 3rd (Regular) Division was attached to VI Corps (GOC Lieutenant-General James Aylmer Lowthorpe Haldane) of Third Army (GOC General Sir Julian Byng) at this time.

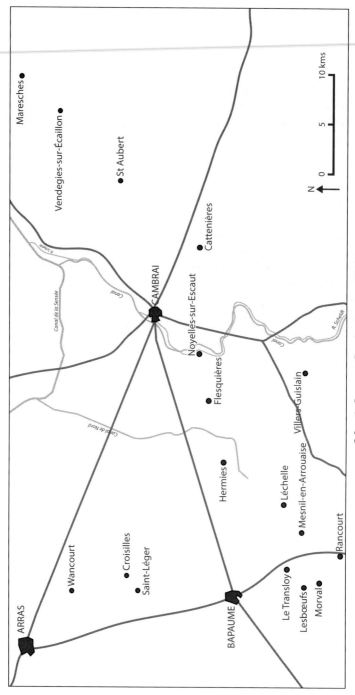

Map 9 Somme–Cambrai sector, 1918.

no help for it so I handed over to Edwards who was then adjutant of the Worcesters and was subsequently appointed Staff Captain.

19/9/18

My dear Dad,
I have been ordered to go to the 3rd Division HQ to officiate (as they put it) as D.A.A.G. i.e. Deputy Assistant Adjutant General. It is rather a bore as I foresee my leave being put off again. I can't very well apply for leave as soon as I get the job. I gather from the way they put it that it is a temporary job only. I hope so, as it means my leaving the Battalion and all the people I know.

If I got the job permanently, it would mean promotion to Major but as I am not a regular, promotion does not interest me.

WD: I left on the 20th and joined the 3rd Division H.Q. at Morchies. Fortunately the D.A.A.G. of the 3rd Division did not leave till the following morning so he was able to tell me what was happening and, as he left a good staff behind him, I was able to carry on all right.

The G.O.C. of this Division was a General called Deverell who had such a temper that the majority of his staff seemed rather afraid of him but as I was used to displays of temper on the part of the B.G. I always managed to get on very well with him.[7]

I stayed with the 3rd Division for exactly a month during which time they had some very heavy fighting crossing the St Quentin Canal and taking the Flesquieres Ridge.[8] Division H.Q. during this time moved successively from Morchies to Hermies then to Flesquières, back to Hermies, again to Flesquières on to Noyelles-sur-Escaut and finally to Cattenières.

22/9/18

My dear Mother,
I am just in the middle of trying to find my feet at my new job. I don't quite know how long it will last for, but the sooner I get settled down, the better. Goodness knows when I shall get my leave now.

---

7   Major-General Cyril John Deverell (1874-1947). Commissioned West Yorkshire Regiment 1895; Ashanti War 1896; Brigade Major 85th Brigade, CO 4th East Yorkshire Regiment 1915; GOC 20th Brigade 1915-16; GOC 3rd Division 1 January 1917.
8   During Walter's brief attachment, 3rd Division were involved in the Battle of the Canal du Nord (27 September-1 October 1918) and Battle of Cambrai (8 October 1918), both "Battles of the Hindenburg Line".

As I have been sitting at the bottom of a very deep dug-out all morning, doing paperwork, I will dry up and go for a walk.

27/9/18

My dear Dad,

There is no news as usual except what you can see in the papers which I am very cheerily reading just now.

I am having a pretty easy time of it just now as my work has practically nothing to do with operations. It is what we call "A" work i.e. it deals with personnel, discipline, casualties etc. I should think it was one of the safest jobs there is. In fact, it is so safe one is apt to be rather ashamed of it. The only thing is that someone has got to do it. What I am afraid of is that, having acted the part here, I may be noted for the job when a proper vacancy occurs. To my mind, Staff Captain is a very much better job.

I have not put up my rank badges as Major yet and have no intention of doing so, unless I am made to. My brain, I have no doubt, works just as well with three stars on my sleeve as with a crown on it and it makes no odds to me whether people think I am still a Captain or not. I have had to take the blue band off my arm, which is rather a bore as it was well sewn on.

I was asked the other day if I would care to go home on a Staff Course. It would mean three months at home and a fortnight's leave afterwards. If I had been in the Regular Army, I would probably have accepted, but as I am not, I refused. I believe it is a good course but I would much rather stay out here. I shall have enough studying to do when the War is over to get up my law again, so meantime I propose to make hay while the sun shines and keep away from schools as much as possible.

The news today is very good. I have no doubt you will have heard about it by the time you get this.

29/9/18

My dear Dad,

Isn't the news all round splendid? Old Hindenburg must be rather scratching his head and wondering what to do next. I only hope the weather keeps decent for a bit yet. We have been very lucky so far and it is now nearly October.

I am fearfully sick at missing both Jack and Hedderwick by being pushed off on this job. I would have been home now if I hadn't been here. If there is anything doing when I get back to the Brigade, I don't know when I shall get home. I should hate to be at home and know the Brigade was in it without me. They could of course get along all right without me but I really rather enjoy being there when there is anything really interesting happening.

I enclose a copy of a poem which I got from a newspaper the other day. It rather amused me, as it is in many ways very true.

A Brigade Staff Captain

Of all the people whom this war
Has smitten with afflictions sore,
Who forge (in rain and mud and gore)
The toils they are entrapped in;
Of all this much-enduring host,
Whom our circumstance has got on toast,
The person that I pity most
Is a Brigade Staff Captain.

Tis his, when all are up the pole,
To comb things out, to make things whole,
And, when his half distracted soul,
Has ceased his strife with gabies [slang: fools]
Tis his to pen (whilst song and spree
Ameliorate the dusks that flee)
Certificates that men are free
From vermin and from scabies.

The Gumboot store, the bomb, the dump,
The leaking hut, the un-drained sump,
Combine to give the man a hump
Stupendous in dimensions.
While in the background they of "Div"
(Their motto: "Live and Don't Let Live")
Preposterous suggestions give
With lordly condescension.

And when, as all men do, he dies,
Perhaps his family heave some sighs;
But "Q" uplifts its voice and cries,
In accent harsh and croaking:
According to the last report
He's fifty pairs of gumboots short,
His iron rations are too few.
Where are those petrol tins he drew?
His strength-returns in knots are tied,
Transport deficits he did hide,
And now the beggar's gone and died.
It's really too provoking.

2/10/18

My dear Jenny,

Many thanks for your letter.

The news, as you say, is excellent but it is rather spoilt as far as I'm concerned by the news I got yesterday that McCosh had died of wounds.[9] He was about the best friend I had left in the Battalion and is a great loss.

We are not exactly living in the lap of luxury just now but it is extraordinarily interesting.

I saw Mr G. Phibbs today wandering round collecting stories and shall be interested to hear what startling yarns he has to produce now. I don't often read what he has to say as when I do he never seems to have anything fresh to say. If you took one of his stories and change the names of places mentioned you would learn about as much as he has to say.

I must stop.

Your loving brother,

Walter J. J. Coats

Edward McCosh. (McCosh family collection)

---

9   On the morning of 26 September 1918, Captain Edward McCosh MC was wounded in the arm and leg by trench mortar fire on Battalion HQ, which was temporarily situated in a sunken road 500 yards south of Villers Guislain. The Glasgow Highlanders' Chaplain, Reverend Arthur J Glossop, wrote to Ted's mother "I was with your boy after he was wounded just before the stretcher started from the line. He then spoke quite strongly and gripped my hand when he went off. We all, including the doctors, thought he would do well. I am now sorry I didn't ask him for a message for you, but I did not want to alarm him, and we thought all was to be well." Edward McCosh died of shock at the Main Dressing Station that evening. He is buried at Five Points Cemetery, Léchelle. Like Walter, he had been offered a staff position earlier in the war, but chose to remain with the Battalion. Brigadier-General Baird observed: "He was quite the best young officer of his rank and service in my Brigade." See TNA WO 95/2431: 1/9th HLI War Diary and Reid, 'Shoulder to Shoulder'; Glossop and Baird letter extracts courtesy of the McCosh family.

4/10/18

My dear Dad,

With any luck, I should get my leave in about a fortnight's time now, though it depends on the situation when I get back to the Brigade. I am looking forward to it very much as it is over seven months had since my last.

I am glad to hear Doug has got prospects of leave at last. I should think he wants it as badly as anyone. When does he get long enough leave to get home?

5/10/18

My dear Jean,

It is so long since I last wrote you and will probably be so long before I write you again. I may as well wish you many happy returns of your next birthday whenever it comes off. If I am more than six months out in my reckoning, you can let me know and I will be sure to write you again in another 4 or 5 months.

I am going strong on my present job and find it about the softest I have struck since I came out here. It is also a very safe one. I have only had one shell anywhere near me since I came here and it only chucked some dirt over my tent. It certainly disturbed my beauty sleep for a few minutes, in fact I lay awake wondering if they were going to send over any more, until the next one passed well over, so I went to sleep again.

10/10/18

My dear Dad,

I have been asked once or twice by the Colonel under whom I am working if I would care to have this job permanently, as he thinks it could be worked if I would like it. I told him I was not the least bit keen on it so I hope to get away very shortly now. What I don't like about it is that it is all paperwork and one never comes in contact with the men at all. I expect I shall be pushed into a job of this sort sooner or later but I mean to stick with my own crowd as long as I can. As I have said before, I am not the least ambitious as a soldier and am quite prepared to go where I am sent without grousing, but I am not going to ask for a job I don't want.

14/10/18

My dear Dad,

The news as usual continues to be good and it is only a matter of time now before the Germans have to give in.

I am at present living in a house that was occupied by the Germans within the last fortnight or so. It is not what one would call a palace but it is very comfortable and warmer than a tent. The further forward one goes now, the better the houses get.

15/10/18

My dear Dad,

Great news. I am being relieved on the 18th and shall probably be back to Brigade on the 19th and then, circumstances permitting, I shall try for leave at once before taking over. Please address my letters to the 100th Brigade again.

The news continues to be splendid and it looks as if the Germans have had about enough. I hope our peace terms are stiff enough.

18/10/18

My dear Mother,

We have just heard here that Lille has been taken and unofficially that we have also got Bruges. It is very interesting to see where he is going to clear from next.

19/10/18

My dear Dad,

I am afraid I have again been done out of my leave as I have received a telephone message to say I have been appointed D.A.A.G. of the 61st Division.[10] It has not been confirmed yet but I am afraid it is likely to be true. It is rather a bore as in the first place I do not want the job and in the second place I do want my leave. I shall have another try for leave as soon as I decently can after getting there.

---

10 61st (2nd South Midland) Division (GOC Major-General Francis John Duncan) was a second-line TF formation deployed in France since late spring 1916. Reduced to cadre by crippling manpower losses sustained during the 1918 German spring offensives, the Division had been rebuilt and attached to XVII Corps (GOC Lieutenant-General Sir Charles Fergusson Bt.). It was subsequently engaged, as part of Third Army in the following "Final Advances in Picardy" battles and engagements before the armistice: Battle of the Selle (17-25 October 1918), Battle of Valenciennes (1-2 November 1918), Battle of the Sambre (4 November 1918) and Passage of the Grand Honnelle (5-7 November 1918). See Sir J.E. Edmonds, *Military Operations France and Belgium 1918 Vol. V* (London: HMSO, 1947).

WD: On the 20th October, the day before we got to Cattenières, it was confirmed that I had been appointed D.A.A.G. of the 61st (South Midland T.F.) Division and I accordingly joined them at Rieux-en-Cambrésis [west of Cambrai] on the 21st.

21/10/18

My dear Dad,

As I thought, I have been appointed D.A.A.G. 61st Division, so my address will now be: H.Q. 61st Div, B.E.F.

I am afraid I am not very keen on the job. It means higher rank and pay etc. but it also means that I have to start and get to know a lot of new people again. What I liked about the Brigade job was that after being Staff Captain for 20 months I knew practically everyone I came across.

I hope you're all going strong at home and that it will not be very long now before I get away on leave.

WD: Next day the Division H.Q. moved to St Aubert where we stayed two days while the Division was fighting its way through Vendegies [Vendegies-sur-Écaillon] and we then moved there after them, via Haussy.

23/10/18

My dear Mother,

I am now with the 61st Division as D.A.A.G. and have been made a temporary Major by virtue of the appointment. I arrived here on the 21st and, so far as I can make out at present, seem to have struck quite a decent lot of fellows. A large proportion of the staff seem to be Scotsmen.

The weather broke down here two or three days ago with the result that the roads are not improved. Today, however, it has cleared up and with any luck we are in for another spell of fine weather. From a personal point of view, the weather does not affect me much now but it makes a big difference to the men and the operations. I wonder when the Germans will decide that they have had enough of it. It is great to know that we are at last definitely considering that it is only a matter of time before the end comes. I have always felt pretty confident that we would win in the long run but until a few months ago, I did not see much prospect of the end.

Everyone is very cheery here just now including yours truly. Among other details, I have a chance of leave in 10 days or a fortnight. I don't want to raise your hopes again, but unless the Germans give in very suddenly, I think I have every chance. I have no chance of a month, I am afraid, and things are moving so quickly just now, that I don't know that I want one. A fortnight will suit me very nicely.

I must stop now and get on with my work, though I am not what I would call busy. I am not looking forward to the demobilisation performance, if I am still on this job. However I may be looking too far ahead.

Would you please send me out 4 cloth crowns to put on the sleeves of my jackets and sufficient braid for 4 sleeves? There is also a thin piece of braid which goes between the broad stuff. I should also like two metal crowns to put on the shoulders of my trench coat.

2/11/18

My dear Dad,

I have at last got settled down after a very unsettled day and as I have very little to do at the moment, I may as well write a short note to let you know I am still going strong.

Many thanks for getting Thompson to send out the crowns and other necessaries so quickly. They arrived today so I shall be able to go home in all my glory. I don't think you have seen me in my red hat yet. I look a fearful Knut and an artist friend of mine has told me that it suits me. Perhaps that was only because he was a friend and knew I was annoyed at having to give up my Glengarry. As a matter of fact, I didn't care whether it suited me or not, I have been ordered to wear it and there was no way out of it.

Letter to Walter from Brigadier General Walter Baird:

3/11/18

HQ 100th Infantry Brigade

My dear Coats,

I was very glad to get your note some days ago and get news of you. I was afraid that your "temp" appointment would develop into something permanent and am very sorry to think that you will not be coming back to us. From your point of view, you are well out of it, however, as I can assure that we have never had a more utterly bothersome and unsatisfactory experience from every point of view than that which we have been undergoing during the past six weeks. It has been truly b…dy and the seems to be no hope of improvement or escape.[11]

---

11 The 33rd Division had, since Walter's departure from 100th Brigade, been involved in the following "Hundred Days" battles and engagements: Battle of the St Quentin Canal (29 September-2 October 1918), Battle of the Beaurevoir Line (3-5 October 1918), Battle of Cambrai (9 October 1918), Pursuit to the Selle (9-12 October 1918) and Battle of the Selle (20-23 October 1918). See Edmonds, *Military Operations France and Belgium 1918 Vol. V.*

You will be sorry to hear that poor Knisley got a nasty wound at the back of the knee on 25th and Balcombe was mortally wounded by the same shell. I got off with two magnificent flesh wounds on both knees, but Knisley writes today that he is afraid that he may have to lose the leg. Tubby has just returned from leave to find that he definitely has been appointed to succeed you – at which we are all very pleased.

The Glasgow Highlanders have done splendidly as usual but the cost has not been light. In 2 days' time we shall be in it again. There is no question of any rest or respite here. The C-in-C has not yet got his K.C.B! Walker is my Brigade Major in place of Innes who has gone to Cambridge – as has fat Foster. I have had a card from Muirhead dated 13/10/18 from Port Said, he is still travelling East. I have lost Perkins to my great regret. We ran into a Boche outpost the other night by mistake and had to clear, and Perkins has been missing ever since. I hope and trust he is a prisoner.[12]

No other news.

Sincerely,

Walter Baird

5/11/18

My dear Mother,

Just a line to let you know I have been told I may go on leave on the ninth, so unless anything very unforeseen happens in the next two days I will be with you on the morning of the 10th.

Today is the fourth anniversary of my arrival out here. I was just thinking last night of all the places I have been to since I came out. I can remember pretty well what region I was in month by month and roughly what we were doing at each place, but that is about the extent of it. I expect by the time I get home for good, I shall have done nearer five than four years out here. Even if Germany cracks up now, it will be a long time before we can all get home.

Do you remember in 1914, there was some little talk about Doug and I going to visit the Rhine for our summer holidays? Imagine how awful it would have been if we had got landed there when the war began and had been stuck there since. I suppose John Monteith is still hung up in Germany.

Your loving son,

Walter JJ Coats

---

12 There are no officers with the surname Perkins recorded as missing or taken prisoner during this time. The lost man, possibly an OR attached to 100th Brigade staff as a batman or in some other capacity, may have been 24-year-old Pte 330357 William George Perkins 1/9th HLI, killed in action 25 October 1918. He is buried in Romeries Communal Cemetery Extension.

WD: When the Division was relieved, we returned to St Aubert where we spent another few days before moving up once more to Vendegies with Brigades at St Martin, Bermerain and Sommaing. This was our last move forward as it was now about the 9th November.

9/11/18

My dear Dad,

I expect Ellie will have told you that the unexpected happened and that the fellow who was to take my place while I was away, went sick at the last moment. He is expected to be out of bed tomorrow and should be fit to take over in about three or four days now. With any luck, therefore, I may get away about the 14th. I didn't think, when I was last home, that it would be nearly nine months before I got leave again.

I have just been reading the newspapers. They are extraordinarily interesting. The history of this year will be very interesting reading.

11/11/18

My dear Dad,

The armistice with Germany came into force about five minutes ago, so I suppose for all practical purposes, at least as far as the fighting is concerned, the war is over. It is very hard to realise.

There is a sort of holiday feeling in the air here today, but otherwise no indication that anything unusual has happened.

I have just been round to see the officer who is to relieve me. He took a turn for the worse again yesterday but seems to be improving again today. I wish he would hurry up and get better as I am very keen to get home on leave. I have no news of any importance except the armistice, which I have no doubt you will have heard of long before you get this.

Hoping it will not be very long now before I get home.

Your loving son,

Walter J.J. Coats

WD: We had a pretty fair idea on the 10th that an armistice would be signed so, when we were eventually informed on the 11th about 7a.m. that hostilities would cease at 11a.m. that day, no one was very surprised. The day of course was celebrated as a holiday but was about the dullest I have ever spent as everyone was feeling very flat.

Letter to Walter from his father:

11th November 1918

198 West George Street, Glasgow

11.15 am

My dear Wat,

I have just got a message from Mr Hedderwick (Citizen), "Armistice signed at 5 o'clock this morning – hostilities ceased at 11.00". I am just waiting to get your Mother on the telephone to tell her. I see the flags going up already. Nisbet's opposite us have just run theirs up. With all my heart I say <u>Thank God</u>!

I have just got Mother. She was so excited she could hardly speak but she echoed my "Thank God" as summing up the thing that is in our minds. What a tremendous change for you and Jack. I am just trying for Esda now, to tell her.

I hear cheering and a band going and I am told there is general excitement down the Town. People have behaved well, no "Mafficking" or that sort of thing in Glasgow at any rate. The feeling is too deep.

I hope we will have you home very soon now.

Your very loving Dad,

John J Coats.

WD: After a few more days at Vendegies, we moved back to billets in Cambrai and I managed to get leave which I felt I was badly in need of as I had had nine pretty strenuous months since my last leave.

10

Getting Home

Goodness knows when I shall get away.

WD: When I got back from leave on December 4th, I found orders waiting for me to report at once to the 17th Corps H.Q. at Beauquesne near Doullens to act as D.A.A.G. there.

7/12/18

My dear Dad,

I have arrived back at last, after wandering round for about three days on this side.

You will be interested to hear that I have once more changed my address. It is now H.Q. 17th Corps. When I arrived back at Div., I was told that I was to report here as D.A.A.G. I don't know whether it is a permanent job or not, and I don't know whether to hope so or not, yet. At any rate, I don't suppose I shall dislike it any more than my last job. Theoretically it is a rise in the world, though my rank and pay remain the same.

PS I hope you were none the worse of seeing me off. I am afraid I left you rather abruptly but I was afraid you would want to get out and hang round a draughty station until the train left.

WD: When I arrived at 17th Corps, I found that the Corps Commander had gone off some days before to take up the appointment of Military Governor in Cologne and had taken with him the D.A. & Q.M.G. and the D.A.A.G. of the Corps and that these officers had taken their Staffs with them. I also found that, since the D.A.A.G. had left, practically all his work had been allowed to accumulate as no one knew how to deal with it. The result was that for the next three months I had to work till 11 or 12 at night every day, including Sundays, in order to keep up to date.

My duties as D.A.A.G. consisted of looking after the following for about 60,000 men viz: Appointments, Burials, Casualties, Cemeteries, Ceremonial, Courts Martial, Courts of Inquiry, Discipline, Interpreters, Law, Leave, Medical Services, Pay, Personal Services,

Police, Promotions, Prisoners of War, Spiritual Welfare, Supply of Personnel, Traffic Control, War Diary and Reinforcements.

12/12/18

My dear Dad,

I am still with the Corps but may go back to the Division any time now. They have applied to get me back and I don't know that the Corps have any right to keep me. Personally, it does not much matter where I go, though on the whole I think I prefer this job.

There is a tremendous lot of paperwork to do here but as I have got eight clerks working for me I am managing to keep up with it.

14/12/18

My dear Mother,

I see a lot of things in the papers about demobilisation. If there is anything that McG D & Co have to do to get me back, I wonder if Dad, if he knows of it, would keep them up to scratch. I am longing to get away from the Army and back to my own job again. At present, my day consists of: 9-1 office; 2-3 office; 3-5 a walk and tea; 5-7.30 office; 7.30-9 dinner; 9-10.30 or 11 office. It varies a little, some days being busier and some less busy but that is about the average. The good old days of 9.30-1 and 2-5.30 with a certain amount of reading after dinner, will suit me much better. Thank goodness however I passed my exams before the war started.

21/12/18

My dear Jean,

Please thank Dad for his trouble about demobilisation. I have done all I can out here, including sending a form, Z15 I think it was, to the 61st Division for them to sign. I shall also take care to see that I am registered here for demobilisation on a register which is being made up. I do not intend to leave any stone unturned to get out early.

The most amusing thing here is in connection with leave. Everyone is shouting out for it and everyone imagines that his particular leave is the only one that matters. They keep ringing up on the phone or coming into the office and saying "What about my leave?" As nine times out of ten I have no idea whom "me" is, and at any rate even if I did know I cannot remember that they ever asked for leave, the result is sometimes very amusing, at least from my point of view.

I have a great pile of paper waiting for me to plough through, so will switch off. As this will probably reach you about Christmas, I may as well wish you all a very merry one, and may I be demobilised by the next.

23/12/18

My dear Mother,
Many thanks for your and everyone else's letters of best wishes for Christmas. I should say the chances of a Merry Christmas are rather greater this year and have been for some time past.

I was rather amused the other day when I picked up a newspaper to read while I was having tea and found I had got a Mention in Dispatches.[1] I think I told Jenny, when I was home on leave last, my opinion as to what it was worth.

26/12/18

My dear Jean,
Isn't it splendid news about the reinforcements the Rowetts have received?[2] What is he going to be called? Please thank Dad and Mother for their congratulations about my Mention. I had a fairly good idea several months ago that I would get it but I had forgotten all about it until, being rather desperate for something to read, I started to read what I thought was a list of casualties or something of that sort and found I was mentioned.

29/12/18

My dear Dad,
I have no news except to wish you all a Happy New Year.

Isn't it splendid Asquith and all the rest of that bunch getting the boot? Everyone here is fearfully pleased. We got a wire giving figures and the names of a choice selection that had been booted this afternoon.

31/12/18

My dear Dad,
It is just about an hour from the New Year, so I may as well wish you all a very happy one. I am still in the office but intend to go to bed when I get this written. I am most fearfully busy just now and find that it takes me all my time to keep my head above paper. I have given up my afternoon walk as I found I simply could not get through the

---

1   *Supplement to the London Gazette of 17th December 1918*, No. 30177, p. 14924, 20 December 1918.
2   Birth of John Penrose Rowett (22 December 1918) to John and Ellie Rowett.

work. To add to the general enjoyment, my head clerk has gone on leave and another clerk is off on special leave tomorrow, as his father has died. I don't expect to see him back. However, there is no use grousing, as I expect it will get much worse when all the clerks get demobilised and we have to carry on with anyone we can find. I believe hard work suits me but I wish it was law. I envy Jack being able to send for his law books to read. All my reading is done either in bed at night or during meals, when I have a squint at the news.

1919

2/1/19

My dear Dad,

I think yesterday was the busiest New Year's Day I have spent since the first one out here. Most of the people here are English who do not celebrate New Year, so business went on as usual, only more so. I was at it from 9.30 AM till 11.00 PM, with breaks for meals. To add to the general excitement, the chief of the clerks who is left has just told me that the work is too much for him. I told him not to worry and go out for a walk every day.

I have written McG D & Co asking them to make me a "Guaranteed Letter man" as I understand that is the quickest way out. If you want particulars of how it is done I have no doubt Mr. Reid will send round my letter if you ask him. It is rather a long job explaining. I must dry up and get a move on.

Your ever cheerful and wouldn't-mind-if-he-was-demobilised son,[3]

Walter J.J. Coats

---

3 Permanent release from the forces applied only to those deemed unfit (wounds, fatigue, etc.) for further duty. The fear that Germany would repudiate the armistice agreement caused the military authorities to hold fit, recently discharged servicemen for recall should hostilities resume. The original wartime demobilisation scheme (1917) proposed that the first to be released should be those previously employed in key branches of industry. However, as these men had been called up during the latter stages of the war, this meant that those with the longest service records were, more often than not, the last to be demobilised. This glaring inequity, as demonstrated by small-scale mutinies at British army camps in Calais and Folkestone and a strident public protest by 3,000 soldiers in London during the final months of 1918 and early 1919, was a source of mounting concern for the Lloyd George government. Thus one of new Secretary of State for War Winston Churchill's first acts was to introduce a revised and more equitable demobilisation scheme based on age, length of service and the number of times a man had been wounded.

18/1/19

My dear Mother,

I wonder if anything can be done about jogging up the authorities with my Guarantee Letter. The situation at present is that other people are getting in ahead of me. I don't mind waiting here a bit, but I do object to seeing people going off who have about half my service out here. I shall be able to take a good holiday when I get off, as I have calculated I will get a gratuity of about £600. Quite a useful little sum.

19/1/19

My dear Dad,

I am writing to the office as this is purely a business letter. My servant, Pte McDonagh, is being demobilised in a few days, as he has over four years' service in France. He came out with the Glasgow Highlanders and has been out here ever since. He tells me that he has no particular job to go back to, as he wants to improve on the job he had before the war, so I have told him that, if he calls you, you might be able to help him. He is a carter and I thought you might know some of the big firms that require carters and who could give him a job. He has been my servant for about two years and has done me extremely well. He is absolutely trustworthy and not afraid of hard work.

I don't know if you can do much but if he calls on you, I hope you'll be able to put him in the way of getting a good job, as he deserves it.

22/1/19

My dear Dad,

I have received my Guarantee Letter at last and have forwarded it onto the proper authorities with a request for early release. Would you please thank McG D & Co the next time you see any of them? I don't think there is anything more to be done now except wait and see. Thank goodness it is not Asquith who is running things now.

Please thank Mother for her last letter which I got today. She said you were very exercised just now, wondering where to go in summer. Personally, if I am with you, I vote for Kirkland Park. If there is not room in the house, I could knock up a very comfortable shack for myself with a few sheets of corrugated iron and some wood. I have slept very comfortably in many worse places. I think Kirkland would be better than Braidwood, though it would be rather amusing ending up the War where I began it. There should be no [TA] camp this year at any rate.

29/1/19

My dear Mother,

I have just heard that my Divisional Commander has no objection to my being demobilised. I am going to try the Corps Commander tonight and will let you know my luck. The only trouble now is to find someone to replace me. Once he is found I am practically a free man.

31/1/19

My dear Dad,

My application to be demobilised has been approved by the Corps Commander and has now gone to the Army. If they find a substitute for me, I may be home almost any time now, if not I should with luck be home in four or five weeks. The prospect is very bright.

On my way home I propose stop in London, if Ellie can take me, to have my MC presented. It will save me going for it later.

12/2/19

My dear Dad,

You will be interested to hear GHQ have refused my application to be demobilised. So much for the wonderful scheme by which the men who had served out here longest were to be demobilised first. Goodness knows when I shall get away. I know you'll be disappointed but I am afraid I can't help it unless I resort to some of the rather doubtful methods of getting out which some people here use but which I have no intention of doing, and I know you have no wish that I should.

Letter to Walter, from Ernest J Whitson:

19/2/19

Queen Alexandra Hospital for Officers
Highgate
London N.6.

My dear old Coats,

I never wrote to congratulate you on your promotion as it took place when I was on leave and afterwards life was a bit of a scrum and I just put it off as usual, and then I went sick.

Do you remember I had a fall from Muirhead's horse one day when you and I shared a room at that sort of Château farm near Ebblinghem, I think it was?[4] Well the cursed thing started giving trouble again, and I suddenly discovered a large hard bump just forward of my hip joint. The M.O. thought it was something serious but luckily it was only a large blood clot caused by the bleeding inside.

I've been in bed over two months now but I shall soon be allowed up in a chair. I've had two operations and I don't want any more.

I hear General Baird has left the 100th. Is it true?[5]

I hear they've started a Glasgow Highlanders' Club in Glasgow. I think they might have waited until the Battalion got home, as they mostly seem to be strangers who are running it.

How d'you like life at Corps? Someone told me you were very bored as you drive about in your Rolls Royce and that you wished you were back being badgered to death in the 100th. I think the happiest hours I spent were as your humble Assistant and O.C. BOMBS "Though I say it as shouldn't". We were a very hot combination, what!

Must stop as I'm going to a concert in the ward.

I hope to see you in Glasgow sometime.

Yours ever,
Ernest Whitson

24/2/19

My dear Dad,
I have no news except that I am very flourishing and waiting patiently to get away. They have given me an extra 35/-per week as I am being retained, so I am now earning £710 per year, which is not bad. I shall be glad however when I get back to £30 as an apprentice. The work will be much more congenial. It would take a good deal more than I am getting to make me adopt the Army as a profession.

Many thanks for the books and the copy of Doug's letter which I got today. Doug seems to be having a pretty thin time of it just now. I wonder what he calls cold? Probably 80° in the shade. I wish we could have a little bit of his cold here.

---

4   Possibly the incident referred to in letter of 13 October 1917.
5   Relinquishing command of 100th Infantry Brigade following the armistice, Brigadier-General Baird later became Military Attaché to Constantinople and Sofia 1921-24. A popular Secretary of the Carlton Club, he died in a motor accident near Winchester on 20 February 1931.

15/3/19

My dear Dad,
Things seem to be brightening up in the demobilisation line and I could clear off tomorrow if someone would only take my place. I hope it will not be very long now before I get away.

Many thanks for various letters I have been receiving. Please do not send any books or anything like that out for a day or two. Things are being stirred up pretty energetically just at the moment and it is a toss-up whether I get home fairly soon or have to stay on a bit. When I know anything definite, I will let you know.

22/3/19

My dear Dad,
The latest news is that I may quite possibly be kept until the 1st of May with no guarantee of getting away even then. The reasons given are that I am indispensable, which is absolute rot. I got into the office this morning at 9.45 AM and have practically finished the day's work by 10.15 except for one or two odd jobs that may turn up. It may be the military idea of indispensable but it is not mine.

3/4/19

My dear Dad,
There is no news here and I am heartily sick of the whole business. My being kept on here is not the least complimentary, it is simply because they can't be bothered finding someone else to do the work. It is easier for them to say I am indispensable, than to take the trouble to see what work I have to do and find someone else to do it. All I have done since tea is to sign my name exactly 395 times. You can imagine how busy I am when I had time to count how often I had signed. I am now practically without work for the rest of the day.

However, I hope it is not long before I am quit of the Army for good.

9/4/19

My dear Mother,
I think I have at last got something definite about my getting away. My chief here told me today that he was going on special leave on the 22nd and that when he got back he would let me go. That means that I should get away about the 7th of May. My own private opinion is that I have been kept all this time so that he can get away and not because of the work. He expects to have a son and heir towards the end of the month

and is running no risk of not being able to get away through lack of someone to take his place. If he had said so from the beginning, I would not have minded so much. What I objected to was being called indispensable when I knew perfectly well that I was not.

20/4/19

My dear Dad,
Very many thanks for your, Mother's and Jenny's good wishes which I got yesterday. It is funny to think it is the fifth birthday I have spent in France. Thank goodness it is likely to be the last. I have had enough soldiering to satisfy me for some time.

20/4/19

My dear Dad,
The Colonel went off on leave yesterday for 14 days, so in a few days over a fortnight now I should be home. It is almost too good to be true. I don't think I have ever been so sick of any job as of this, except possibly trying to pass some of my exams in Glasgow.

Please thank mother for the cake, biscuits and sweets which arrived in excellent condition and have been greatly appreciated. We can buy fancy 1d cakes in the shops here now, at half a franc each, ie 2½d a mouthful. Personally, I prefer plain cake, so I don't think the French will make much profit out of me in that line.

2/5/19

My dear Dad,
I have no news except that I have been writing a sort of outline of a diary of the war since 1914. So far, I have got the general outline as far as December 1916, and I think with the help of my letters home, I should manage a fairly connected diary.

The only other news is that I have to give evidence tomorrow at a General Court Martial on an Officer. It is rather a disagreeable job, as he is a perfectly harmless sort of creature and I think innocent of any guilty intention.

I am looking at the papers every day to see if the Colonel's baby has arrived, as he will not come back from leave until it does. However, it should not be long before I get home again for good. I meant to wait in London on my way home and get my MC but I think I saw in some paper the other day that the King was leaving London about that time. If he does, then I am afraid my MC will have to be sent to me by post. It has occurred to me that I have only been on leave once in the last 14 months, so the sooner I get home the better.

The entrance hall at 27 Woodside Place, Glasgow, the Coats family home where the vast majority of Walter's letters were sent. (WJJC collection)

8/5/19

My dear Dad,

The Colonel's baby has arrived at last and GHQ have sanctioned my being demobilised, so as soon as the Colonel comes back I shall push off.

It may interest you to know that my address is now changed. As a matter of fact, it has been changed for some time but I did not worry to let you know as I get my letters just as quickly under the old one. It is:

H.Q. 17 Corps Group Packet

British Troops in France and Flanders

We have so few troops left, they call us a Corps Group Packet instead of a Corps.

12/5/19

My dear Dad,
I enclose the Fettes Roll of Honour form. I don't quite know what they mean by "Regiment" and "Duration of Service" and I can't remember the year I went to Fettes but they can easily look it up. If they want particulars of what I was doing at Brigade Headquarters etc., I was Staff Captain, 100 Brigade, a/DAAG 3rd Division, DAAG 61st Division, and am now a/DAAG 17th Corps.

19/5/19 Monday

My dear Ellie,
Just a short note to say that I hope to reach London on Friday night.

I don't know if you are going to be in London then, but I shall come to your house on the chance of finding you in and if I can arrange to have my MC presented, I shall stay with you for a few days.

As the boat crosses about 4.00 PM, I expect to reach London about 8.00 PM. Please don't keep dinner for me or anything of that sort.

There is no more news except that I really think I'm going to get home this time.
Your loving brother,
Walter J.J. Coats

WD: It was accordingly not until the 24th of May 1919, after 4 years and 7 months service in France, that I was finally demobilised.

11

Epilogue

This is the fiftieth anniversary of the start of the Battle of the Somme.

All four Coats boys survived the War. Walter returned to Glasgow and completed his apprenticeship at McGrigor, Donald & Co. In 1921 he joined the family law firm, A J and A Graham, where he worked for the rest of his life, becoming senior partner in 1949. During all this time Walter continued to live at 27 Woodside Place, which he bought over in 1932 when his father died. As Ellie described it, he kept "as a kind of family headquarters", and his sisters Jean and Janet also lived there. In the late 1930's, he bought a house called Bardykes, at Fairlie on the Ayshire coast, from where he spent much of his leisure time sailing his boat, *Ladybird*.[1]

During the Second World War, Jean and Jint spent most of their time in Bardykes, to be away from air raid danger, while Walter stayed in Glasgow and served in the Home Guard. In May 1942, Walter's sister Ellie Rowett wrote to Graham cousins in New Zealand, "Walter is now in the Anti-Aircraft branch of the Home Guard. His earlier war work was in organising the H.G. somewhere. He is now a private and enjoying it enormously. He says it is renewing his youth and he is delighted with the weapons that they have – I can't say more than that. He rose to the height of divisional staff officer during the last war, and he loves to be a private with no responsibilities but to toe the line. As a matter of fact, he has just been appointed as an instructor so he will have more responsibilities now. He is very funny about his battle dress. He told someone that he looks exactly like a convict in rompers and always hopes he won't meet a client when out in it."

Walter never married and lived a fairly reclusive lifestyle. However, he was extremely fond of and much loved by his enlarged family of nephews and nieces. Although the older Walter might have seemed somewhat shy and retiring, he unselfishly helped and cared for a great many people, family, friends, and relative strangers alike.

It seems clear, though, that he carried the memories and effects of the war for the remainder of his life. The shell at High Wood might have exploded or been inches

---

1   A likely reference to the ladybird, 100th Brigade's adopted unit sign. See Christmas card page 292.

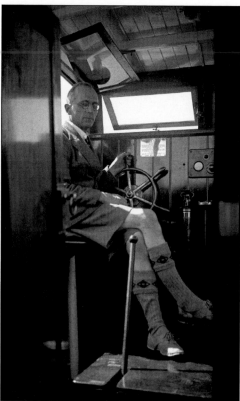

Walter at the helm of
Ladybird in the late 1930s.
(WJJC Collection)

Walter aboard *Ladybird* in the late 1930s. (WJJC Collection)

closer; he might have not taken the staff officer post in 1917 and remained with the Battalion and been killed, like Ted McCosh; or the sniper's bullet might have got him and not John Collier Stormonth-Darling.

11 July 1966

My dear Ellie,

Please thank Caroline [Ellie's daughter, b. 1922, and mother of the Editor JC] for the programme of the Sovereign's Parade Sandhurst which was very interesting. I presume she has another copy but if not I shall return it.

It is funny to remember that we actually took our swords out to France. Mine might have cut butter on a hot day but I doubt it would have done so with butter from the fridge. Incidentally, none of us had the foggiest idea how to use a sword and the only use mine had was that I could stick it in the ground and use the shiny part of the hilt as a shaving mirror. Fortunately they took them away from us fairly soon and sent them home and I never saw mine again.

The Tattoo programme refers to those who just disappeared in the mud and this reminded me of a case of another Brigade in our Division when a patrol one night found a man stuck in the mud. They could not get him out that night so went out the next night with shovels but could not find him. The night following they did find him and got him out and he was able to walk down to the dressing station. Even now fly paper gives me cold shivers.

This is the fiftieth anniversary of the start of the Battle of the Somme. We were thrown in about the middle of July and by the end of August had lost 25 officers and over 800 men out of a nominal 30 officers and 1000 men. Even then we were simply reinforced and kept in it till November and I do not know how many more we lost. As a matter of fact, I nearly missed the battle because the first day I was in it I was walking across the open when a low trajectory shell took a divot out of the ground in front of me an went whizzing off into space. Fortunately it came from the side but if I had been a step further forward it would have taken my leg off or if it had exploded it would have removed other bits as well. In any event I would not have had to take much further interest in the battle. One of my luckiest escapes was when I was sent up to take Mathew Anderson's company out of the action, as it was pitch dark and I had only the vaguest idea of where to find them. I went forward in what I guessed might have been their line of attack till I came to an empty trench when I hesitated whether to turn right or left. I had hardly turned right when I was challenged and I found I was between blocks that had been set up by each side in the same trench. If I had turned left I would have had it.

In light of this, I think you will understand why I do not feel I am being unselfish by being content with my sanity and present home comforts.

Love to all,

Your affectionate brother

Walter J.J. Coats

Walter Coats died in Glasgow on 25 August 1969. His brother Jim died in Devon on the same day. Douglas had died in 1938 and Jack passed away in 1973.

---

2 September 1969 – *The Glasgow Herald*

A friend writes:

To those who were not privileged to enjoy his close friendship, Walter Coats might have seemed austere and somewhat forbidding. His manner, like his faultless attire, tended to be formal and becomingly old fashioned. Behind that façade, however, lay an exceptionally warm heart, a lively sense of humour, and a profound understanding and tolerance of human frailty and folly which might well have been found lacking in a man who, in his journey through life, had plotted for himself the course of unswerving rectitude.

Nurtured in the finest traditions of his high calling, his early professional years were interrupted by the outbreak of the First World War, in which he immediately took up arms, serving with distinction and gallantry and attaining field rank. When the War ended he returned, still in his twenties, to McGrigor Donald and Co to complete the apprenticeship in Law which he had begun before his military service.

By 1921 he had qualified as a solicitor and joined the firm of A J and A Graham in which his father, Mr. John Jackson Coats, and his uncle, Mr. James Graham, were partners and with which he remained until the day of his death, having been senior partner since 1949.

It is particularly sad to know that Walter's death on August 25th terminates a long and honourable line of direct descendants of John Graham of Kittochside whose family connection with A.J. and A. Graham began in the 18th century. It is also a tragic and ironical coincidence that his brother James, who lived in England, died on the same day.

Modest and self-denying to a fault, he allowed himself but few personal indulgences. Travel appealed to him and he was an adept amateur photographer. But his voyages were rare, for with his tremendous sense of duty he was seldom absent from his office desk.

Sailing was his main recreation, and it is typical of the thoroughness with which he tackled every task which came his way that he underwent a course of study at a school of motoring simply because he wished to learn the intricacies of the mechanism of the internal combustion engine which propelled the boat he maintained at Fairlie. His instructors were soon astonished when he made it clear to them that he had not the faintest desire to learn how to drive a motor car and courteously refused the offers of tuition.

For those of us who survive and knew and loved him the memory of him will not soon fade. In an even wider circle, his name will always be revered.

Annex

Walter Coats Military Service Record

Served with Territorial Army (TF), 1/9th HLI (Glasgow Highlanders) from (approximately) January 1910.
Commissioned 2nd Lieutenant 24 January 1910 (Commission decree dated 23 July 1910)
1st Lieutenant 1/9th Battalion, HLI (Glasgow Highlanders) by 1914
France and Flanders from 5 November 1914 to 24 May 1919
1/9 HLI in 5th Brigade until 29 May 1916, when, replacing 1/6th Cameronians, it was assigned to 100th Brigade, 33rd Division
Captain: May 1916, backdated to 27 September 1915
Attached 98th Brigade 12 December 1916 – 4 January 1917
Staff Captain 100th Brigade 4 January 1917 – 20 September 1918
Acting Brigade Major 100th Brigade from c 25 May – June 1917.
Acting Deputy Assistant Adjutant General (DAAG) 3rd Division, 20 September 1918 – 21 October 1918
Mentioned in Despatches 8 November 1918 (*London Gazette* No. 31077, 17 December 1918, p. 14924)
DAAG 61st Division 21 October 1918 – 4 December 1918
DAAG XVII Corps 4 December 1918 – 24 May 1919
Temporary Major from 17 November 1918
Demobilised 24 May 1919

Decorations
Military Cross June 1917 (*London Gazette* No. 30111, 1 June 1917, p. 5478)
1914 Star (See letter 28 November 1917)
British War Medal
Victory Medal

Bibliography

Archival Sources

The National Archives (Kew)
TNA: WO 95/1343-2, 5th Brigade War Diary
TNA: WO 95/2406: 33rd Division War Diary
TNA: TNA WO 95/2428 and WO 95/2429: 100th Brigade War Diary
TNA: WO 95/2431: 1/9th HLI (Glasgow Highlanders) War Diary
TNA: WO 339/95859: Lieutenant Frank Watt SANDEMAN [1914-22]

British Library
General Sir Aylmer Hunter-Weston Papers

Imperial War Museum
General Sir Reginald John Pinney Diary

Durham County Record Office
Cuthbert Headlam Papers

Printed Sources

Alex Aiken, *Courage Past* (Glasgow: George Outram, 1971).
Anon, *Fifty Years of Fettes: Memories of Old Fettesians, 1870-1920* (Edinburgh: Constable, 1931).
Chris Baker, *The Battle for Flanders: German Defeat on the Lys 1918* (Barnsley: Pen & Sword, 2011).
Peter Barton, *The Battlefields of the First World War: Unseen Panoramas of the Western Front* (London: Constable, 2013).
Major A.F. Becke, *Order of Battle of Divisions Part I – The Regular British Divisions* (London: HMSO, 1935).
—— *Order of Battle Divisions: Part 3B. New Army Divisions (30-41); & 63rd (RN) Division)* (London: HMSO, 1945).
—— *Order of Battle: Part 4. The Army Council, GHQs, Armies and Corps 1914-1918* (London: HMSO, 1945).

Ian F.W. Beckett, *Riflemen Form! A Study of the Rifle Volunteer Movement 1859-1908* (Barnsley: Pen & Sword, 2007).

Edmund Blunden, *Undertones of War* (London: Penguin, 2000).

Jon Cooksey & Jerry Murland, *The Battles of French Flanders: Neuve Chapelle, Aubers Ridge, Festubert, Loos and Fromelles* (Barnsley: Pen & Sword, 2015).

Richard Devonald-Lewis (ed), *From the Somme to the Armistice: The Memoirs of Captain Stormont-Gibbs MC* (London: William Kimber, 1986).

Captain J.C. Dunn, *The War the Infantry Knew: A Chronicle of Service in France and Belgium* (London: Jane's, 1987).

Sir J.E. Edmonds, *Military Operations France and Belgium 1915 Vol. I* (London: Macmillan, 1927).

—— *Military Operations France and Belgium 1915 Vol. II* (London: Macmillan, 1928)

—— *Military Operations France and Belgium 1916 Vol. I* (London: Macmillan, 1932).

—— *Military Operations France and Belgium 1918 Vol I* (London: Macmillan, 1935).

—— *Military Operations France and Belgium 1918 Vol. III* (London: Macmillan, 1939).

—— *Military Operations France and Belgium 1918 Vol. V* (London: HMSO, 1947).

—— *Military Operations France and Belgium 1917 Vol. II* (London: HMSO, 1948).

Cyril Falls, *Military Operations France Belgium 1917 Vol. I* (London: Macmillan, 1940).

Gerald Gliddon, *Somme 1916: A Battlefield Companion* (Thrupp – Stroud: Sutton, 2006).

Robert Graves, *Goodbye to All That* (London: Penguin, 2000).

Paul Harris, *The Men Who Planned the War: A Study of the Staff of the British Army on the Western Front, 1914-1918* (Farnham: Ashgate, 2015).

Lieutenant-Colonel Graham Seton Hutchison, *The Thirty-Third Division in France and Flanders 1915-1919* (London: Warlow & Sons, 1921).

—— *Footslogger: An Autobiography* (London: Hutchinson & Co., 1931).

Spencer Jones (ed), *Stemming the Tide: Officers and Leadership in the British Expeditionary Force 1914* (Solihull: Helion & Company, 2013).

—— (ed), *Courage Without Glory: The British Army on the Western Front 1915* (Solihull: Helion & Company, 2015).

Abraham Kingdon (ed), *Patriotic Poems* (Winnipeg: The Kingdon Printing Co., Limited, 1916).

Peter Liddle (ed), *Passchendaele in Perspective: The Third Battle of Ypres* (London: Leo Cooper, 1997).

Nick Lloyd, *Loos 1915* (Stroud: History Press, 2008).

Michael LoCicero, *A Moonlight Massacre: The Night Operation on the Passchendaele Ridge, 2 December 1917* (Solihull: Helion & Company, 2014).

Compton Mackenzie, *Gallipoli Memories* (London: Cassell, 1929).

Chris McCarthy, *Passchendaele: The Day-by-Day Account* (London: Arms & Armour Press, 1995).

Elaine McFarland, *A Slashing Man of Action: The Life of Lieutenant General Sir Aylmer Hunter-Weston MP* (Oxford: Peter Lang, 2014).

Michael Meighan, *Glasgow: A History* (Stroud: Amberley, 2013).

Martin Middlebrook, *The Kaiser's Battle* (Barnsley: Pen & Sword, 2007).

Captain Wilfred Miles, *Military Operations France and Belgium 1916 Vol. II* (London: Macmillan, 1938).

K.W. Mitchinson, *England's Last Hope: The Territorial Force, 1908-14* (London: Palgrave Macmillan, 2008).

—— *The Territorial Force at War, 1914-16* (London: Palgrave Macmillan, 2014).

Christopher Moore-Bick, *Playing the Game: The British Junior Officer on the Western Front 1914-18* (Solihull: Helion & Company, 2011).

James Hamilton Muir, *Glasgow 1901* (Dorchester: White Cockade Publishing, 2001).

David Murphy, *Breaking Point of the French Army: The Nivelle Offensive of 1917* (Barnsley: Pen & Sword, 2015)

Terry Norman, *The Hell They Called High Wood: The Somme 1916* (Barnsley: Pen & Sword, 2009).

Robin Prior & Trevor Wilson, *Passchendaele: The Untold Story* (New Haven: Yale Nota Bene, 2002).

Andrew Rawson, *The Somme Campaign* (Barnsley: Pen & Sword, 2014).

Anthony Saunders, *Raiding on the Western Front* (Barnsley: Pen & Sword, 2012).

Michael Senior, *Haking: A Dutiful Soldier, Lt. General Sir Richard Haking, XI Corps Commander 1915-18: A Study in Corps Command* (Barnsley: Pen & Sword, 2012).

Peter Simkins, *Kitchener's Army: The Raising of the New Armies 1914-1916* (Barnsley: Pen & Sword, 2007).

Lieutenant-Colonel R.R. Thompson, *The Fifty-Second Lowland Division 1914-1918* (Glasgow: Maclehose, Jackson & Co., 1923).

Fred W. Ward, *The 23rd (Service) Battalion Royal Fusiliers (First Sportsman's) During the First World War 1914-1918* (Driffield: Leonaur, 2010).

Alec Weir, *Come on Highlanders!: Glasgow Territorials in the Great War* (Thrupp – Stroud: Sutton, 2005).

Everard Wyrall, *The History of the Second Division 1914-1918 Vol. I* (London: Thomas Nelson & Sons, 1921).

Mitchell A. Yockelson, *Borrowed Soldiers: Americans Under British Command, 1918* (Norman, Oklahoma: University of Oklahoma Press, 2008).

David Zabecki, *The German 1918 Offensives: A Case Study in the Operational Level of War* (London: Routledge, 2006).

Journals and Periodicals

Fettesian
Glasgow Herald
London Gazette

Unpublished Sources

Colonel Alexander Kirkwood Reid, 'Shoulder to Shoulder: History of the 1/9th HLI' (1988).

Electronic Sources

BBC Guides <http://www.bbc.co.uk/guides/zqtmyrd>
British Postal Museum and Archive <ww.postalheritage.org.uk>
Edwardian Promenade <http://www.edwardianpromenade.com/>
Friends of Glasgow Necropolis <http://www.glasgownecropolis.org/>
Long, Long Trail <http://www.longlongtrail.co.uk/>
Riviera Reporter <http://www.rivierareporter.com/>
University of Glasgow Story <http://www.universitystory.gla.ac.uk/>
White Fox Rare Books and Antiques <http://www.whitefoxrarebooks.com/ci_384.html

Index

PEOPLE

PLACES

FORMATIONS & UNITS